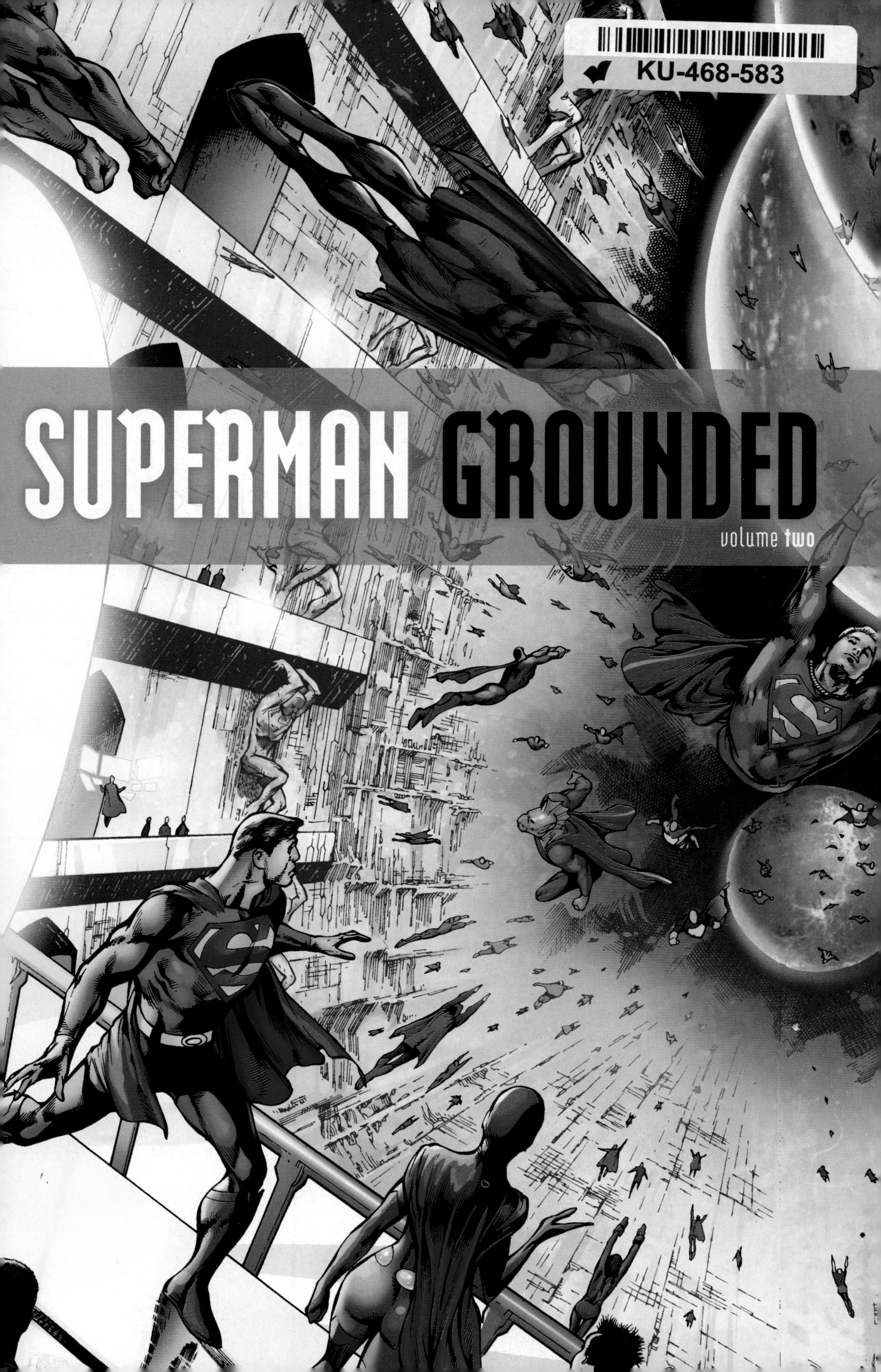
SUPERMAN GROUNDED
volume two

Matt Idelson Editor – Original Series / Wil Moss Associate Editor – Original Series
Peter Hamboussi Editor / Robbin Brosterman Design Director – Books

Bob Harras VP – Editor-in-Chief

Diane Nelson President / Dan DiDio and Jim Lee Co-Publishers / Geoff Johns Chief Creative Officer / John Rood Executive VP – Sales, Marketing and Business Development
Amy Genkins Senior VP – Business and Legal Affairs / Nairi Gardiner Senior VP – Finance / Jeff Boison VP – Publishing Operations / Mark Chiarello VP – Art Direction and Design
John Cunningham VP – Marketing / Terri Cunningham VP – Talent Relations and Services / Alison Gill Senior VP – Manufacturing and Operations / Hank Kanalz Senior VP – Digital
Jay Kogan VP – Business and Legal Affairs, Publishing / Jack Mahan VP – Business Affairs, Talent / Nick Napolitano VP – Manufacturing Administration
Sue Pohja VP – Book Sales / Courtney Simmons Senior VP – Publicity / Bob Wayne Senior VP – Sales

SUPERMAN: GROUNDED, Volume 2
Published by DC Comics.

DC Comics, 1700 Broadway, New York, NY 10019
A Warner Bros. Entertainment Company.
Printed by RR Donnelley, Salem, VA, USA. 11/02/12. First Printing.
ISBN: 978-1-4012-3532-1

SUSTAINABLE FORESTRY INITIATIVE
Certified Chain of Custody
At Least 25% Certified Forest Content
www.sfiprogram.org
SFI-01042
APPLIES TO TEXT STOCK ONLY

DES MOINES, IOWA.

"IT'S BEEN A SLOW MORNING.

"SINCE REACHING TOWN, I'VE HELPED A POLICE OFFICER STOP A BANK ROBBERY...

"...KEPT A FREIGHT TRAIN FROM RUNNING OVER A LITTLE GIRL WHO RAN ONTO THE TRACK CHASING A LOST BALLOON...

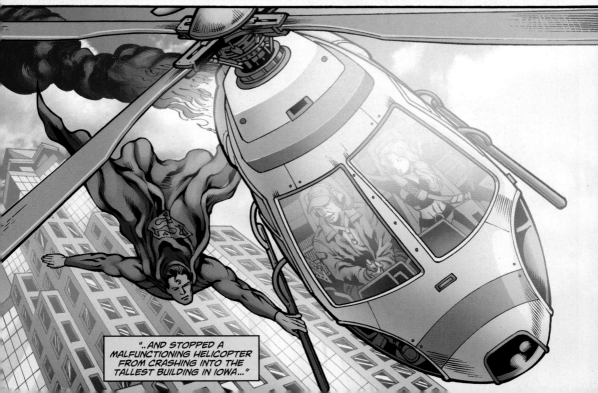

"...AND STOPPED A MALFUNCTIONING HELICOPTER FROM CRASHING INTO THE TALLEST BUILDING IN IOWA..."

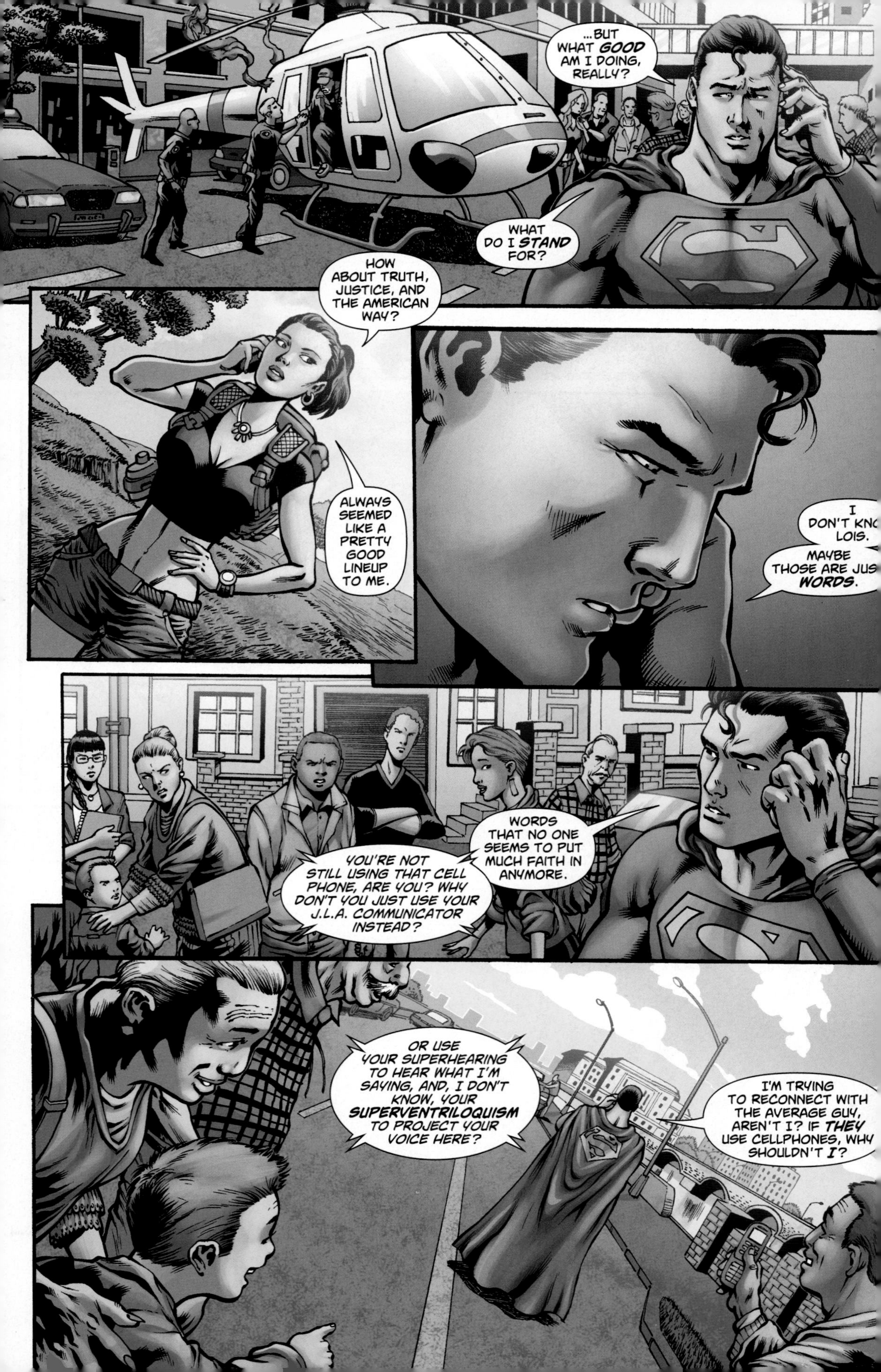
...BUT WHAT GOOD AM I DOING, REALLY?
WHAT DO I STAND FOR?
HOW ABOUT TRUTH, JUSTICE, AND THE AMERICAN WAY?
ALWAYS SEEMED LIKE A PRETTY GOOD LINEUP TO ME.
I DON'T KNO LOIS.
MAYBE THOSE ARE JUS WORDS.
WORDS THAT NO ONE SEEMS TO PUT MUCH FAITH IN ANYMORE.
YOU'RE NOT STILL USING THAT CELL PHONE, ARE YOU? WHY DON'T YOU JUST USE YOUR J.L.A. COMMUNICATOR INSTEAD?
OR USE YOUR SUPERHEARING TO HEAR WHAT I'M SAYING, AND, I DON'T KNOW, YOUR SUPERVENTRILOQUISM TO PROJECT YOUR VOICE HERE?
I'M TRYING TO RECONNECT WITH THE AVERAGE GUY, AREN'T I? IF THEY USE CELLPHONES, WHY SHOULDN'T I?

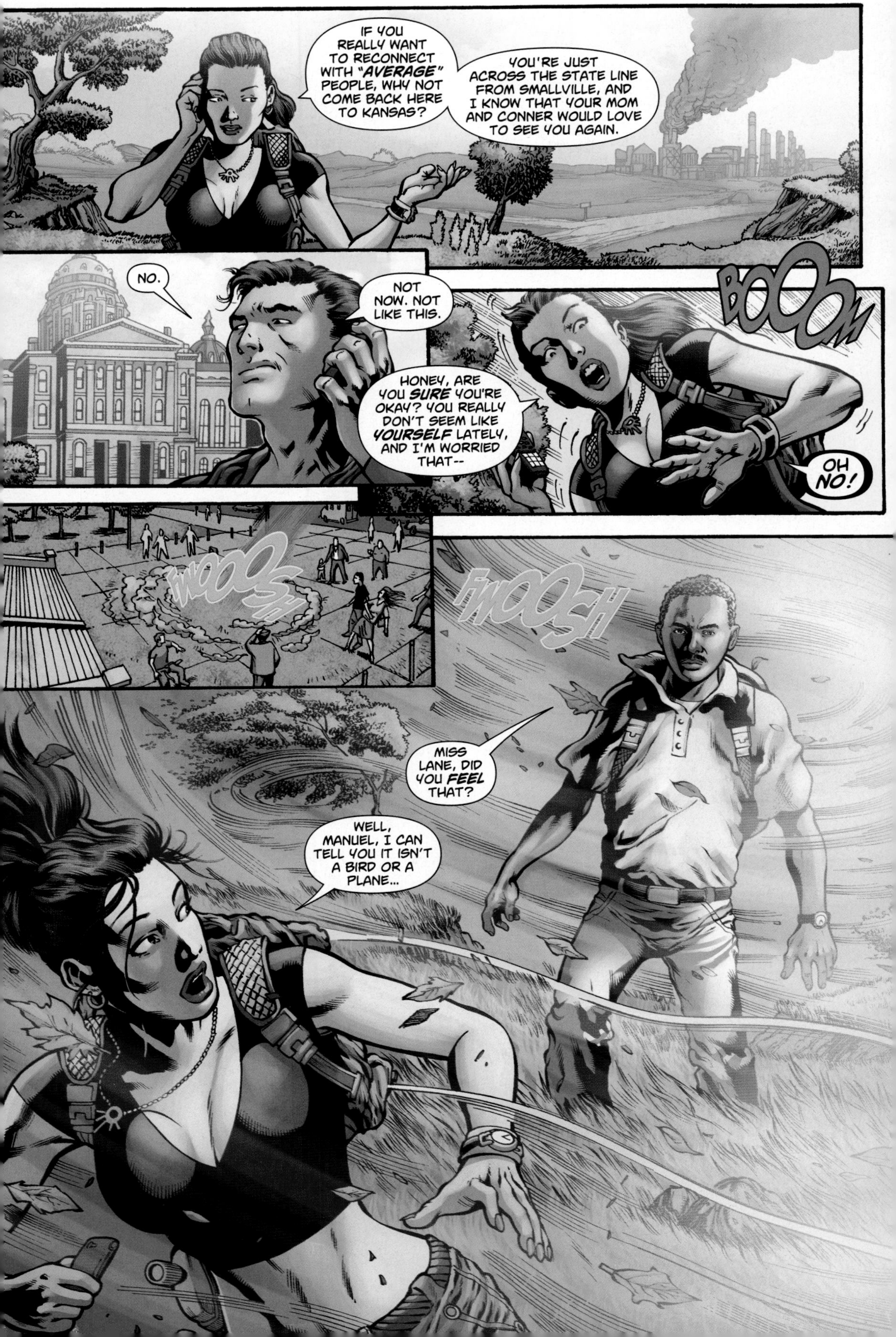

IF YOU REALLY WANT TO RECONNECT WITH "AVERAGE" PEOPLE, WHY NOT COME BACK HERE TO KANSAS?
YOU'RE JUST ACROSS THE STATE LINE FROM SMALLVILLE, AND I KNOW THAT YOUR MOM AND CONNER WOULD LOVE TO SEE YOU AGAIN.
NO.
NOT NOW. NOT LIKE THIS.
HONEY, ARE YOU SURE YOU'RE OKAY? YOU REALLY DON'T SEEM LIKE YOURSELF LATELY, AND I'M WORRIED THAT--
BOOOOM
OH NO!
FWOOOSH
FWOOSH
MISS LANE, DID YOU FEEL THAT?
WELL, MANUEL, I CAN TELL YOU IT ISN'T A BIRD OR A PLANE...

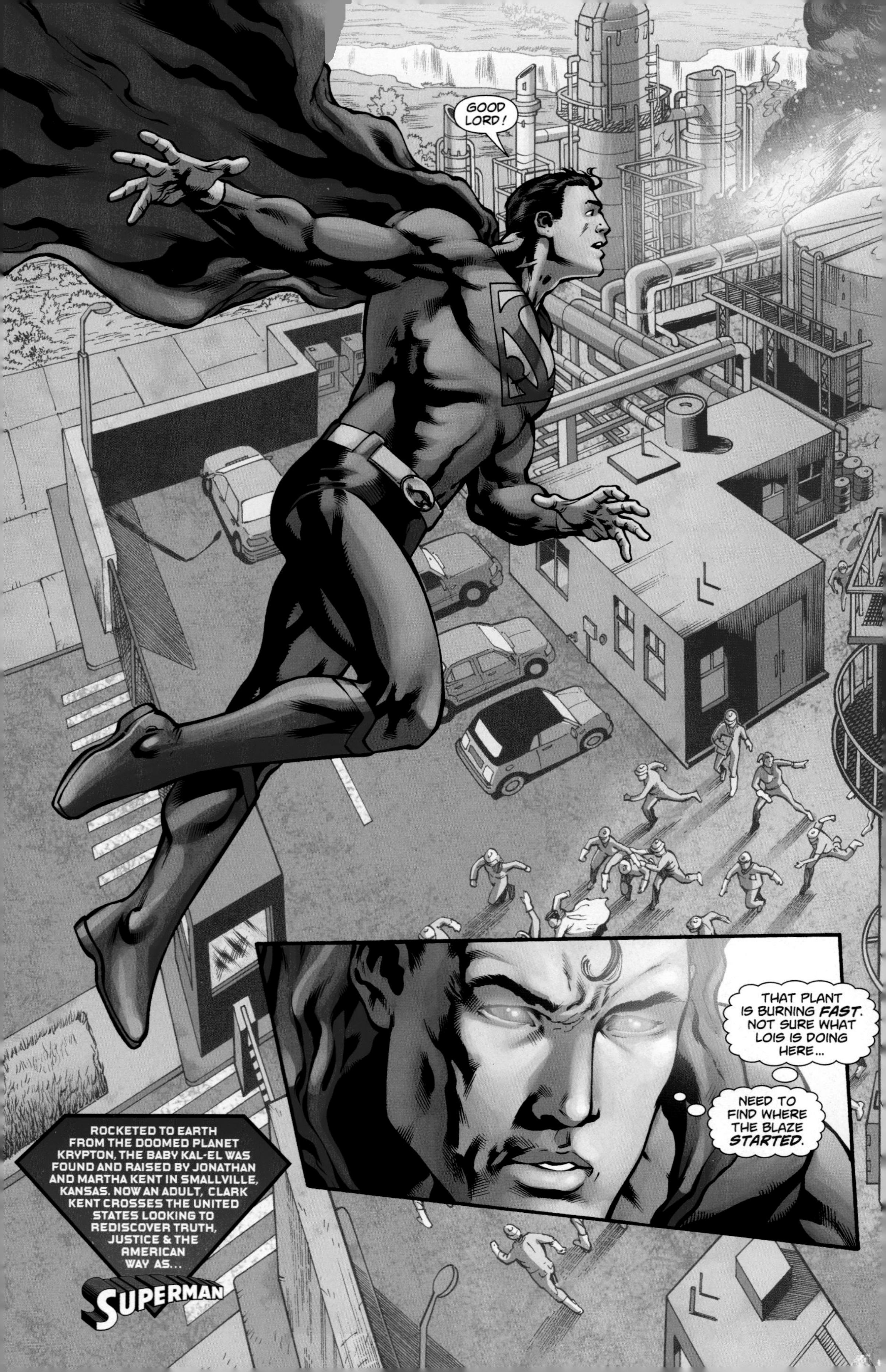
GOOD LORD!
THAT PLANT IS BURNING FAST. NOT SURE WHAT LOIS IS DOING HERE...
NEED TO FIND WHERE THE BLAZE STARTED.
ROCKETED TO EARTH FROM THE DOOMED PLANET KRYPTON, THE BABY KAL-EL WAS FOUND AND RAISED BY JONATHAN AND MARTHA KENT IN SMALLVILLE, KANSAS. NOW AN ADULT, CLARK KENT CROSSES THE UNITED STATES LOOKING TO REDISCOVER TRUTH, JUSTICE & THE AMERICAN WAY AS...
SUPERMAN

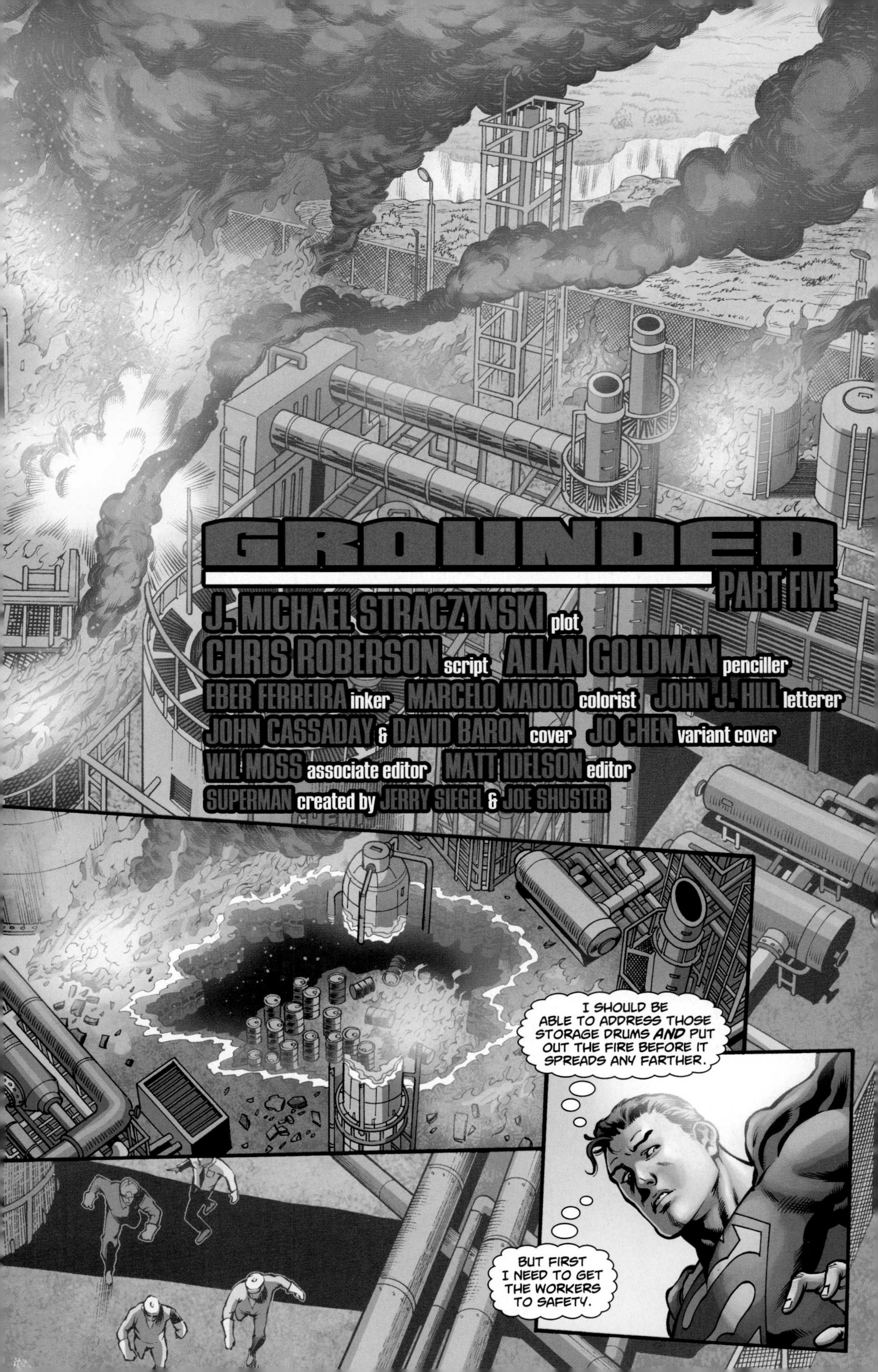
GROUNDED
PART FIVE
J. MICHAEL STRACZYNSKI plot
CHRIS ROBERSON script ALLAN GOLDMAN penciller
EBER FERREIRA inker MARCELO MAIOLO colorist JOHN J. HILL letterer
JOHN CASSADAY & DAVID BARON cover JO CHEN variant cover
WIL MOSS associate editor MATT IDELSON editor
SUPERMAN created by JERRY SIEGEL & JOE SHUSTER
I SHOULD BE ABLE TO ADDRESS THOSE STORAGE DRUMS AND PUT OUT THE FIRE BEFORE IT SPREADS ANY FARTHER.
BUT FIRST I NEED TO GET THE WORKERS TO SAFETY.

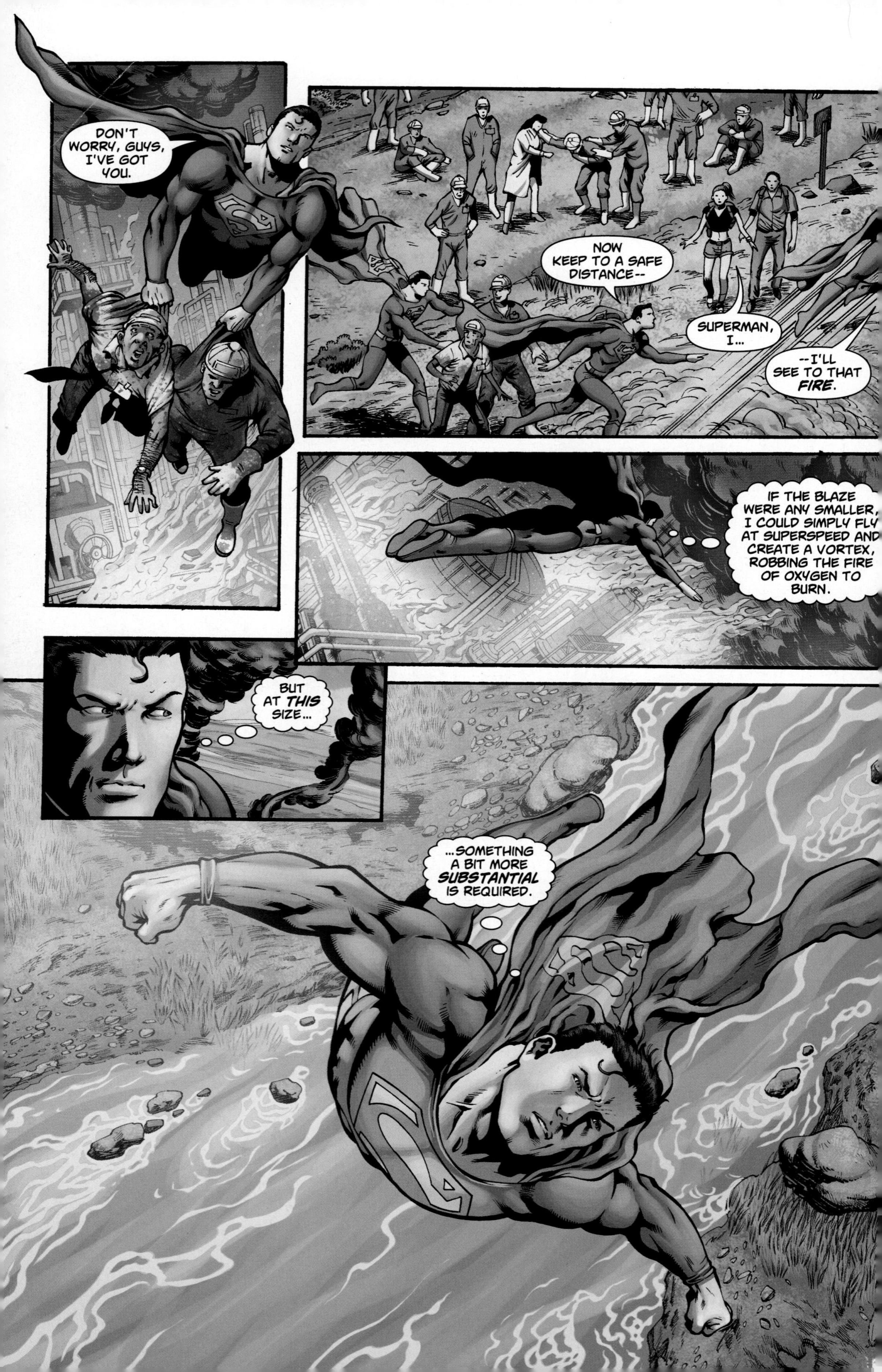
DON'T WORRY, GUYS, I'VE GOT YOU.
NOW KEEP TO A SAFE DISTANCE--
SUPERMAN, I...
--I'LL SEE TO THAT FIRE.
IF THE BLAZE WERE ANY SMALLER, I COULD SIMPLY FLY AT SUPERSPEED AND CREATE A VORTEX, ROBBING THE FIRE OF OXYGEN TO BURN.
BUT AT THIS SIZE...
...SOMETHING A BIT MORE SUBSTANTIAL IS REQUIRED.

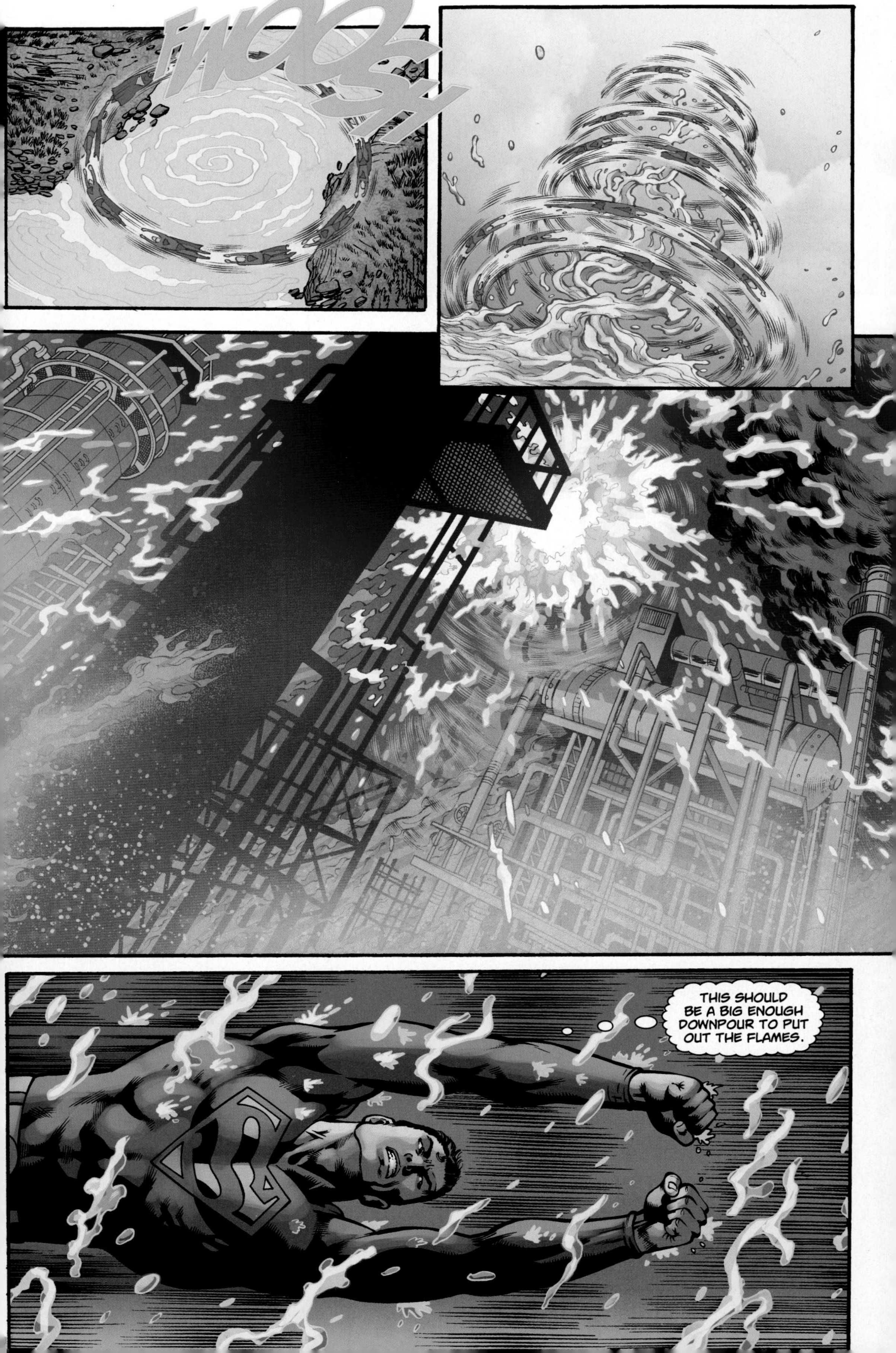
FWOOSH
THIS SHOULD BE A BIG ENOUGH DOWNPOUR TO PUT OUT THE FLAMES.

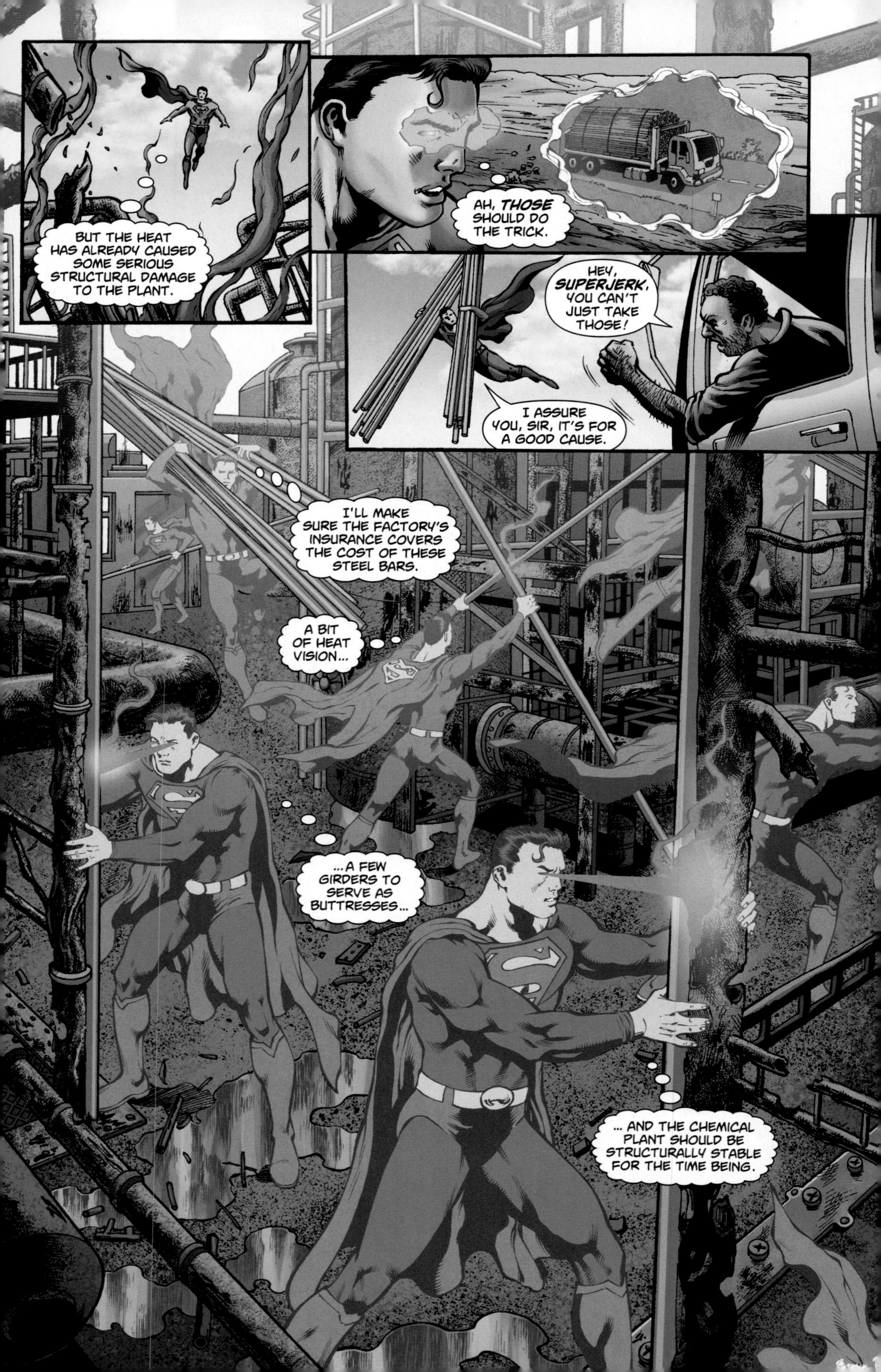
BUT THE HEAT HAS ALREADY CAUSED SOME SERIOUS STRUCTURAL DAMAGE TO THE PLANT.
AH, THOSE SHOULD DO THE TRICK.
HEY, SUPERJERK, YOU CAN'T JUST TAKE THOSE!
I ASSURE YOU, SIR, IT'S FOR A GOOD CAUSE.
I'LL MAKE SURE THE FACTORY'S INSURANCE COVERS THE COST OF THESE STEEL BARS.
A BIT OF HEAT VISION...
...A FEW GIRDERS TO SERVE AS BUTTRESSES...
... AND THE CHEMICAL PLANT SHOULD BE STRUCTURALLY STABLE FOR THE TIME BEING.

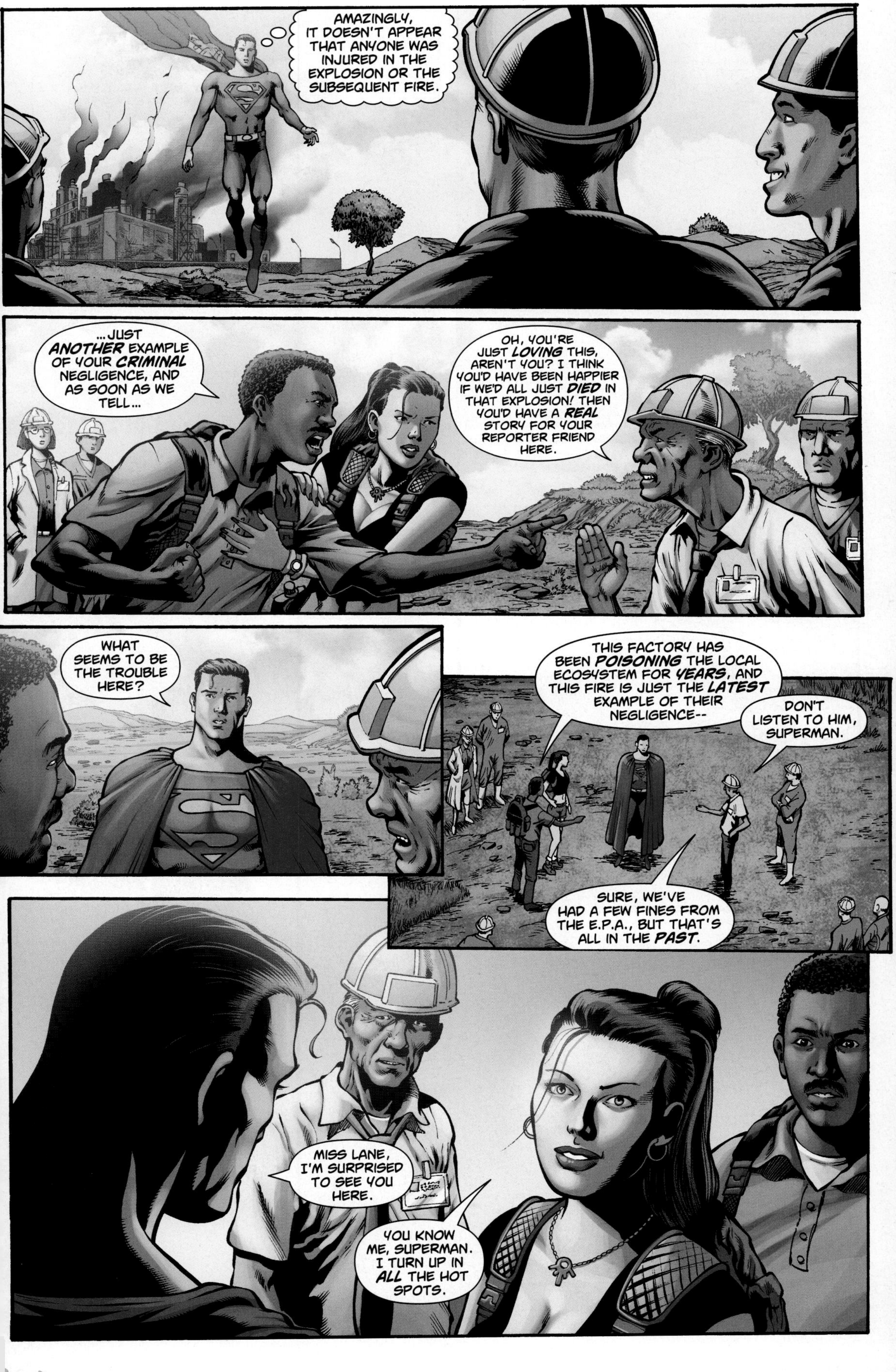
AMAZINGLY, IT DOESN'T APPEAR THAT ANYONE WAS INJURED IN THE EXPLOSION OR THE SUBSEQUENT FIRE.
...JUST ANOTHER EXAMPLE OF YOUR CRIMINAL NEGLIGENCE, AND AS SOON AS WE TELL...
OH, YOU'RE JUST LOVING THIS, AREN'T YOU? I THINK YOU'D HAVE BEEN HAPPIER IF WE'D ALL JUST DIED IN THAT EXPLOSION! THEN YOU'D HAVE A REAL STORY FOR YOUR REPORTER FRIEND HERE.
WHAT SEEMS TO BE THE TROUBLE HERE?
THIS FACTORY HAS BEEN POISONING THE LOCAL ECOSYSTEM FOR YEARS, AND THIS FIRE IS JUST THE LATEST EXAMPLE OF THEIR NEGLIGENCE--
DON'T LISTEN TO HIM, SUPERMAN.
SURE, WE'VE HAD A FEW FINES FROM THE E.P.A., BUT THAT'S ALL IN THE PAST.
MISS LANE, I'M SURPRISED TO SEE YOU HERE.
YOU KNOW ME, SUPERMAN. I TURN UP IN ALL THE HOT SPOTS.

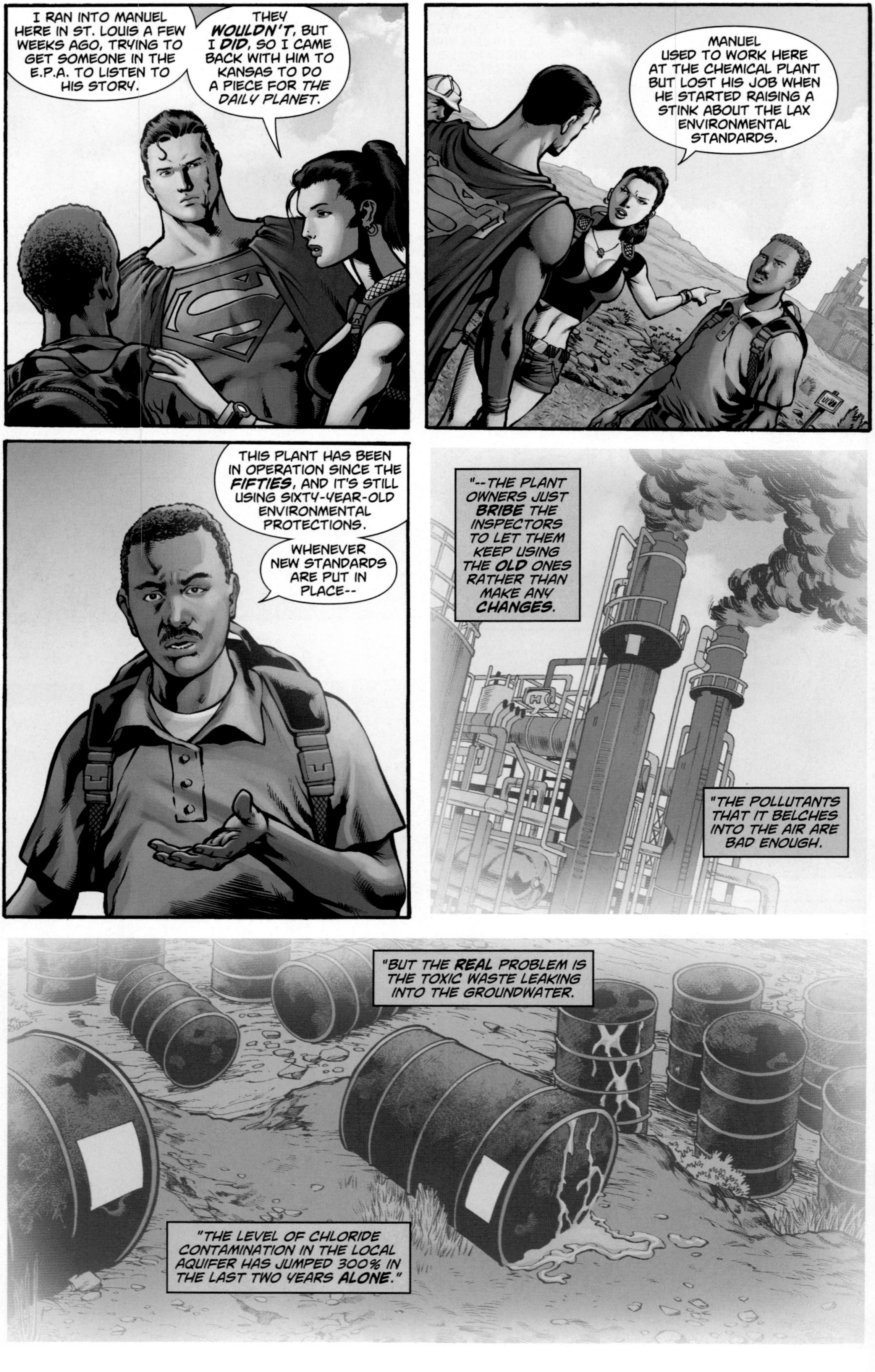
I RAN INTO MANUEL HERE IN ST. LOUIS A FEW WEEKS AGO, TRYING TO GET SOMEONE IN THE E.P.A. TO LISTEN TO HIS STORY.
THEY *WOULDN'T*, BUT I *DID*, SO I CAME BACK WITH HIM TO KANSAS TO DO A PIECE FOR *THE DAILY PLANET*.
MANUEL USED TO WORK HERE AT THE CHEMICAL PLANT BUT LOST HIS JOB WHEN HE STARTED RAISING A STINK ABOUT THE LAX ENVIRONMENTAL STANDARDS.
THIS PLANT HAS BEEN IN OPERATION SINCE THE *FIFTIES*, AND IT'S STILL USING SIXTY-YEAR-OLD ENVIRONMENTAL PROTECTIONS.
WHENEVER NEW STANDARDS ARE PUT IN PLACE--
"--THE PLANT OWNERS JUST *BRIBE* THE INSPECTORS TO LET THEM KEEP USING THE *OLD* ONES RATHER THAN MAKE ANY *CHANGES*.
"THE POLLUTANTS THAT IT BELCHES INTO THE AIR ARE BAD ENOUGH.
"BUT THE *REAL* PROBLEM IS THE TOXIC WASTE LEAKING INTO THE GROUNDWATER.
"THE LEVEL OF CHLORIDE CONTAMINATION IN THE LOCAL AQUIFER HAS JUMPED 300% IN THE LAST TWO YEARS *ALONE*."

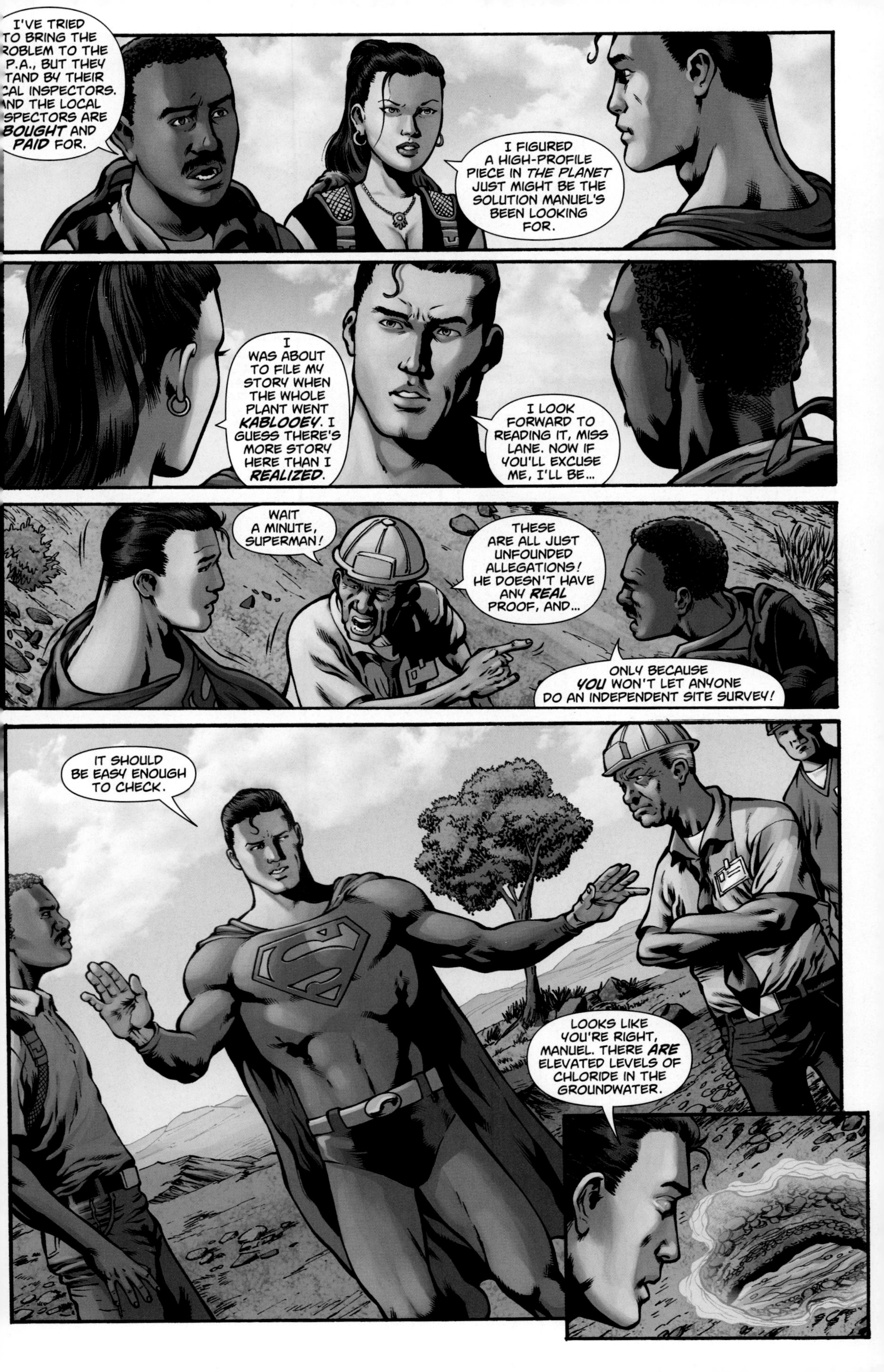
I'VE TRIED TO BRING THE PROBLEM TO THE E.P.A., BUT THEY STAND BY THEIR LOCAL INSPECTORS. AND THE LOCAL INSPECTORS ARE BOUGHT AND PAID FOR.
I FIGURED A HIGH-PROFILE PIECE IN THE PLANET JUST MIGHT BE THE SOLUTION MANUEL'S BEEN LOOKING FOR.
I WAS ABOUT TO FILE MY STORY WHEN THE WHOLE PLANT WENT KABLOOEY. I GUESS THERE'S MORE STORY HERE THAN I REALIZED.
I LOOK FORWARD TO READING IT, MISS LANE. NOW IF YOU'LL EXCUSE ME, I'LL BE...
WAIT A MINUTE, SUPERMAN!
THESE ARE ALL JUST UNFOUNDED ALLEGATIONS! HE DOESN'T HAVE ANY REAL PROOF, AND...
ONLY BECAUSE YOU WON'T LET ANYONE DO AN INDEPENDENT SITE SURVEY!
IT SHOULD BE EASY ENOUGH TO CHECK.
LOOKS LIKE YOU'RE RIGHT, MANUEL. THERE ARE ELEVATED LEVELS OF CHLORIDE IN THE GROUNDWATER.

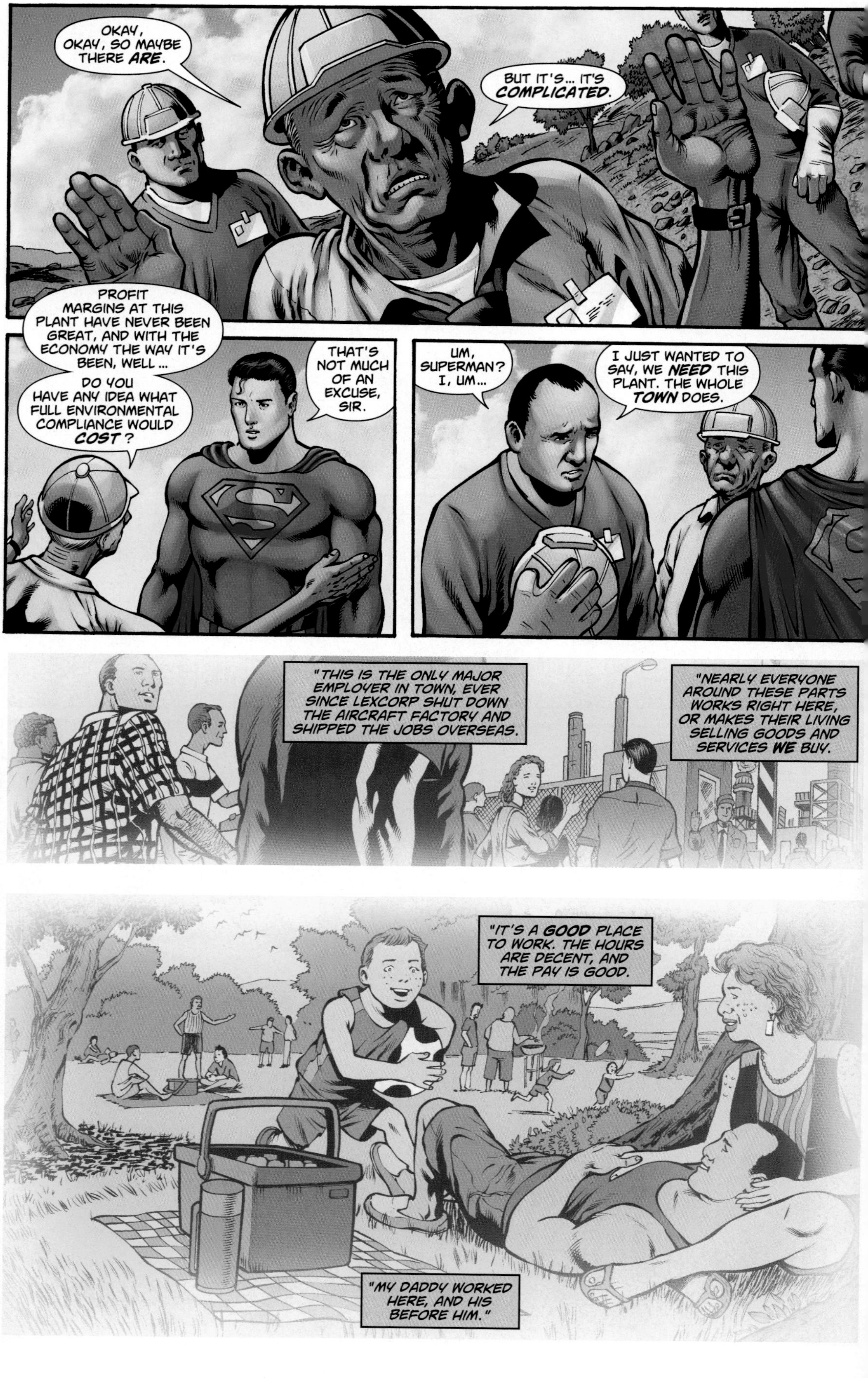
OKAY, OKAY, SO MAYBE THERE ARE.
BUT IT'S... IT'S COMPLICATED.
PROFIT MARGINS AT THIS PLANT HAVE NEVER BEEN GREAT, AND WITH THE ECONOMY THE WAY IT'S BEEN, WELL ...
DO YOU HAVE ANY IDEA WHAT FULL ENVIRONMENTAL COMPLIANCE WOULD COST?
THAT'S NOT MUCH OF AN EXCUSE, SIR.
UM, SUPERMAN? I, UM...
I JUST WANTED TO SAY, WE NEED THIS PLANT. THE WHOLE TOWN DOES.
"THIS IS THE ONLY MAJOR EMPLOYER IN TOWN, EVER SINCE LEXCORP SHUT DOWN THE AIRCRAFT FACTORY AND SHIPPED THE JOBS OVERSEAS.
"NEARLY EVERYONE AROUND THESE PARTS WORKS RIGHT HERE, OR MAKES THEIR LIVING SELLING GOODS AND SERVICES WE BUY.
"IT'S A GOOD PLACE TO WORK. THE HOURS ARE DECENT, AND THE PAY IS GOOD.
"MY DADDY WORKED HERE, AND HIS BEFORE HIM."

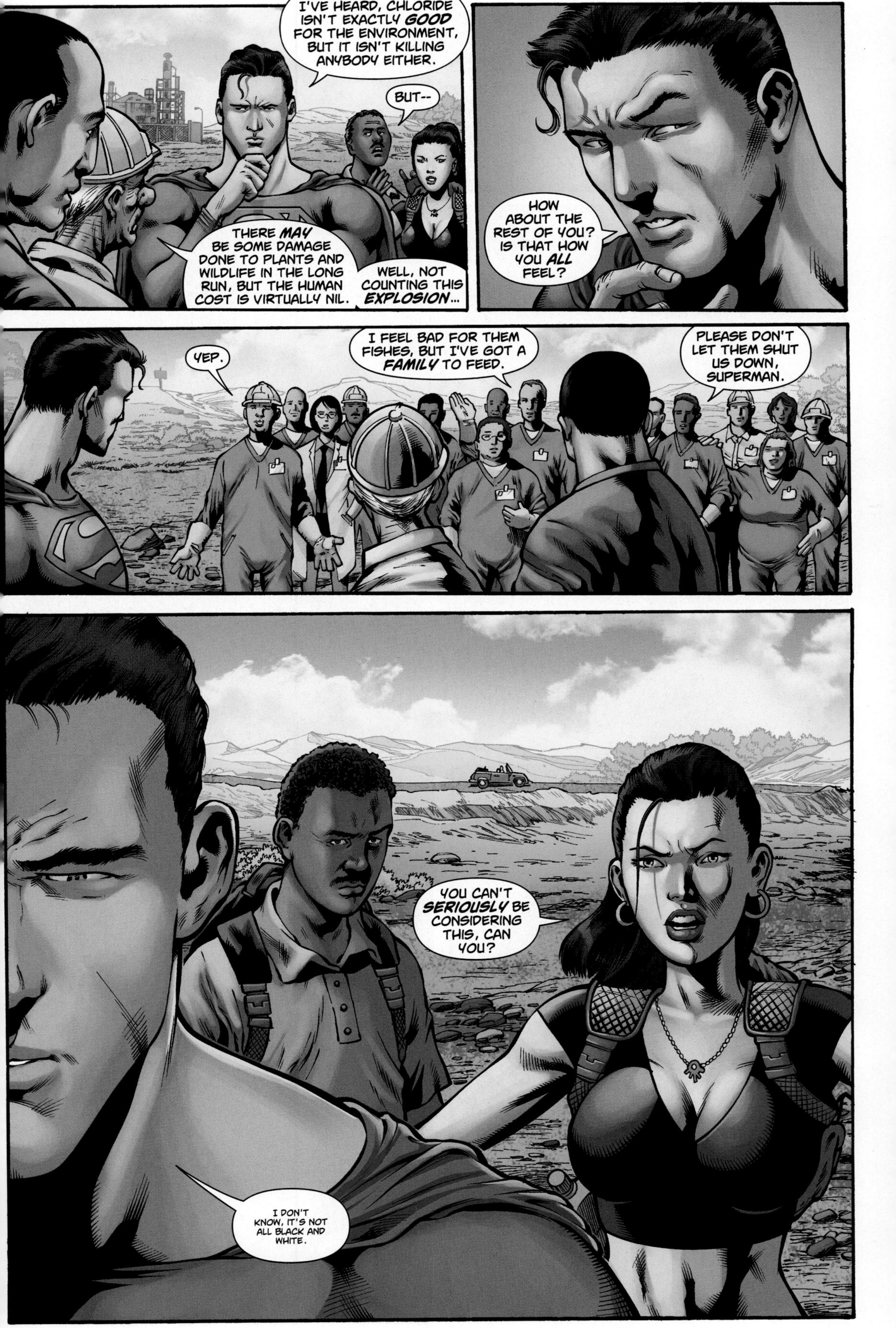
FROM WHAT I'VE HEARD, CHLORIDE ISN'T EXACTLY GOOD FOR THE ENVIRONMENT, BUT IT ISN'T KILLING ANYBODY EITHER.
BUT--
THERE MAY BE SOME DAMAGE DONE TO PLANTS AND WILDLIFE IN THE LONG RUN, BUT THE HUMAN COST IS VIRTUALLY NIL.
WELL, NOT COUNTING THIS EXPLOSION...
HOW ABOUT THE REST OF YOU? IS THAT HOW YOU ALL FEEL?
YEP.
I FEEL BAD FOR THEM FISHES, BUT I'VE GOT A FAMILY TO FEED.
PLEASE DON'T LET THEM SHUT US DOWN, SUPERMAN.
YOU CAN'T SERIOUSLY BE CONSIDERING THIS, CAN YOU?
I DON'T KNOW, IT'S NOT ALL BLACK AND WHITE.

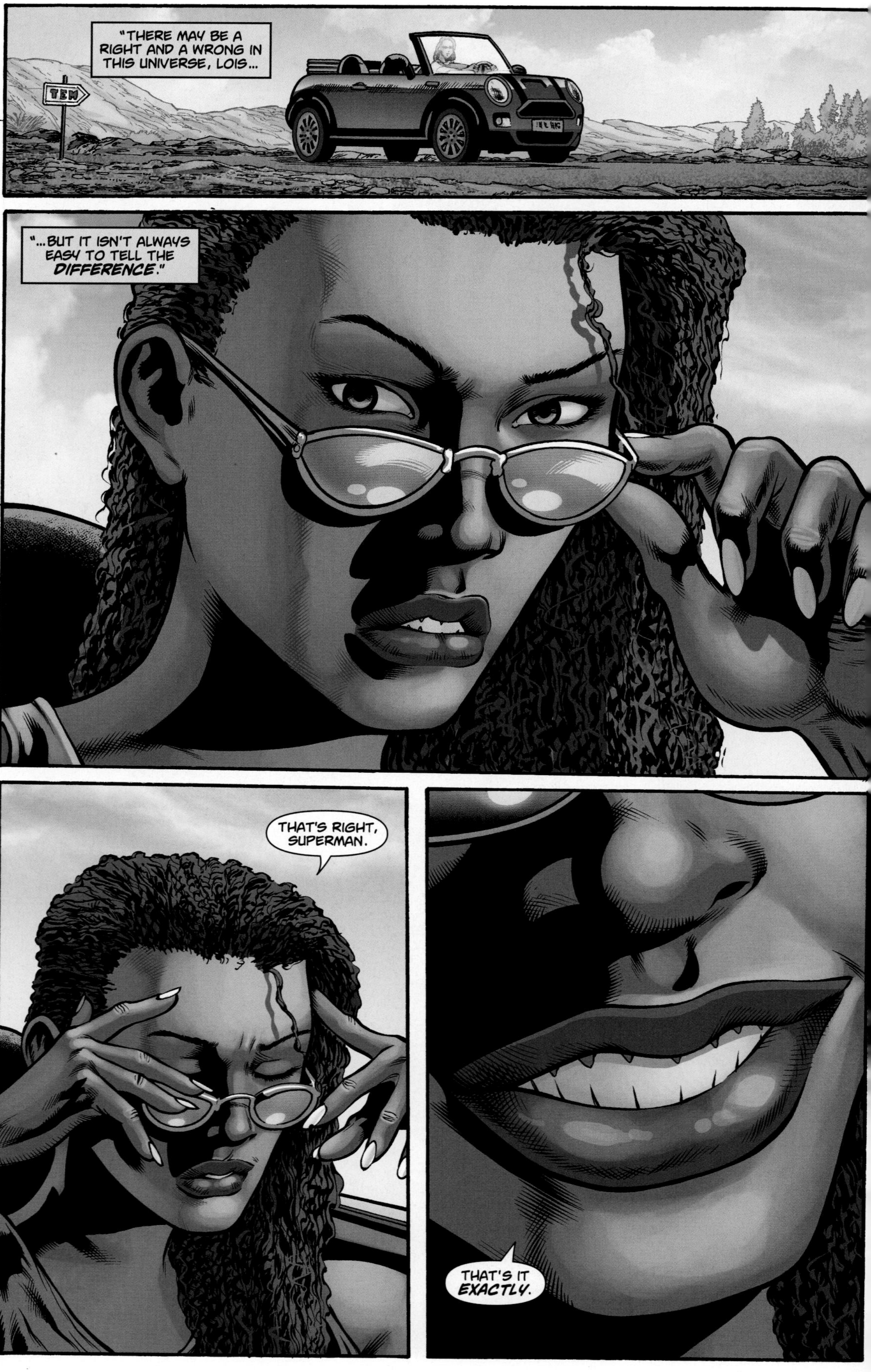
"THERE MAY BE A RIGHT AND A WRONG IN THIS UNIVERSE, LOIS...
TEM
"...BUT IT ISN'T ALWAYS EASY TO TELL THE *DIFFERENCE*."
THAT'S RIGHT, SUPERMAN.
THAT'S IT *EXACTLY*.

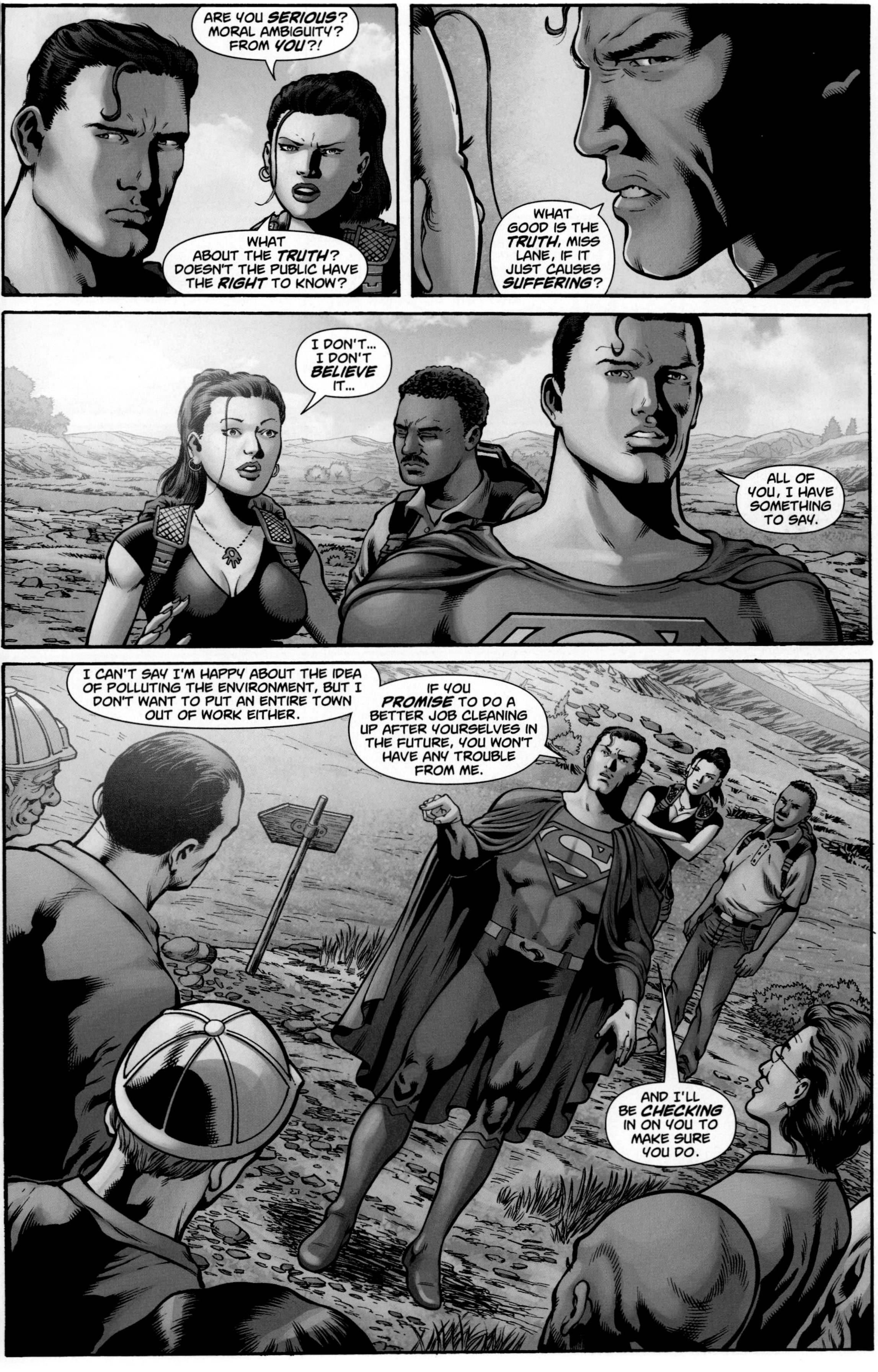
ARE YOU SERIOUS? MORAL AMBIGUITY? FROM YOU?!
WHAT ABOUT THE TRUTH? DOESN'T THE PUBLIC HAVE THE RIGHT TO KNOW?
WHAT GOOD IS THE TRUTH, MISS LANE, IF IT JUST CAUSES SUFFERING?
I DON'T... I DON'T BELIEVE IT...
ALL OF YOU, I HAVE SOMETHING TO SAY.
I CAN'T SAY I'M HAPPY ABOUT THE IDEA OF POLLUTING THE ENVIRONMENT, BUT I DON'T WANT TO PUT AN ENTIRE TOWN OUT OF WORK EITHER.
IF YOU PROMISE TO DO A BETTER JOB CLEANING UP AFTER YOURSELVES IN THE FUTURE, YOU WON'T HAVE ANY TROUBLE FROM ME.
AND I'LL BE CHECKING IN ON YOU TO MAKE SURE YOU DO.

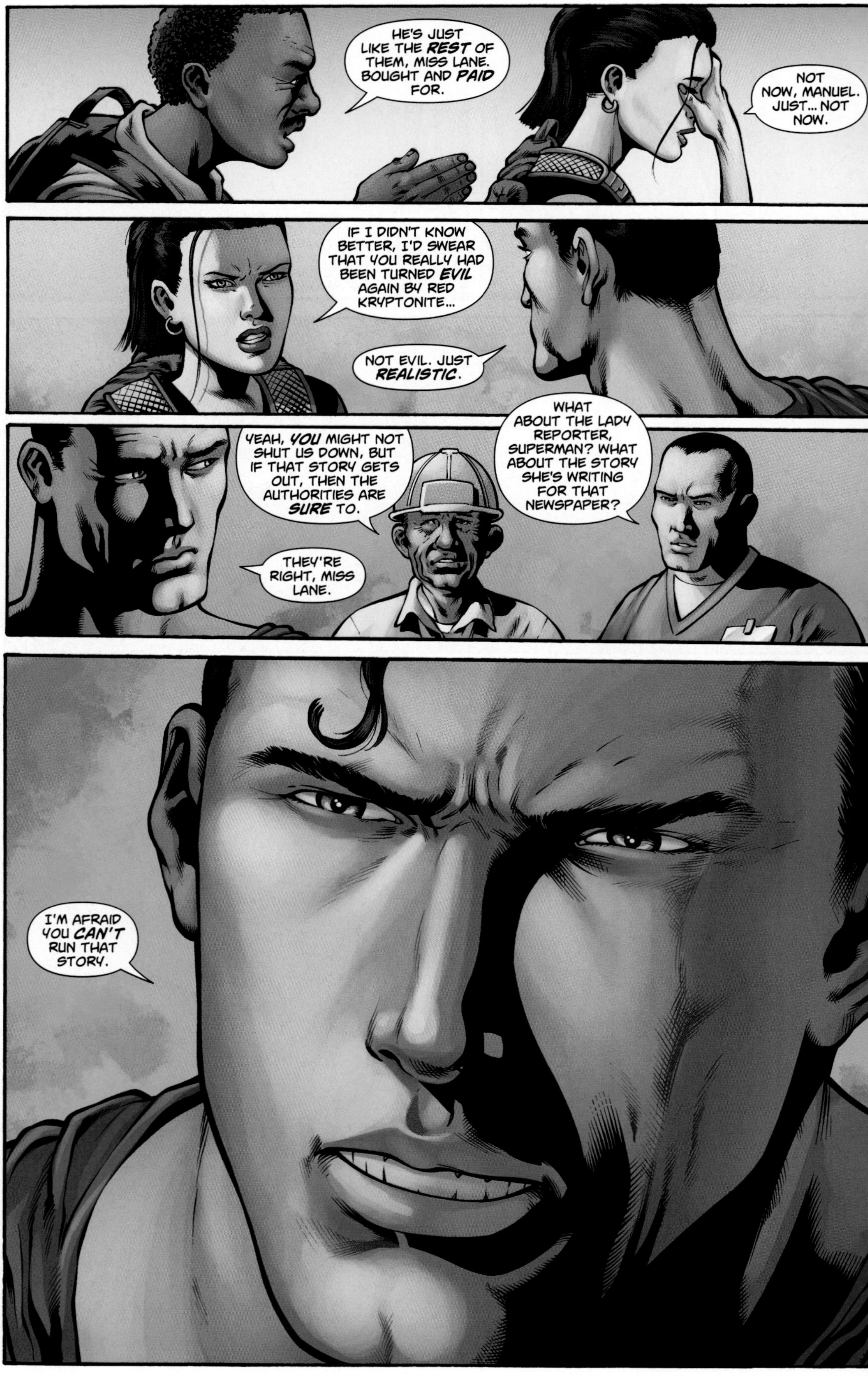
HE'S JUST LIKE THE REST OF THEM, MISS LANE. BOUGHT AND PAID FOR.
NOT NOW, MANUEL. JUST... NOT NOW.
IF I DIDN'T KNOW BETTER, I'D SWEAR THAT YOU REALLY HAD BEEN TURNED EVIL AGAIN BY RED KRYPTONITE...
NOT EVIL. JUST REALISTIC.
YEAH, YOU MIGHT NOT SHUT US DOWN, BUT IF THAT STORY GETS OUT, THEN THE AUTHORITIES ARE SURE TO.
WHAT ABOUT THE LADY REPORTER, SUPERMAN? WHAT ABOUT THE STORY SHE'S WRITING FOR THAT NEWSPAPER?
THEY'RE RIGHT, MISS LANE.
I'M AFRAID YOU CAN'T RUN THAT STORY.

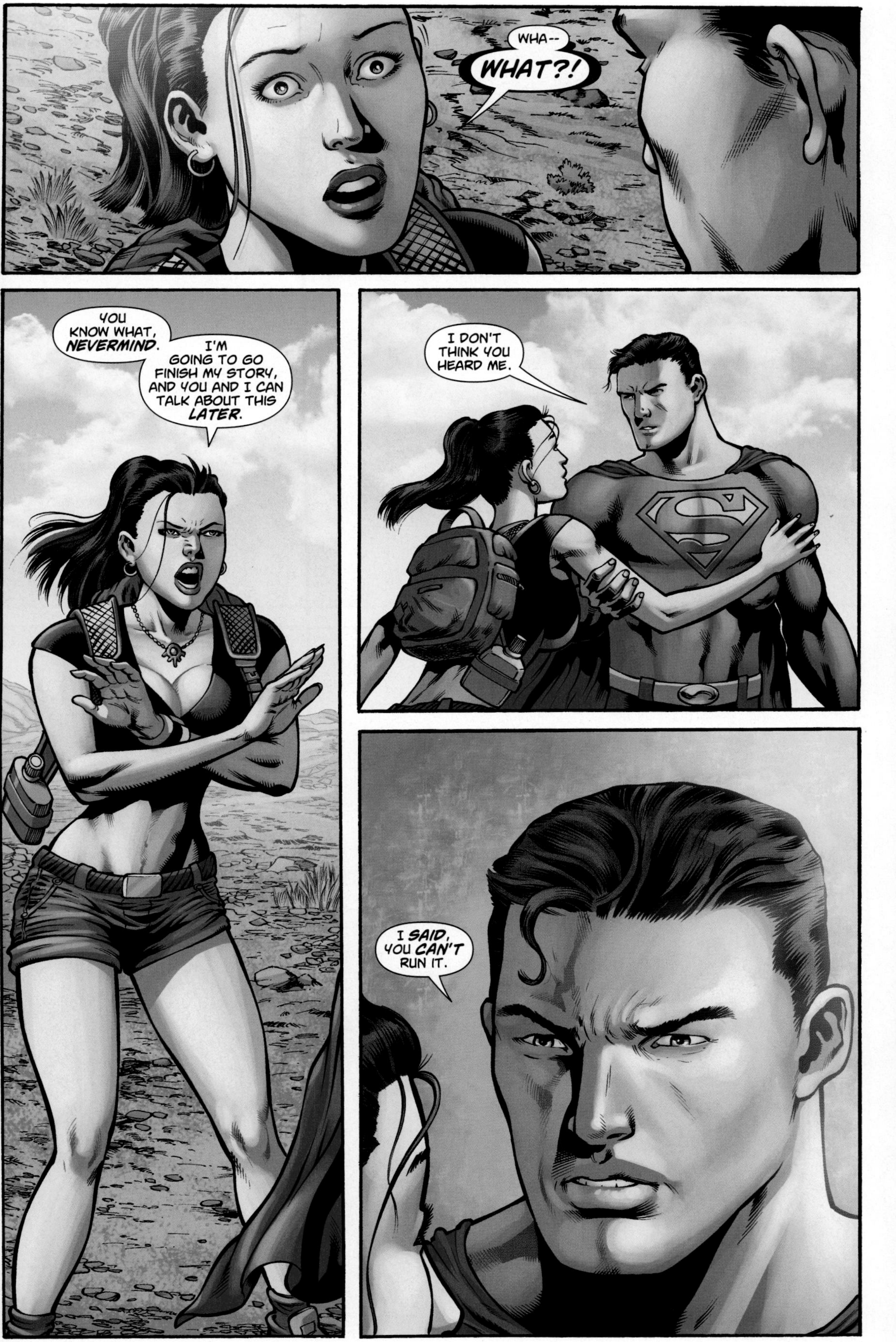
WHA--
WHAT?!
YOU KNOW WHAT, NEVERMIND.
I'M GOING TO GO FINISH MY STORY, AND YOU AND I CAN TALK ABOUT THIS LATER.
I DON'T THINK YOU HEARD ME.
I SAID, YOU CAN'T RUN IT.

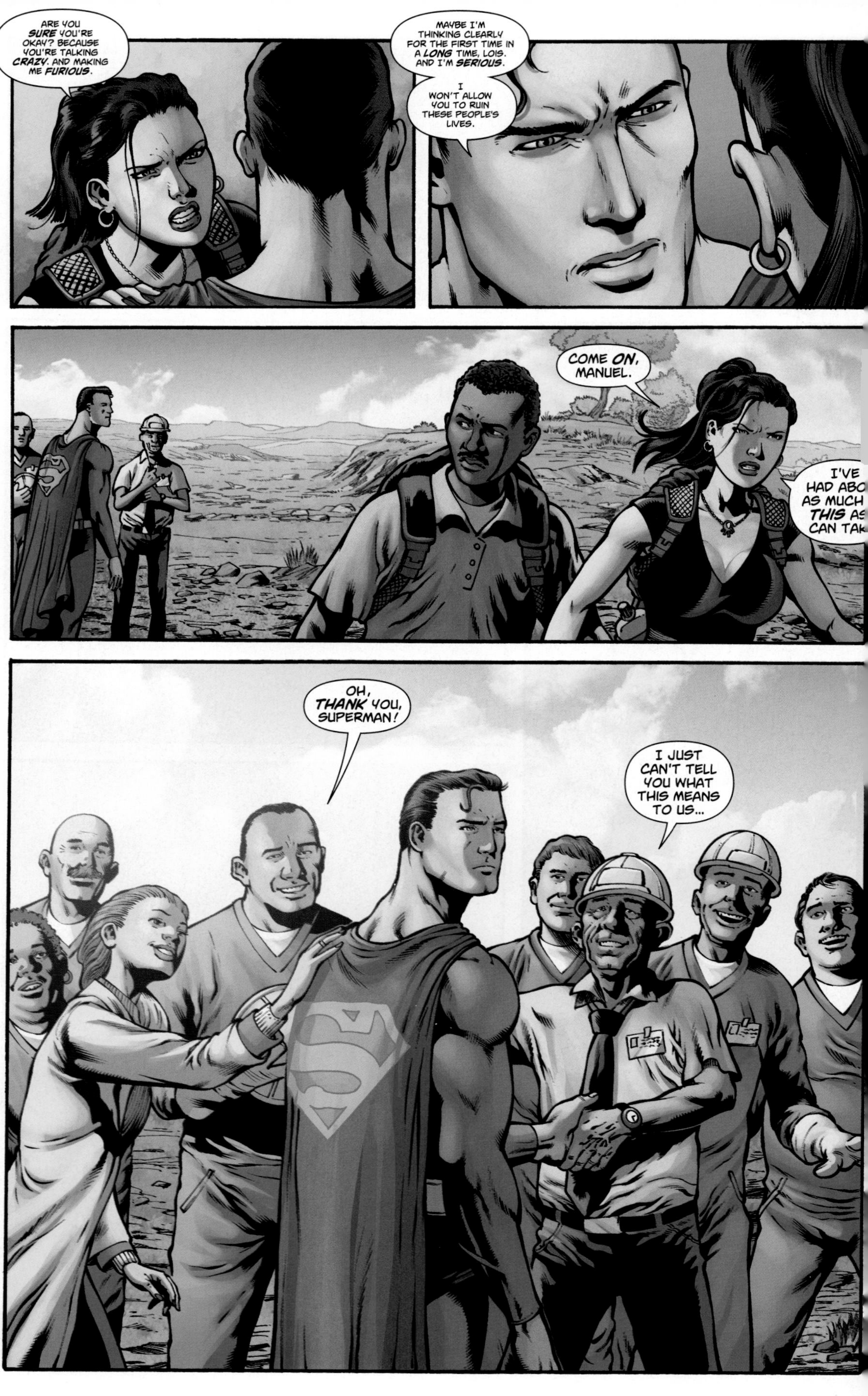
ARE YOU SURE YOU'RE OKAY? BECAUSE YOU'RE TALKING CRAZY. AND MAKING ME FURIOUS.
MAYBE I'M THINKING CLEARLY FOR THE FIRST TIME IN A LONG TIME, LOIS. AND I'M SERIOUS.
I WON'T ALLOW YOU TO RUIN THESE PEOPLE'S LIVES.
COME ON, MANUEL.
I'VE HAD ABO AS MUCH THIS AS CAN TAK
OH, THANK YOU, SUPERMAN!
I JUST CAN'T TELL YOU WHAT THIS MEANS TO US...

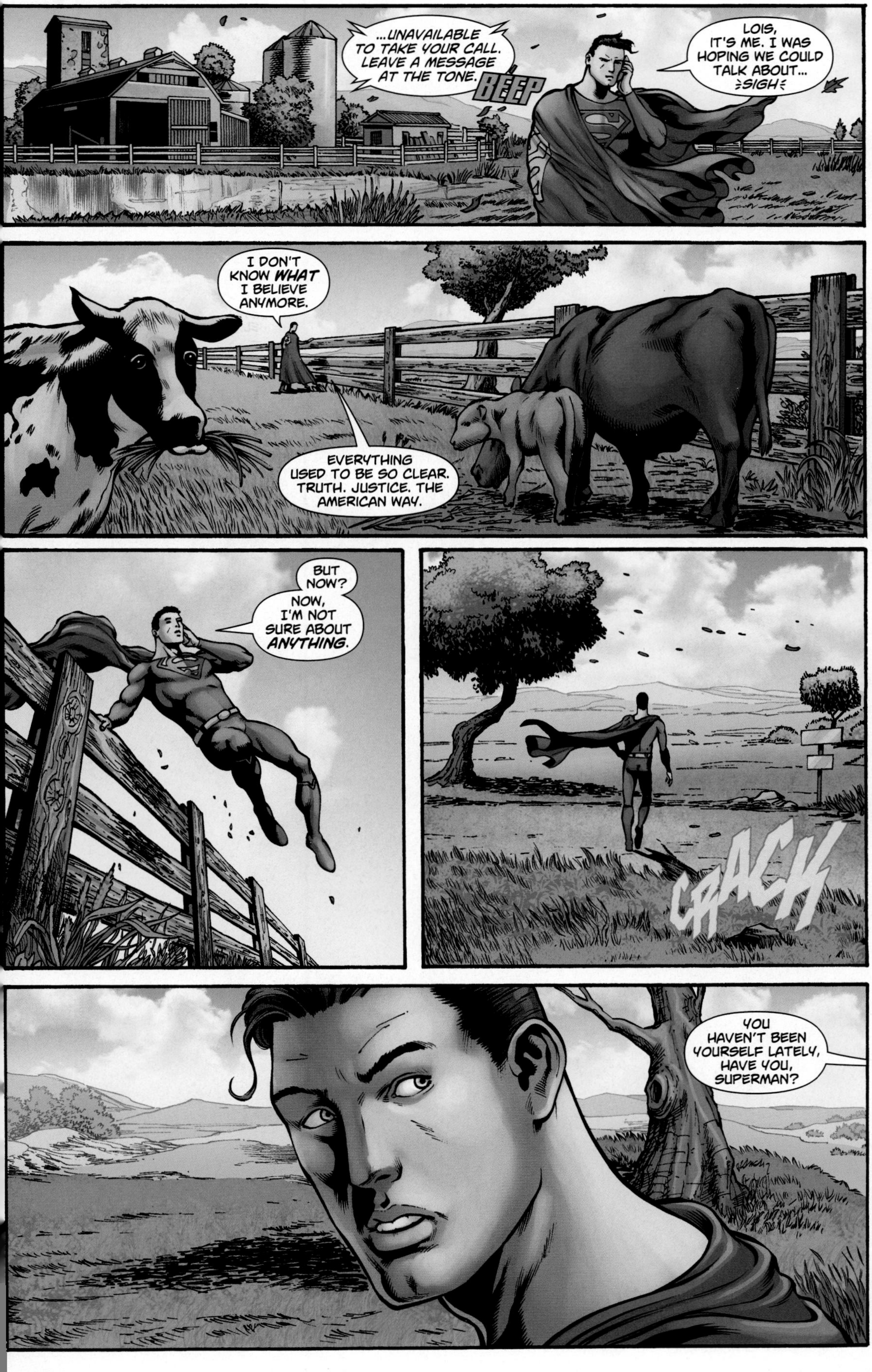
...UNAVAILABLE TO TAKE YOUR CALL. LEAVE A MESSAGE AT THE TONE.
BEEP
LOIS, IT'S ME. I WAS HOPING WE COULD TALK ABOUT... SIGH
I DON'T KNOW WHAT I BELIEVE ANYMORE.
EVERYTHING USED TO BE SO CLEAR. TRUTH. JUSTICE. THE AMERICAN WAY.
BUT NOW? NOW, I'M NOT SURE ABOUT ANYTHING.
CRACK
YOU HAVEN'T BEEN YOURSELF LATELY, HAVE YOU, SUPERMAN?

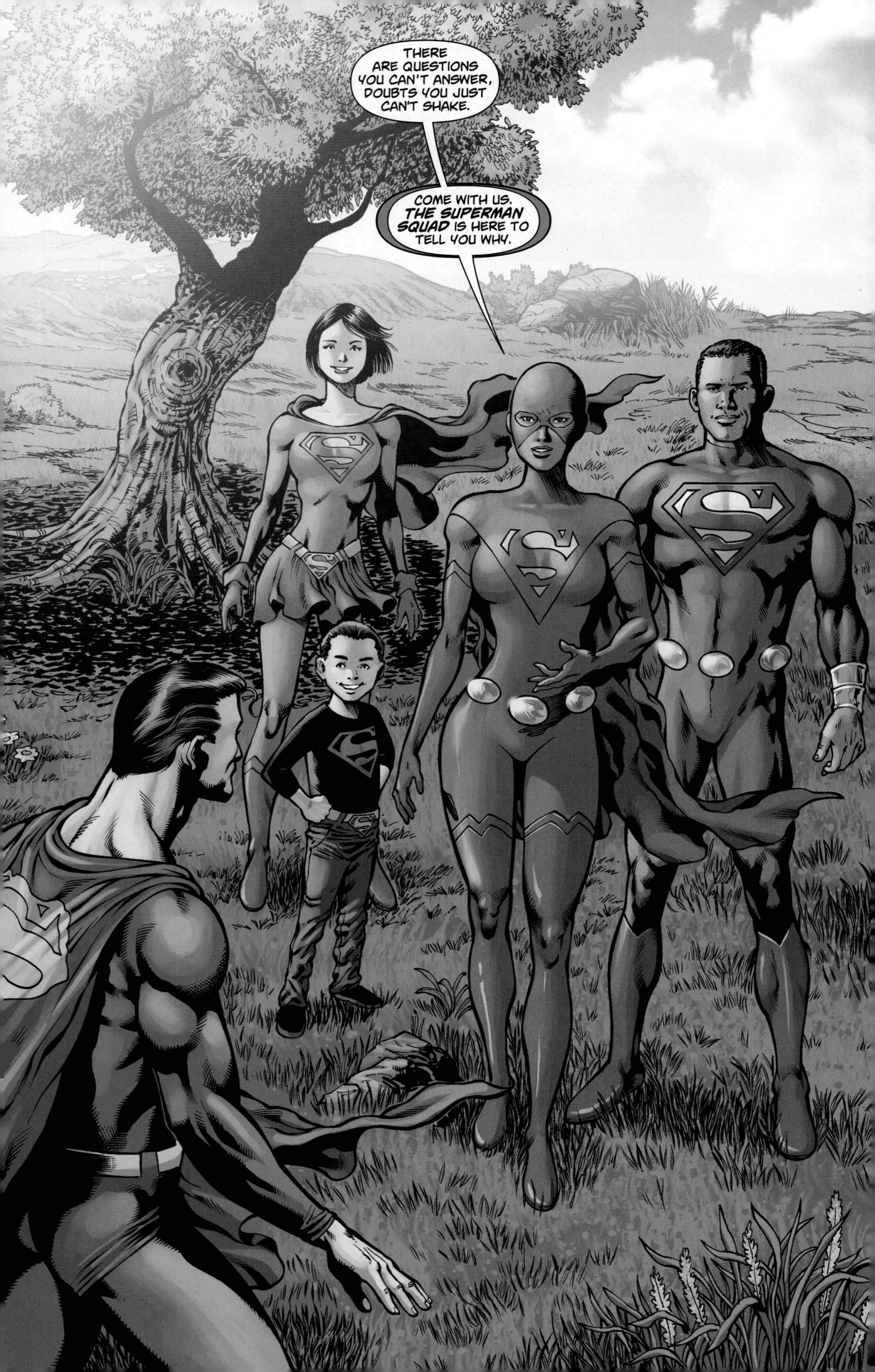
THERE ARE QUESTIONS YOU CAN'T ANSWER, DOUBTS YOU JUST CAN'T SHAKE.
COME WITH US. ***THE SUPERMAN SQUAD*** IS HERE TO TELL YOU WHY.

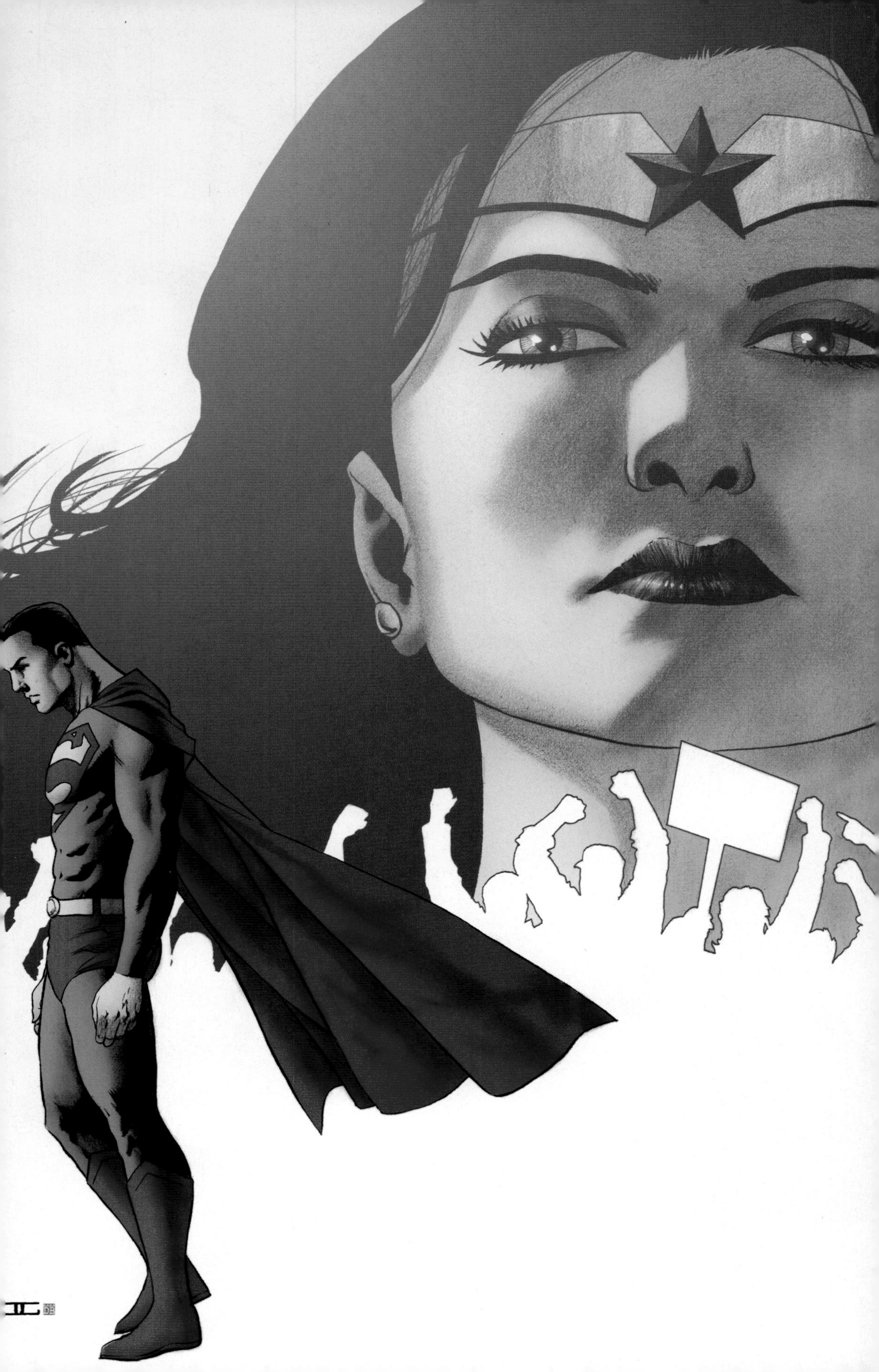

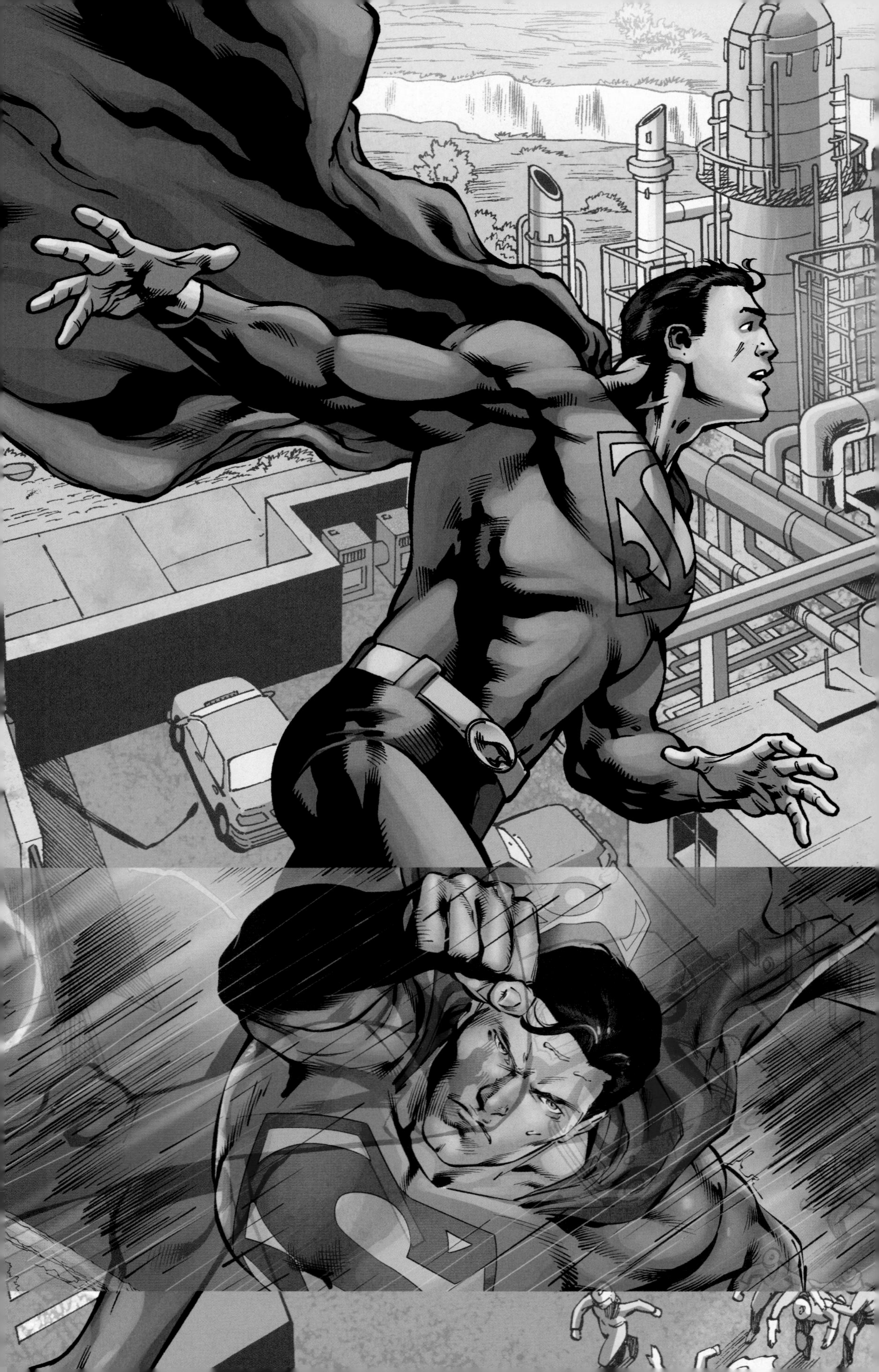

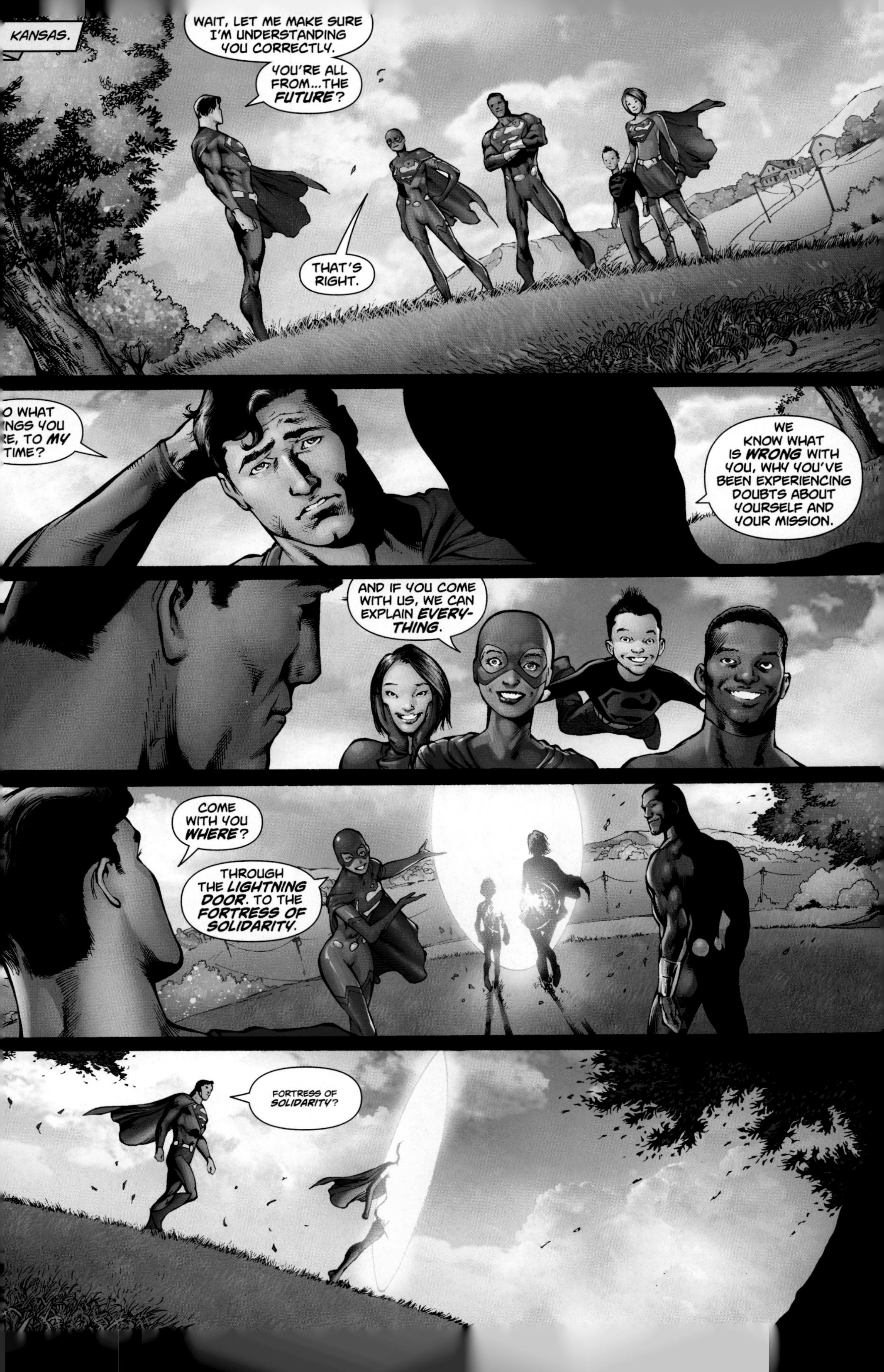
KANSAS.
WAIT, LET ME MAKE SURE I'M UNDERSTANDING YOU CORRECTLY.
YOU'RE ALL FROM...THE FUTURE?
THAT'S RIGHT.
O WHAT NGS YOU RE, TO MY TIME?
WE KNOW WHAT IS WRONG WITH YOU, WHY YOU'VE BEEN EXPERIENCING DOUBTS ABOUT YOURSELF AND YOUR MISSION.
AND IF YOU COME WITH US, WE CAN EXPLAIN EVERY-THING.
COME WITH YOU WHERE?
THROUGH THE LIGHTNING DOOR. TO THE FORTRESS OF SOLIDARITY.
FORTRESS OF SOLIDARITY?

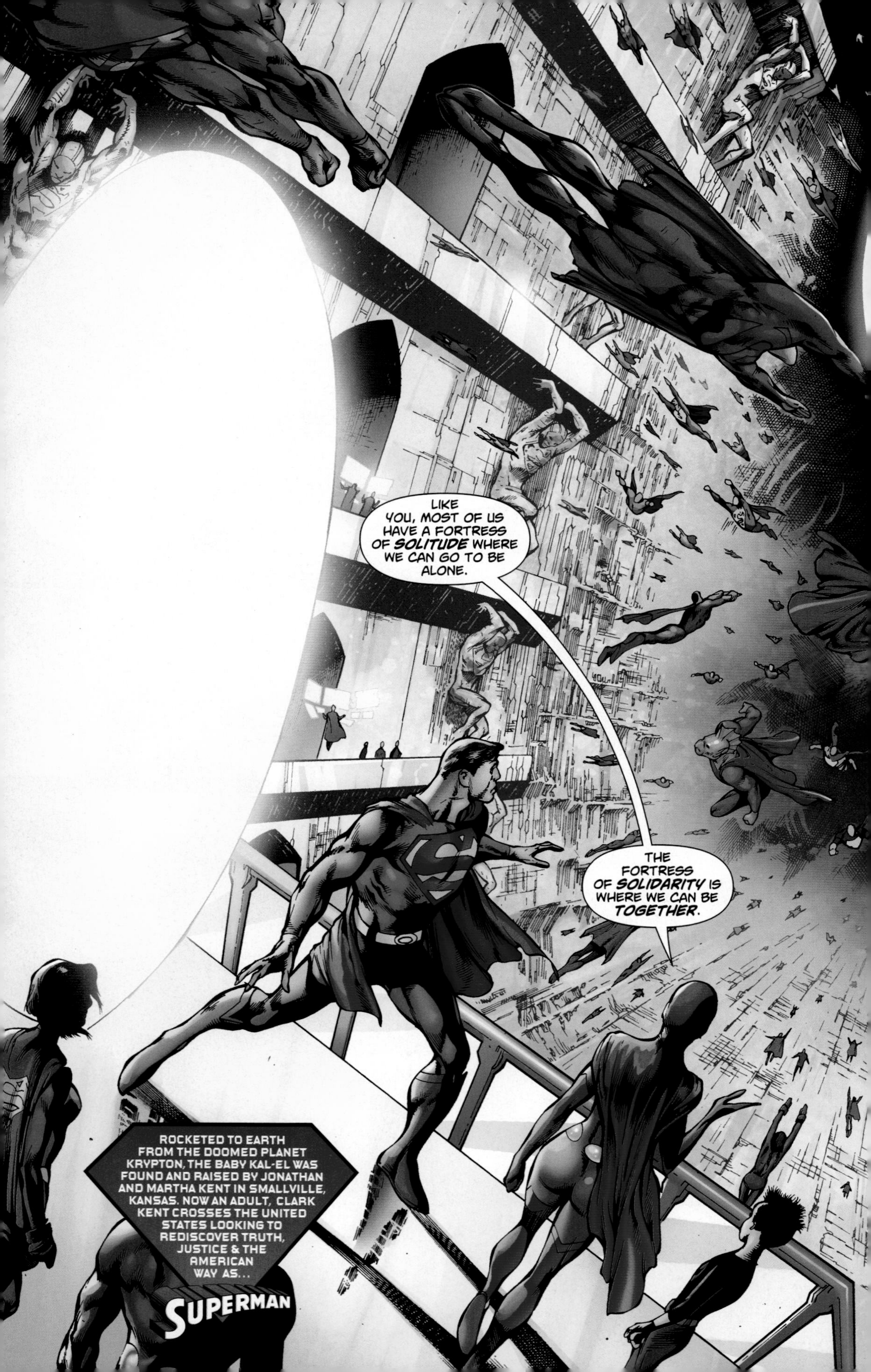

LIKE YOU, MOST OF US HAVE A FORTRESS OF SOLITUDE WHERE WE CAN GO TO BE ALONE.
THE FORTRESS OF SOLIDARITY IS WHERE WE CAN BE TOGETHER.
ROCKETED TO EARTH FROM THE DOOMED PLANET KRYPTON, THE BABY KAL-EL WAS FOUND AND RAISED BY JONATHAN AND MARTHA KENT IN SMALLVILLE, KANSAS. NOW AN ADULT, CLARK KENT CROSSES THE UNITED STATES LOOKING TO REDISCOVER TRUTH, JUSTICE & THE AMERICAN WAY AS...
SUPERMAN

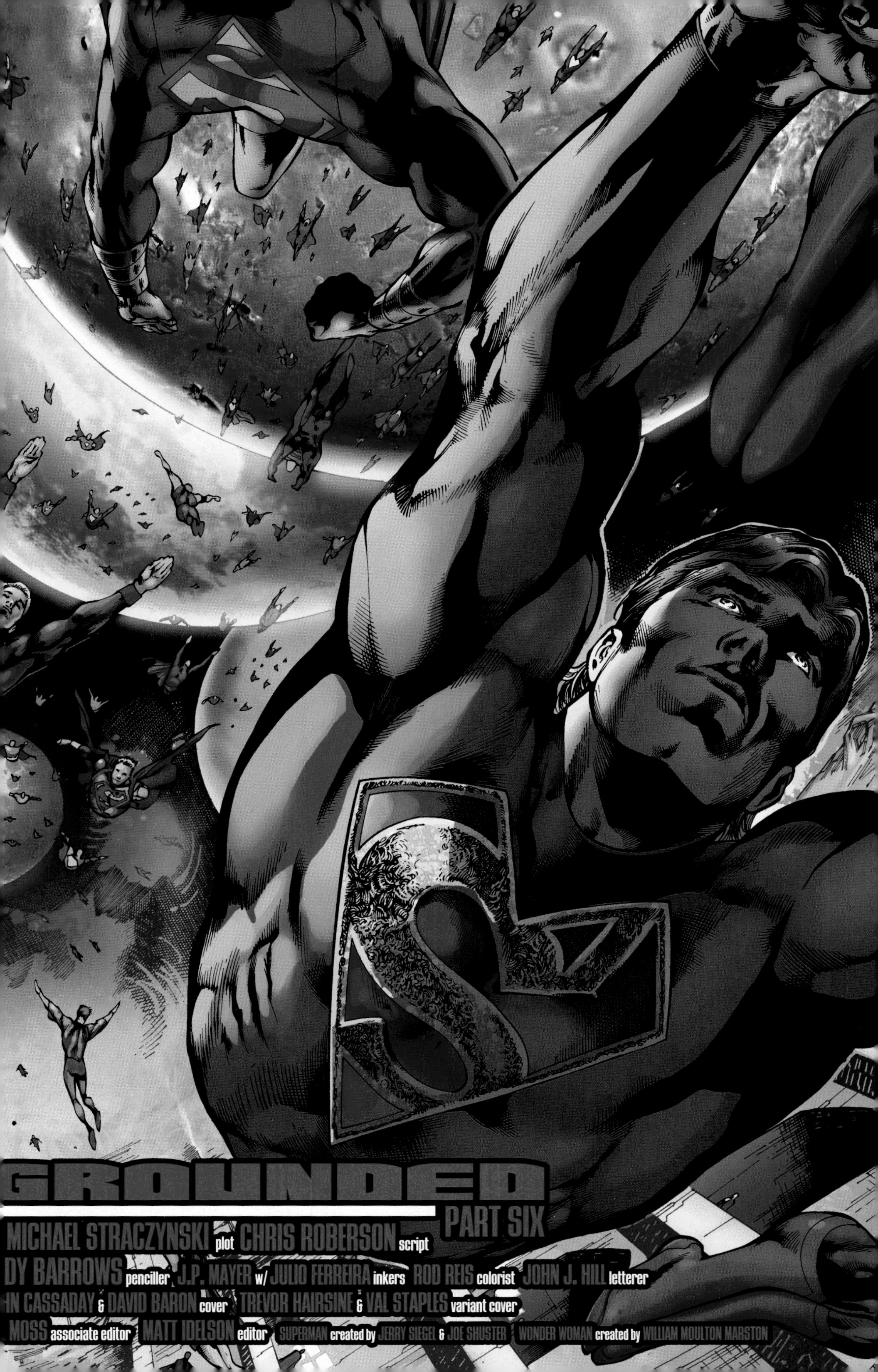
GROUNDED
PART SIX
MICHAEL STRACZYNSKI plot CHRIS ROBERSON script
DY BARROWS penciller J.P. MAYER w/ JULIO FERREIRA inkers ROD REIS colorist JOHN J. HILL letterer
IN CASSADAY & DAVID BARON cover TREVOR HAIRSINE & VAL STAPLES variant cover
MOSS associate editor MATT IDELSON editor SUPERMAN created by JERRY SIEGEL & JOE SHUSTER WONDER WOMAN created by WILLIAM MOULTON MARSTON

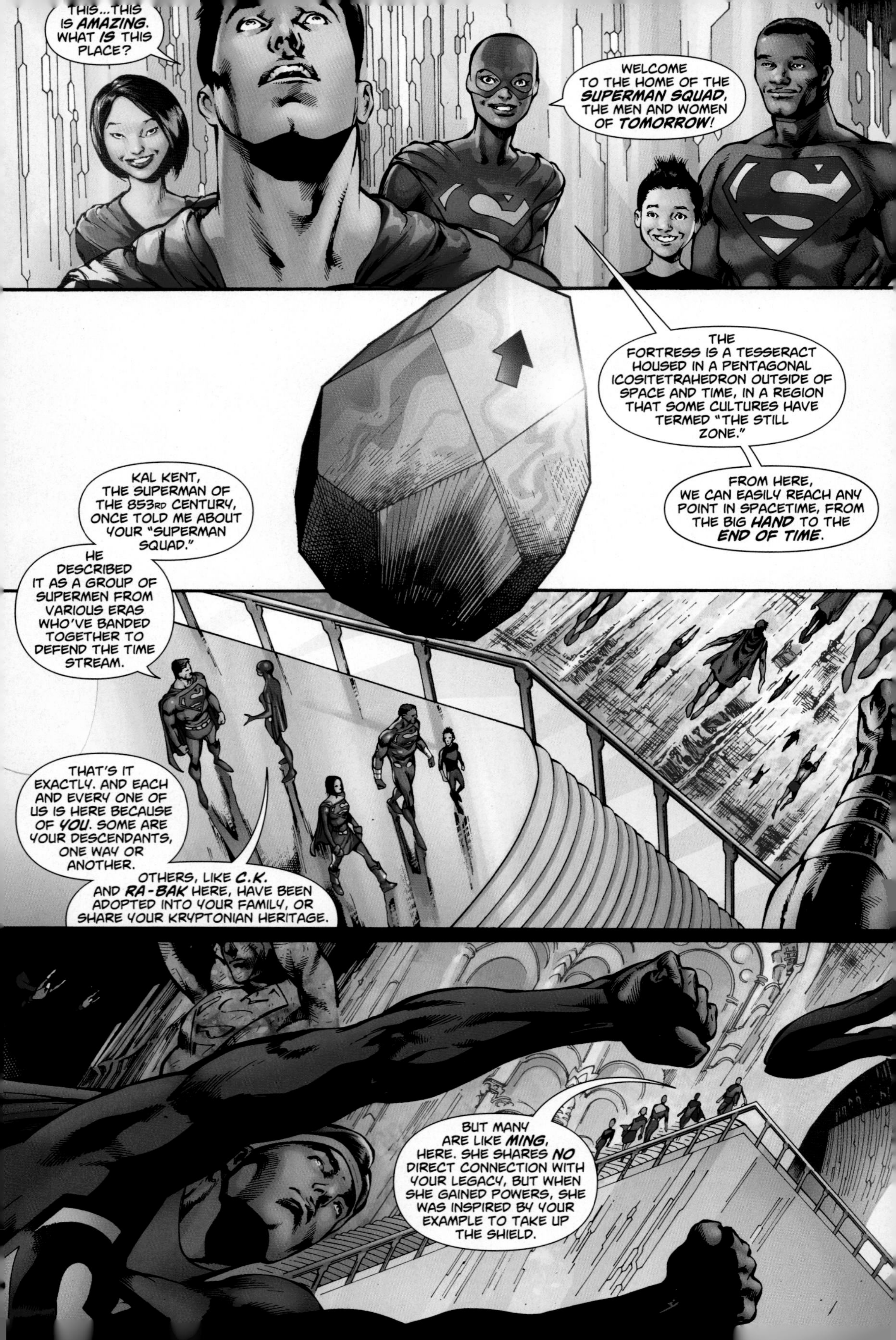

THIS...THIS IS AMAZING. WHAT IS THIS PLACE?
WELCOME TO THE HOME OF THE SUPERMAN SQUAD, THE MEN AND WOMEN OF TOMORROW!
THE FORTRESS IS A TESSERACT HOUSED IN A PENTAGONAL ICOSITETRAHEDRON OUTSIDE OF SPACE AND TIME, IN A REGION THAT SOME CULTURES HAVE TERMED "THE STILL ZONE."
FROM HERE, WE CAN EASILY REACH ANY POINT IN SPACETIME, FROM THE BIG HAND TO THE END OF TIME.
KAL KENT, THE SUPERMAN OF THE 853RD CENTURY, ONCE TOLD ME ABOUT YOUR "SUPERMAN SQUAD."
HE DESCRIBED IT AS A GROUP OF SUPERMEN FROM VARIOUS ERAS WHO'VE BANDED TOGETHER TO DEFEND THE TIME STREAM.
THAT'S IT EXACTLY. AND EACH AND EVERY ONE OF US IS HERE BECAUSE OF YOU. SOME ARE YOUR DESCENDANTS, ONE WAY OR ANOTHER.
OTHERS, LIKE C.K. AND RA-BAK HERE, HAVE BEEN ADOPTED INTO YOUR FAMILY, OR SHARE YOUR KRYPTONIAN HERITAGE.
BUT MANY ARE LIKE MING, HERE. SHE SHARES NO DIRECT CONNECTION WITH YOUR LEGACY, BUT WHEN SHE GAINED POWERS, SHE WAS INSPIRED BY YOUR EXAMPLE TO TAKE UP THE SHIELD.

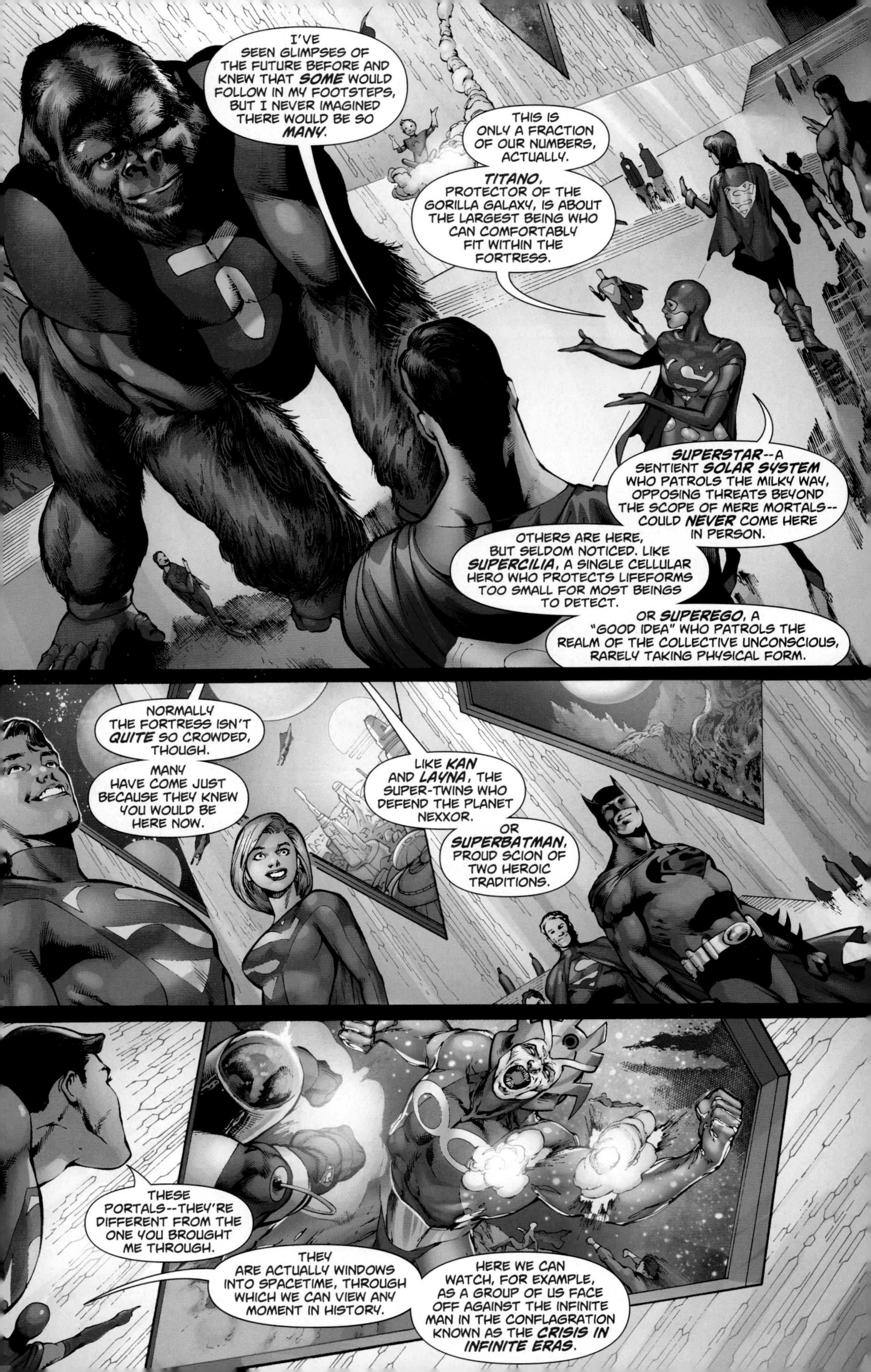
I'VE SEEN GLIMPSES OF THE FUTURE BEFORE AND KNEW THAT SOME WOULD FOLLOW IN MY FOOTSTEPS, BUT I NEVER IMAGINED THERE WOULD BE SO MANY.
THIS IS ONLY A FRACTION OF OUR NUMBERS, ACTUALLY.
TITANO, PROTECTOR OF THE GORILLA GALAXY, IS ABOUT THE LARGEST BEING WHO CAN COMFORTABLY FIT WITHIN THE FORTRESS.
SUPERSTAR--A SENTIENT SOLAR SYSTEM WHO PATROLS THE MILKY WAY, OPPOSING THREATS BEYOND THE SCOPE OF MERE MORTALS--COULD NEVER COME HERE IN PERSON.
OTHERS ARE HERE, BUT SELDOM NOTICED. LIKE SUPERCILIA, A SINGLE CELLULAR HERO WHO PROTECTS LIFEFORMS TOO SMALL FOR MOST BEINGS TO DETECT.
OR SUPEREGO, A "GOOD IDEA" WHO PATROLS THE REALM OF THE COLLECTIVE UNCONSCIOUS, RARELY TAKING PHYSICAL FORM.
NORMALLY THE FORTRESS ISN'T QUITE SO CROWDED, THOUGH.
MANY HAVE COME JUST BECAUSE THEY KNEW YOU WOULD BE HERE NOW.
LIKE KAN AND LAYNA, THE SUPER-TWINS WHO DEFEND THE PLANET NEXXOR.
OR SUPERBATMAN, PROUD SCION OF TWO HEROIC TRADITIONS.
THESE PORTALS--THEY'RE DIFFERENT FROM THE ONE YOU BROUGHT ME THROUGH.
THEY ARE ACTUALLY WINDOWS INTO SPACETIME, THROUGH WHICH WE CAN VIEW ANY MOMENT IN HISTORY.
HERE WE CAN WATCH, FOR EXAMPLE, AS A GROUP OF US FACE OFF AGAINST THE INFINITE MAN IN THE CONFLAGRATION KNOWN AS THE CRISIS IN INFINITE ERAS.

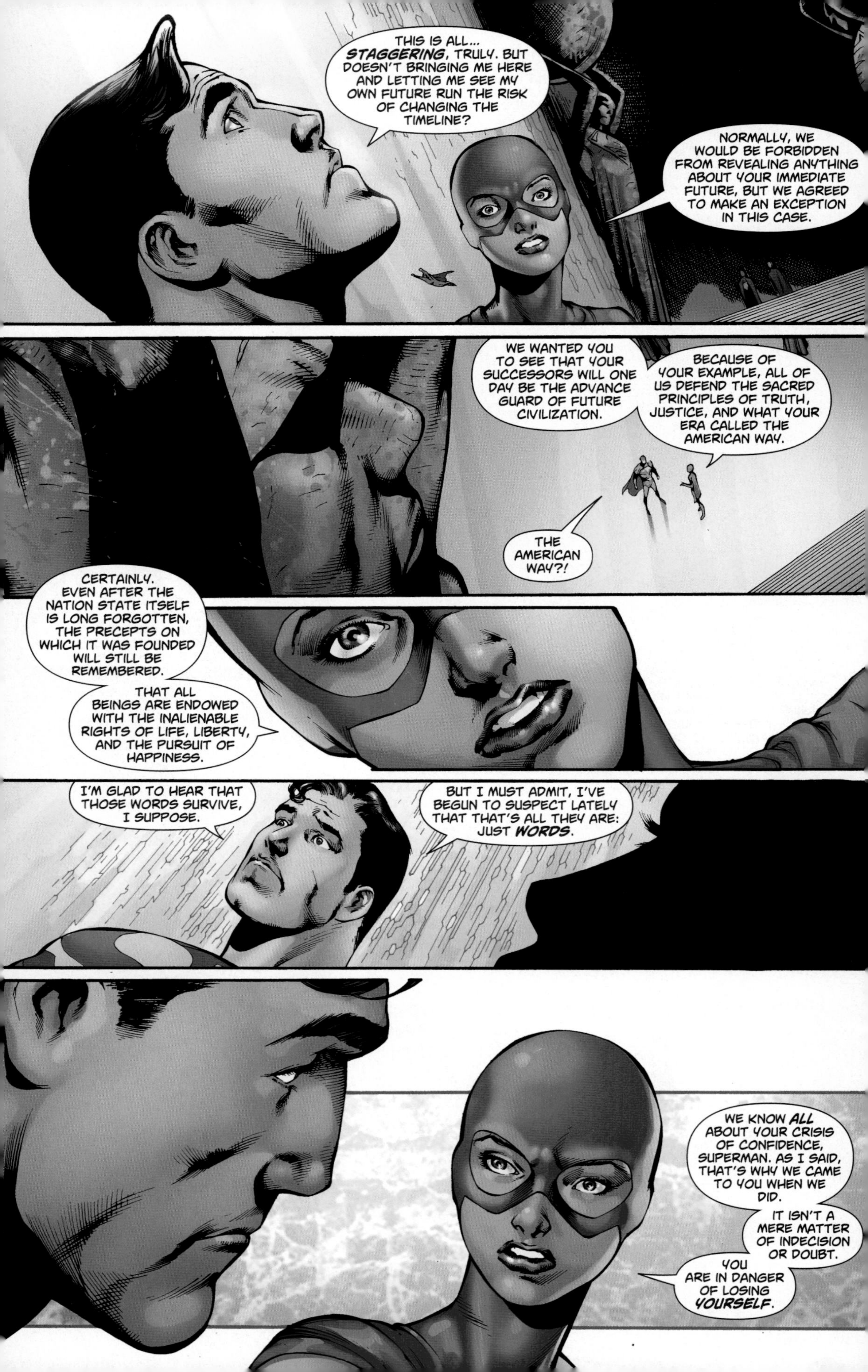
THIS IS ALL... STAGGERING, TRULY. BUT DOESN'T BRINGING ME HERE AND LETTING ME SEE MY OWN FUTURE RUN THE RISK OF CHANGING THE TIMELINE?
NORMALLY, WE WOULD BE FORBIDDEN FROM REVEALING ANYTHING ABOUT YOUR IMMEDIATE FUTURE, BUT WE AGREED TO MAKE AN EXCEPTION IN THIS CASE.
WE WANTED YOU TO SEE THAT YOUR SUCCESSORS WILL ONE DAY BE THE ADVANCE GUARD OF FUTURE CIVILIZATION.
BECAUSE OF YOUR EXAMPLE, ALL OF US DEFEND THE SACRED PRINCIPLES OF TRUTH, JUSTICE, AND WHAT YOUR ERA CALLED THE AMERICAN WAY.
THE AMERICAN WAY?!
CERTAINLY. EVEN AFTER THE NATION STATE ITSELF IS LONG FORGOTTEN, THE PRECEPTS ON WHICH IT WAS FOUNDED WILL STILL BE REMEMBERED.
THAT ALL BEINGS ARE ENDOWED WITH THE INALIENABLE RIGHTS OF LIFE, LIBERTY, AND THE PURSUIT OF HAPPINESS.
I'M GLAD TO HEAR THAT THOSE WORDS SURVIVE, I SUPPOSE.
BUT I MUST ADMIT, I'VE BEGUN TO SUSPECT LATELY THAT THAT'S ALL THEY ARE: JUST WORDS.
WE KNOW ALL ABOUT YOUR CRISIS OF CONFIDENCE, SUPERMAN. AS I SAID, THAT'S WHY WE CAME TO YOU WHEN WE DID.
IT ISN'T A MERE MATTER OF INDECISION OR DOUBT.
YOU ARE IN DANGER OF LOSING YOURSELF.

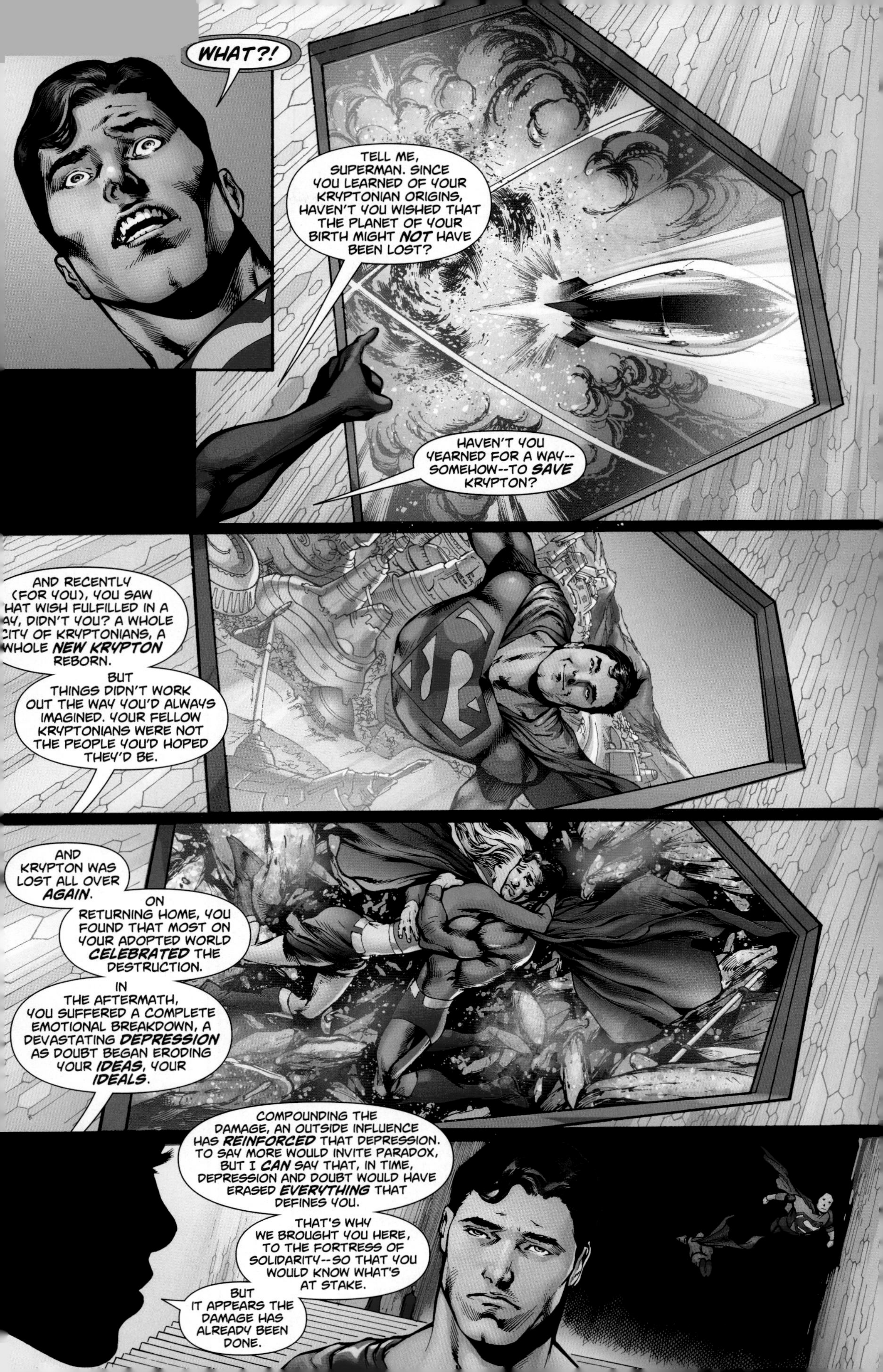
WHAT?!
TELL ME, SUPERMAN. SINCE YOU LEARNED OF YOUR KRYPTONIAN ORIGINS, HAVEN'T YOU WISHED THAT THE PLANET OF YOUR BIRTH MIGHT NOT HAVE BEEN LOST?
HAVEN'T YOU YEARNED FOR A WAY--SOMEHOW--TO SAVE KRYPTON?
AND RECENTLY (FOR YOU), YOU SAW THAT WISH FULFILLED IN A WAY, DIDN'T YOU? A WHOLE CITY OF KRYPTONIANS, A WHOLE NEW KRYPTON REBORN.
BUT THINGS DIDN'T WORK OUT THE WAY YOU'D ALWAYS IMAGINED. YOUR FELLOW KRYPTONIANS WERE NOT THE PEOPLE YOU'D HOPED THEY'D BE.
AND KRYPTON WAS LOST ALL OVER AGAIN.
ON RETURNING HOME, YOU FOUND THAT MOST ON YOUR ADOPTED WORLD CELEBRATED THE DESTRUCTION.
IN THE AFTERMATH, YOU SUFFERED A COMPLETE EMOTIONAL BREAKDOWN, A DEVASTATING DEPRESSION AS DOUBT BEGAN ERODING YOUR IDEAS, YOUR IDEALS.
COMPOUNDING THE DAMAGE, AN OUTSIDE INFLUENCE HAS REINFORCED THAT DEPRESSION. TO SAY MORE WOULD INVITE PARADOX, BUT I CAN SAY THAT, IN TIME, DEPRESSION AND DOUBT WOULD HAVE ERASED EVERYTHING THAT DEFINES YOU.
THAT'S WHY WE BROUGHT YOU HERE, TO THE FORTRESS OF SOLIDARITY--SO THAT YOU WOULD KNOW WHAT'S AT STAKE.
BUT IT APPEARS THE DAMAGE HAS ALREADY BEEN DONE.

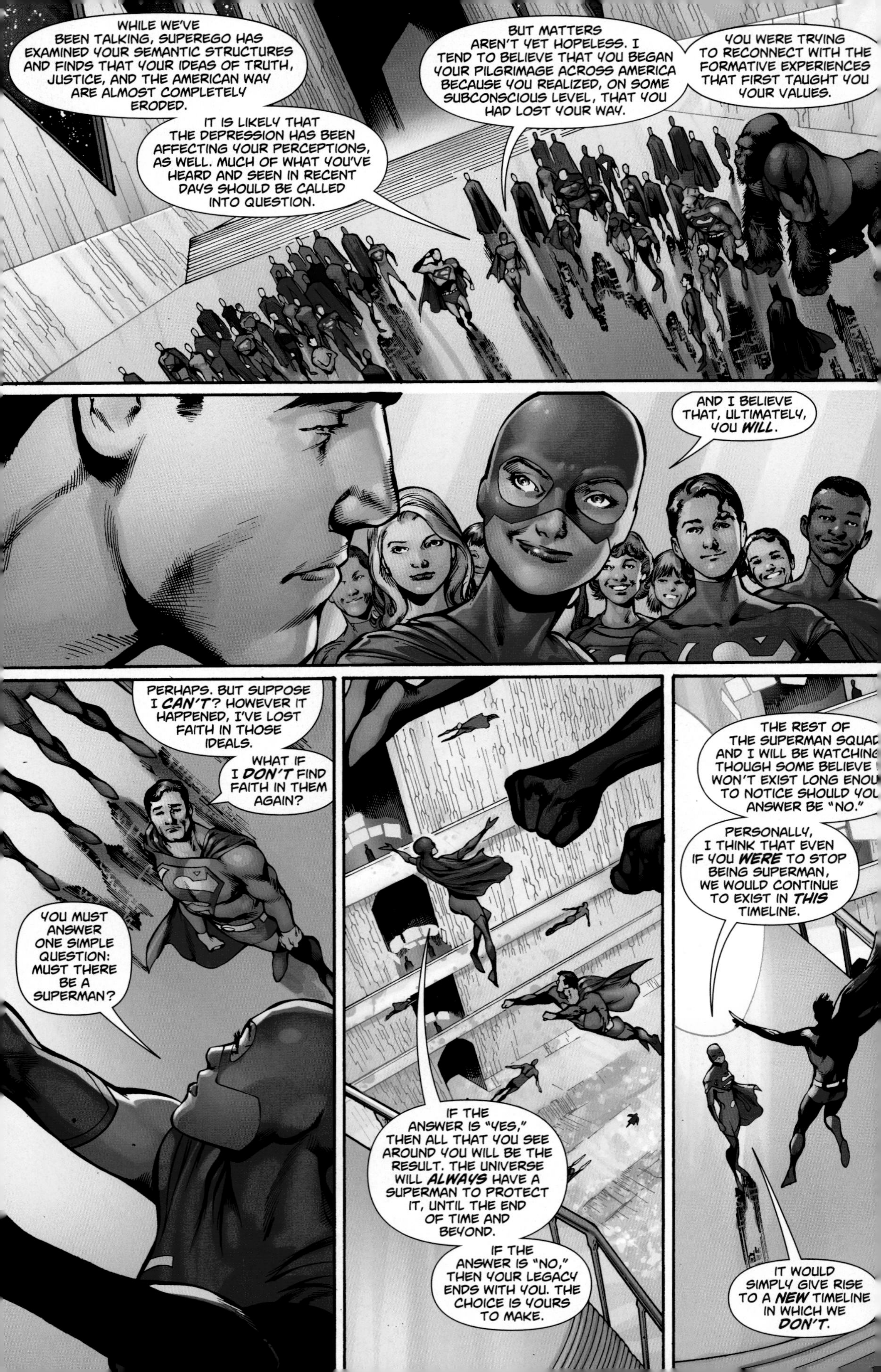

WHILE WE'VE BEEN TALKING, SUPEREGO HAS EXAMINED YOUR SEMANTIC STRUCTURES AND FINDS THAT YOUR IDEAS OF TRUTH, JUSTICE, AND THE AMERICAN WAY ARE ALMOST COMPLETELY ERODED.
IT IS LIKELY THAT THE DEPRESSION HAS BEEN AFFECTING YOUR PERCEPTIONS, AS WELL. MUCH OF WHAT YOU'VE HEARD AND SEEN IN RECENT DAYS SHOULD BE CALLED INTO QUESTION.
BUT MATTERS AREN'T YET HOPELESS. I TEND TO BELIEVE THAT YOU BEGAN YOUR PILGRIMAGE ACROSS AMERICA BECAUSE YOU REALIZED, ON SOME SUBCONSCIOUS LEVEL, THAT YOU HAD LOST YOUR WAY.
YOU WERE TRYING TO RECONNECT WITH THE FORMATIVE EXPERIENCES THAT FIRST TAUGHT YOU YOUR VALUES.
AND I BELIEVE THAT, ULTIMATELY, YOU *WILL*.
PERHAPS. BUT SUPPOSE I *CAN'T*? HOWEVER IT HAPPENED, I'VE LOST FAITH IN THOSE IDEALS.
WHAT IF I *DON'T* FIND FAITH IN THEM AGAIN?
YOU MUST ANSWER ONE SIMPLE QUESTION: MUST THERE BE A SUPERMAN?
IF THE ANSWER IS "YES," THEN ALL THAT YOU SEE AROUND YOU WILL BE THE RESULT. THE UNIVERSE WILL *ALWAYS* HAVE A SUPERMAN TO PROTECT IT, UNTIL THE END OF TIME AND BEYOND.
IF THE ANSWER IS "NO," THEN YOUR LEGACY ENDS WITH YOU. THE CHOICE IS YOURS TO MAKE.
THE REST OF THE SUPERMAN SQUAD AND I WILL BE WATCHING THOUGH SOME BELIEVE WON'T EXIST LONG ENOU TO NOTICE SHOULD YOU ANSWER BE "NO."
PERSONALLY, I THINK THAT EVEN IF YOU *WERE* TO STOP BEING SUPERMAN, WE WOULD CONTINUE TO EXIST IN *THIS* TIMELINE.
IT WOULD SIMPLY GIVE RISE TO A *NEW* TIMELINE IN WHICH WE *DON'T*.

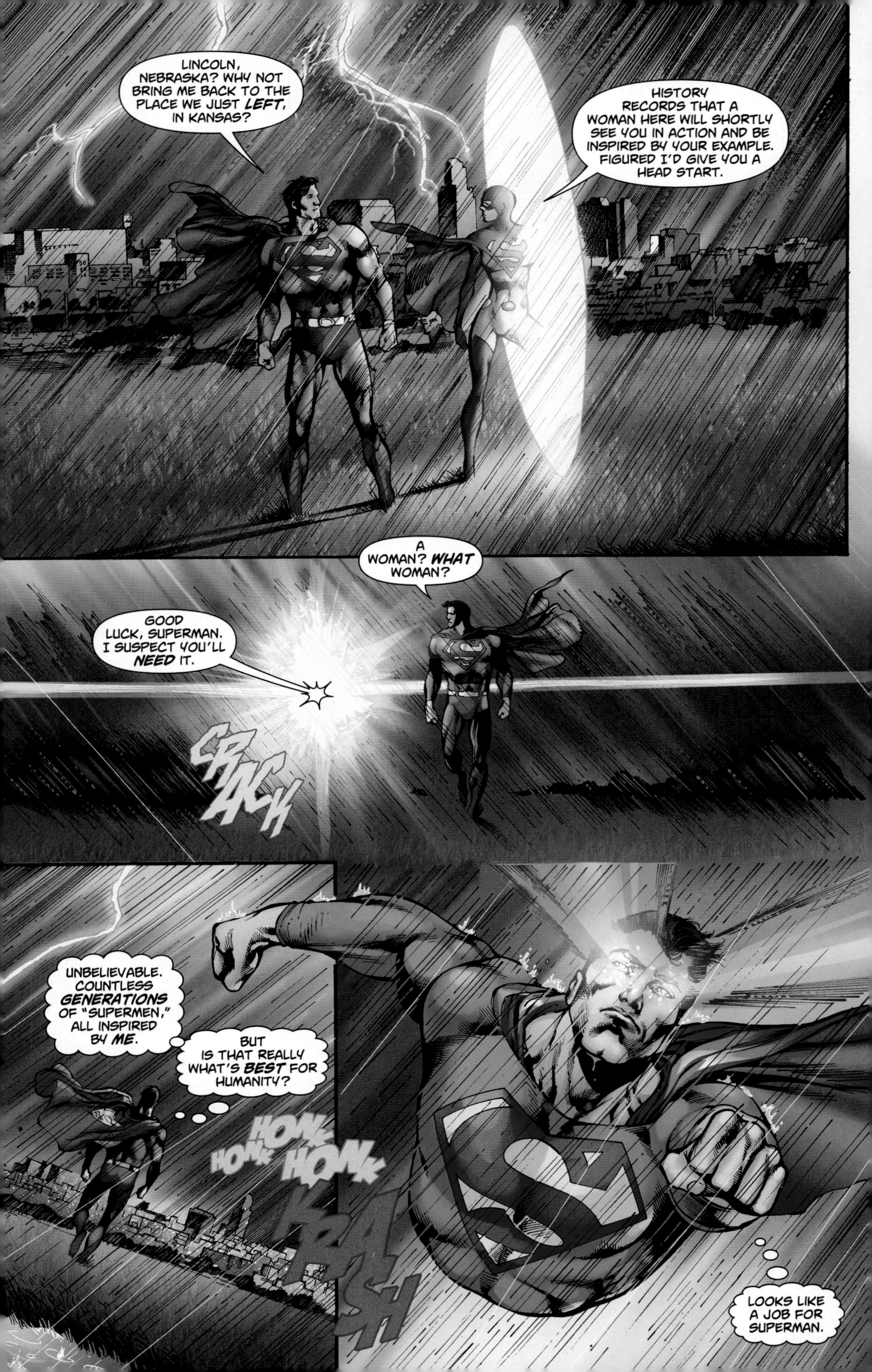

LINCOLN, NEBRASKA? WHY NOT BRING ME BACK TO THE PLACE WE JUST *LEFT*, IN KANSAS?
HISTORY RECORDS THAT A WOMAN HERE WILL SHORTLY SEE YOU IN ACTION AND BE INSPIRED BY YOUR EXAMPLE. FIGURED I'D GIVE YOU A HEAD START.
A WOMAN? *WHAT* WOMAN?
GOOD LUCK, SUPERMAN. I SUSPECT YOU'LL *NEED* IT.
CRACK
UNBELIEVABLE. COUNTLESS *GENERATIONS* OF "SUPERMEN," ALL INSPIRED BY *ME*.
BUT IS THAT REALLY WHAT'S *BEST* FOR HUMANITY?
HONK HONK HONK
KRASH
LOOKS LIKE A JOB FOR SUPERMAN.

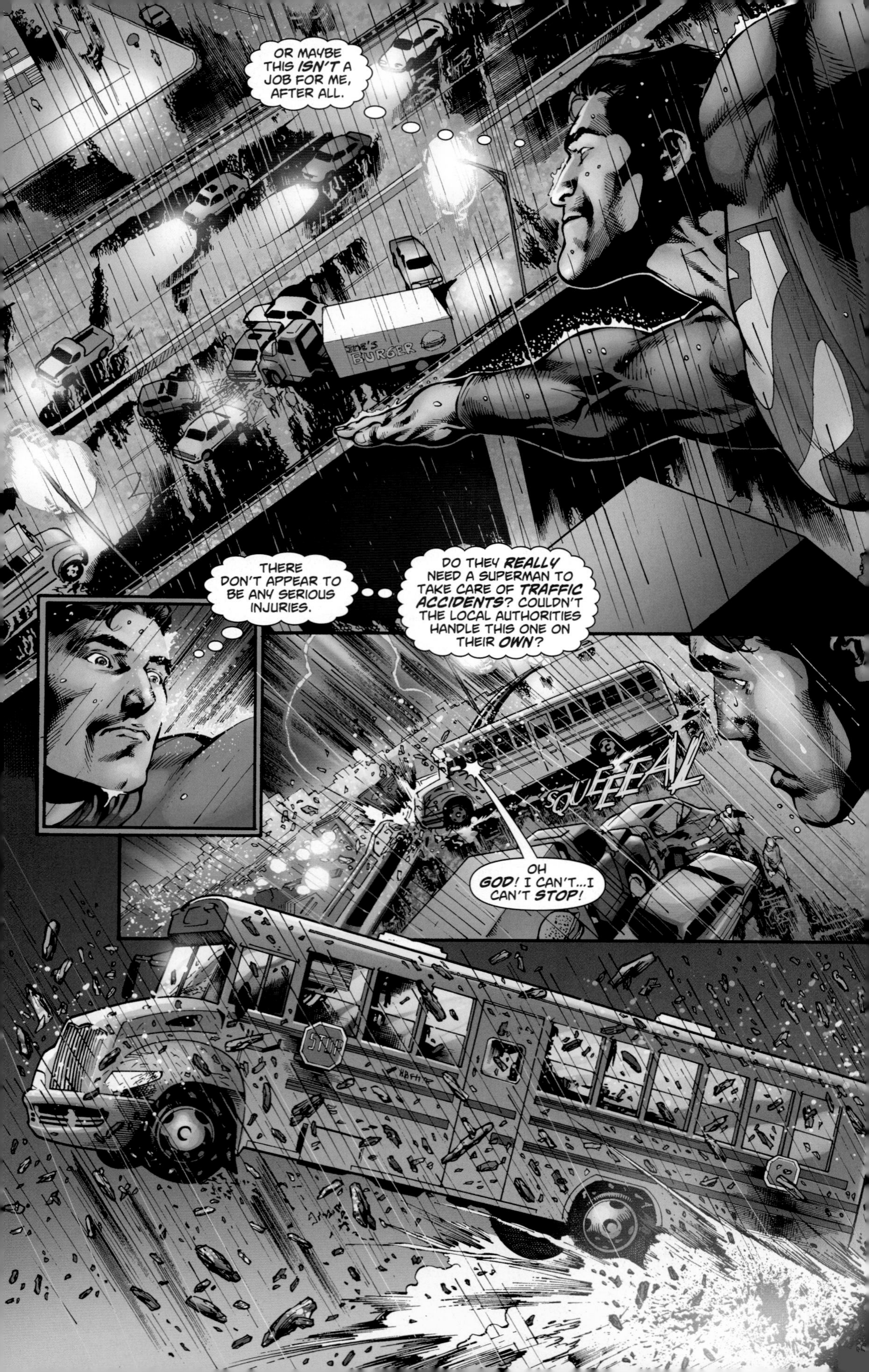
OR MAYBE THIS ISN'T A JOB FOR ME, AFTER ALL.
THERE DON'T APPEAR TO BE ANY SERIOUS INJURIES.
DO THEY REALLY NEED A SUPERMAN TO TAKE CARE OF TRAFFIC ACCIDENTS? COULDN'T THE LOCAL AUTHORITIES HANDLE THIS ONE ON THEIR OWN?
SQUEEEEAL
OH GOD! I CAN'T...I CAN'T STOP!
JOE'S BURGER
STOP

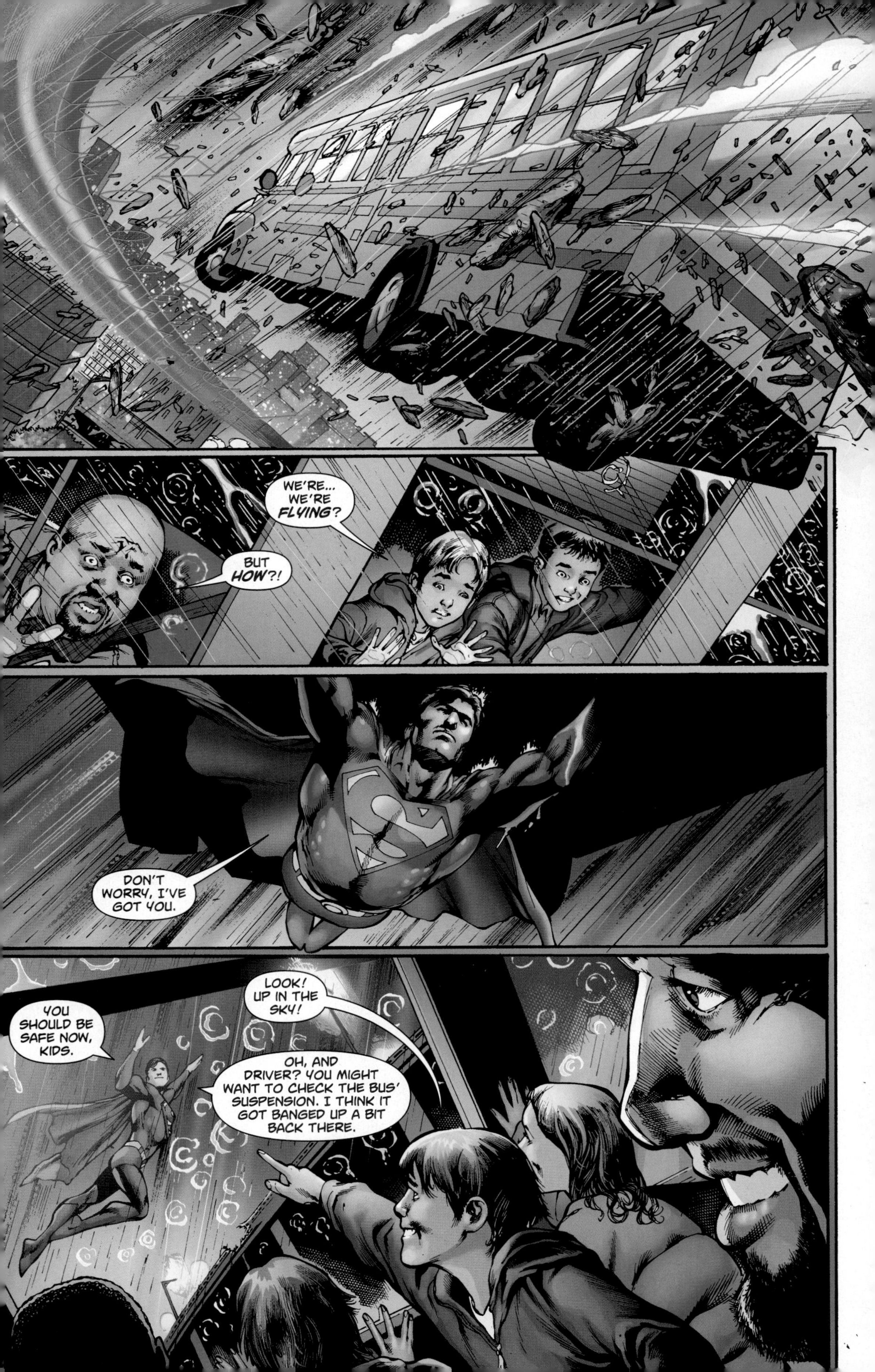
WE'RE... WE'RE FLYING?
BUT HOW?!
DON'T WORRY, I'VE GOT YOU.
YOU SHOULD BE SAFE NOW, KIDS.
LOOK! UP IN THE SKY!
OH, AND DRIVER? YOU MIGHT WANT TO CHECK THE BUS' SUSPENSION. I THINK IT GOT BANGED UP A BIT BACK THERE.

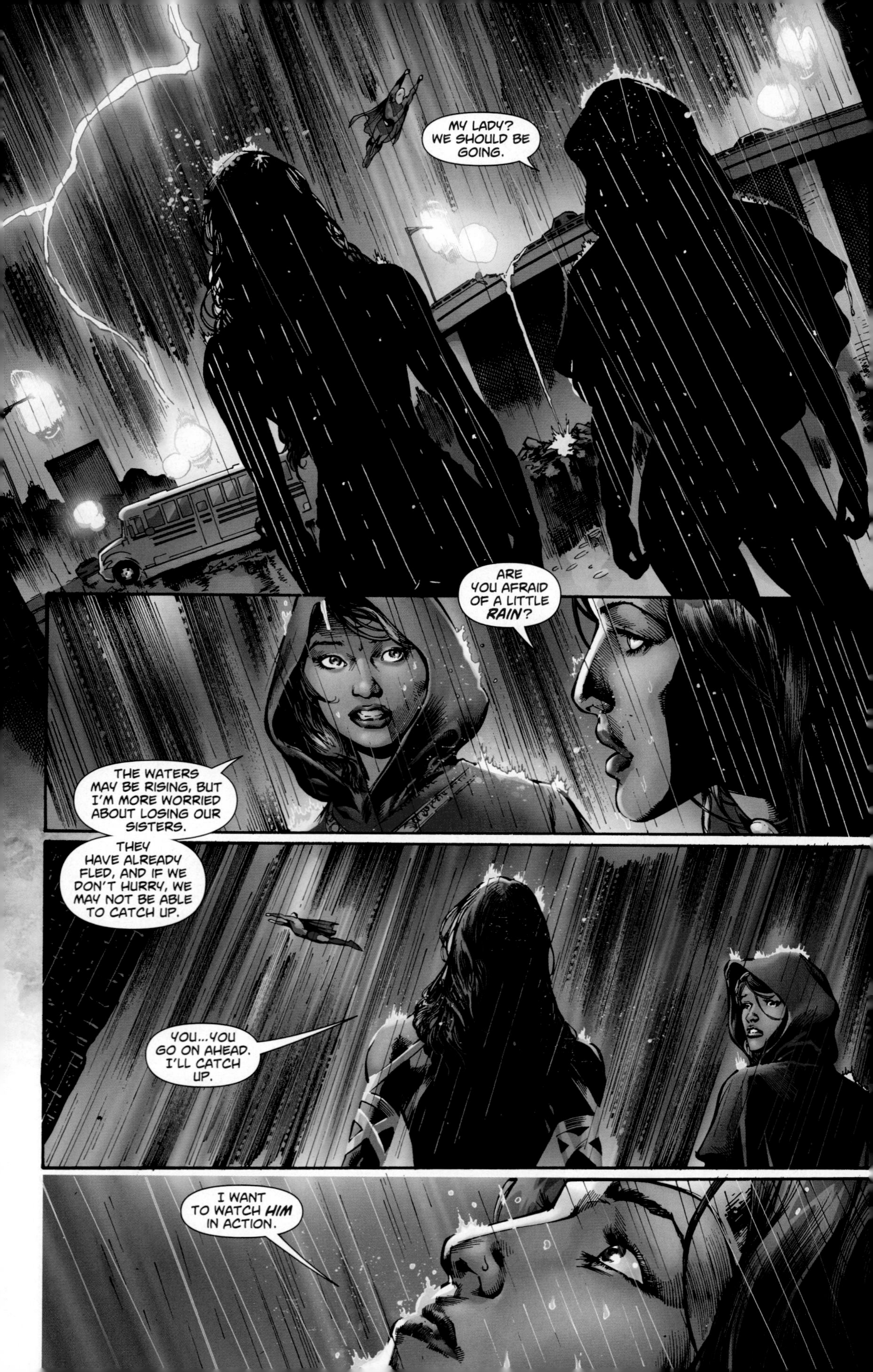
MY LADY? WE SHOULD BE GOING.
ARE YOU AFRAID OF A LITTLE RAIN?
THE WATERS MAY BE RISING, BUT I'M MORE WORRIED ABOUT LOSING OUR SISTERS.
THEY HAVE ALREADY FLED, AND IF WE DON'T HURRY, WE MAY NOT BE ABLE TO CATCH UP.
YOU...YOU GO ON AHEAD. I'LL CATCH UP.
I WANT TO WATCH HIM IN ACTION.

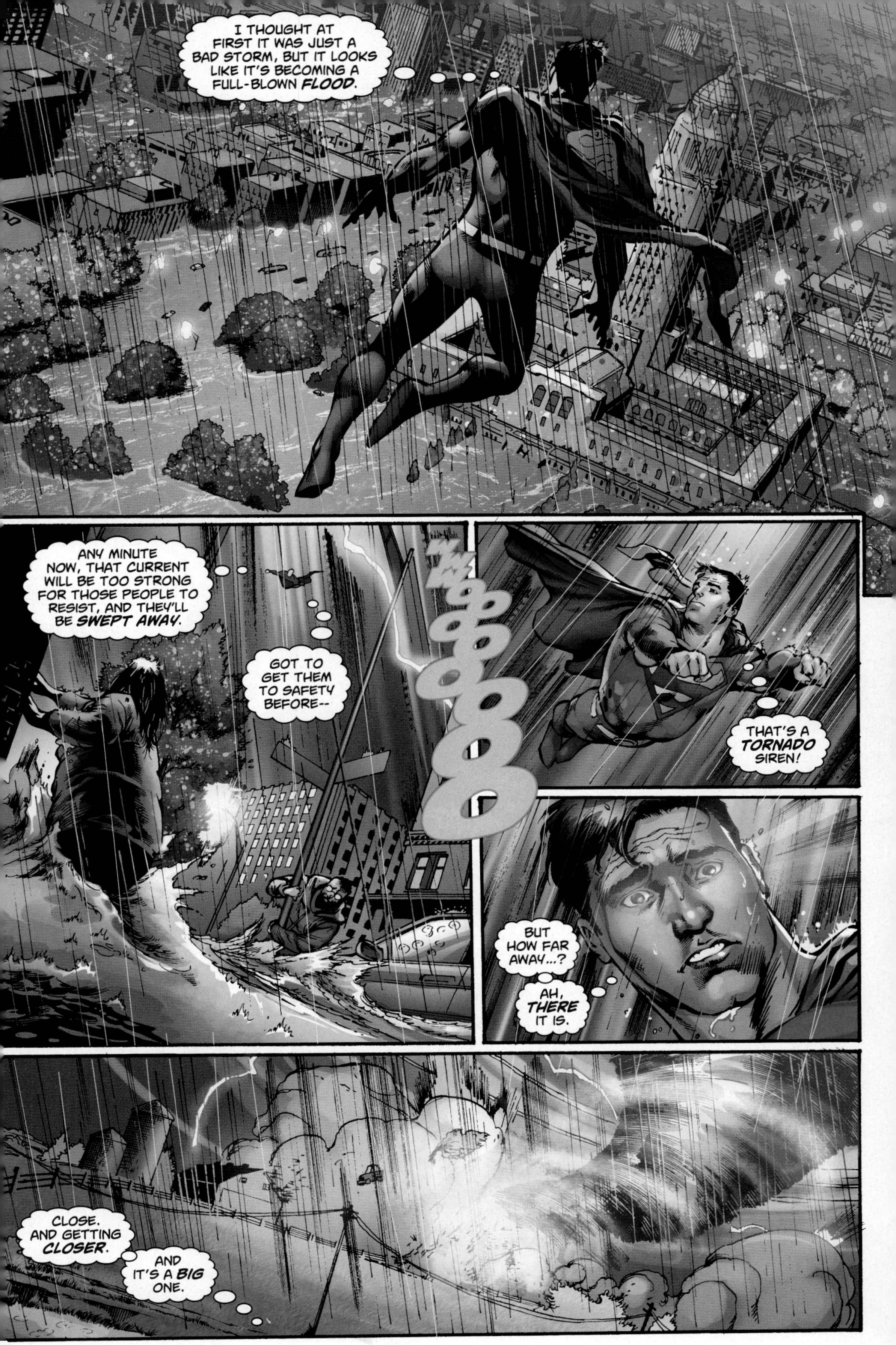
I THOUGHT AT FIRST IT WAS JUST A BAD STORM, BUT IT LOOKS LIKE IT'S BECOMING A FULL-BLOWN FLOOD.
ANY MINUTE NOW, THAT CURRENT WILL BE TOO STRONG FOR THOSE PEOPLE TO RESIST, AND THEY'LL BE SWEPT AWAY.
GOT TO GET THEM TO SAFETY BEFORE--
WHOOOOOOO
THAT'S A TORNADO SIREN!
BUT HOW FAR AWAY...?
AH, THERE IT IS.
CLOSE. AND GETTING CLOSER.
AND IT'S A BIG ONE.

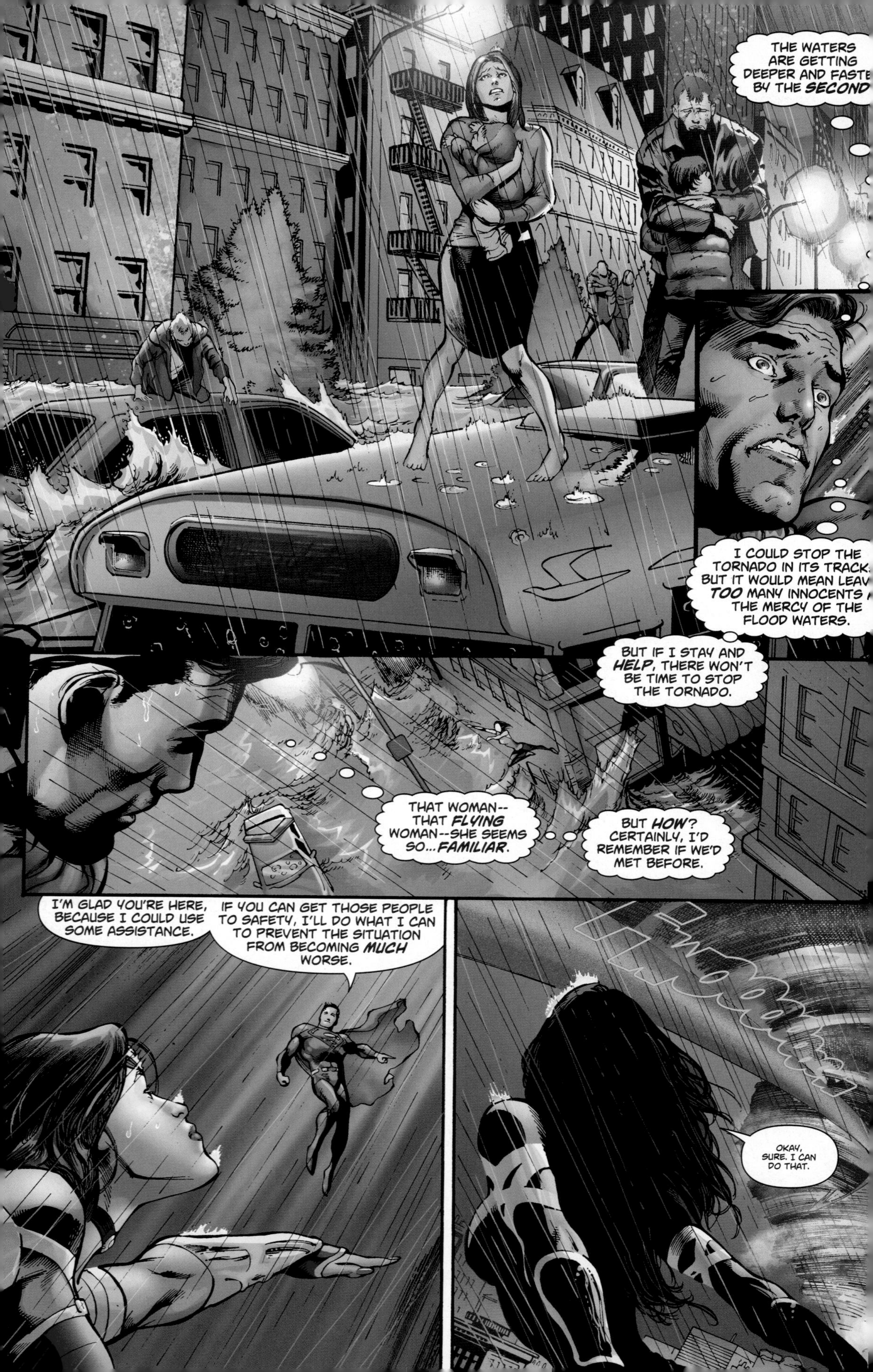
THE WATERS ARE GETTING DEEPER AND FASTE BY THE *SECOND*
I COULD STOP THE TORNADO IN ITS TRACK BUT IT WOULD MEAN LEAV *TOO* MANY INNOCENTS THE MERCY OF THE FLOOD WATERS.
BUT IF I STAY AND *HELP*, THERE WON'T BE TIME TO STOP THE TORNADO.
THAT WOMAN-- THAT *FLYING* WOMAN--SHE SEEMS SO...*FAMILIAR*.
BUT *HOW*? CERTAINLY, I'D REMEMBER IF WE'D MET BEFORE.
I'M GLAD YOU'RE HERE, BECAUSE I COULD USE SOME ASSISTANCE.
IF YOU CAN GET THOSE PEOPLE TO SAFETY, I'LL DO WHAT I CAN TO PREVENT THE SITUATION FROM BECOMING *MUCH* WORSE.
OKAY, SURE. I CAN DO THAT.

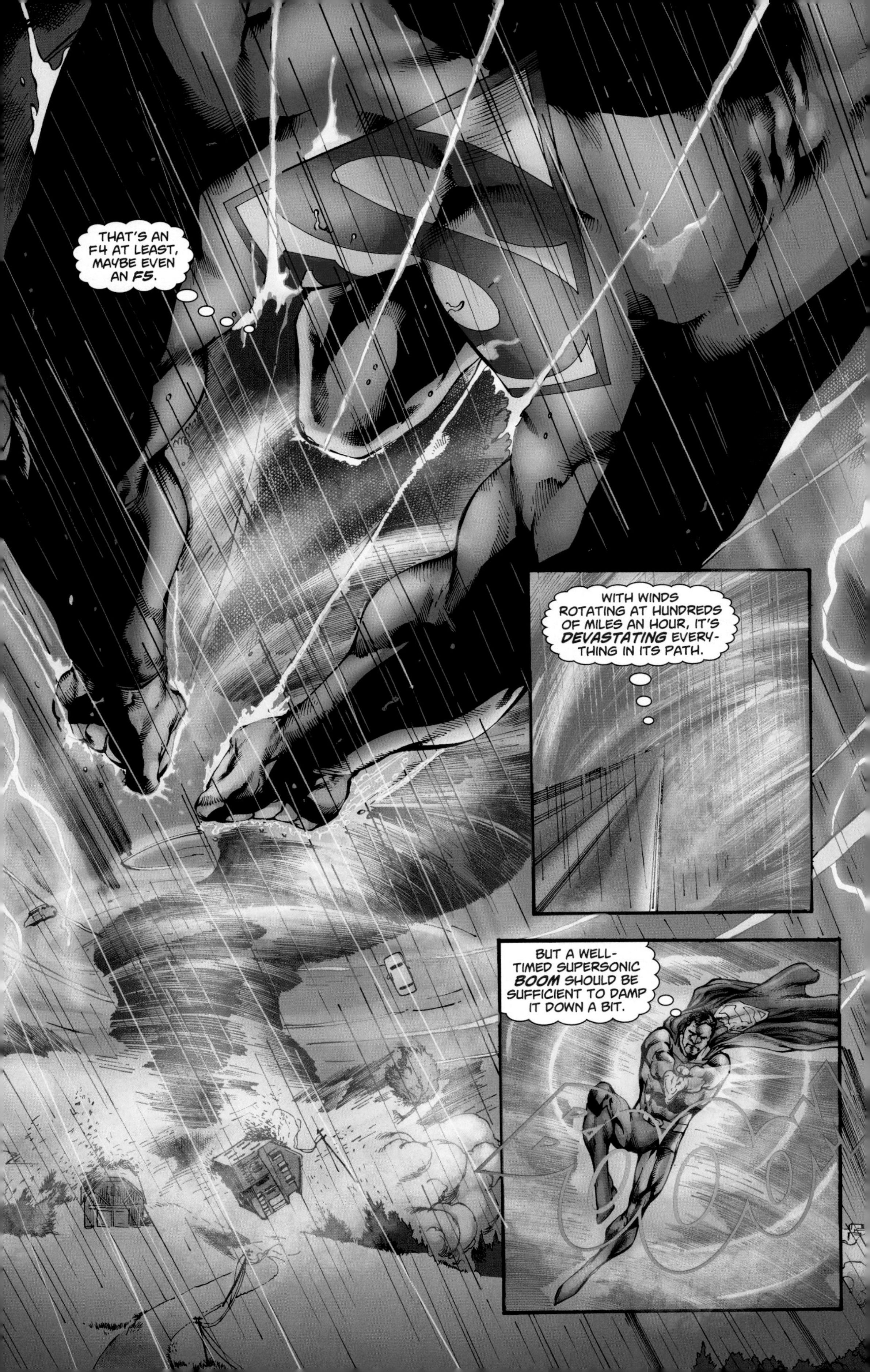
THAT'S AN F4 AT LEAST, MAYBE EVEN AN F5.
WITH WINDS ROTATING AT HUNDREDS OF MILES AN HOUR, IT'S DEVASTATING EVERY-THING IN ITS PATH.
BUT A WELL-TIMED SUPERSONIC BOOM SHOULD BE SUFFICIENT TO DAMP IT DOWN A BIT.

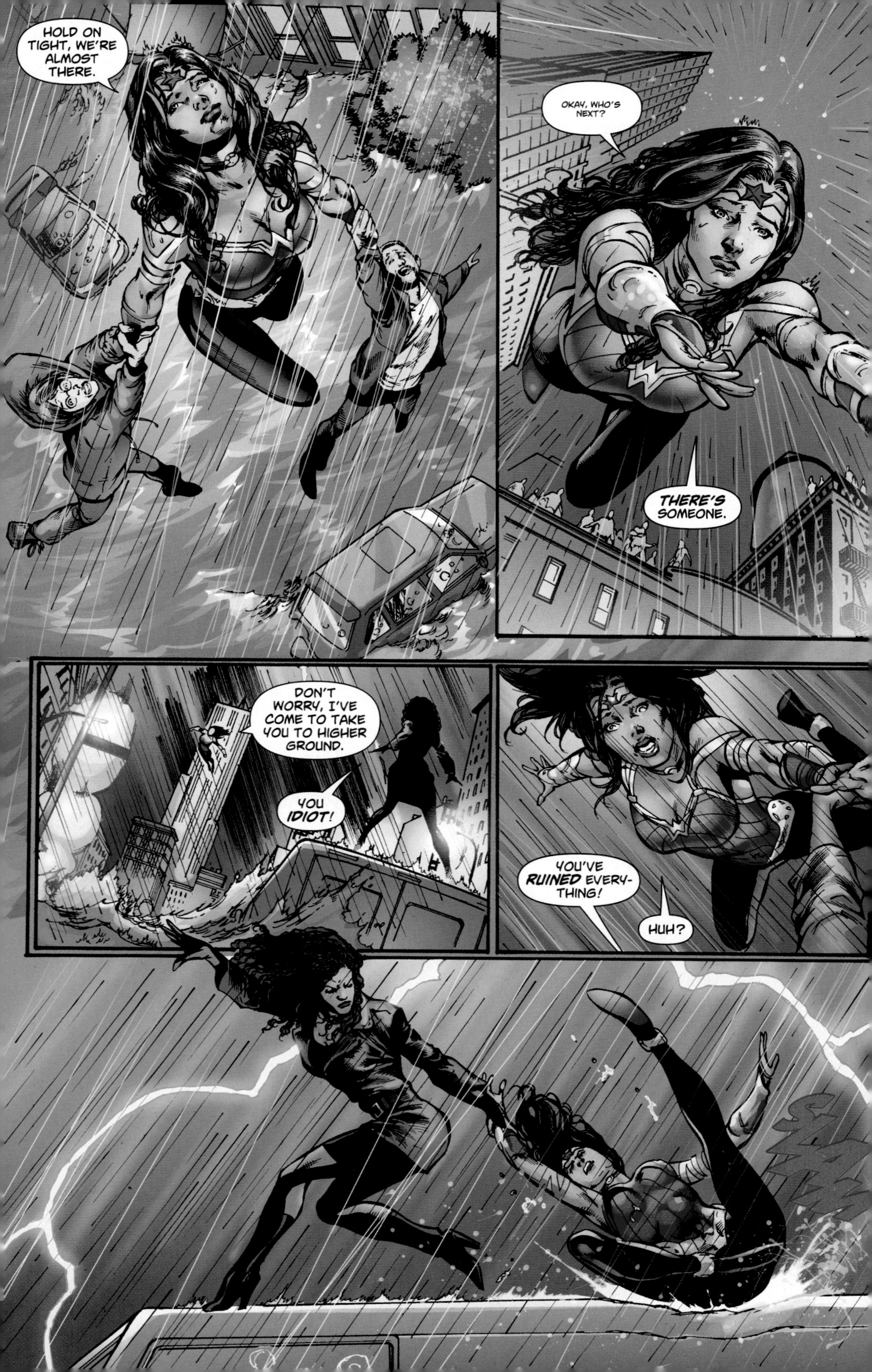
HOLD ON TIGHT, WE'RE ALMOST THERE.
OKAY, WHO'S NEXT?
THERE'S SOMEONE.
DON'T WORRY, I'VE COME TO TAKE YOU TO HIGHER GROUND.
YOU IDIOT!
YOU'VE RUINED EVERY-THING!
HUH?

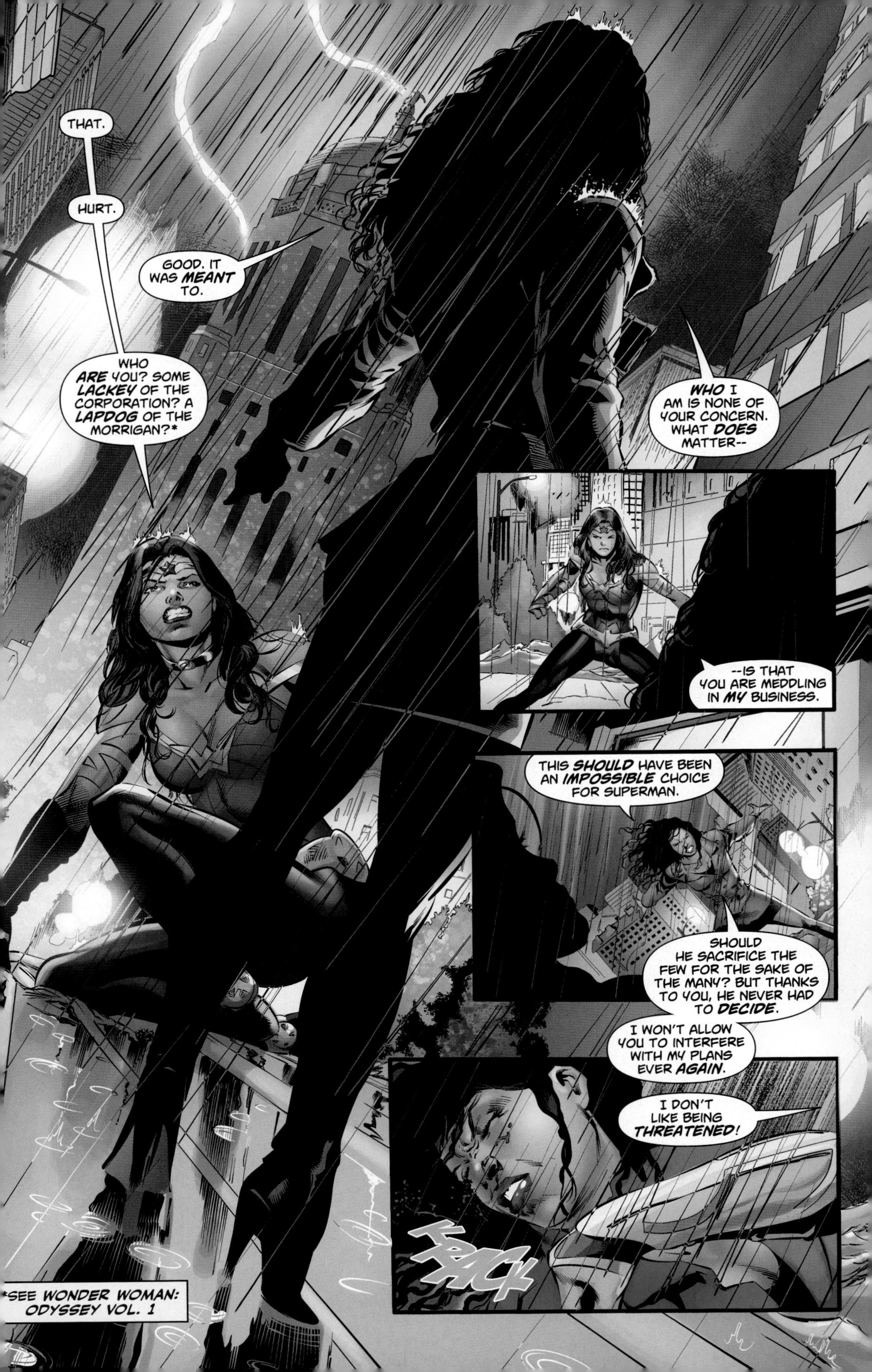
THAT.
HURT.
GOOD. IT WAS MEANT TO.
WHO ARE YOU? SOME LACKEY OF THE CORPORATION? A LAPDOG OF THE MORRIGAN?*
WHO I AM IS NONE OF YOUR CONCERN. WHAT DOES MATTER--
--IS THAT YOU ARE MEDDLING IN MY BUSINESS.
THIS SHOULD HAVE BEEN AN IMPOSSIBLE CHOICE FOR SUPERMAN.
SHOULD HE SACRIFICE THE FEW FOR THE SAKE OF THE MANY? BUT THANKS TO YOU, HE NEVER HAD TO DECIDE.
I WON'T ALLOW YOU TO INTERFERE WITH MY PLANS EVER AGAIN.
I DON'T LIKE BEING THREATENED!
KRACK
*SEE WONDER WOMAN: ODYSSEY VOL. 1

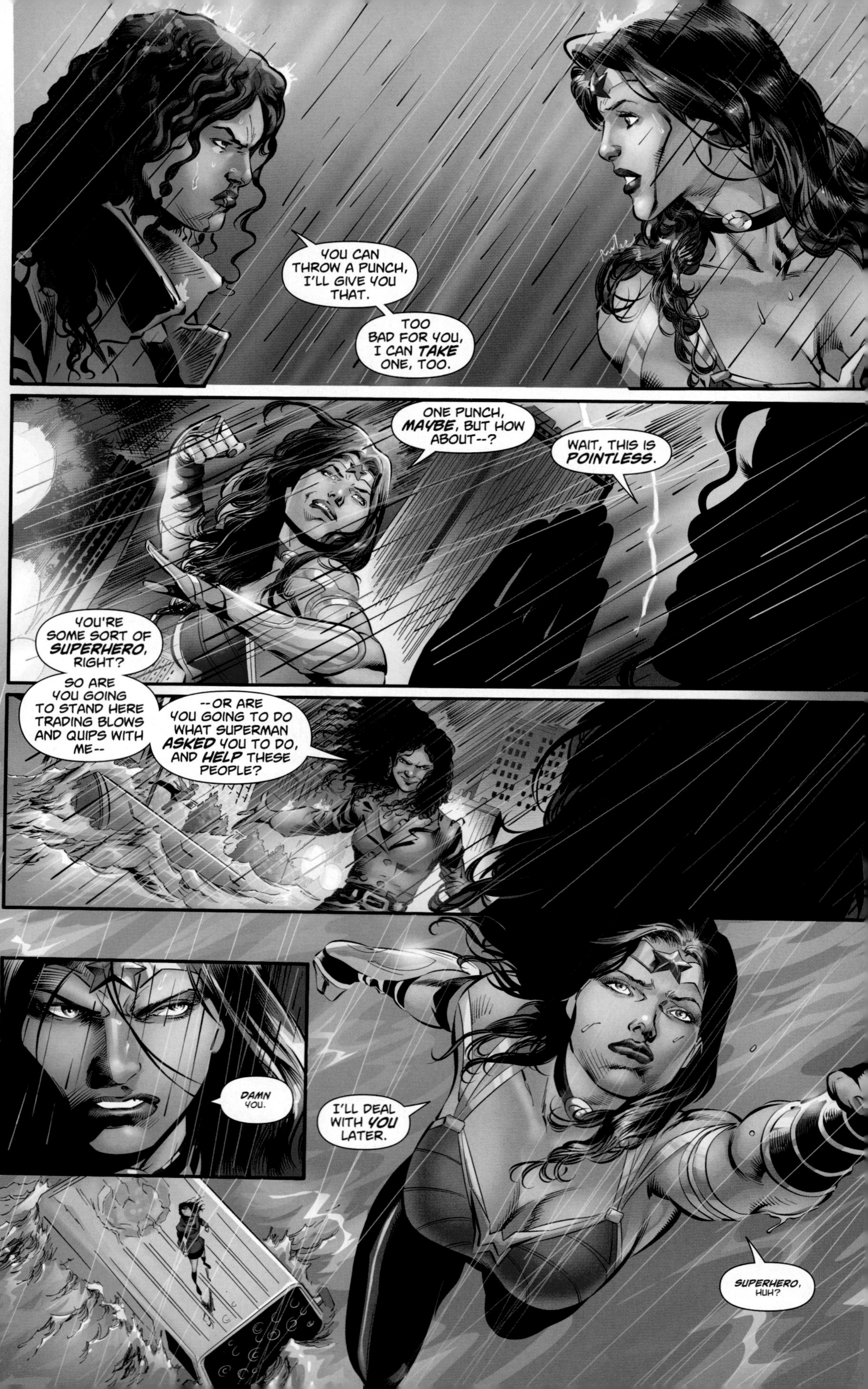
YOU CAN THROW A PUNCH, I'LL GIVE YOU THAT.
TOO BAD FOR YOU, I CAN TAKE ONE, TOO.
ONE PUNCH, MAYBE, BUT HOW ABOUT--?
WAIT, THIS IS POINTLESS.
YOU'RE SOME SORT OF SUPERHERO, RIGHT?
SO ARE YOU GOING TO STAND HERE TRADING BLOWS AND QUIPS WITH ME--
--OR ARE YOU GOING TO DO WHAT SUPERMAN ASKED YOU TO DO, AND HELP THESE PEOPLE?
DAMN YOU.
I'LL DEAL WITH YOU LATER.
SUPERHERO, HUH?

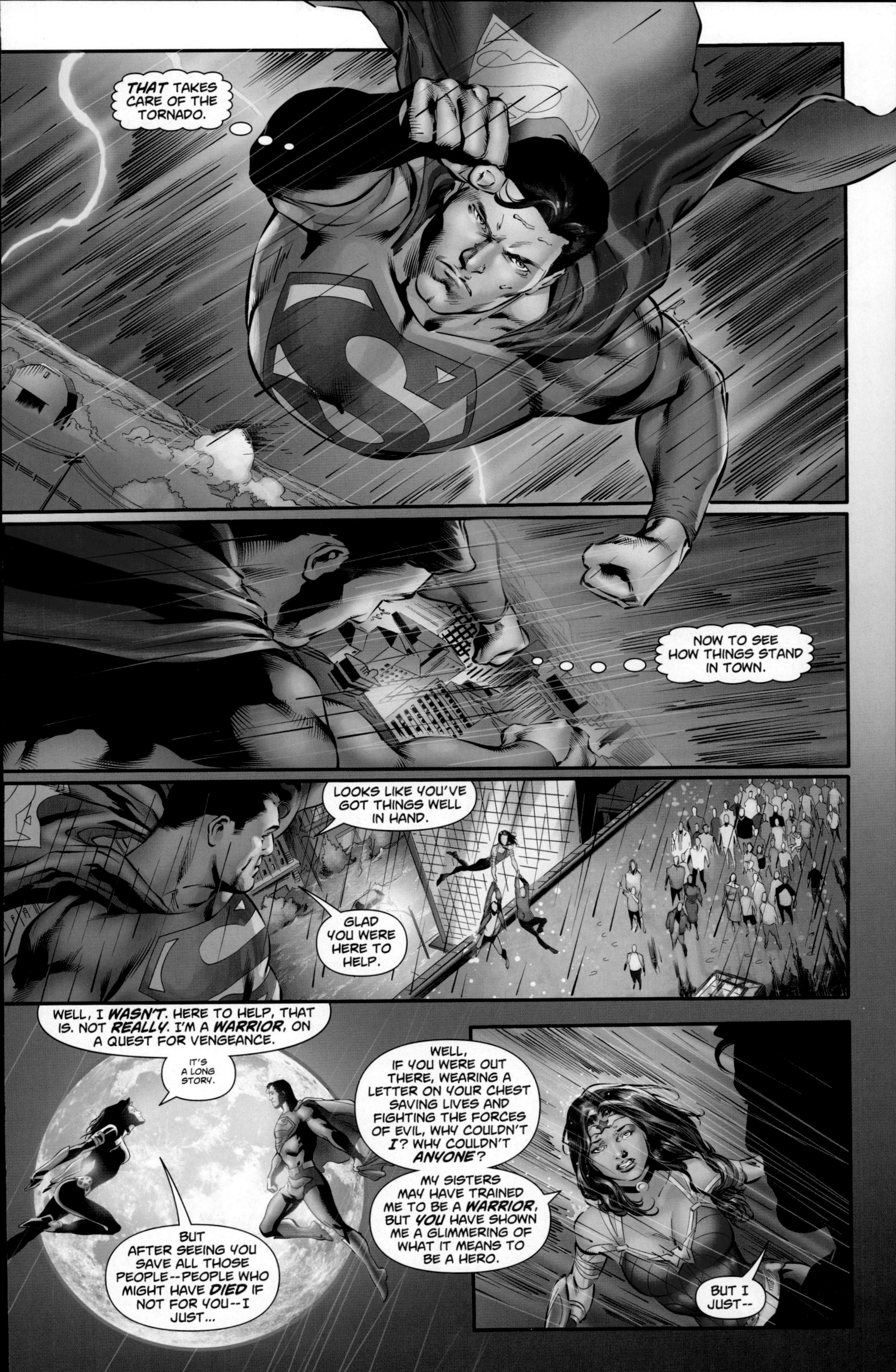

THAT TAKES CARE OF THE TORNADO.
NOW TO SEE HOW THINGS STAND IN TOWN.
LOOKS LIKE YOU'VE GOT THINGS WELL IN HAND.
GLAD YOU WERE HERE TO HELP.
WELL, I WASN'T. HERE TO HELP, THAT IS. NOT REALLY. I'M A WARRIOR, ON A QUEST FOR VENGEANCE.
IT'S A LONG STORY.
BUT AFTER SEEING YOU SAVE ALL THOSE PEOPLE--PEOPLE WHO MIGHT HAVE DIED IF NOT FOR YOU--I JUST...
WELL, IF YOU WERE OUT THERE, WEARING A LETTER ON YOUR CHEST SAVING LIVES AND FIGHTING THE FORCES OF EVIL, WHY COULDN'T I? WHY COULDN'T ANYONE?
MY SISTERS MAY HAVE TRAINED ME TO BE A WARRIOR, BUT YOU HAVE SHOWN ME A GLIMMERING OF WHAT IT MEANS TO BE A HERO.
BUT I JUST--

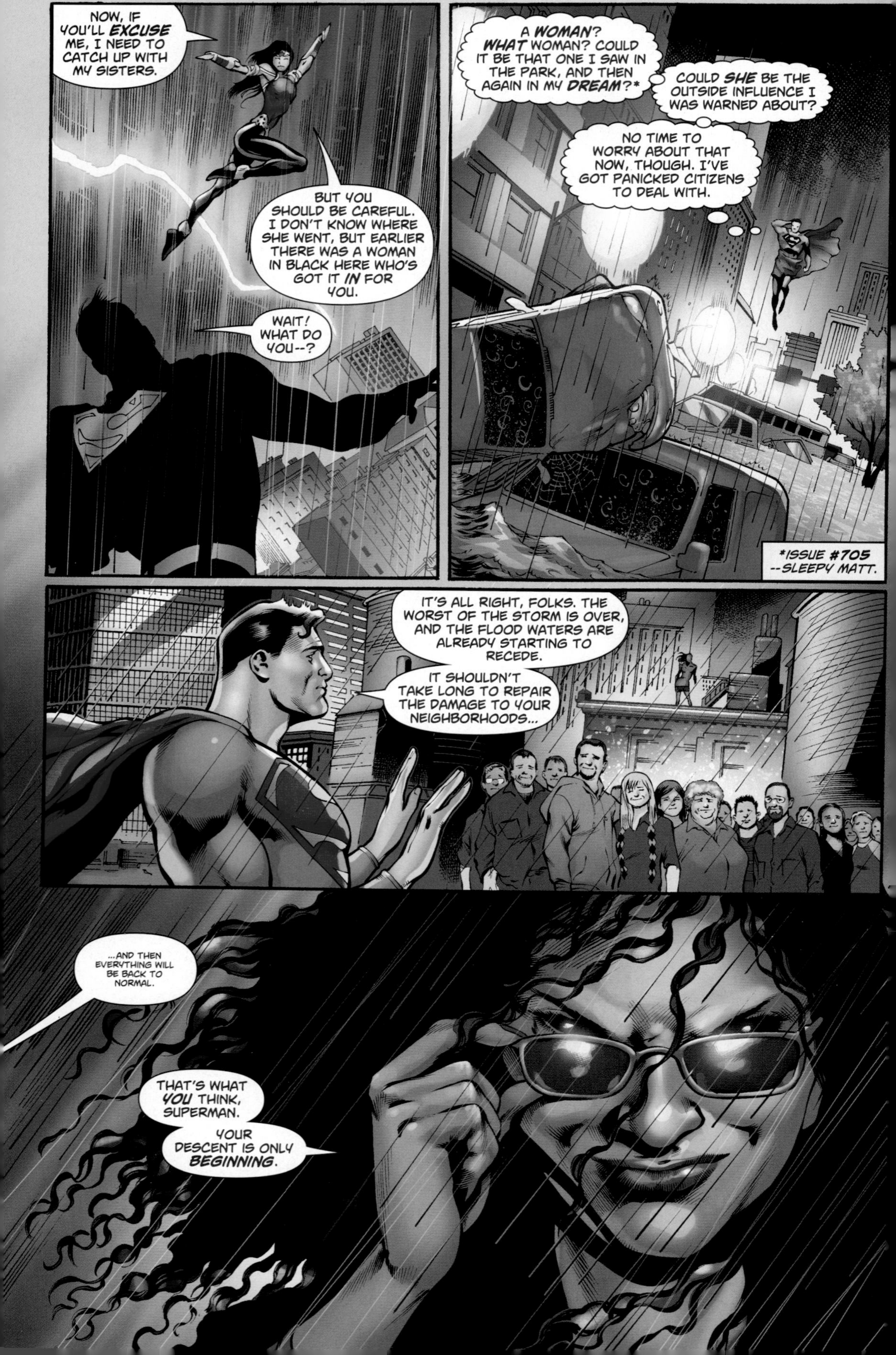
NOW, IF YOU'LL EXCUSE ME, I NEED TO CATCH UP WITH MY SISTERS.
BUT YOU SHOULD BE CAREFUL. I DON'T KNOW WHERE SHE WENT, BUT EARLIER THERE WAS A WOMAN IN BLACK HERE WHO'S GOT IT IN FOR YOU.
WAIT! WHAT DO YOU--?
A WOMAN? WHAT WOMAN? COULD IT BE THAT ONE I SAW IN THE PARK, AND THEN AGAIN IN MY DREAM?*
COULD SHE BE THE OUTSIDE INFLUENCE I WAS WARNED ABOUT?
NO TIME TO WORRY ABOUT THAT NOW, THOUGH. I'VE GOT PANICKED CITIZENS TO DEAL WITH.
*ISSUE #705 --SLEEPY MATT.
IT'S ALL RIGHT, FOLKS. THE WORST OF THE STORM IS OVER, AND THE FLOOD WATERS ARE ALREADY STARTING TO RECEDE.
IT SHOULDN'T TAKE LONG TO REPAIR THE DAMAGE TO YOUR NEIGHBORHOODS...
...AND THEN EVERYTHING WILL BE BACK TO NORMAL.
THAT'S WHAT YOU THINK, SUPERMAN.
YOUR DESCENT IS ONLY BEGINNING.

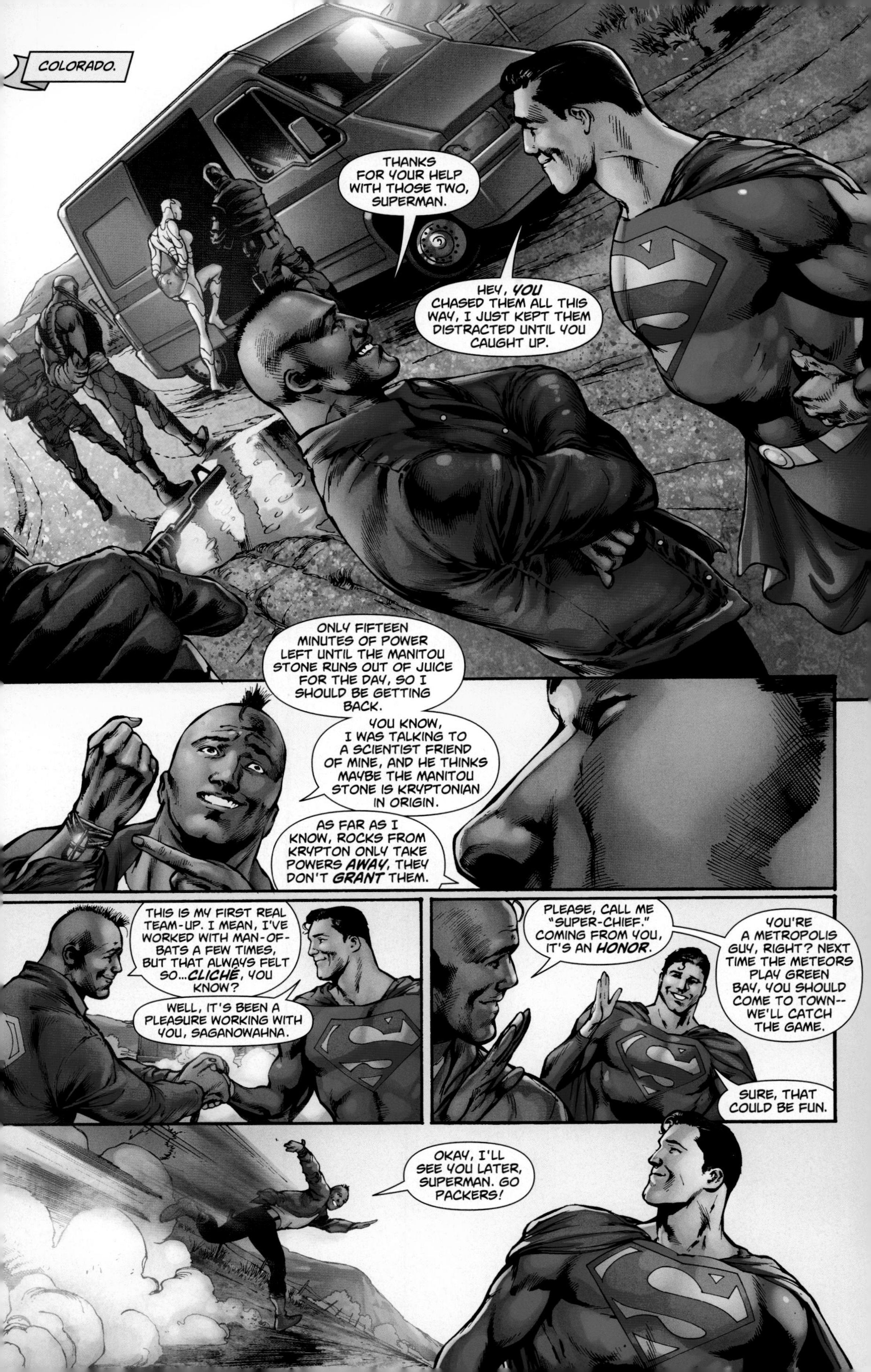
COLORADO.
THANKS FOR YOUR HELP WITH THOSE TWO, SUPERMAN.
HEY, YOU CHASED THEM ALL THIS WAY, I JUST KEPT THEM DISTRACTED UNTIL YOU CAUGHT UP.
ONLY FIFTEEN MINUTES OF POWER LEFT UNTIL THE MANITOU STONE RUNS OUT OF JUICE FOR THE DAY, SO I SHOULD BE GETTING BACK.
YOU KNOW, I WAS TALKING TO A SCIENTIST FRIEND OF MINE, AND HE THINKS MAYBE THE MANITOU STONE IS KRYPTONIAN IN ORIGIN.
AS FAR AS I KNOW, ROCKS FROM KRYPTON ONLY TAKE POWERS AWAY, THEY DON'T GRANT THEM.
THIS IS MY FIRST REAL TEAM-UP. I MEAN, I'VE WORKED WITH MAN-OF-BATS A FEW TIMES, BUT THAT ALWAYS FELT SO...CLICHÉ, YOU KNOW?
WELL, IT'S BEEN A PLEASURE WORKING WITH YOU, SAGANOWAHNA.
PLEASE, CALL ME "SUPER-CHIEF." COMING FROM YOU, IT'S AN HONOR.
YOU'RE A METROPOLIS GUY, RIGHT? NEXT TIME THE METEORS PLAY GREEN BAY, YOU SHOULD COME TO TOWN-- WE'LL CATCH THE GAME.
SURE, THAT COULD BE FUN.
OKAY, I'LL SEE YOU LATER, SUPERMAN. GO PACKERS!

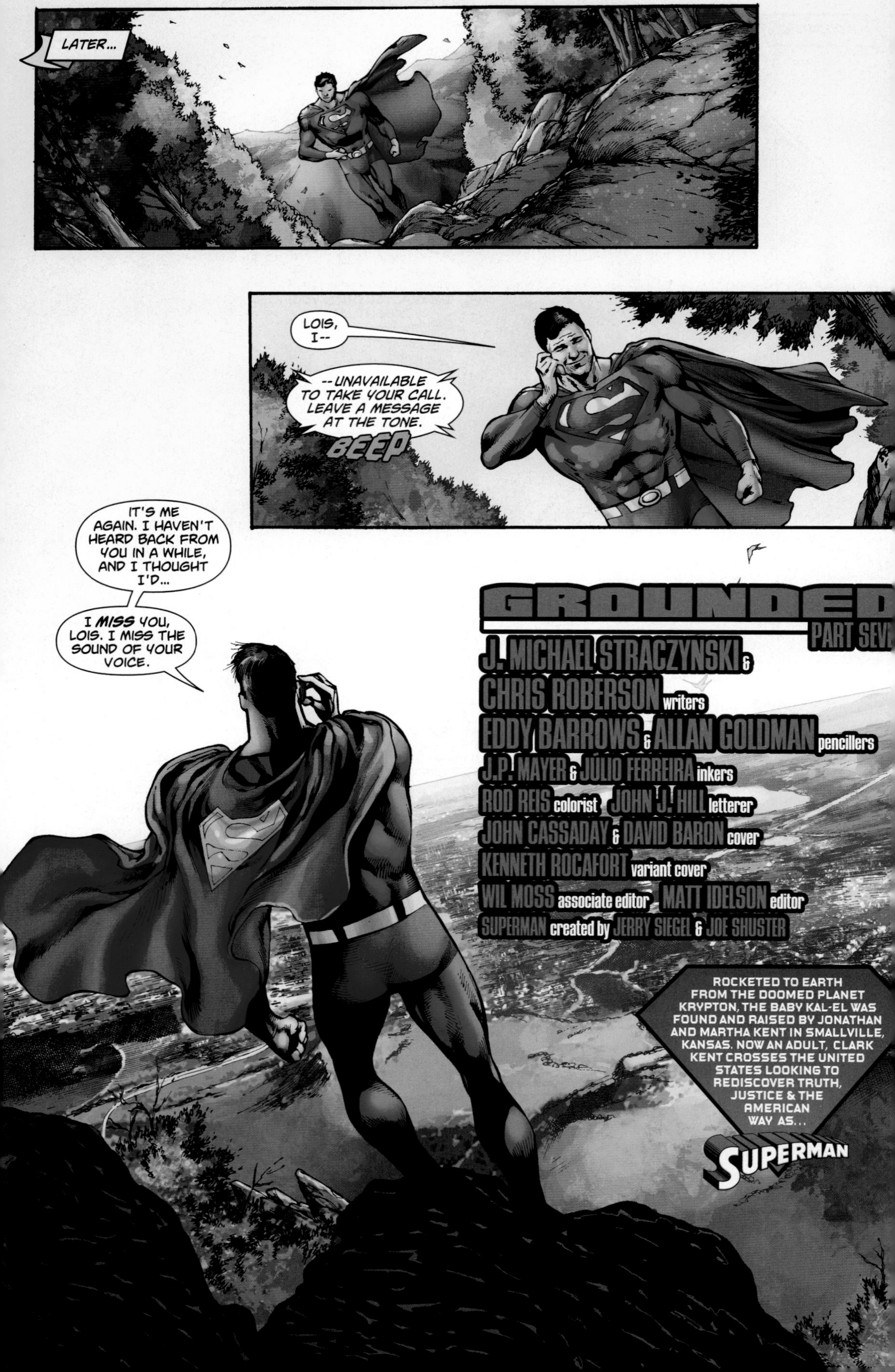
LATER...
LOIS, I--
--UNAVAILABLE TO TAKE YOUR CALL. LEAVE A MESSAGE AT THE TONE.
BEEP
IT'S ME AGAIN. I HAVEN'T HEARD BACK FROM YOU IN A WHILE, AND I THOUGHT I'D...
I MISS YOU, LOIS. I MISS THE SOUND OF YOUR VOICE.
GROUNDED
PART SEVEN
J. MICHAEL STRACZYNSKI & CHRIS ROBERSON writers
EDDY BARROWS & ALLAN GOLDMAN pencillers
J.P. MAYER & JULIO FERREIRA inkers
ROD REIS colorist JOHN J. HILL letterer
JOHN CASSADAY & DAVID BARON cover
KENNETH ROCAFORT variant cover
WIL MOSS associate editor MATT IDELSON editor
SUPERMAN created by JERRY SIEGEL & JOE SHUSTER
ROCKETED TO EARTH FROM THE DOOMED PLANET KRYPTON, THE BABY KAL-EL WAS FOUND AND RAISED BY JONATHAN AND MARTHA KENT IN SMALLVILLE, KANSAS. NOW AN ADULT, CLARK KENT CROSSES THE UNITED STATES LOOKING TO REDISCOVER TRUTH, JUSTICE & THE AMERICAN WAY AS...
SUPERMAN

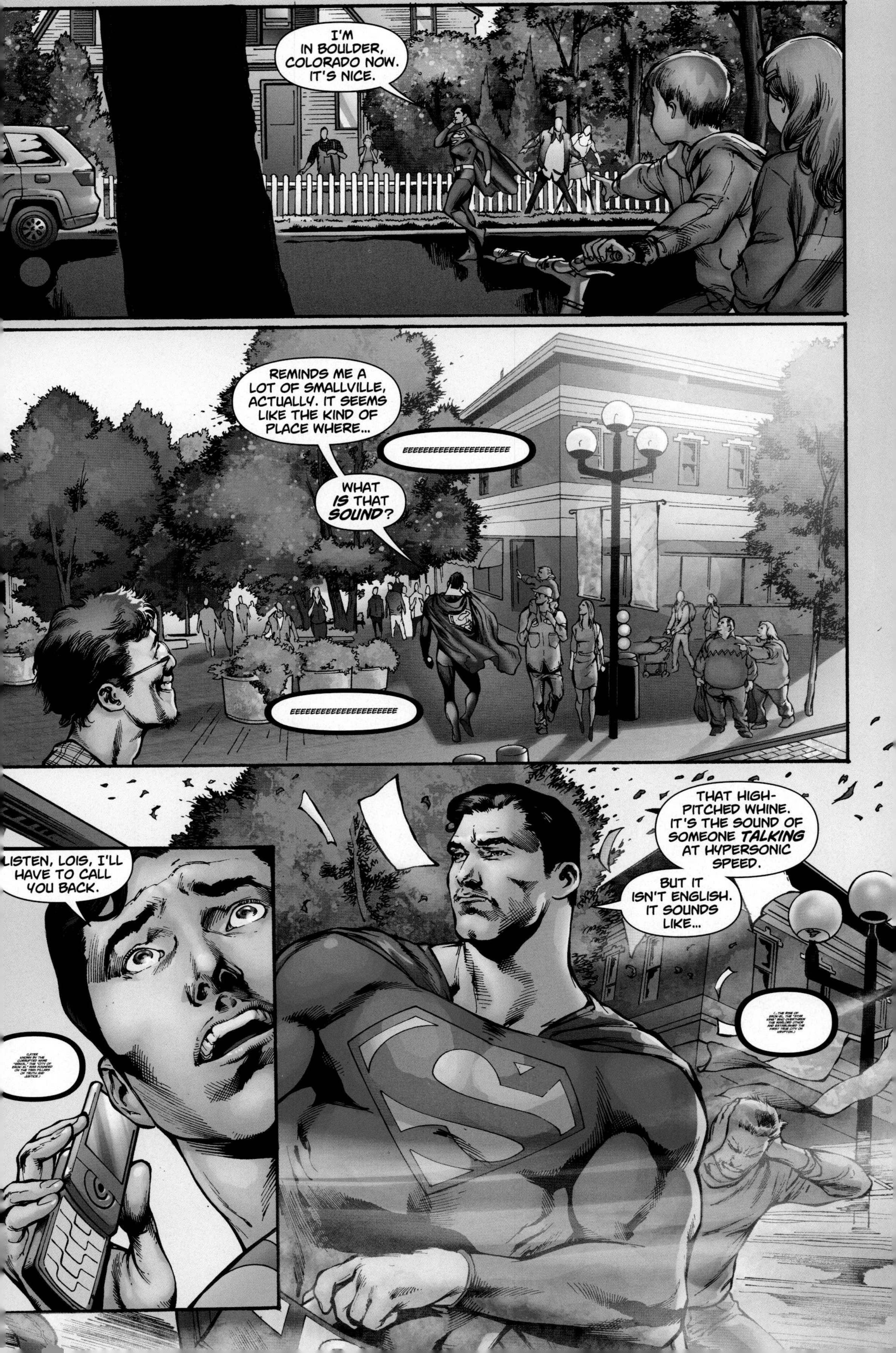
I'M IN BOULDER, COLORADO NOW. IT'S NICE.
REMINDS ME A LOT OF SMALLVILLE, ACTUALLY. IT SEEMS LIKE THE KIND OF PLACE WHERE...
EEEEEEEEEEEEEEEEEEEE
WHAT IS THAT SOUND?
EEEEEEEEEEEEEEEEEEEE
LISTEN, LOIS, I'LL HAVE TO CALL YOU BACK.
THAT HIGH-PITCHED WHINE. IT'S THE SOUND OF SOMEONE TALKING AT HYPERSONIC SPEED.
BUT IT ISN'T ENGLISH. IT SOUNDS LIKE...
(...THE RISE OF EROK-EL, THE "STAR KING" WHO OVERTHREW THE WARLORD UTHOR AND ESTABLISHED THE FIRST TRUE CITY ON KRYPTON.)
(LATER KNOWN BY THE CORRUPTED NAME "ERKOL," THE "CITY OF EROK-EL" WAS FOUNDED ON THE TWIN PILLARS OF TRUTH AND JUSTICE.)

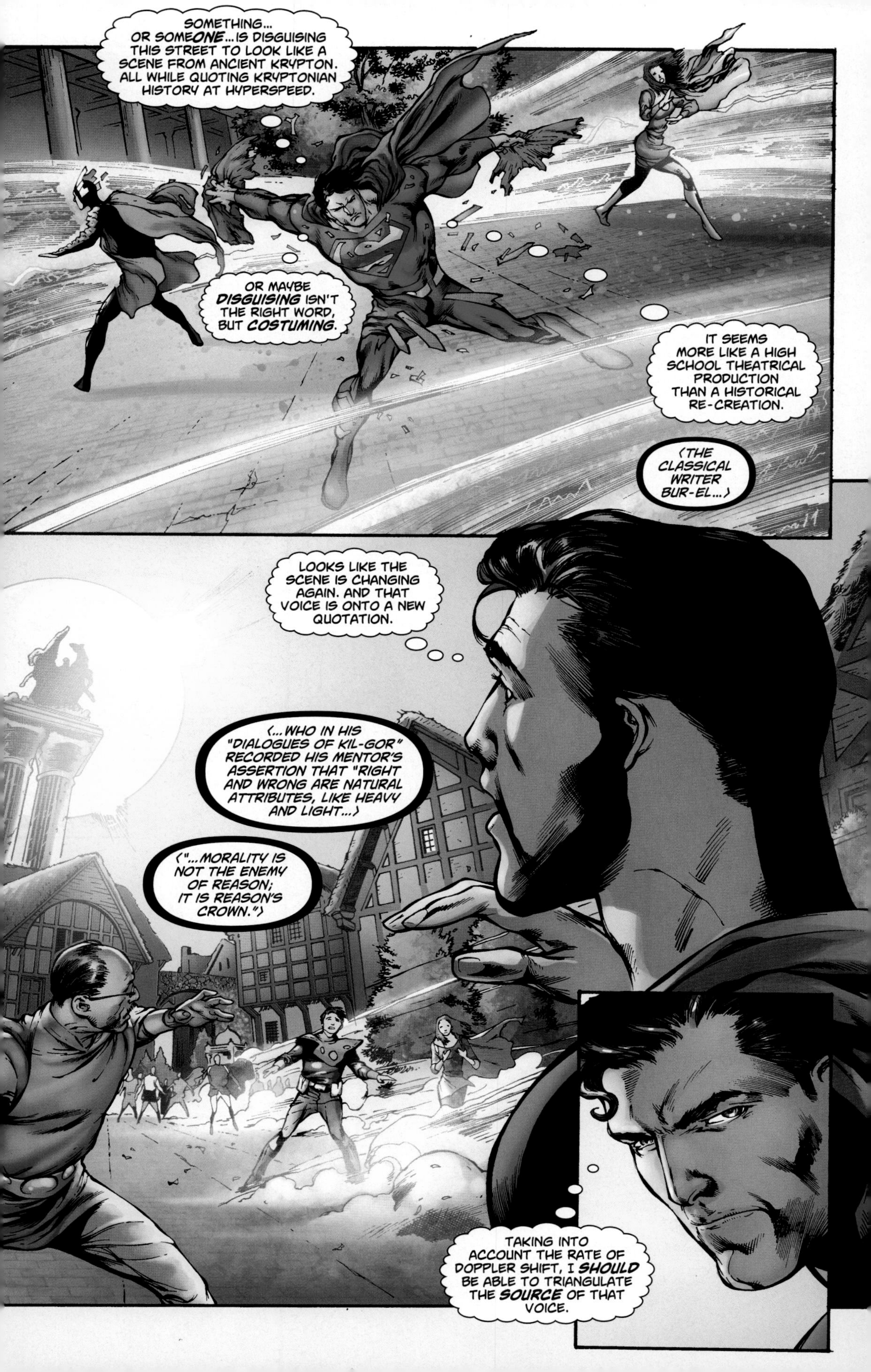
SOMETHING... OR SOMEONE...IS DISGUISING THIS STREET TO LOOK LIKE A SCENE FROM ANCIENT KRYPTON. ALL WHILE QUOTING KRYPTONIAN HISTORY AT HYPERSPEED.
OR MAYBE DISGUISING ISN'T THE RIGHT WORD, BUT COSTUMING.
IT SEEMS MORE LIKE A HIGH SCHOOL THEATRICAL PRODUCTION THAN A HISTORICAL RE-CREATION.
<THE CLASSICAL WRITER BUR-EL...>
LOOKS LIKE THE SCENE IS CHANGING AGAIN. AND THAT VOICE IS ONTO A NEW QUOTATION.
<...WHO IN HIS "DIALOGUES OF KIL-GOR" RECORDED HIS MENTOR'S ASSERTION THAT "RIGHT AND WRONG ARE NATURAL ATTRIBUTES, LIKE HEAVY AND LIGHT...>
<"...MORALITY IS NOT THE ENEMY OF REASON; IT IS REASON'S CROWN.">
TAKING INTO ACCOUNT THE RATE OF DOPPLER SHIFT, I SHOULD BE ABLE TO TRIANGULATE THE SOURCE OF THAT VOICE.

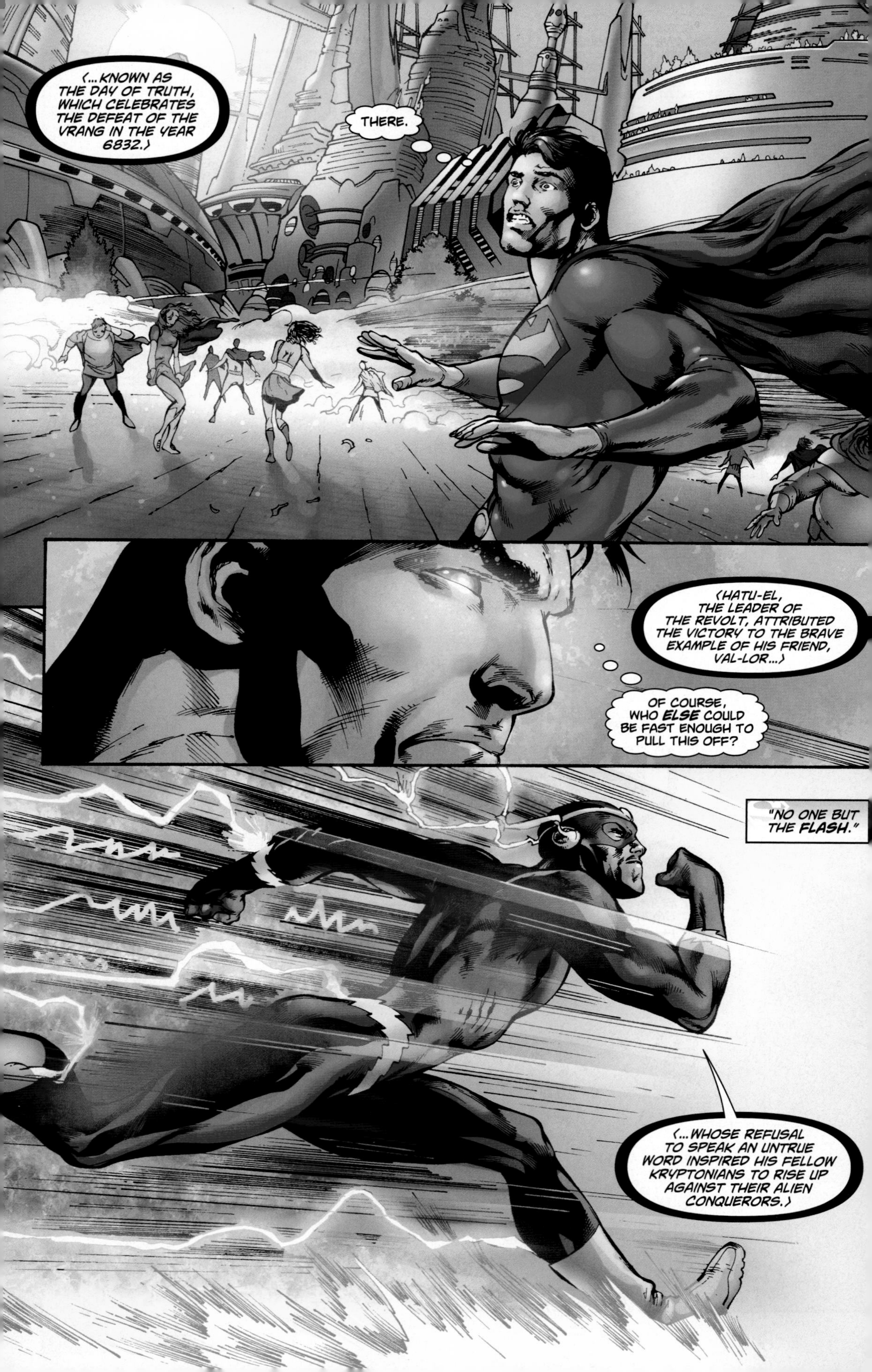
‹...KNOWN AS THE DAY OF TRUTH, WHICH CELEBRATES THE DEFEAT OF THE VRANG IN THE YEAR 6832.›
THERE.
‹HATU-EL, THE LEADER OF THE REVOLT, ATTRIBUTED THE VICTORY TO THE BRAVE EXAMPLE OF HIS FRIEND, VAL-LOR...›
OF COURSE, WHO ELSE COULD BE FAST ENOUGH TO PULL THIS OFF?
"NO ONE BUT THE FLASH."
‹...WHOSE REFUSAL TO SPEAK AN UNTRUE WORD INSPIRED HIS FELLOW KRYPTONIANS TO RISE UP AGAINST THEIR ALIEN CONQUERORS.›

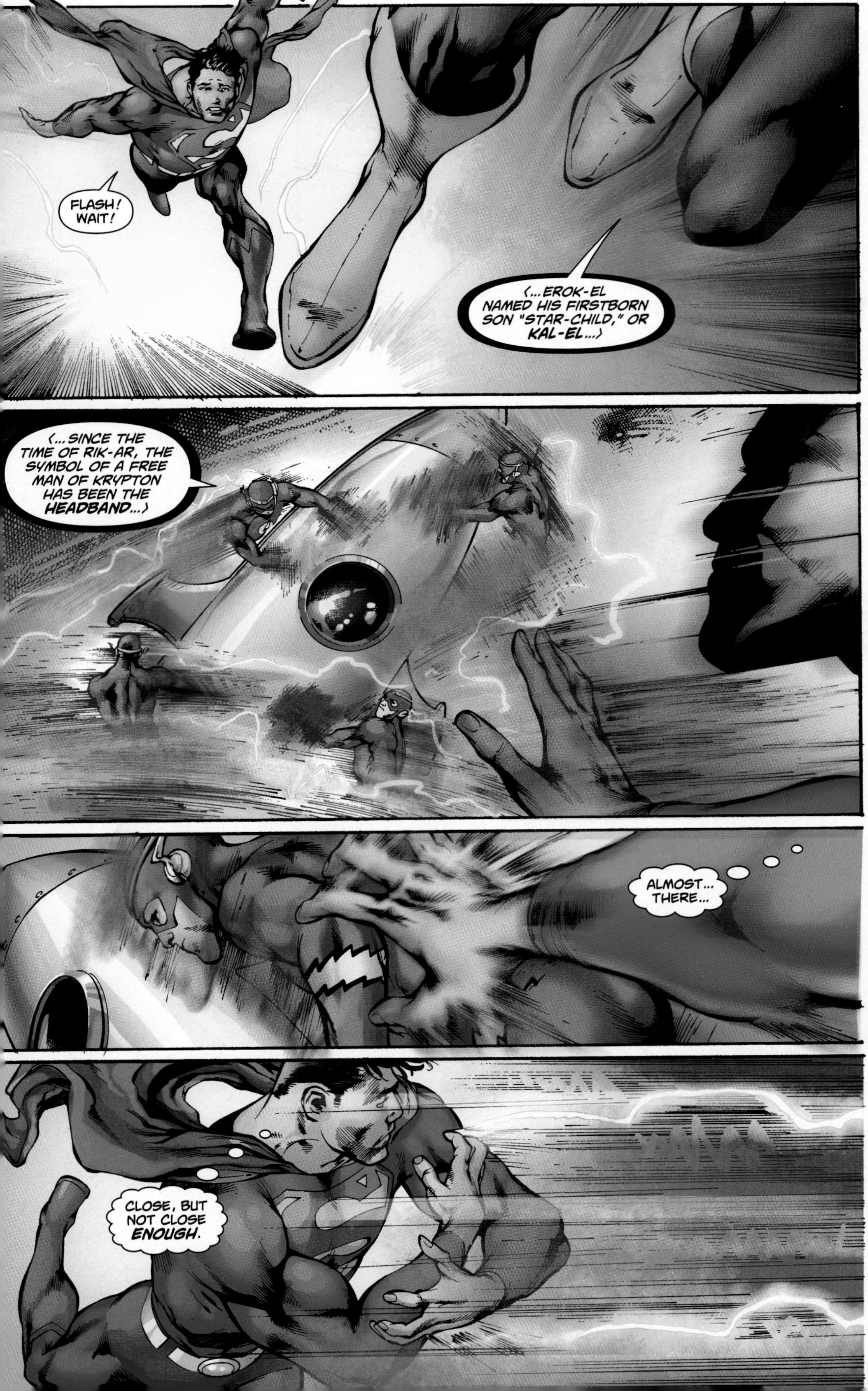
FLASH! WAIT!
‹...EROK-EL NAMED HIS FIRSTBORN SON "STAR-CHILD," OR **KAL-EL**...›
‹...SINCE THE TIME OF RIK-AR, THE SYMBOL OF A FREE MAN OF KRYPTON HAS BEEN THE **HEADBAND**...›
ALMOST... THERE...
CLOSE, BUT NOT CLOSE **ENOUGH**.

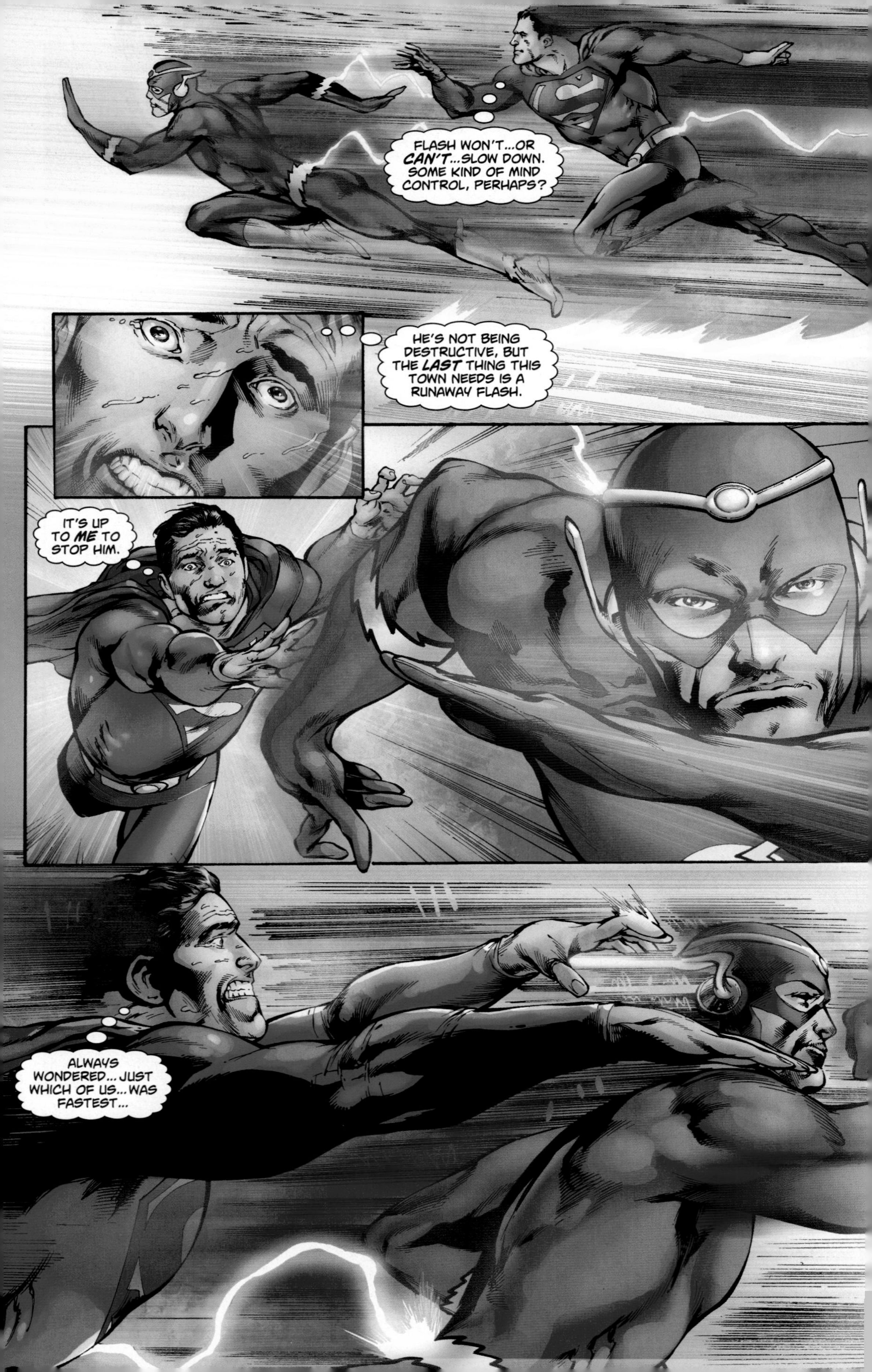
FLASH WON'T...OR CAN'T...SLOW DOWN. SOME KIND OF MIND CONTROL, PERHAPS?
HE'S NOT BEING DESTRUCTIVE, BUT THE LAST THING THIS TOWN NEEDS IS A RUNAWAY FLASH.
IT'S UP TO ME TO STOP HIM.
ALWAYS WONDERED... JUST WHICH OF US...WAS FASTEST...

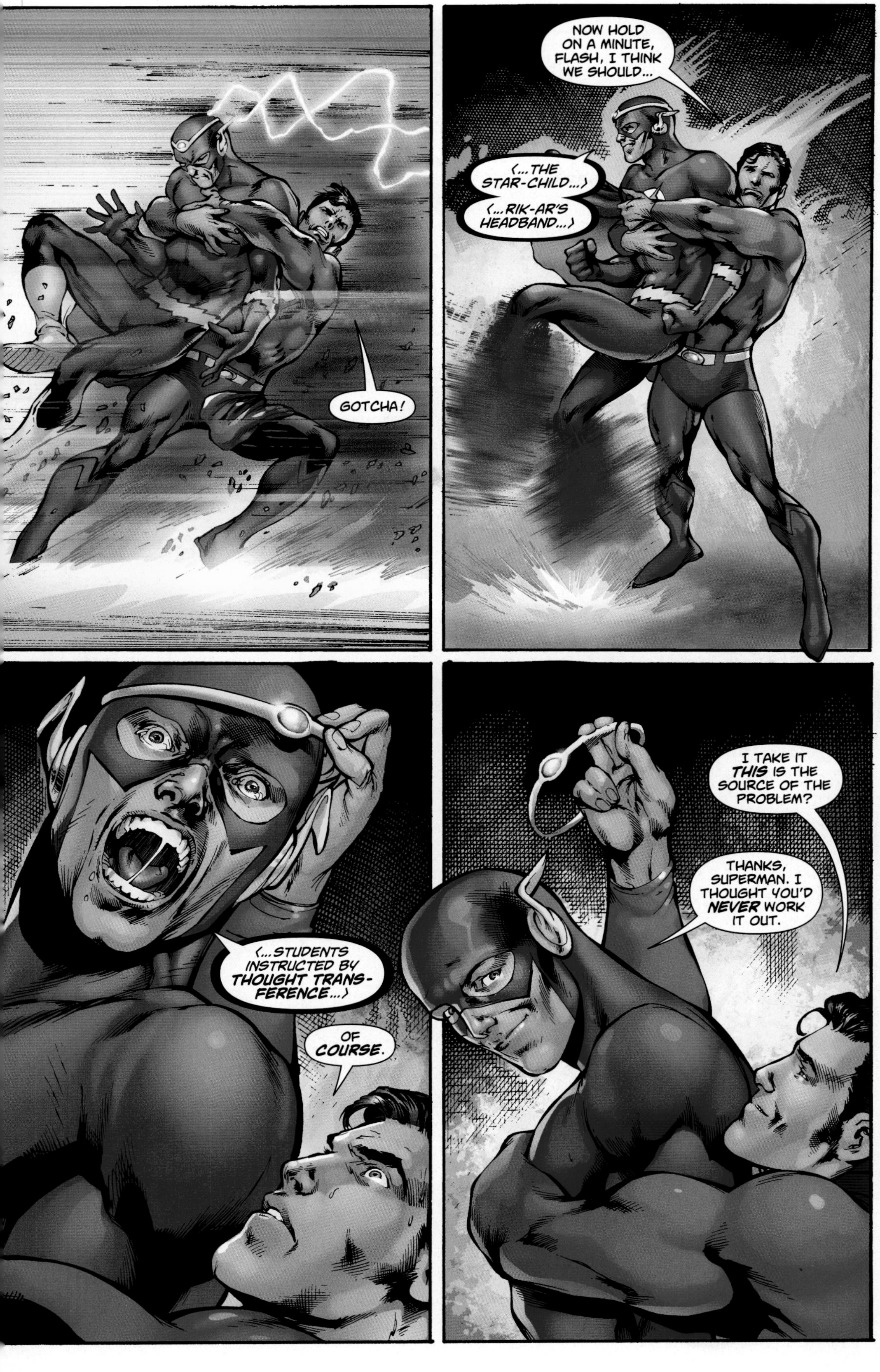
GOTCHA!
NOW HOLD ON A MINUTE, FLASH, I THINK WE SHOULD...
‹...THE STAR-CHILD...›
‹...RIK-AR'S HEADBAND...›
‹...STUDENTS INSTRUCTED BY THOUGHT TRANS-FERENCE...›
OF COURSE.
I TAKE IT THIS IS THE SOURCE OF THE PROBLEM?
THANKS, SUPERMAN. I THOUGHT YOU'D NEVER WORK IT OUT.

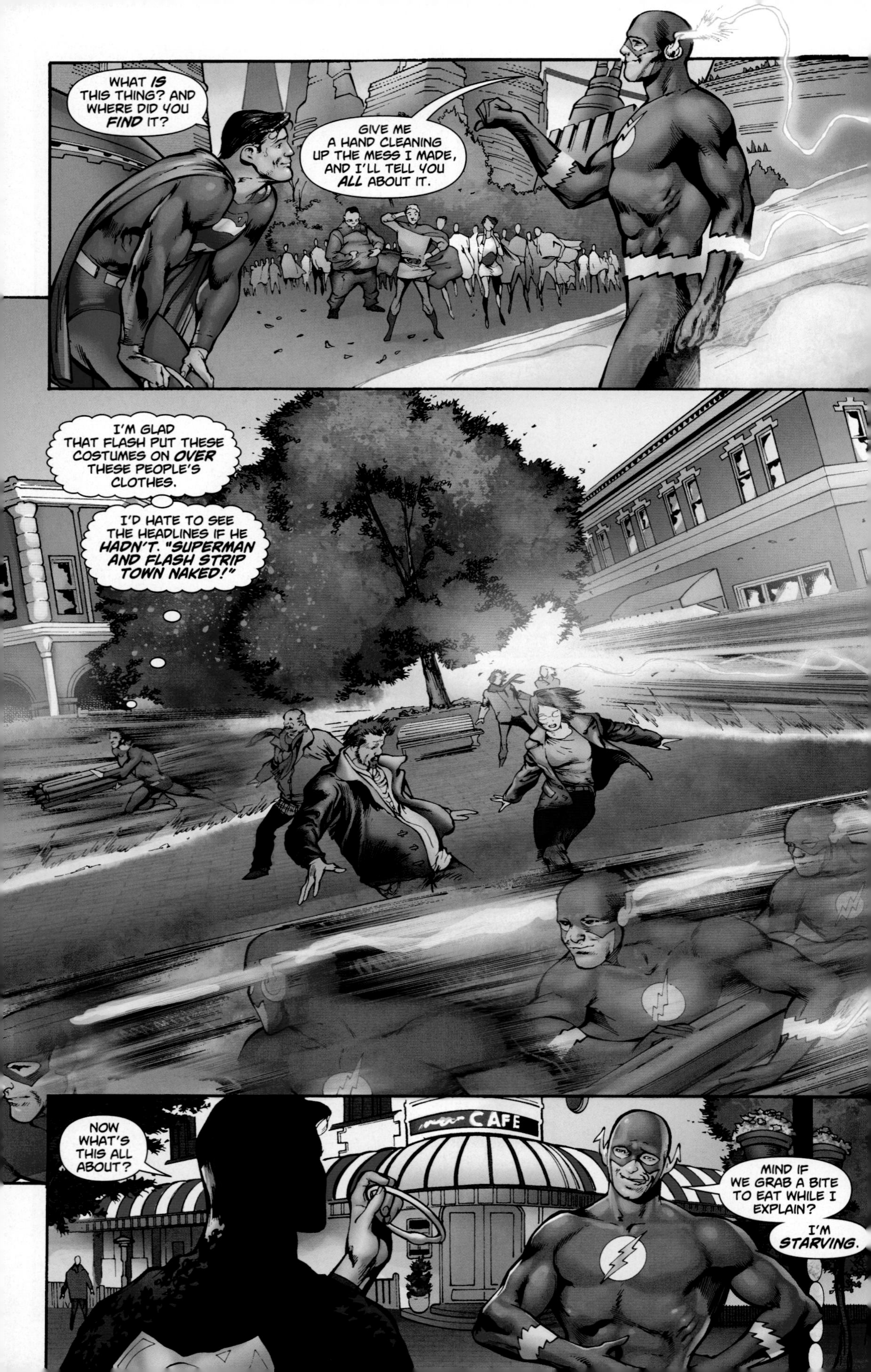
WHAT *IS* THIS THING? AND WHERE DID YOU *FIND* IT?
GIVE ME A HAND CLEANING UP THE MESS I MADE, AND I'LL TELL YOU *ALL* ABOUT IT.
I'M GLAD THAT FLASH PUT THESE COSTUMES ON *OVER* THESE PEOPLE'S CLOTHES.
I'D HATE TO SEE THE HEADLINES IF HE *HADN'T. "SUPERMAN AND FLASH STRIP TOWN NAKED!"*
CAFE
NOW WHAT'S THIS ALL ABOUT?
MIND IF WE GRAB A BITE TO EAT WHILE I EXPLAIN?
I'M *STARVING*.

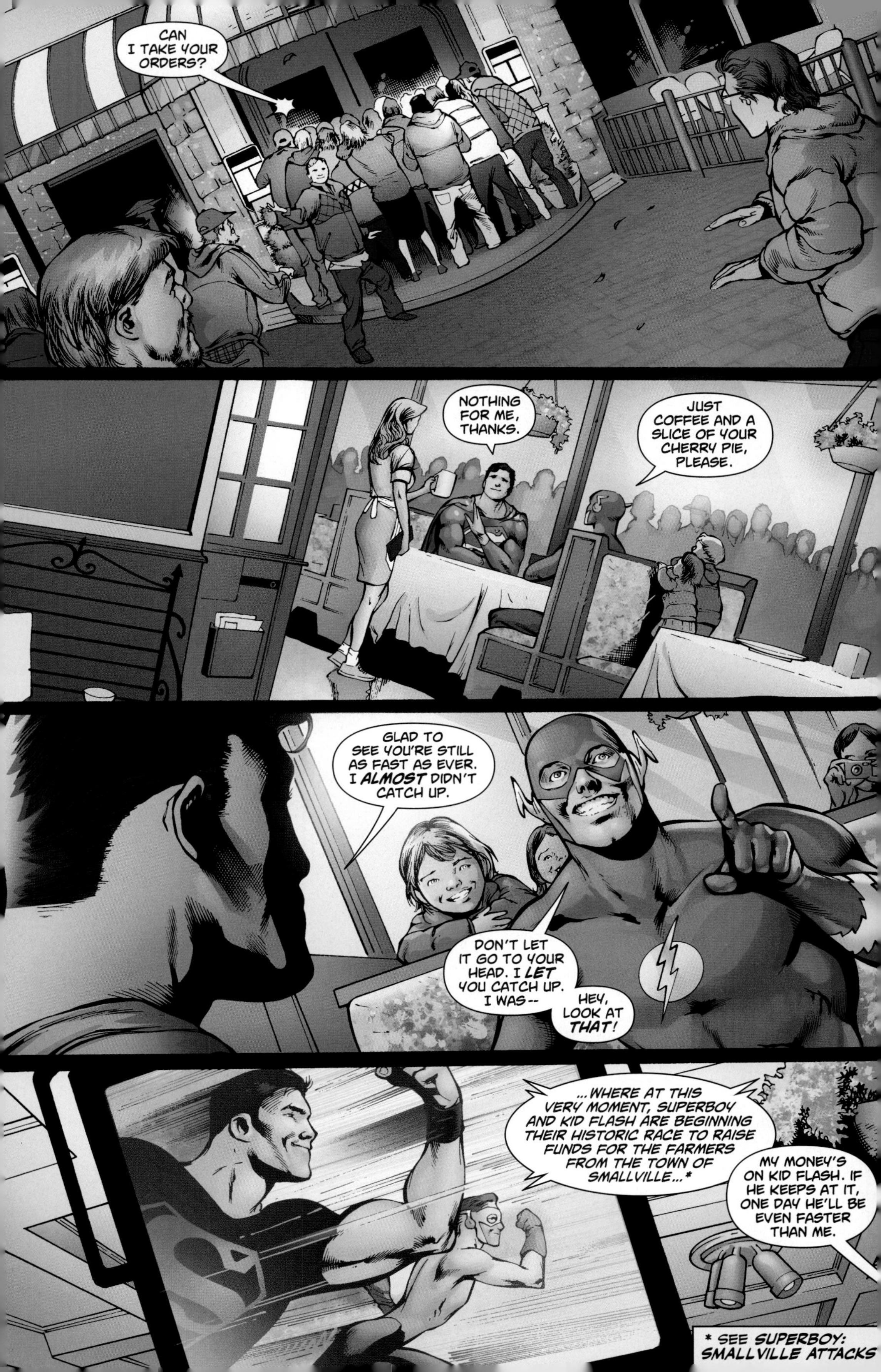
CAN I TAKE YOUR ORDERS?
NOTHING FOR ME, THANKS.
JUST COFFEE AND A SLICE OF YOUR CHERRY PIE, PLEASE.
GLAD TO SEE YOU'RE STILL AS FAST AS EVER. I *ALMOST* DIDN'T CATCH UP.
DON'T LET IT GO TO YOUR HEAD. I *LET* YOU CATCH UP. I WAS--
HEY, LOOK AT *THAT!*
...WHERE AT THIS VERY MOMENT, SUPERBOY AND KID FLASH ARE BEGINNING THEIR HISTORIC RACE TO RAISE FUNDS FOR THE FARMERS FROM THE TOWN OF SMALLVILLE...*
MY MONEY'S ON KID FLASH. IF HE KEEPS AT IT, ONE DAY HE'LL BE EVEN FASTER THAN ME.
* SEE *SUPERBOY: SMALLVILLE ATTACKS*

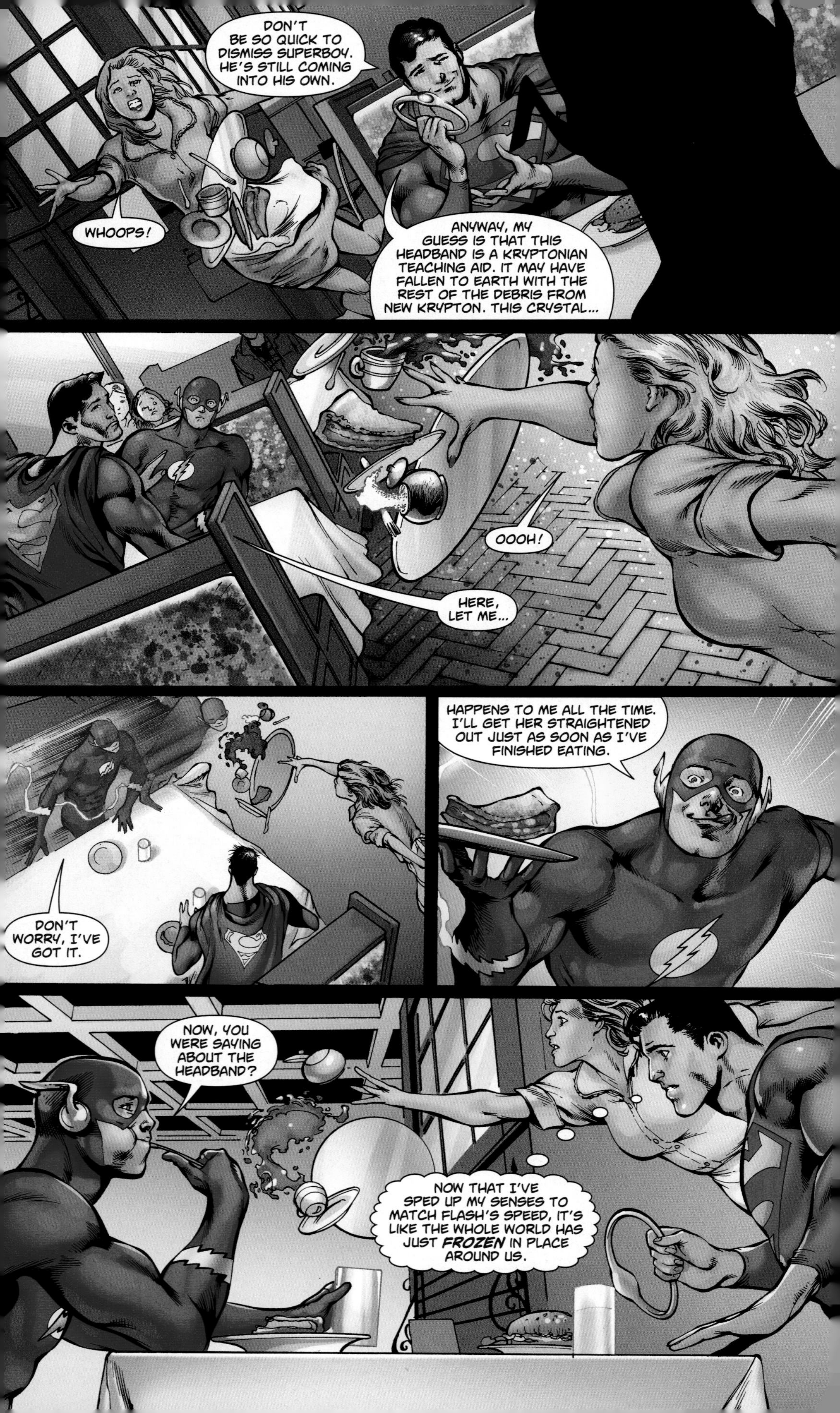

DON'T BE SO QUICK TO DISMISS SUPERBOY. HE'S STILL COMING INTO HIS OWN.
WHOOPS!
ANYWAY, MY GUESS IS THAT THIS HEADBAND IS A KRYPTONIAN TEACHING AID. IT MAY HAVE FALLEN TO EARTH WITH THE REST OF THE DEBRIS FROM NEW KRYPTON. THIS CRYSTAL...
OOOH!
HERE, LET ME...
DON'T WORRY, I'VE GOT IT.
HAPPENS TO ME ALL THE TIME. I'LL GET HER STRAIGHTENED OUT JUST AS SOON AS I'VE FINISHED EATING.
NOW, YOU WERE SAYING ABOUT THE HEADBAND?
NOW THAT I'VE SPED UP MY SENSES TO MATCH FLASH'S SPEED, IT'S LIKE THE WHOLE WORLD HAS JUST FROZEN IN PLACE AROUND US.

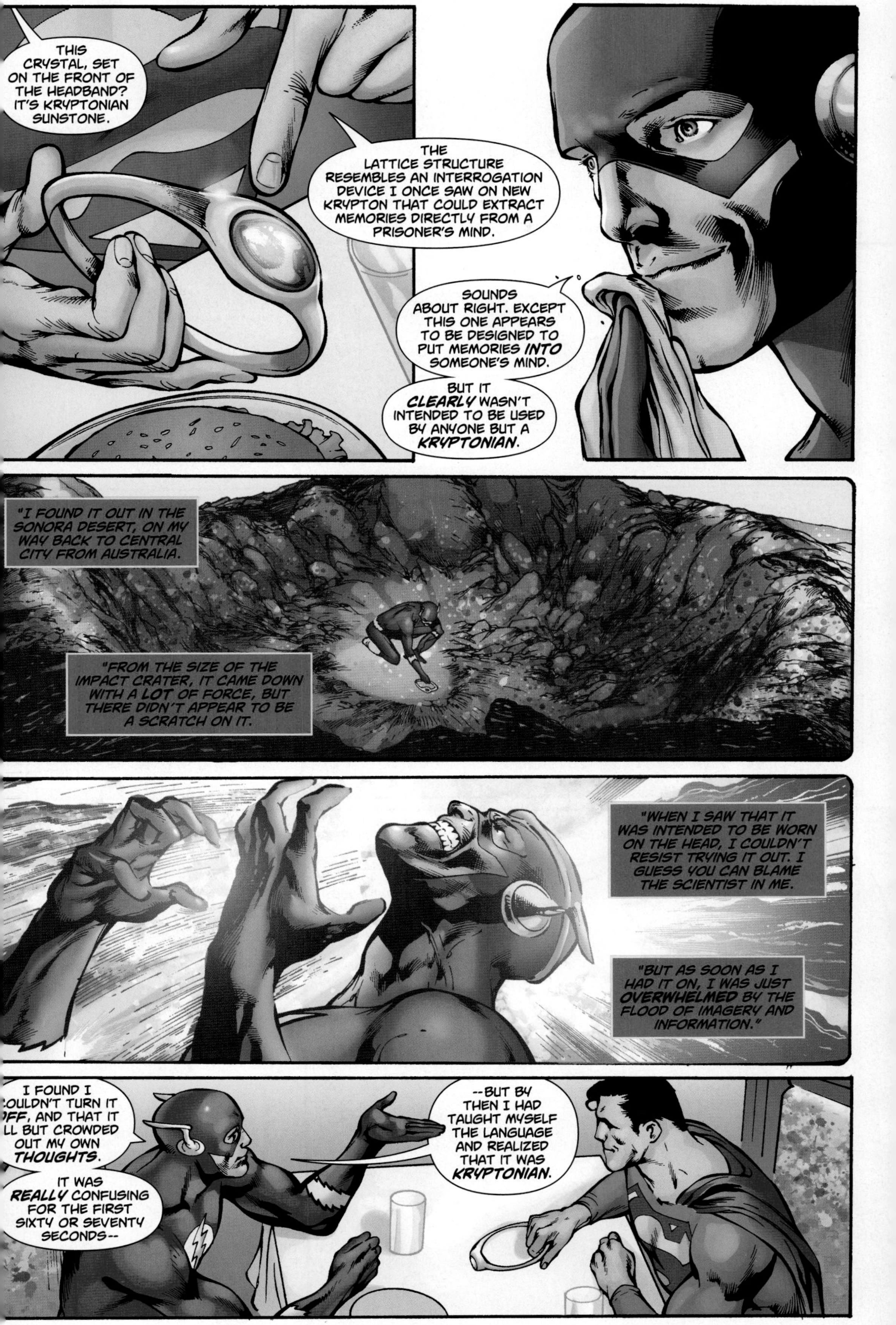

THIS CRYSTAL, SET ON THE FRONT OF THE HEADBAND? IT'S KRYPTONIAN SUNSTONE.
THE LATTICE STRUCTURE RESEMBLES AN INTERROGATION DEVICE I ONCE SAW ON NEW KRYPTON THAT COULD EXTRACT MEMORIES DIRECTLY FROM A PRISONER'S MIND.
SOUNDS ABOUT RIGHT. EXCEPT THIS ONE APPEARS TO BE DESIGNED TO PUT MEMORIES *INTO* SOMEONE'S MIND.
BUT IT *CLEARLY* WASN'T INTENDED TO BE USED BY ANYONE BUT A *KRYPTONIAN*.
"I FOUND IT OUT IN THE SONORA DESERT, ON MY WAY BACK TO CENTRAL CITY FROM AUSTRALIA.
"FROM THE SIZE OF THE IMPACT CRATER, IT CAME DOWN WITH A *LOT* OF FORCE, BUT THERE DIDN'T APPEAR TO BE A SCRATCH ON IT.
"WHEN I SAW THAT IT WAS INTENDED TO BE WORN ON THE HEAD, I COULDN'T RESIST TRYING IT OUT. I GUESS YOU CAN BLAME THE SCIENTIST IN ME.
"BUT AS SOON AS I HAD IT ON, I WAS JUST *OVERWHELMED* BY THE FLOOD OF IMAGERY AND INFORMATION."
I FOUND I COULDN'T TURN IT OFF, AND THAT IT ALL BUT CROWDED OUT MY OWN *THOUGHTS*.
IT WAS *REALLY* CONFUSING FOR THE FIRST SIXTY OR SEVENTY SECONDS--
--BUT BY THEN I HAD TAUGHT MYSELF THE LANGUAGE AND REALIZED THAT IT WAS *KRYPTONIAN*.

I COULD BARELY MANAGE TO *THINK* WITH ALL OF THESE KRYPTONIAN FACTS AND IMAGES FLOODING INTO MY HEAD. I COULDN'T EVEN TAKE THE HEADBAND *OFF.*

BUT I KNEW THAT IF THERE WAS [ONE] PERSON ON *EA[RTH]* WHO COULD HEL[P, IT] WOULD BE *YO[U.]*

TOOK ME *FOREVER* TO FIND YOU. I CRISSCROSSED NORTH AMERICA FIVE TIMES IN THE SECONDS IT TOOK TO TRACK YOU DOWN.

AND ONCE YOU *FOUND* ME, YOU HAD TO FIND SOME WAY OF *COMMUNICATING* WITH ME.

I'M SORRY I DIDN'T CATCH ON SOONER.

THE REFERENCES TO THE HOUSE OF EL, AND TO "CROWNS" AND "HEADBANDS." TO OVERTHROWING "ALIEN CONQUERORS."

YOU WERE TALKING *TO* ME.

SINCE ALL I COULD *THINK* OF WERE THESE BITS OF KRYPTONIAN HISTORY, I COULD ONLY SPEAK IN QUOTATIONS.

THE COSTUMES AND SCENERY WERE JUS[T] TO ATTRACT YOU[R] ATTENTION.

IS THAT THE ONLY REASON YOU CHOSE THOSE BITS TO REPEAT? YOU SEEMED TO MENTION "TRUTH" AND "MORALITY" AN AWFUL LOT.

DID I? DIDN'T MEAN TO. I GUESS THOSE IDEAS JUST CROP UP A LOT IN KRYPTONIAN HISTORY.

I WONDER... THAT QUOTE FROM THE "DIALOGUES OF KIL-GOR" IN PARTICULAR, ABOUT MORALITY BEING A NATURAL LAW?

I COULDN'T HELP THINKING ABOUT SOMETHING MY FATHER-- MY *ADOPTIVE* FATHER-- USED TO SAY. OR RATHER, ABOUT WHAT A CLASSMATE OF MINE ONCE *SAID* ABOUT IT.

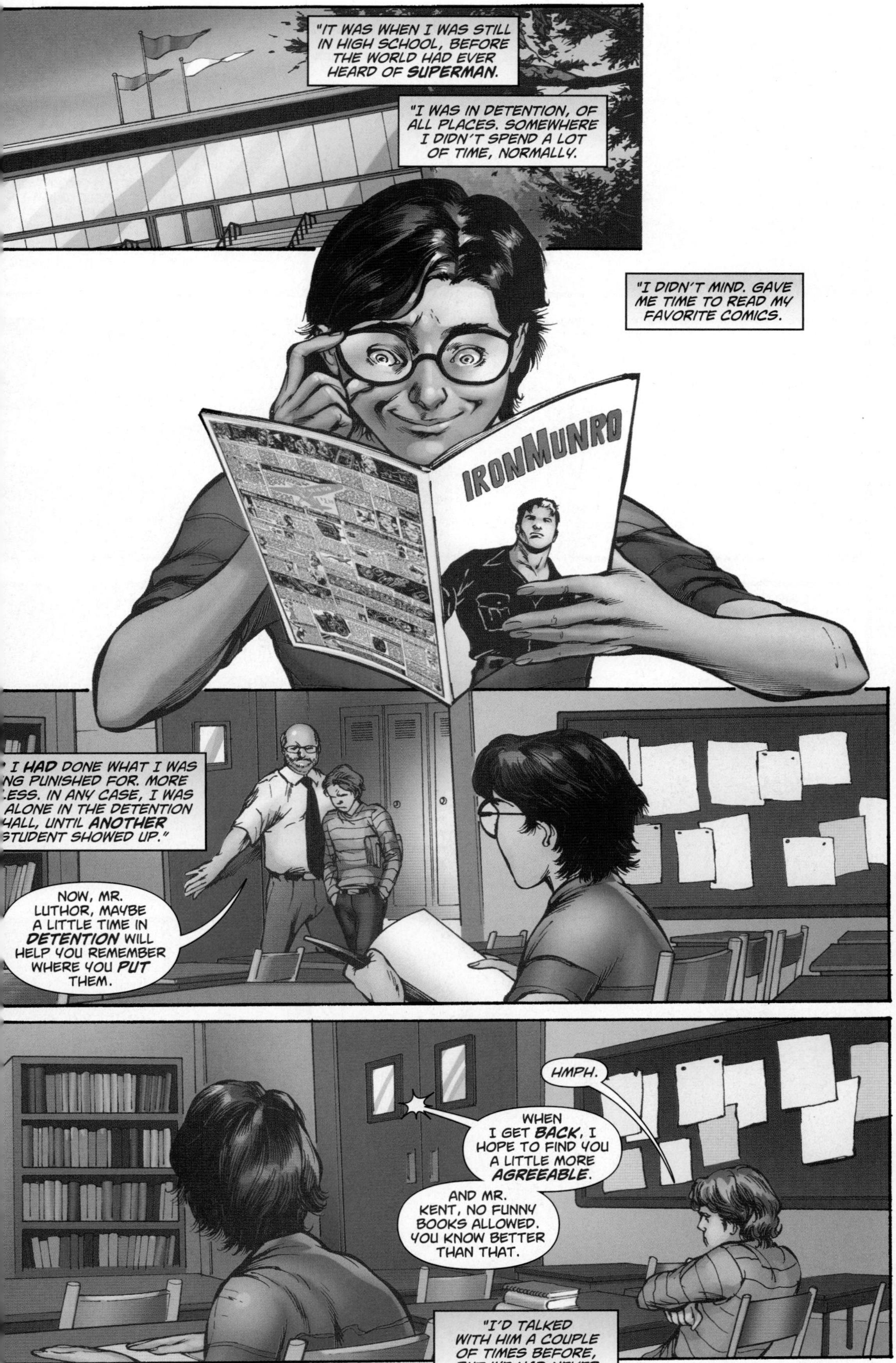
"IT WAS WHEN I WAS STILL IN HIGH SCHOOL, BEFORE THE WORLD HAD EVER HEARD OF SUPERMAN.
"I WAS IN DETENTION, OF ALL PLACES. SOMEWHERE I DIDN'T SPEND A LOT OF TIME, NORMALLY.
"I DIDN'T MIND. GAVE ME TIME TO READ MY FAVORITE COMICS.
IRONMUNRO
I HAD DONE WHAT I WAS NG PUNISHED FOR. MORE LESS. IN ANY CASE, I WAS ALONE IN THE DETENTION HALL, UNTIL ANOTHER STUDENT SHOWED UP."
NOW, MR. LUTHOR, MAYBE A LITTLE TIME IN DETENTION WILL HELP YOU REMEMBER WHERE YOU PUT THEM.
HMPH.
WHEN I GET BACK, I HOPE TO FIND YOU A LITTLE MORE AGREEABLE.
AND MR. KENT, NO FUNNY BOOKS ALLOWED. YOU KNOW BETTER THAN THAT.
"I'D TALKED WITH HIM A COUPLE OF TIMES BEFORE, BUT WE HAD NEVER REALLY BEEN FRIENDS.

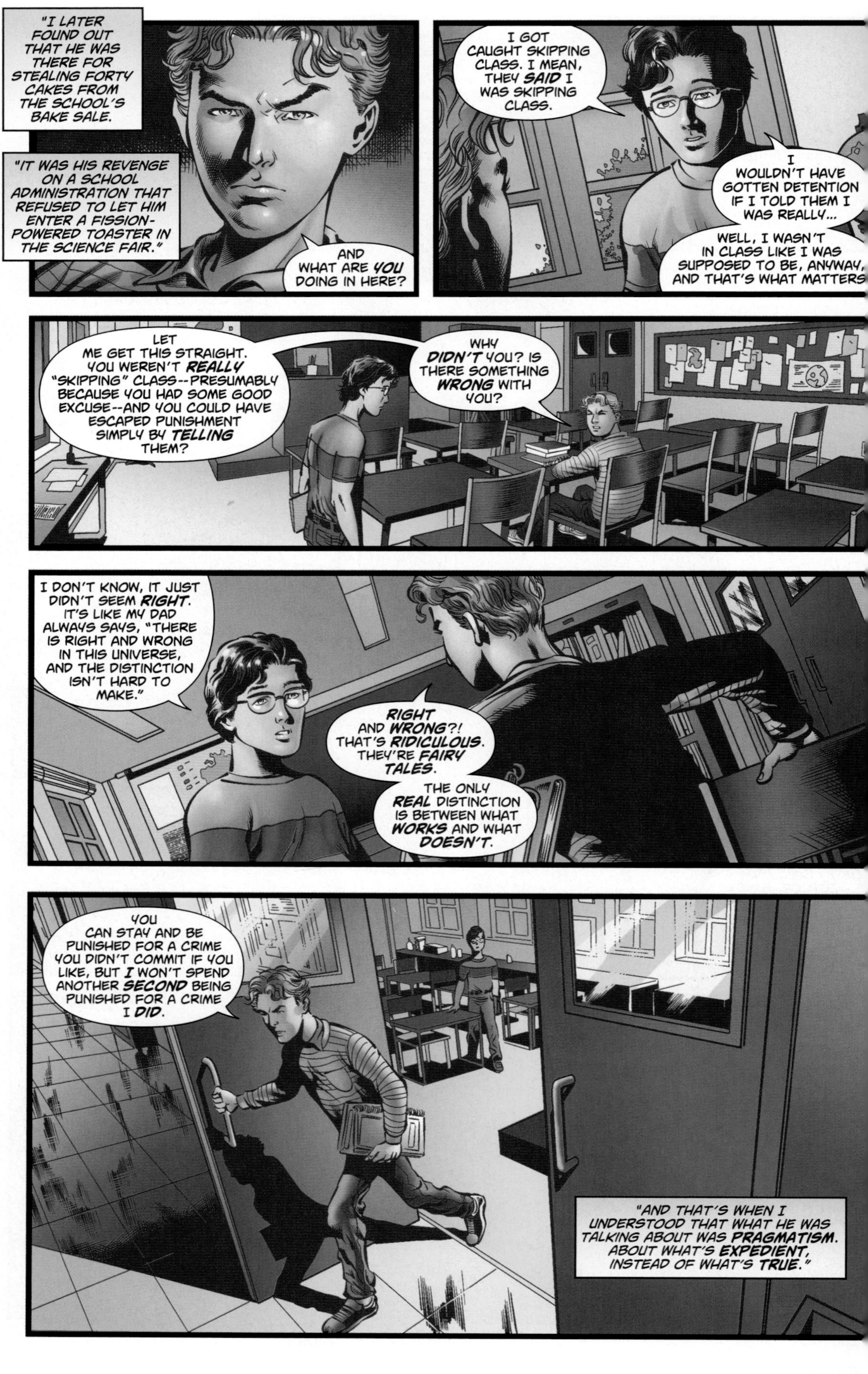
"I LATER FOUND OUT THAT HE WAS THERE FOR STEALING FORTY CAKES FROM THE SCHOOL'S BAKE SALE.
"IT WAS HIS REVENGE ON A SCHOOL ADMINISTRATION THAT REFUSED TO LET HIM ENTER A FISSION-POWERED TOASTER IN THE SCIENCE FAIR."
AND WHAT ARE YOU DOING IN HERE?
I GOT CAUGHT SKIPPING CLASS. I MEAN, THEY SAID I WAS SKIPPING CLASS.
I WOULDN'T HAVE GOTTEN DETENTION IF I TOLD THEM I WAS REALLY...
WELL, I WASN'T IN CLASS LIKE I WAS SUPPOSED TO BE, ANYWAY, AND THAT'S WHAT MATTERS
LET ME GET THIS STRAIGHT. YOU WEREN'T REALLY "SKIPPING" CLASS--PRESUMABLY BECAUSE YOU HAD SOME GOOD EXCUSE--AND YOU COULD HAVE ESCAPED PUNISHMENT SIMPLY BY TELLING THEM?
WHY DIDN'T YOU? IS THERE SOMETHING WRONG WITH YOU?
I DON'T KNOW, IT JUST DIDN'T SEEM RIGHT. IT'S LIKE MY DAD ALWAYS SAYS, "THERE IS RIGHT AND WRONG IN THIS UNIVERSE, AND THE DISTINCTION ISN'T HARD TO MAKE."
RIGHT AND WRONG?! THAT'S RIDICULOUS. THEY'RE FAIRY TALES.
THE ONLY REAL DISTINCTION IS BETWEEN WHAT WORKS AND WHAT DOESN'T.
YOU CAN STAY AND BE PUNISHED FOR A CRIME YOU DIDN'T COMMIT IF YOU LIKE, BUT I WON'T SPEND ANOTHER SECOND BEING PUNISHED FOR A CRIME I DID.
"AND THAT'S WHEN I UNDERSTOOD THAT WHAT HE WAS TALKING ABOUT WAS PRAGMATISM. ABOUT WHAT'S EXPEDIENT, INSTEAD OF WHAT'S TRUE."

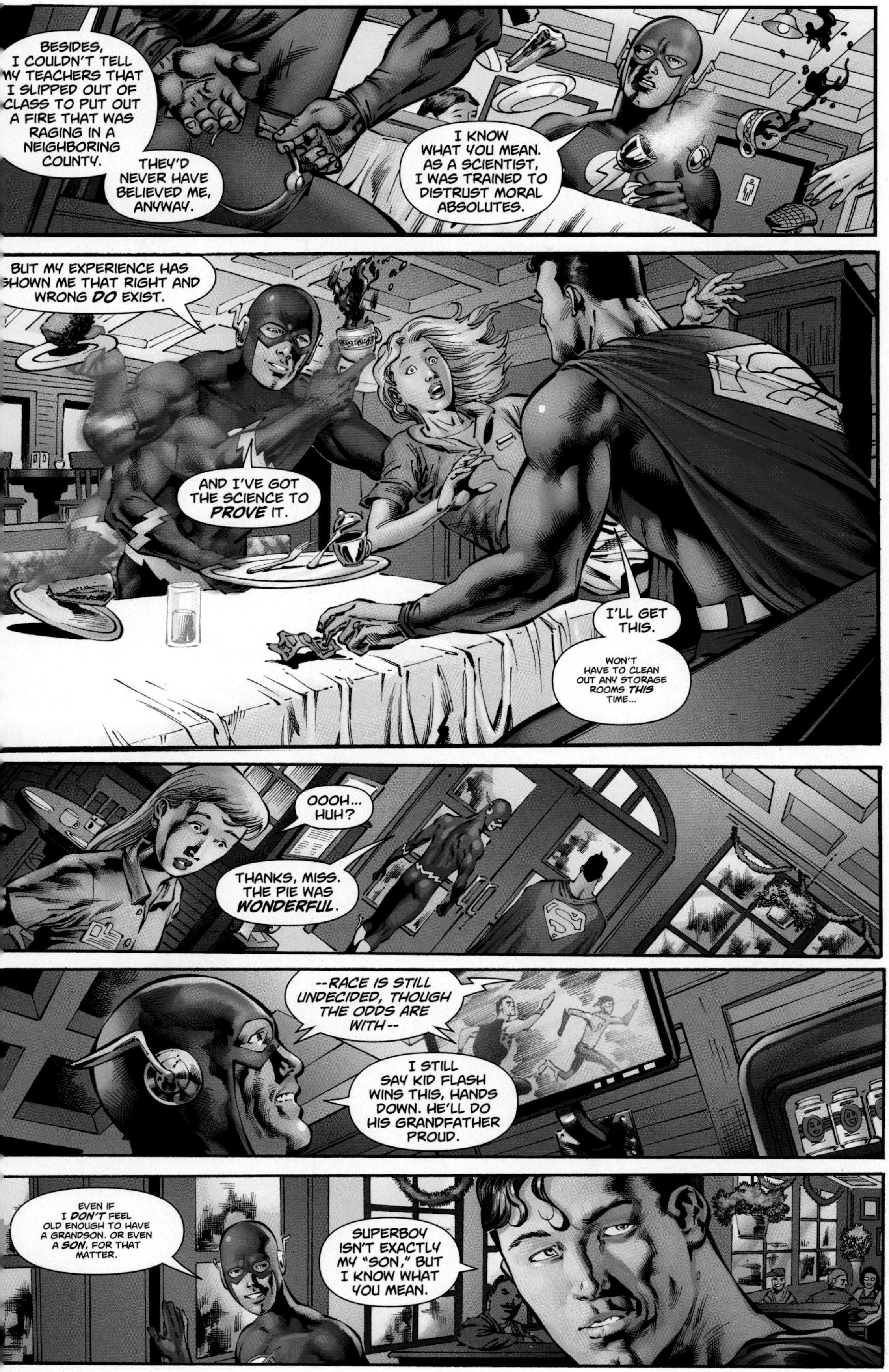
BESIDES, I COULDN'T TELL MY TEACHERS THAT I SLIPPED OUT OF CLASS TO PUT OUT A FIRE THAT WAS RAGING IN A NEIGHBORING COUNTY.
THEY'D NEVER HAVE BELIEVED ME, ANYWAY.
I KNOW WHAT YOU MEAN. AS A SCIENTIST, I WAS TRAINED TO DISTRUST MORAL ABSOLUTES.
BUT MY EXPERIENCE HAS SHOWN ME THAT RIGHT AND WRONG DO EXIST.
AND I'VE GOT THE SCIENCE TO PROVE IT.
I'LL GET THIS.
WON'T HAVE TO CLEAN OUT ANY STORAGE ROOMS THIS TIME...
OOOH... HUH?
THANKS, MISS. THE PIE WAS WONDERFUL.
--RACE IS STILL UNDECIDED, THOUGH THE ODDS ARE WITH--
I STILL SAY KID FLASH WINS THIS, HANDS DOWN. HE'LL DO HIS GRANDFATHER PROUD.
EVEN IF I DON'T FEEL OLD ENOUGH TO HAVE A GRANDSON. OR EVEN A SON, FOR THAT MATTER.
SUPERBOY ISN'T EXACTLY MY "SON," BUT I KNOW WHAT YOU MEAN.

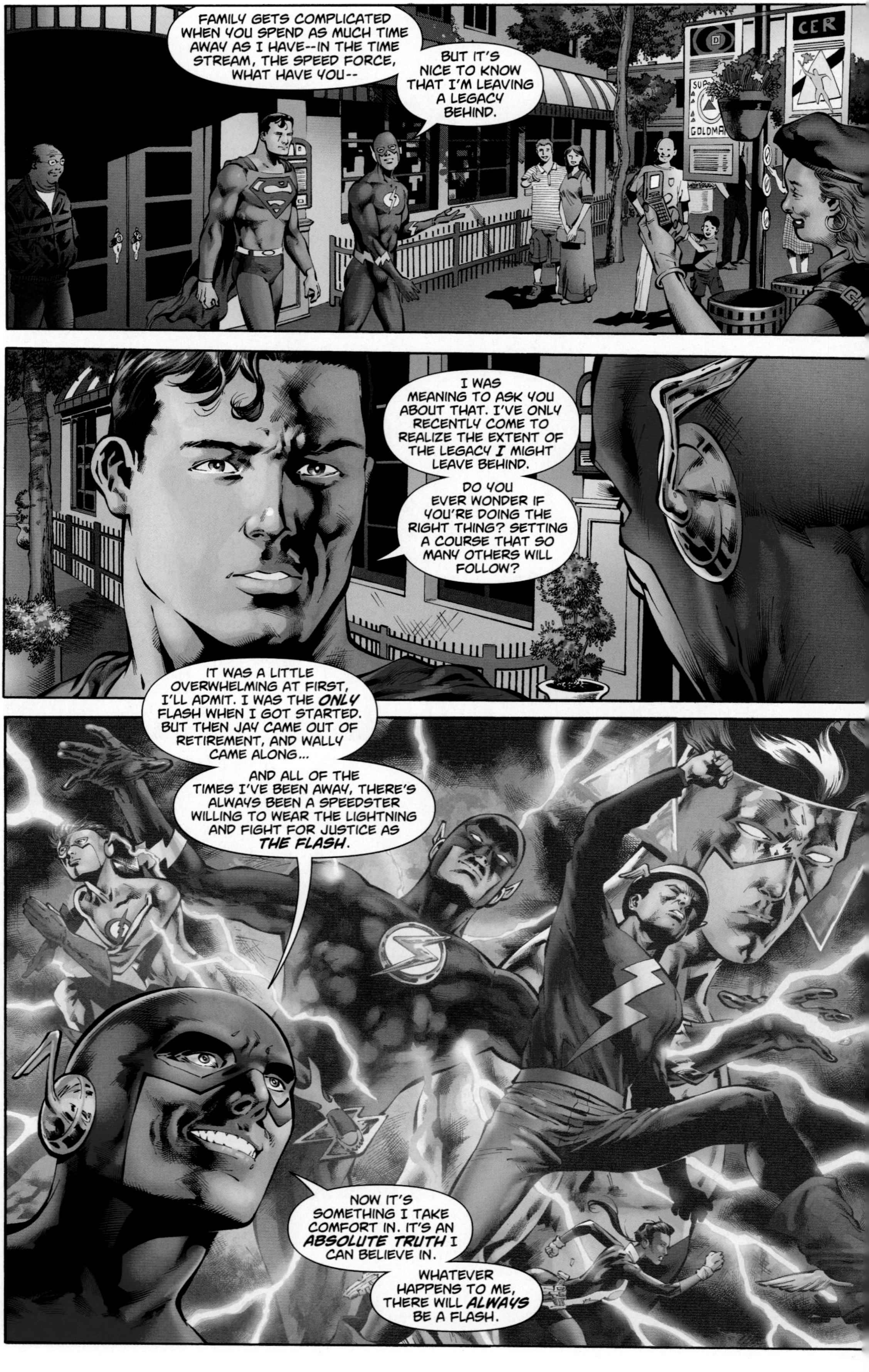
FAMILY GETS COMPLICATED WHEN YOU SPEND AS MUCH TIME AWAY AS I HAVE--IN THE TIME STREAM, THE SPEED FORCE, WHAT HAVE YOU--
BUT IT'S NICE TO KNOW THAT I'M LEAVING A LEGACY BEHIND.
I WAS MEANING TO ASK YOU ABOUT THAT. I'VE ONLY RECENTLY COME TO REALIZE THE EXTENT OF THE LEGACY *I* MIGHT LEAVE BEHIND.
DO YOU EVER WONDER IF YOU'RE DOING THE RIGHT THING? SETTING A COURSE THAT SO MANY OTHERS WILL FOLLOW?
IT WAS A LITTLE OVERWHELMING AT FIRST, I'LL ADMIT. I WAS THE *ONLY* FLASH WHEN I GOT STARTED. BUT THEN JAY CAME OUT OF RETIREMENT, AND WALLY CAME ALONG...
AND ALL OF THE TIMES I'VE BEEN AWAY, THERE'S ALWAYS BEEN A SPEEDSTER WILLING TO WEAR THE LIGHTNING AND FIGHT FOR JUSTICE AS ***THE FLASH***.
NOW IT'S SOMETHING I TAKE COMFORT IN. IT'S AN ***ABSOLUTE TRUTH*** I CAN BELIEVE IN.
WHATEVER HAPPENS TO ME, THERE WILL ***ALWAYS*** BE A FLASH.

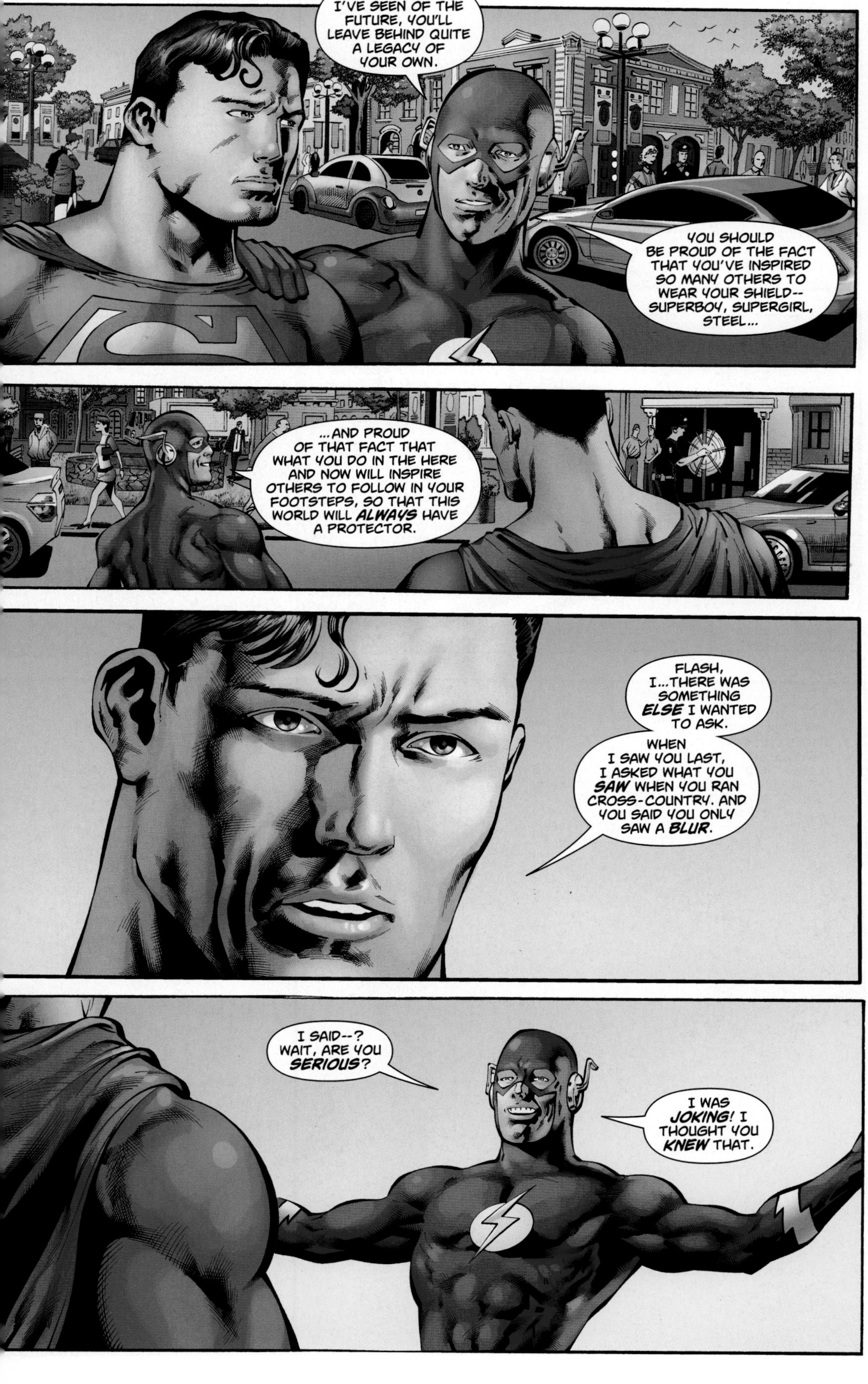
FROM WHAT I'VE SEEN OF THE FUTURE, YOU'LL LEAVE BEHIND QUITE A LEGACY OF YOUR OWN.
YOU SHOULD BE PROUD OF THE FACT THAT YOU'VE INSPIRED SO MANY OTHERS TO WEAR YOUR SHIELD-- SUPERBOY, SUPERGIRL, STEEL...
...AND PROUD OF THAT FACT THAT WHAT YOU DO IN THE HERE AND NOW WILL INSPIRE OTHERS TO FOLLOW IN YOUR FOOTSTEPS, SO THAT THIS WORLD WILL ALWAYS HAVE A PROTECTOR.
FLASH, I...THERE WAS SOMETHING ELSE I WANTED TO ASK.
WHEN I SAW YOU LAST, I ASKED WHAT YOU SAW WHEN YOU RAN CROSS-COUNTRY. AND YOU SAID YOU ONLY SAW A BLUR.
I SAID--? WAIT, ARE YOU SERIOUS?
I WAS JOKING! I THOUGHT YOU KNEW THAT.

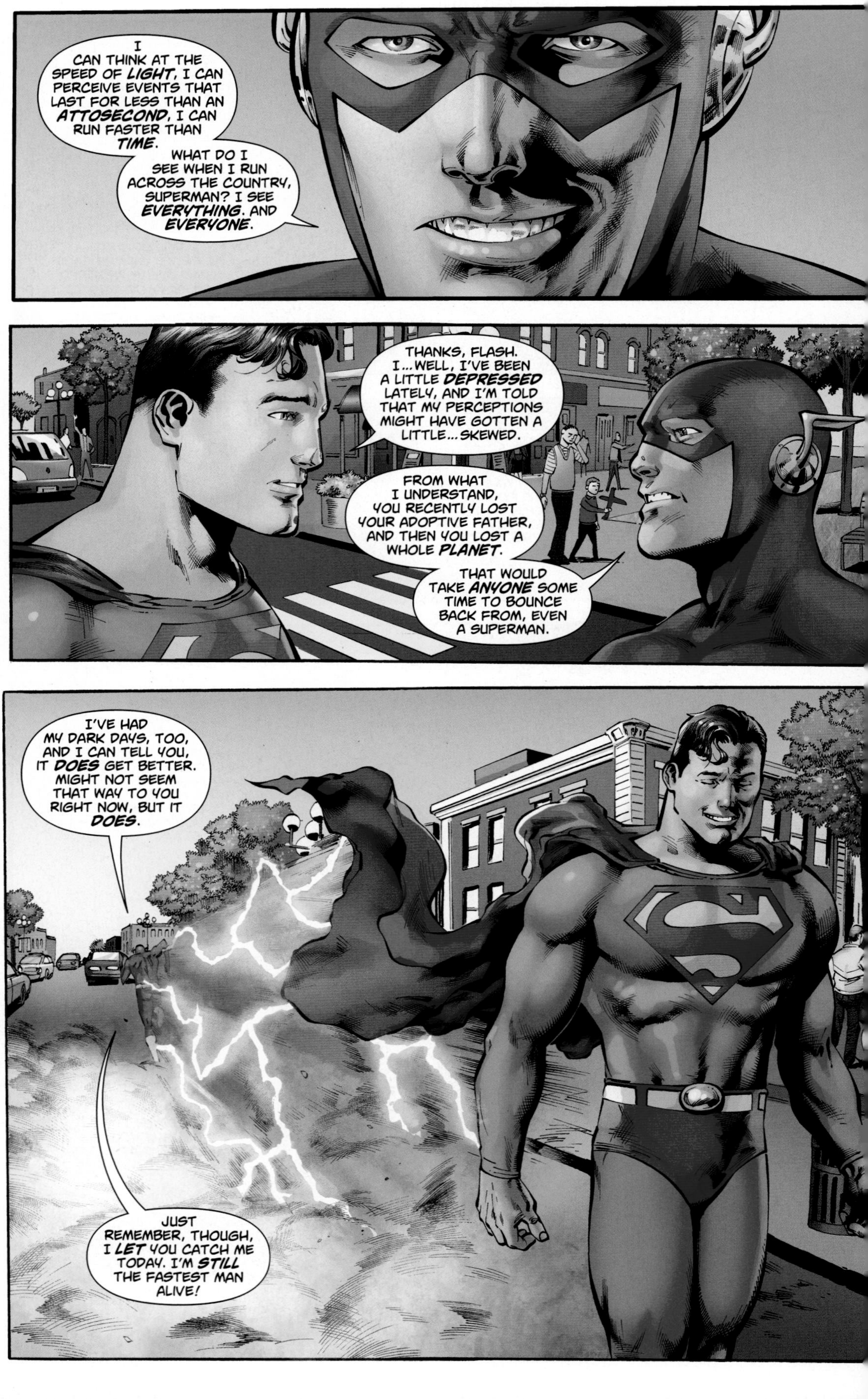
I CAN THINK AT THE SPEED OF LIGHT, I CAN PERCEIVE EVENTS THAT LAST FOR LESS THAN AN ATTOSECOND, I CAN RUN FASTER THAN TIME.
WHAT DO I SEE WHEN I RUN ACROSS THE COUNTRY, SUPERMAN? I SEE EVERYTHING. AND EVERYONE.
THANKS, FLASH. I... WELL, I'VE BEEN A LITTLE DEPRESSED LATELY, AND I'M TOLD THAT MY PERCEPTIONS MIGHT HAVE GOTTEN A LITTLE... SKEWED.
FROM WHAT I UNDERSTAND, YOU RECENTLY LOST YOUR ADOPTIVE FATHER, AND THEN YOU LOST A WHOLE PLANET.
THAT WOULD TAKE ANYONE SOME TIME TO BOUNCE BACK FROM, EVEN A SUPERMAN.
I'VE HAD MY DARK DAYS, TOO, AND I CAN TELL YOU, IT DOES GET BETTER. MIGHT NOT SEEM THAT WAY TO YOU RIGHT NOW, BUT IT DOES.
JUST REMEMBER, THOUGH, I LET YOU CATCH ME TODAY. I'M STILL THE FASTEST MAN ALIVE!

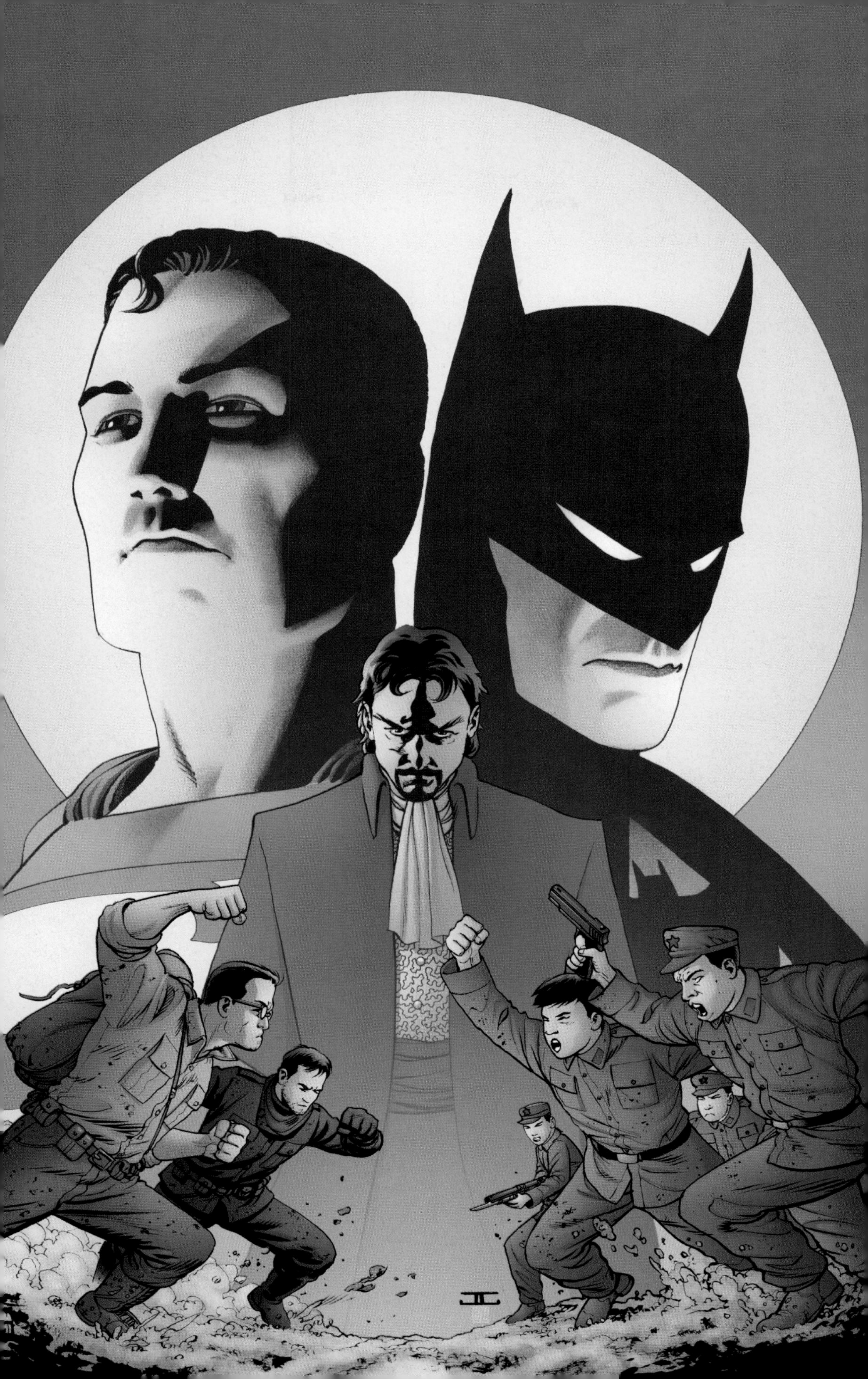

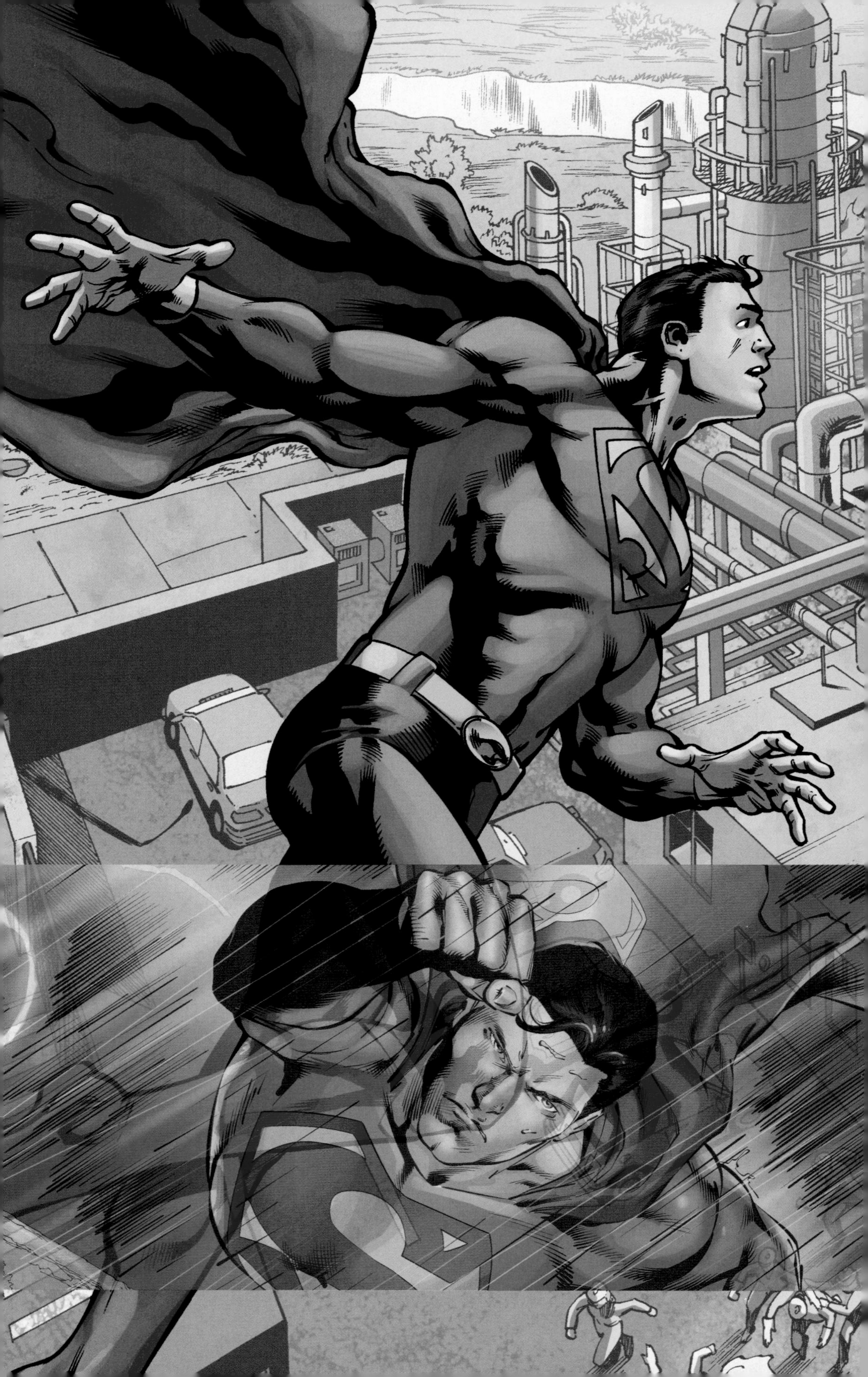

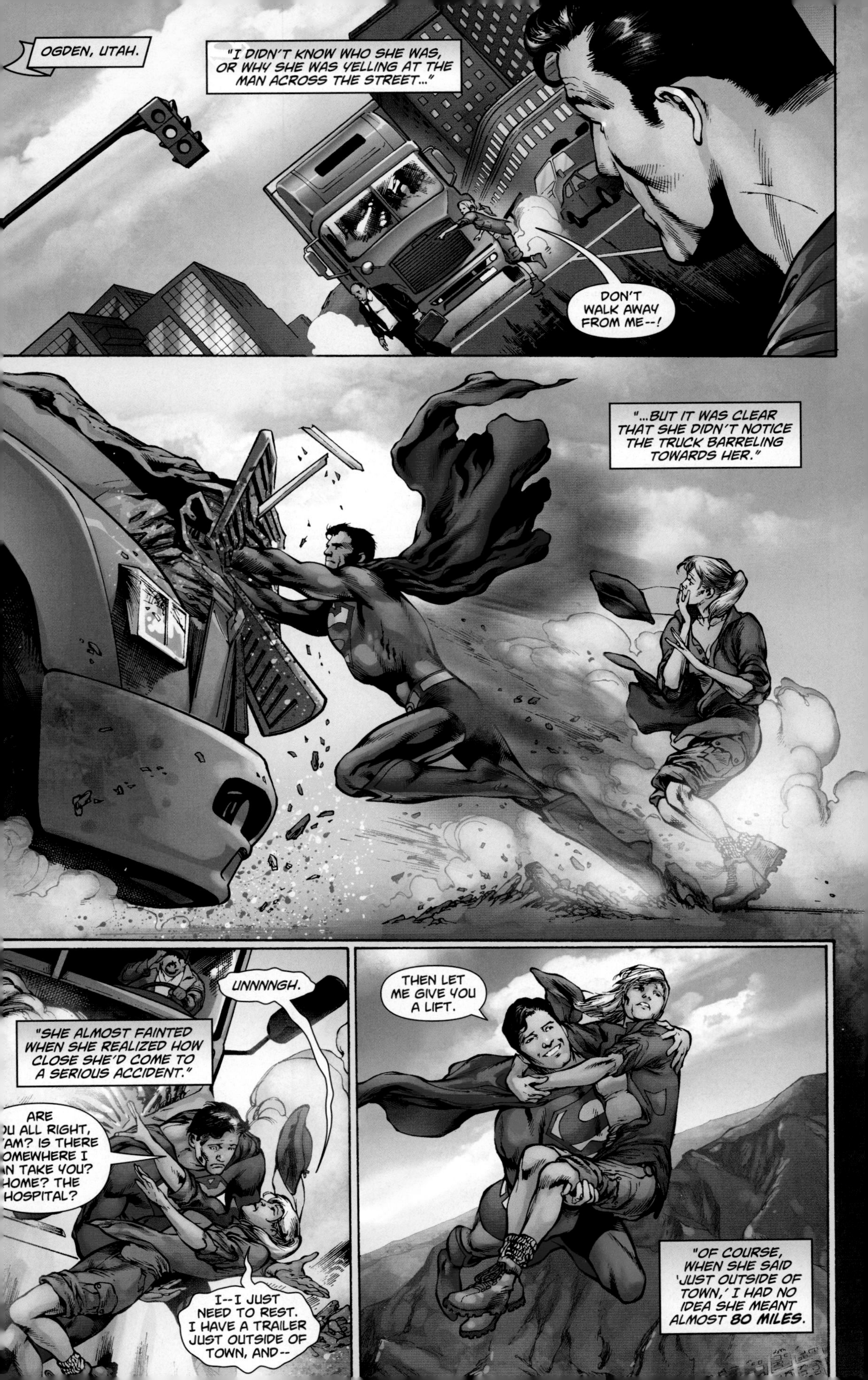

OGDEN, UTAH.
"I DIDN'T KNOW WHO SHE WAS, OR WHY SHE WAS YELLING AT THE MAN ACROSS THE STREET..."
DON'T WALK AWAY FROM ME--!
"...BUT IT WAS CLEAR THAT SHE DIDN'T NOTICE THE TRUCK BARRELING TOWARDS HER."
UNNNNGH.
"SHE ALMOST FAINTED WHEN SHE REALIZED HOW CLOSE SHE'D COME TO A SERIOUS ACCIDENT."
ARE OU ALL RIGHT, 'AM? IS THERE OMEWHERE I N TAKE YOU? HOME? THE HOSPITAL?
I--I JUST NEED TO REST. I HAVE A TRAILER JUST OUTSIDE OF TOWN, AND--
THEN LET ME GIVE YOU A LIFT.
"OF COURSE, WHEN SHE SAID 'JUST OUTSIDE OF TOWN,' I HAD NO IDEA SHE MEANT ALMOST 80 MILES.

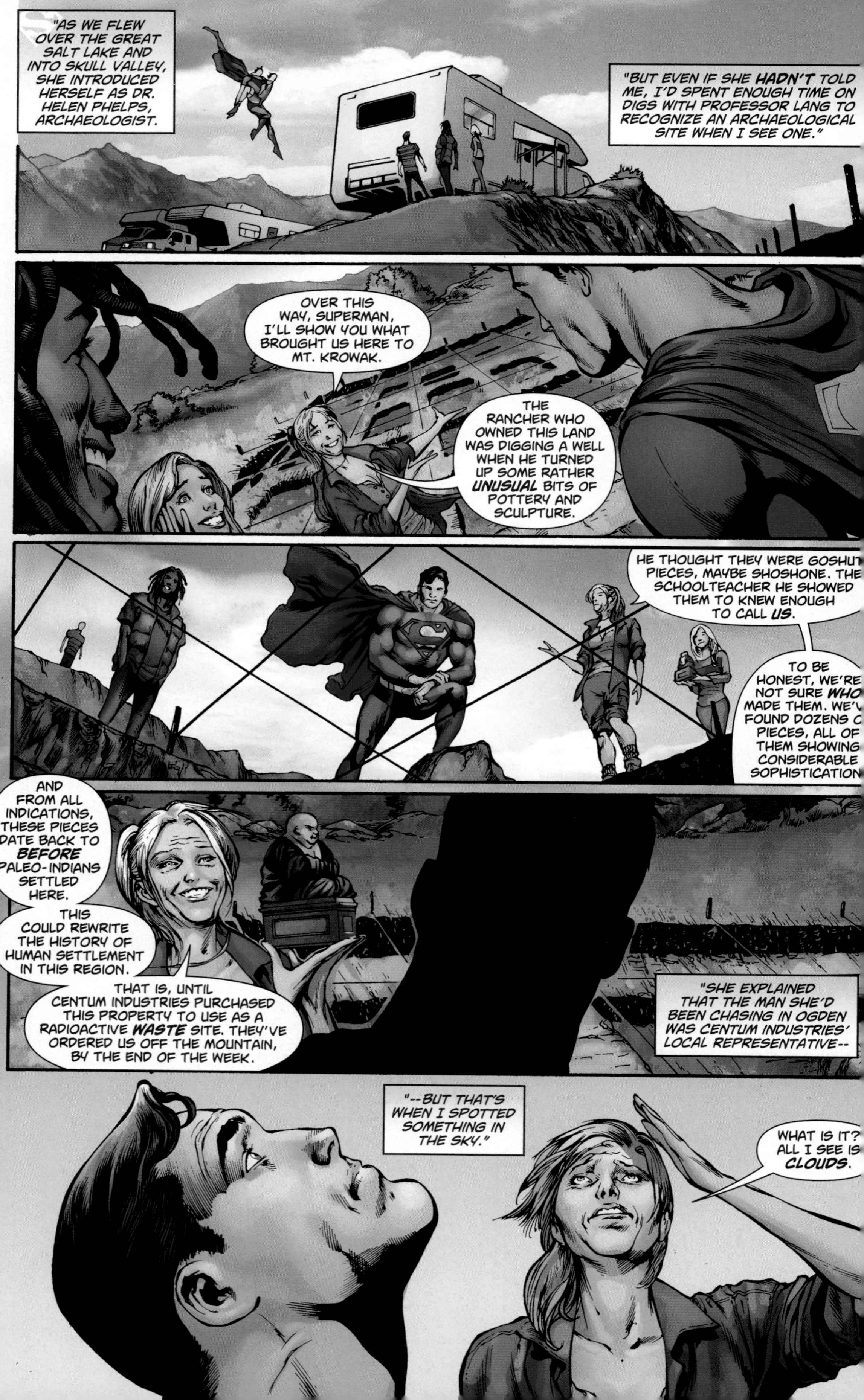
"AS WE FLEW OVER THE GREAT SALT LAKE AND INTO SKULL VALLEY, SHE INTRODUCED HERSELF AS DR. HELEN PHELPS, ARCHAEOLOGIST.
"BUT EVEN IF SHE HADN'T TOLD ME, I'D SPENT ENOUGH TIME ON DIGS WITH PROFESSOR LANG TO RECOGNIZE AN ARCHAEOLOGICAL SITE WHEN I SEE ONE."
OVER THIS WAY, SUPERMAN, I'LL SHOW YOU WHAT BROUGHT US HERE TO MT. KROWAK.
THE RANCHER WHO OWNED THIS LAND WAS DIGGING A WELL WHEN HE TURNED UP SOME RATHER UNUSUAL BITS OF POTTERY AND SCULPTURE.
HE THOUGHT THEY WERE GOSHUT PIECES, MAYBE SHOSHONE. THE SCHOOLTEACHER HE SHOWED THEM TO KNEW ENOUGH TO CALL US.
TO BE HONEST, WE'RE NOT SURE WHO MADE THEM. WE'V FOUND DOZENS O PIECES, ALL OF THEM SHOWING CONSIDERABLE SOPHISTICATION
AND FROM ALL INDICATIONS, THESE PIECES DATE BACK TO BEFORE PALEO-INDIANS SETTLED HERE.
THIS COULD REWRITE THE HISTORY OF HUMAN SETTLEMENT IN THIS REGION.
THAT IS, UNTIL CENTUM INDUSTRIES PURCHASED THIS PROPERTY TO USE AS A RADIOACTIVE WASTE SITE. THEY'VE ORDERED US OFF THE MOUNTAIN, BY THE END OF THE WEEK.
"SHE EXPLAINED THAT THE MAN SHE'D BEEN CHASING IN OGDEN WAS CENTUM INDUSTRIES' LOCAL REPRESENTATIVE--
"--BUT THAT'S WHEN I SPOTTED SOMETHING IN THE SKY."
WHAT IS IT? ALL I SEE IS CLOUDS.

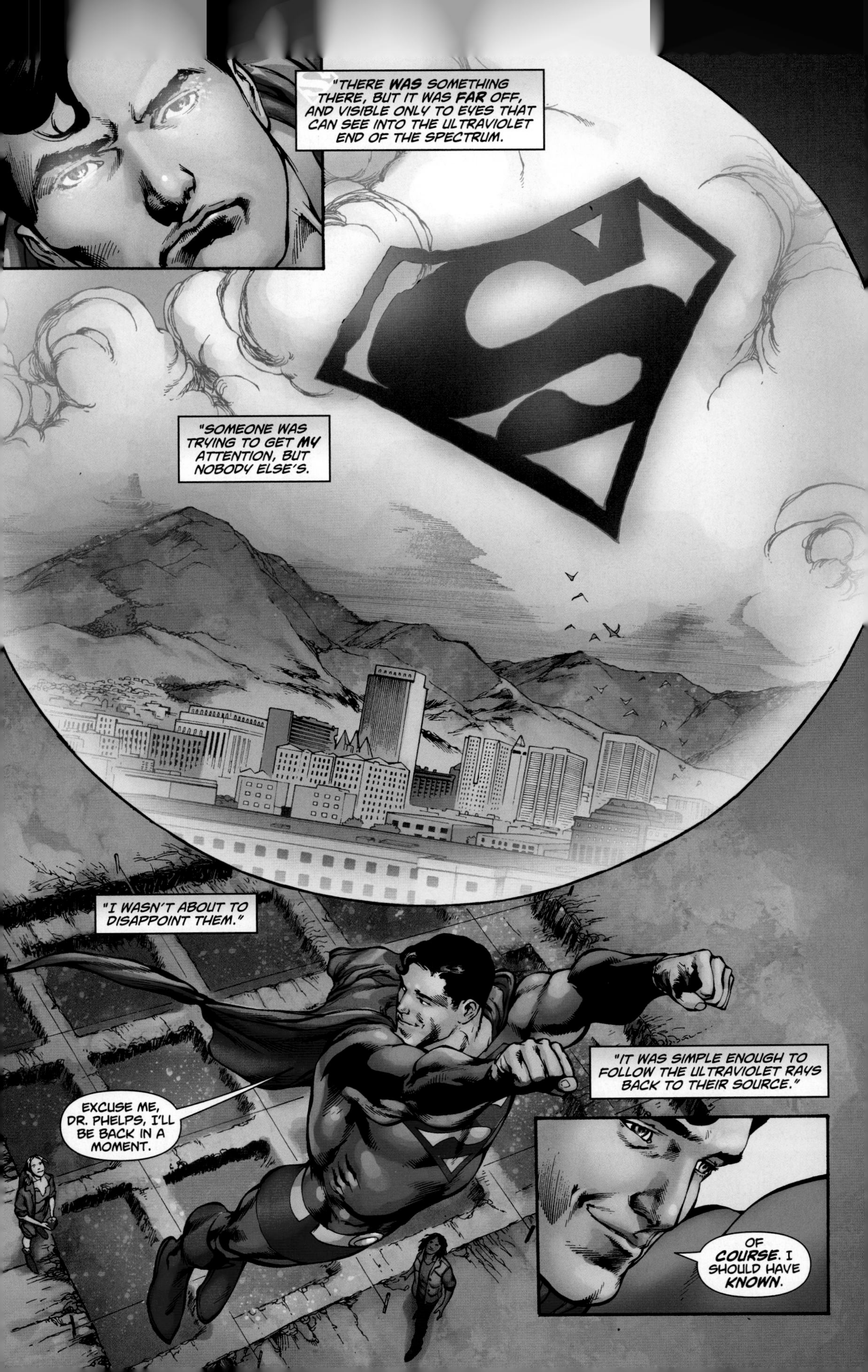
"THERE WAS SOMETHING THERE, BUT IT WAS FAR OFF, AND VISIBLE ONLY TO EYES THAT CAN SEE INTO THE ULTRAVIOLET END OF THE SPECTRUM.
"SOMEONE WAS TRYING TO GET MY ATTENTION, BUT NOBODY ELSE'S.
"I WASN'T ABOUT TO DISAPPOINT THEM."
EXCUSE ME, DR. PHELPS, I'LL BE BACK IN A MOMENT.
"IT WAS SIMPLE ENOUGH TO FOLLOW THE ULTRAVIOLET RAYS BACK TO THEIR SOURCE."
OF COURSE. I SHOULD HAVE KNOWN.

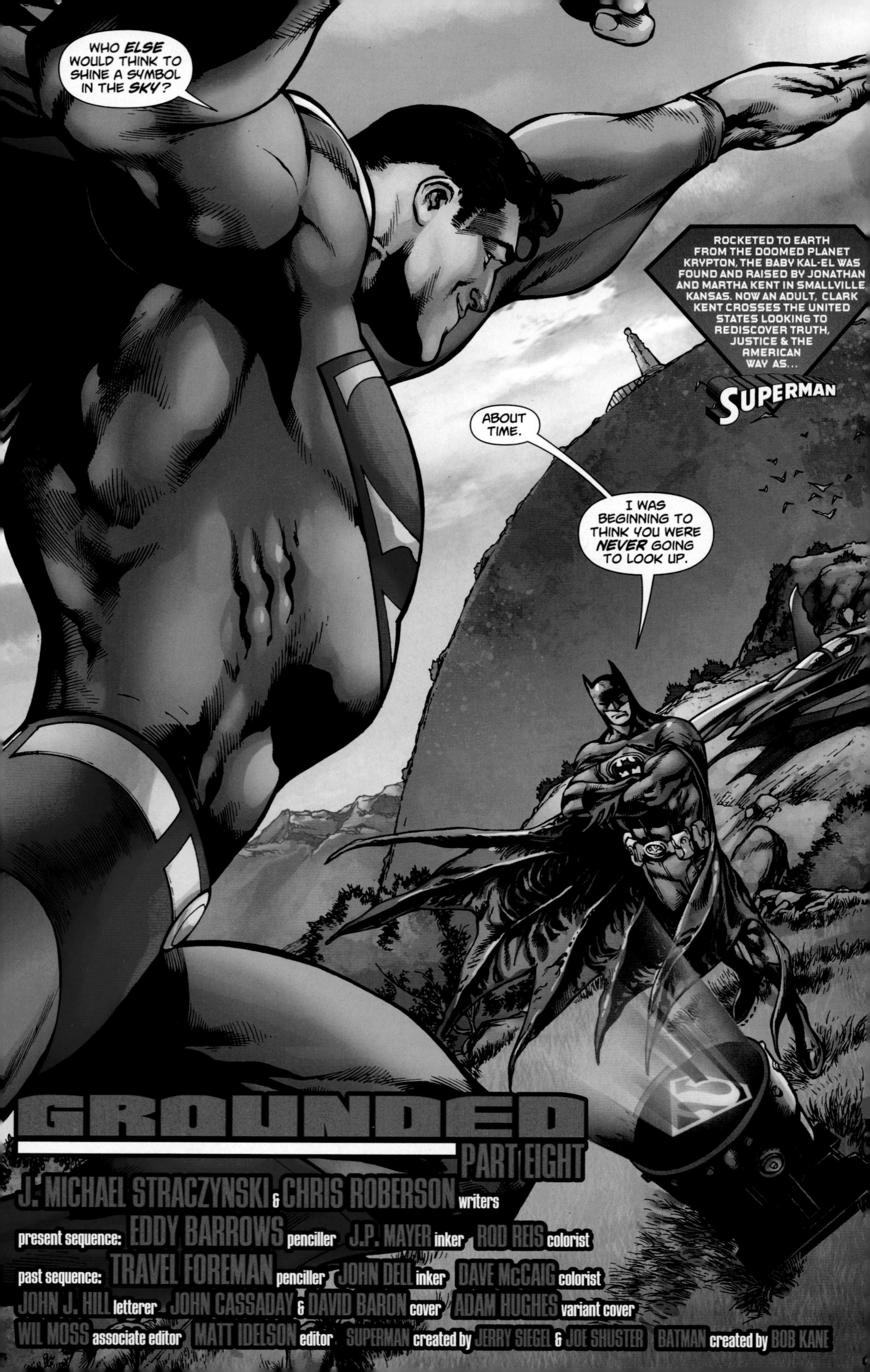
WHO ELSE WOULD THINK TO SHINE A SYMBOL IN THE SKY?
ROCKETED TO EARTH FROM THE DOOMED PLANET KRYPTON, THE BABY KAL-EL WAS FOUND AND RAISED BY JONATHAN AND MARTHA KENT IN SMALLVILLE KANSAS. NOW AN ADULT, CLARK KENT CROSSES THE UNITED STATES LOOKING TO REDISCOVER TRUTH, JUSTICE & THE AMERICAN WAY AS...
SUPERMAN
ABOUT TIME.
I WAS BEGINNING TO THINK YOU WERE NEVER GOING TO LOOK UP.
GROUNDED
PART EIGHT
J. MICHAEL STRACZYNSKI & CHRIS ROBERSON writers
present sequence: EDDY BARROWS penciller J.P. MAYER inker ROD REIS colorist
past sequence: TRAVEL FOREMAN penciller JOHN DELL inker DAVE McCAIG colorist
JOHN J. HILL letterer JOHN CASSADAY & DAVID BARON cover ADAM HUGHES variant cover
WIL MOSS associate editor MATT IDELSON editor SUPERMAN created by JERRY SIEGEL & JOE SHUSTER BATMAN created by BOB KANE

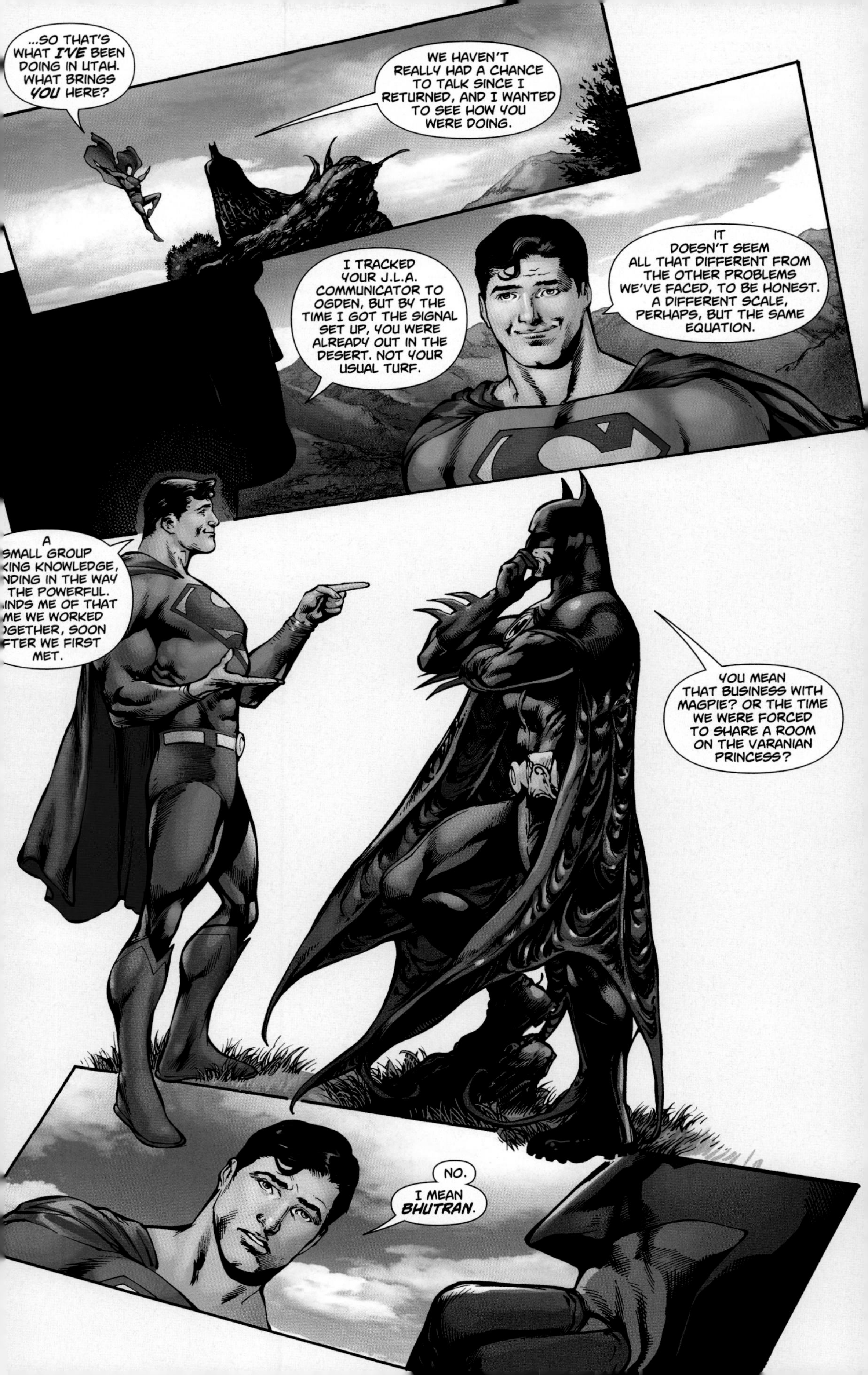
...SO THAT'S WHAT I'VE BEEN DOING IN UTAH. WHAT BRINGS YOU HERE?
WE HAVEN'T REALLY HAD A CHANCE TO TALK SINCE I RETURNED, AND I WANTED TO SEE HOW YOU WERE DOING.
I TRACKED YOUR J.L.A. COMMUNICATOR TO OGDEN, BUT BY THE TIME I GOT THE SIGNAL SET UP, YOU WERE ALREADY OUT IN THE DESERT. NOT YOUR USUAL TURF.
IT DOESN'T SEEM ALL THAT DIFFERENT FROM THE OTHER PROBLEMS WE'VE FACED, TO BE HONEST. A DIFFERENT SCALE, PERHAPS, BUT THE SAME EQUATION.
A SMALL GROUP ...KING KNOWLEDGE, ...NDING IN THE WAY ...THE POWERFUL. ...INDS ME OF THAT ...ME WE WORKED ...OGETHER, SOON ...FTER WE FIRST MET.
YOU MEAN THAT BUSINESS WITH MAGPIE? OR THE TIME WE WERE FORCED TO SHARE A ROOM ON THE VARANIAN PRINCESS?
NO.
I MEAN BHUTRAN.

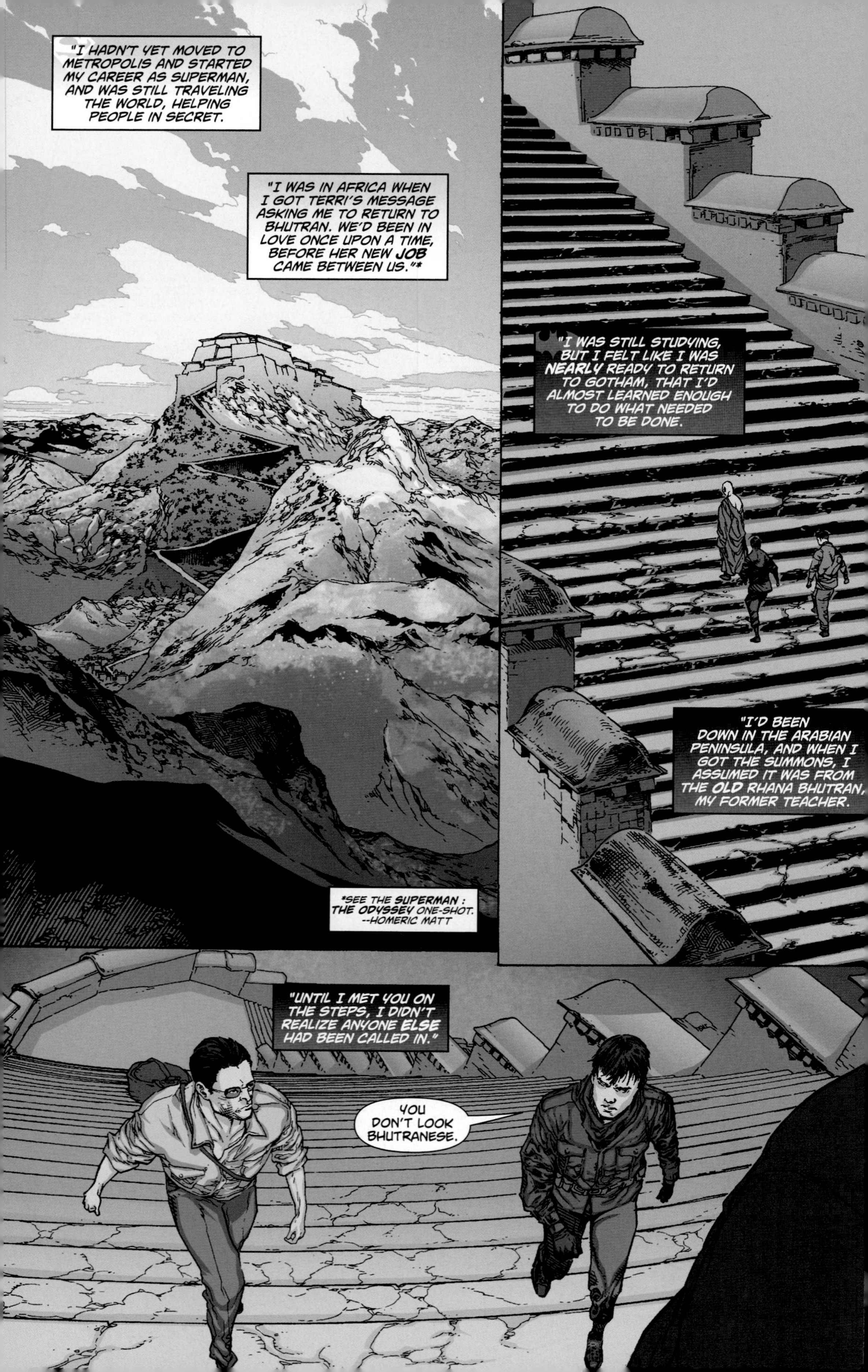
"I HADN'T YET MOVED TO METROPOLIS AND STARTED MY CAREER AS SUPERMAN, AND WAS STILL TRAVELING THE WORLD, HELPING PEOPLE IN SECRET.
"I WAS IN AFRICA WHEN I GOT TERRI'S MESSAGE ASKING ME TO RETURN TO BHUTRAN. WE'D BEEN IN LOVE ONCE UPON A TIME, BEFORE HER NEW JOB CAME BETWEEN US."*
*SEE THE SUPERMAN : THE ODYSSEY ONE-SHOT. --HOMERIC MATT
"I WAS STILL STUDYING, BUT I FELT LIKE I WAS NEARLY READY TO RETURN TO GOTHAM, THAT I'D ALMOST LEARNED ENOUGH TO DO WHAT NEEDED TO BE DONE.
"I'D BEEN DOWN IN THE ARABIAN PENINSULA, AND WHEN I GOT THE SUMMONS, I ASSUMED IT WAS FROM THE OLD RHANA BHUTRAN, MY FORMER TEACHER.
"UNTIL I MET YOU ON THE STEPS, I DIDN'T REALIZE ANYONE ELSE HAD BEEN CALLED IN."
YOU DON'T LOOK BHUTRANESE.

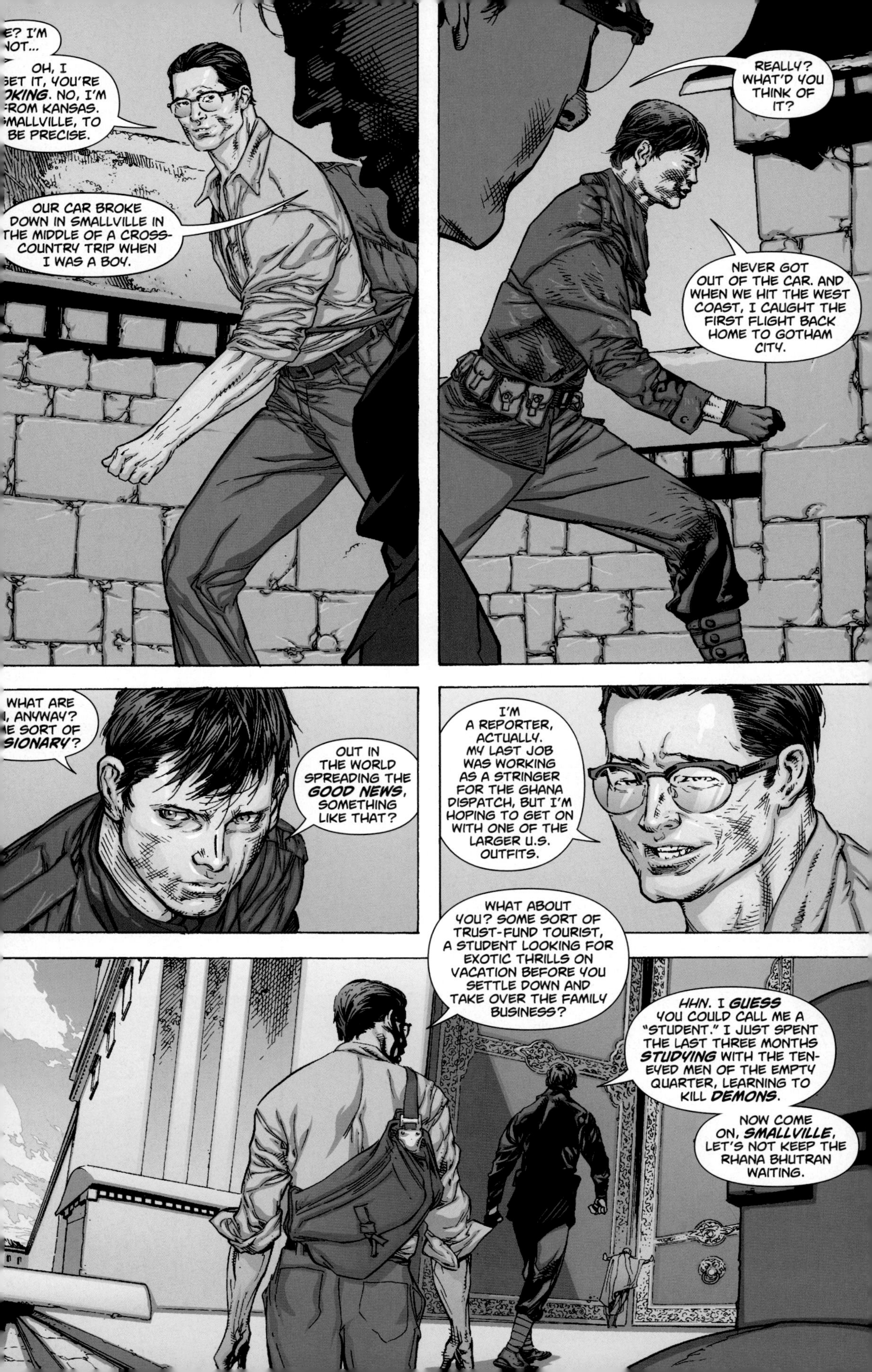

E? I'M NOT...
OH, I GET IT, YOU'RE JOKING. NO, I'M FROM KANSAS. SMALLVILLE, TO BE PRECISE.
REALLY? WHAT'D YOU THINK OF IT?
OUR CAR BROKE DOWN IN SMALLVILLE IN THE MIDDLE OF A CROSS-COUNTRY TRIP WHEN I WAS A BOY.
NEVER GOT OUT OF THE CAR. AND WHEN WE HIT THE WEST COAST, I CAUGHT THE FIRST FLIGHT BACK HOME TO GOTHAM CITY.
WHAT ARE , ANYWAY? E SORT OF SIONARY?
OUT IN THE WORLD SPREADING THE GOOD NEWS, SOMETHING LIKE THAT?
I'M A REPORTER, ACTUALLY. MY LAST JOB WAS WORKING AS A STRINGER FOR THE GHANA DISPATCH, BUT I'M HOPING TO GET ON WITH ONE OF THE LARGER U.S. OUTFITS.
WHAT ABOUT YOU? SOME SORT OF TRUST-FUND TOURIST, A STUDENT LOOKING FOR EXOTIC THRILLS ON VACATION BEFORE YOU SETTLE DOWN AND TAKE OVER THE FAMILY BUSINESS?
HHN. I GUESS YOU COULD CALL ME A "STUDENT." I JUST SPENT THE LAST THREE MONTHS STUDYING WITH THE TEN-EYED MEN OF THE EMPTY QUARTER, LEARNING TO KILL DEMONS.
NOW COME ON, SMALLVILLE, LET'S NOT KEEP THE RHANA BHUTRAN WAITING.

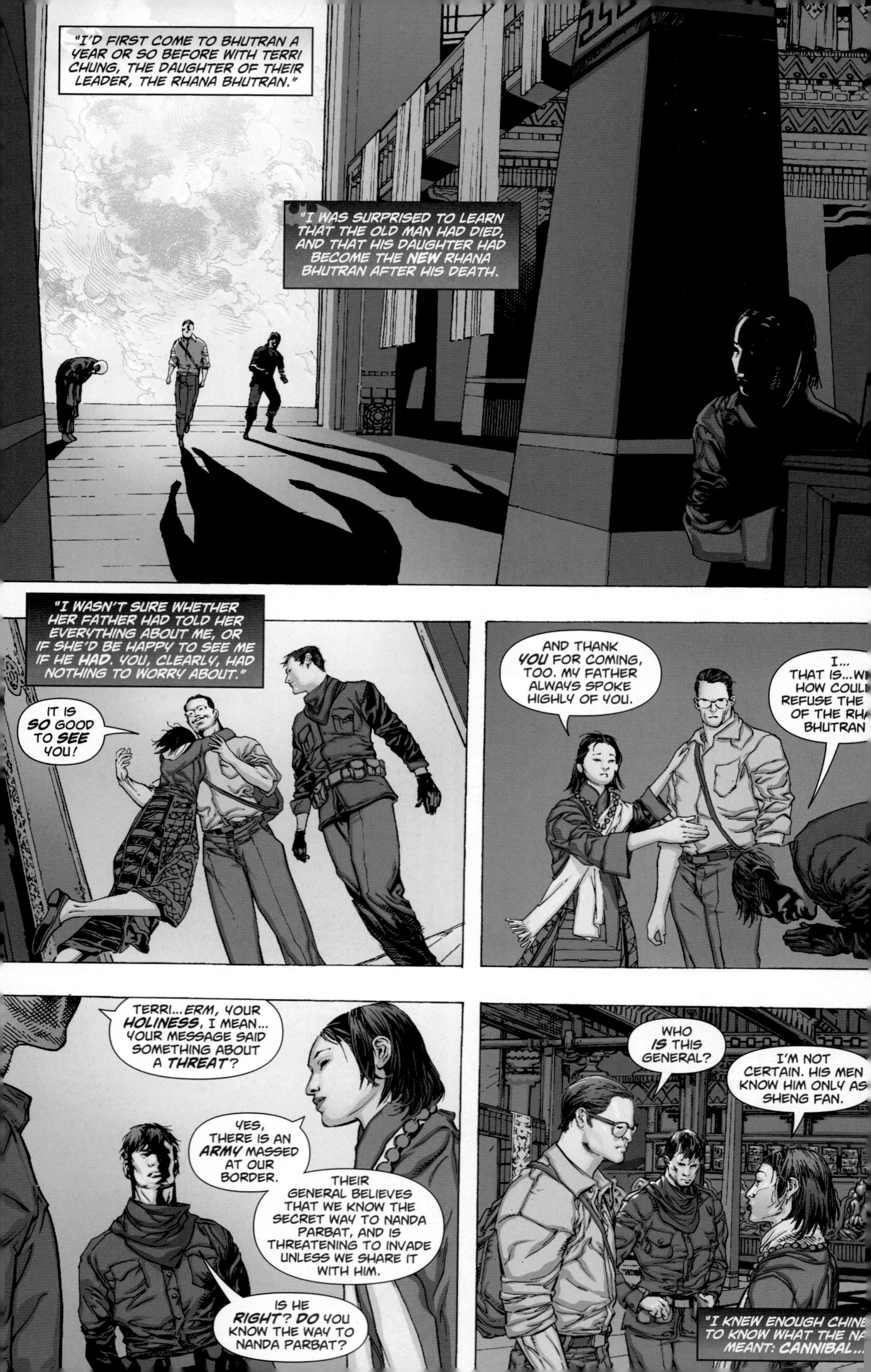
"I'D FIRST COME TO BHUTRAN A YEAR OR SO BEFORE WITH TERRI CHUNG, THE DAUGHTER OF THEIR LEADER, THE RHANA BHUTRAN."
"I WAS SURPRISED TO LEARN THAT THE OLD MAN HAD DIED, AND THAT HIS DAUGHTER HAD BECOME THE NEW RHANA BHUTRAN AFTER HIS DEATH.
"I WASN'T SURE WHETHER HER FATHER HAD TOLD HER EVERYTHING ABOUT ME, OR IF SHE'D BE HAPPY TO SEE ME IF HE HAD. YOU, CLEARLY, HAD NOTHING TO WORRY ABOUT."
IT IS SO GOOD TO SEE YOU!
AND THANK YOU FOR COMING, TOO. MY FATHER ALWAYS SPOKE HIGHLY OF YOU.
I... THAT IS...
HOW COUL
REFUSE THE
OF THE RH
BHUTRAN
TERRI... ERM, YOUR HOLINESS, I MEAN... YOUR MESSAGE SAID SOMETHING ABOUT A THREAT?
YES, THERE IS AN ARMY MASSED AT OUR BORDER.
THEIR GENERAL BELIEVES THAT WE KNOW THE SECRET WAY TO NANDA PARBAT, AND IS THREATENING TO INVADE UNLESS WE SHARE IT WITH HIM.
IS HE RIGHT? DO YOU KNOW THE WAY TO NANDA PARBAT?
WHO IS THIS GENERAL?
I'M NOT CERTAIN. HIS MEN KNOW HIM ONLY AS SHENG FAN.
"I KNEW ENOUGH CHINE
TO KNOW WHAT THE NA
MEANT: CANNIBAL...

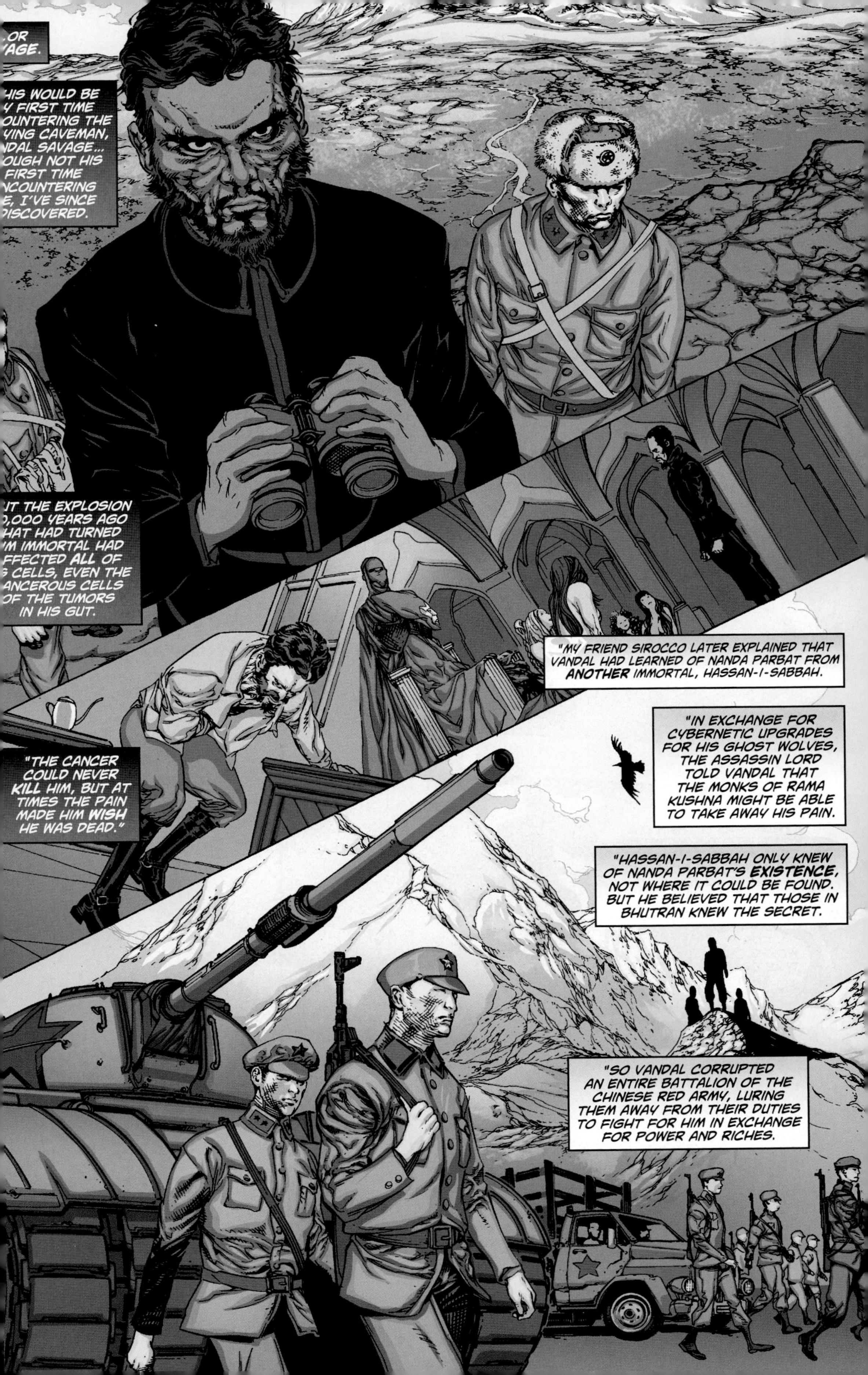

...OR
...AGE.
...HIS WOULD BE
...Y FIRST TIME
...OUNTERING THE
...YING CAVEMAN,
...NDAL SAVAGE...
...OUGH NOT HIS
FIRST TIME
...NCOUNTERING
...E, I'VE SINCE
...DISCOVERED.
...UT THE EXPLOSION
...0,000 YEARS AGO
...HAT HAD TURNED
...IM IMMORTAL HAD
...FFECTED ALL OF
...S CELLS, EVEN THE
...ANCEROUS CELLS
OF THE TUMORS
IN HIS GUT.
"MY FRIEND SIROCCO LATER EXPLAINED THAT VANDAL HAD LEARNED OF NANDA PARBAT FROM ANOTHER IMMORTAL, HASSAN-I-SABBAH.
"THE CANCER COULD NEVER KILL HIM, BUT AT TIMES THE PAIN MADE HIM WISH HE WAS DEAD."
"IN EXCHANGE FOR CYBERNETIC UPGRADES FOR HIS GHOST WOLVES, THE ASSASSIN LORD TOLD VANDAL THAT THE MONKS OF RAMA KUSHNA MIGHT BE ABLE TO TAKE AWAY HIS PAIN.
"HASSAN-I-SABBAH ONLY KNEW OF NANDA PARBAT'S EXISTENCE, NOT WHERE IT COULD BE FOUND. BUT HE BELIEVED THAT THOSE IN BHUTRAN KNEW THE SECRET.
"SO VANDAL CORRUPTED AN ENTIRE BATTALION OF THE CHINESE RED ARMY, LURING THEM AWAY FROM THEIR DUTIES TO FIGHT FOR HIM IN EXCHANGE FOR POWER AND RICHES.

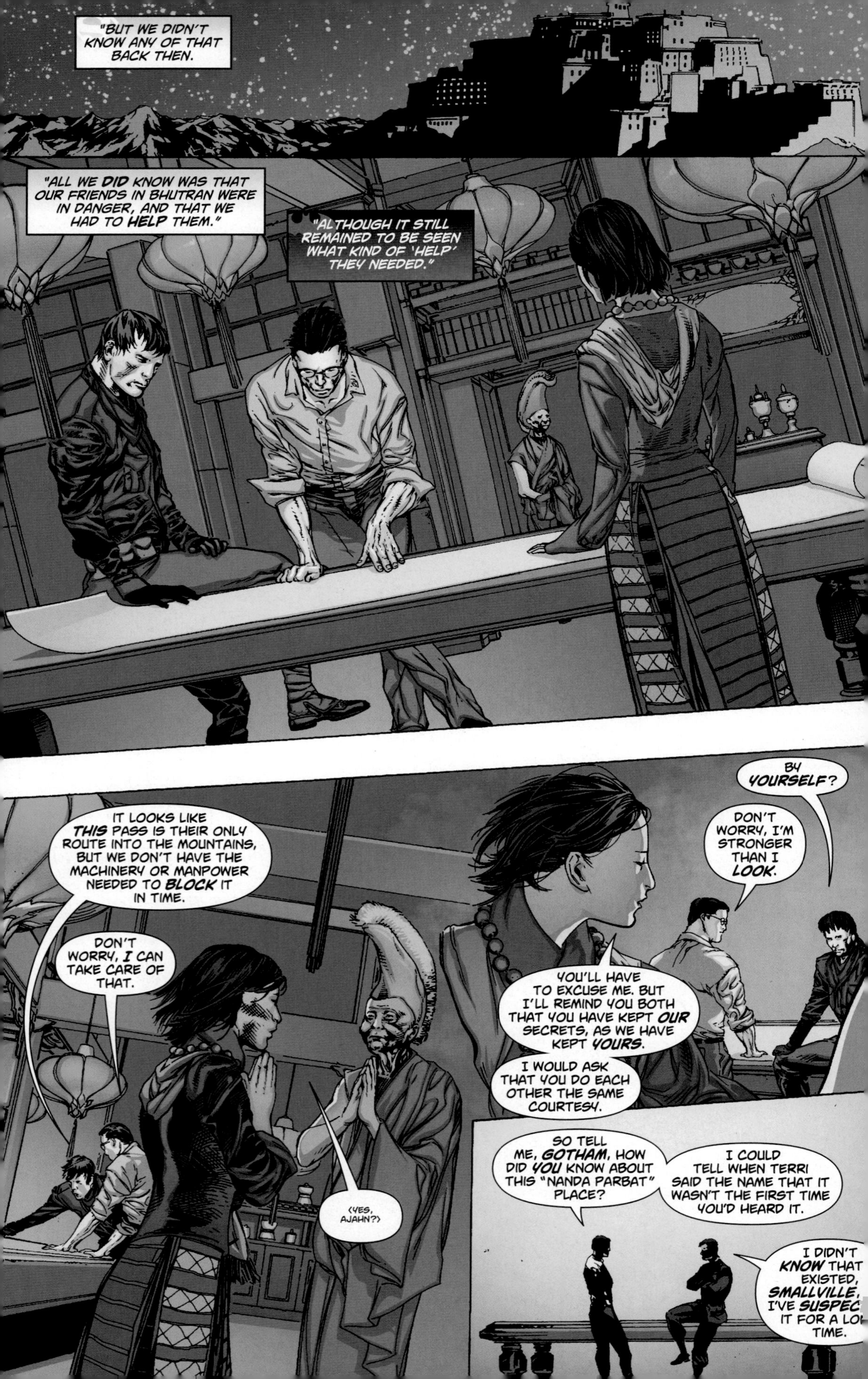
"BUT WE DIDN'T KNOW ANY OF THAT BACK THEN.
"ALL WE DID KNOW WAS THAT OUR FRIENDS IN BHUTRAN WERE IN DANGER, AND THAT WE HAD TO HELP THEM."
"ALTHOUGH IT STILL REMAINED TO BE SEEN WHAT KIND OF 'HELP' THEY NEEDED."
IT LOOKS LIKE THIS PASS IS THEIR ONLY ROUTE INTO THE MOUNTAINS, BUT WE DON'T HAVE THE MACHINERY OR MANPOWER NEEDED TO BLOCK IT IN TIME.
DON'T WORRY, I CAN TAKE CARE OF THAT.
‹YES, AJAHN?›
BY YOURSELF?
DON'T WORRY, I'M STRONGER THAN I LOOK.
YOU'LL HAVE TO EXCUSE ME. BUT I'LL REMIND YOU BOTH THAT YOU HAVE KEPT OUR SECRETS, AS WE HAVE KEPT YOURS.
I WOULD ASK THAT YOU DO EACH OTHER THE SAME COURTESY.
SO TELL ME, GOTHAM, HOW DID YOU KNOW ABOUT THIS "NANDA PARBAT" PLACE?
I COULD TELL WHEN TERRI SAID THE NAME THAT IT WASN'T THE FIRST TIME YOU'D HEARD IT.

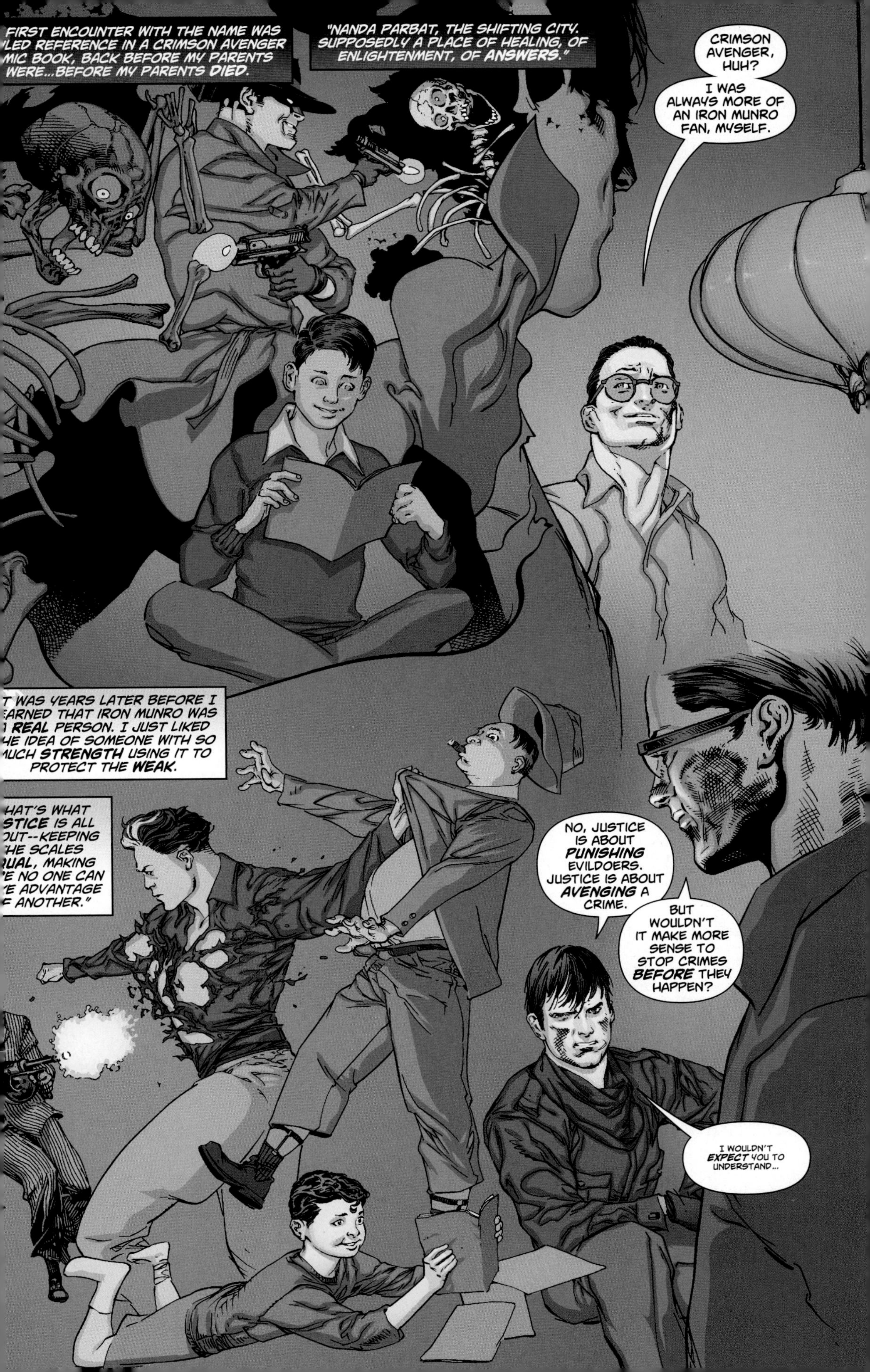
FIRST ENCOUNTER WITH THE NAME WAS 'LED REFERENCE IN A CRIMSON AVENGER MIC BOOK, BACK BEFORE MY PARENTS WERE...BEFORE MY PARENTS DIED.
"NANDA PARBAT, THE SHIFTING CITY. SUPPOSEDLY A PLACE OF HEALING, OF ENLIGHTENMENT, OF ANSWERS."
CRIMSON AVENGER, HUH?
I WAS ALWAYS MORE OF AN IRON MUNRO FAN, MYSELF.
T WAS YEARS LATER BEFORE I EARNED THAT IRON MUNRO WAS REAL PERSON. I JUST LIKED HE IDEA OF SOMEONE WITH SO MUCH STRENGTH USING IT TO PROTECT THE WEAK.
HAT'S WHAT STICE IS ALL OUT--KEEPING HE SCALES UAL, MAKING E NO ONE CAN E ADVANTAGE F ANOTHER."
NO, JUSTICE IS ABOUT PUNISHING EVILDOERS. JUSTICE IS ABOUT AVENGING A CRIME.
BUT WOULDN'T IT MAKE MORE SENSE TO STOP CRIMES BEFORE THEY HAPPEN?
I WOULDN'T EXPECT YOU TO UNDERSTAND...

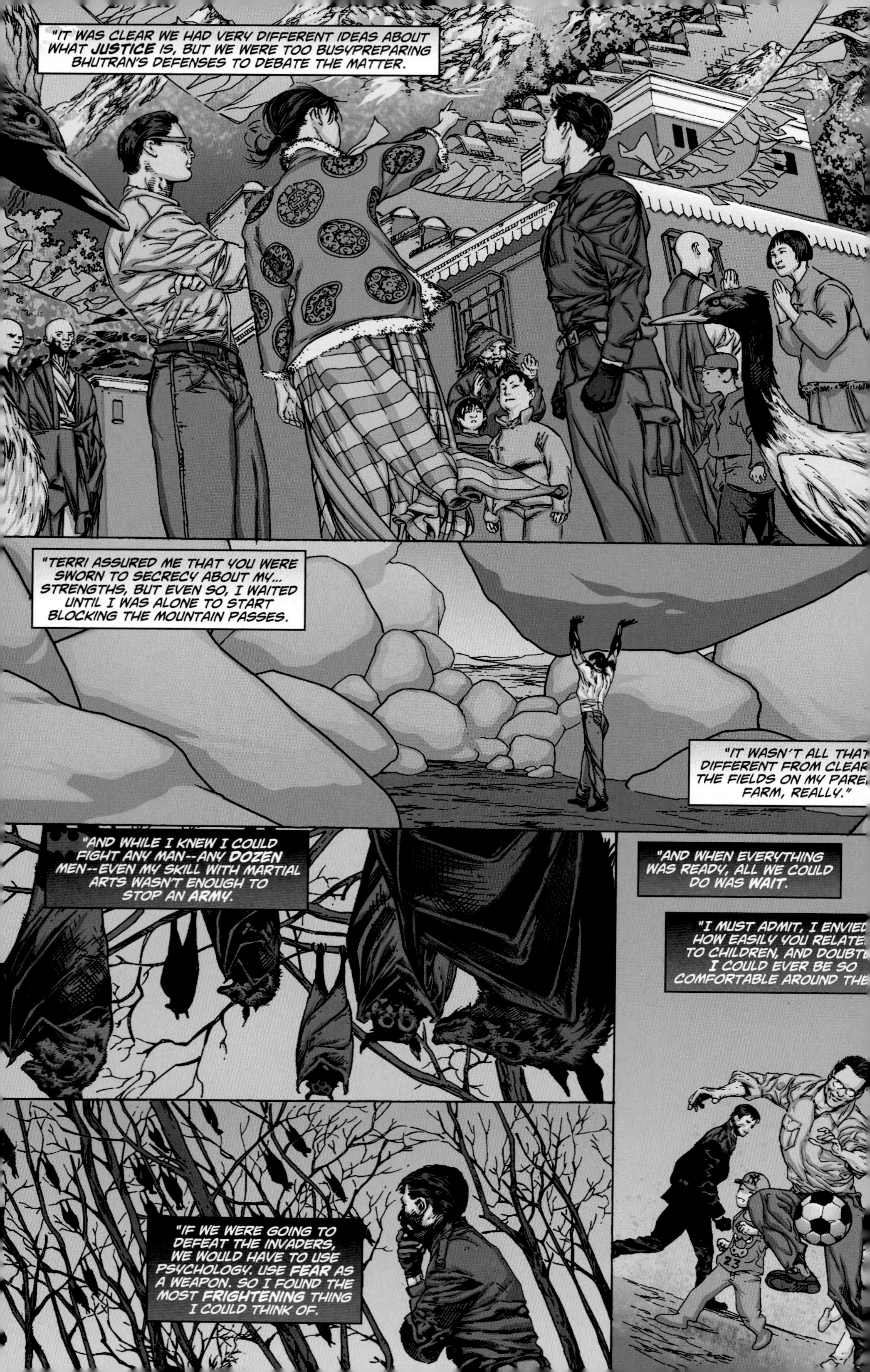
"IT WAS CLEAR WE HAD VERY DIFFERENT IDEAS ABOUT WHAT JUSTICE IS, BUT WE WERE TOO BUSYPREPARING BHUTRAN'S DEFENSES TO DEBATE THE MATTER.
"TERRI ASSURED ME THAT YOU WERE SWORN TO SECRECY ABOUT MY... STRENGTHS, BUT EVEN SO, I WAITED UNTIL I WAS ALONE TO START BLOCKING THE MOUNTAIN PASSES.
"IT WASN'T ALL THAT DIFFERENT FROM CLEAR THE FIELDS ON MY PARE FARM, REALLY."
"AND WHILE I KNEW I COULD FIGHT ANY MAN--ANY DOZEN MEN--EVEN MY SKILL WITH MARTIAL ARTS WASN'T ENOUGH TO STOP AN ARMY.
"IF WE WERE GOING TO DEFEAT THE INVADERS, WE WOULD HAVE TO USE PSYCHOLOGY. USE FEAR AS A WEAPON. SO I FOUND THE MOST FRIGHTENING THING I COULD THINK OF.
"AND WHEN EVERYTHING WAS READY, ALL WE COULD DO WAS WAIT.
"I MUST ADMIT, I ENVIE HOW EASILY YOU RELATE TO CHILDREN, AND DOUBTE I COULD EVER BE SO COMFORTABLE AROUND THE

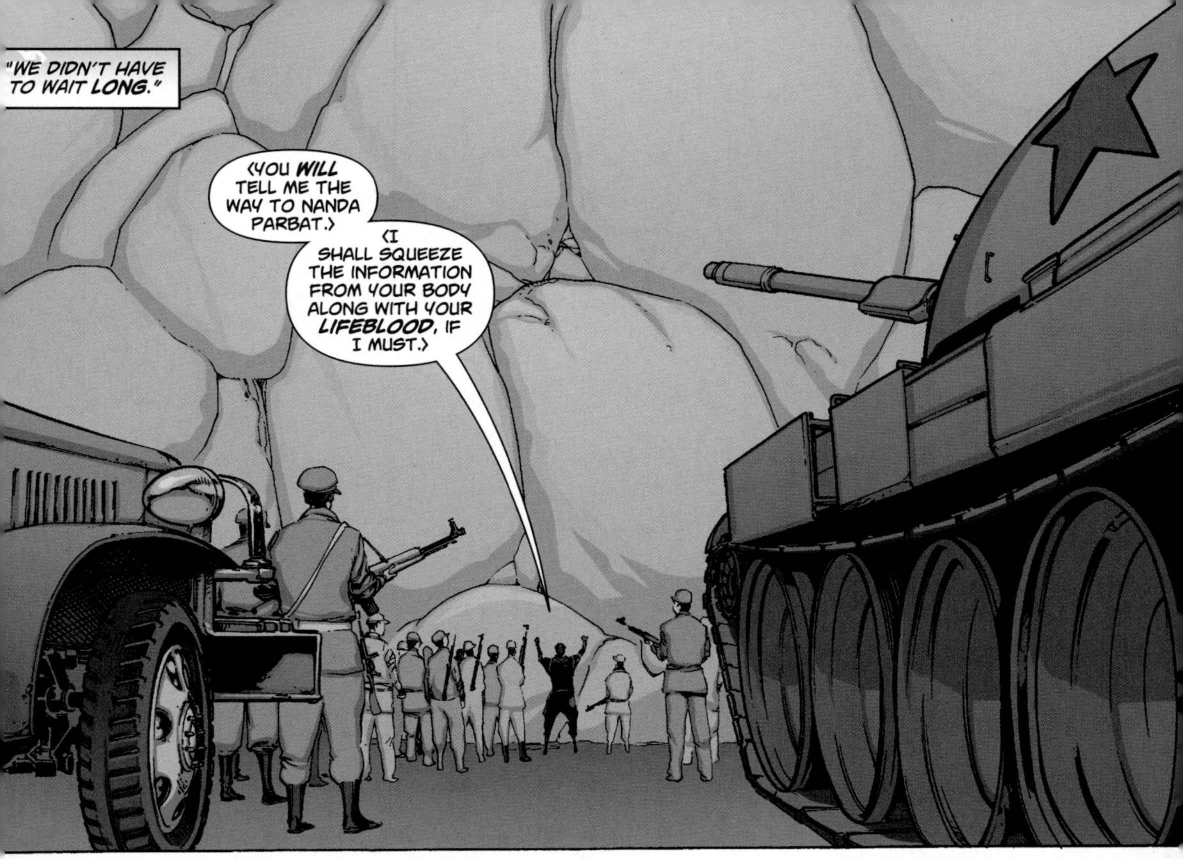
"WE DIDN'T HAVE TO WAIT LONG."
‹YOU WILL TELL ME THE WAY TO NANDA PARBAT.›
‹I SHALL SQUEEZE THE INFORMATION FROM YOUR BODY ALONG WITH YOUR LIFEBLOOD, IF I MUST.›

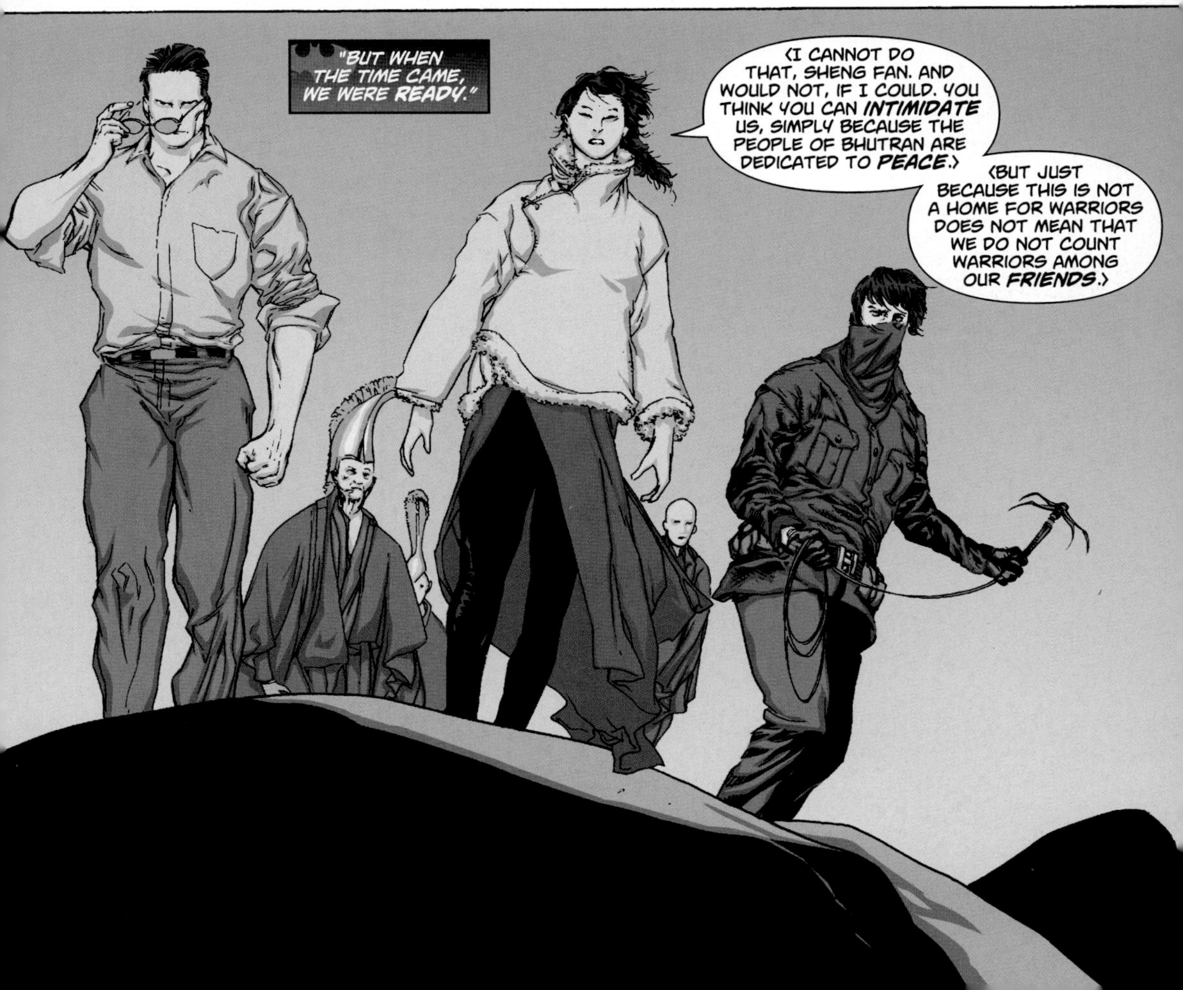
"BUT WHEN THE TIME CAME, WE WERE READY."
‹I CANNOT DO THAT, SHENG FAN. AND WOULD NOT, IF I COULD. YOU THINK YOU CAN INTIMIDATE US, SIMPLY BECAUSE THE PEOPLE OF BHUTRAN ARE DEDICATED TO PEACE.›
‹BUT JUST BECAUSE THIS IS NOT A HOME FOR WARRIORS DOES NOT MEAN THAT WE DO NOT COUNT WARRIORS AMONG OUR FRIENDS.›

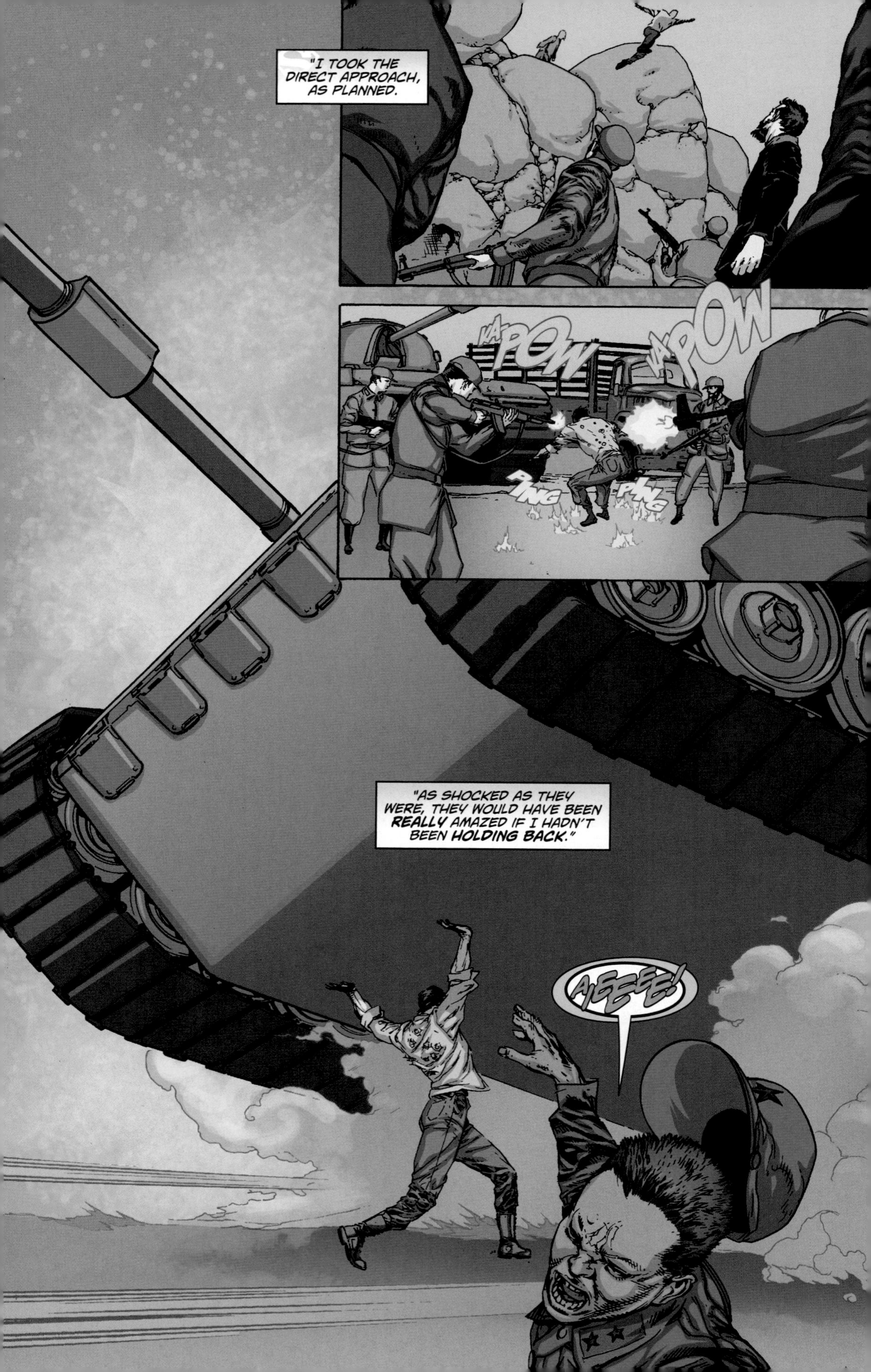
"I TOOK THE DIRECT APPROACH, AS PLANNED.
KA-POW
KA-POW
PING
PING
"AS SHOCKED AS THEY WERE, THEY WOULD HAVE BEEN REALLY AMAZED IF I HADN'T BEEN HOLDING BACK."
AIEEEE!

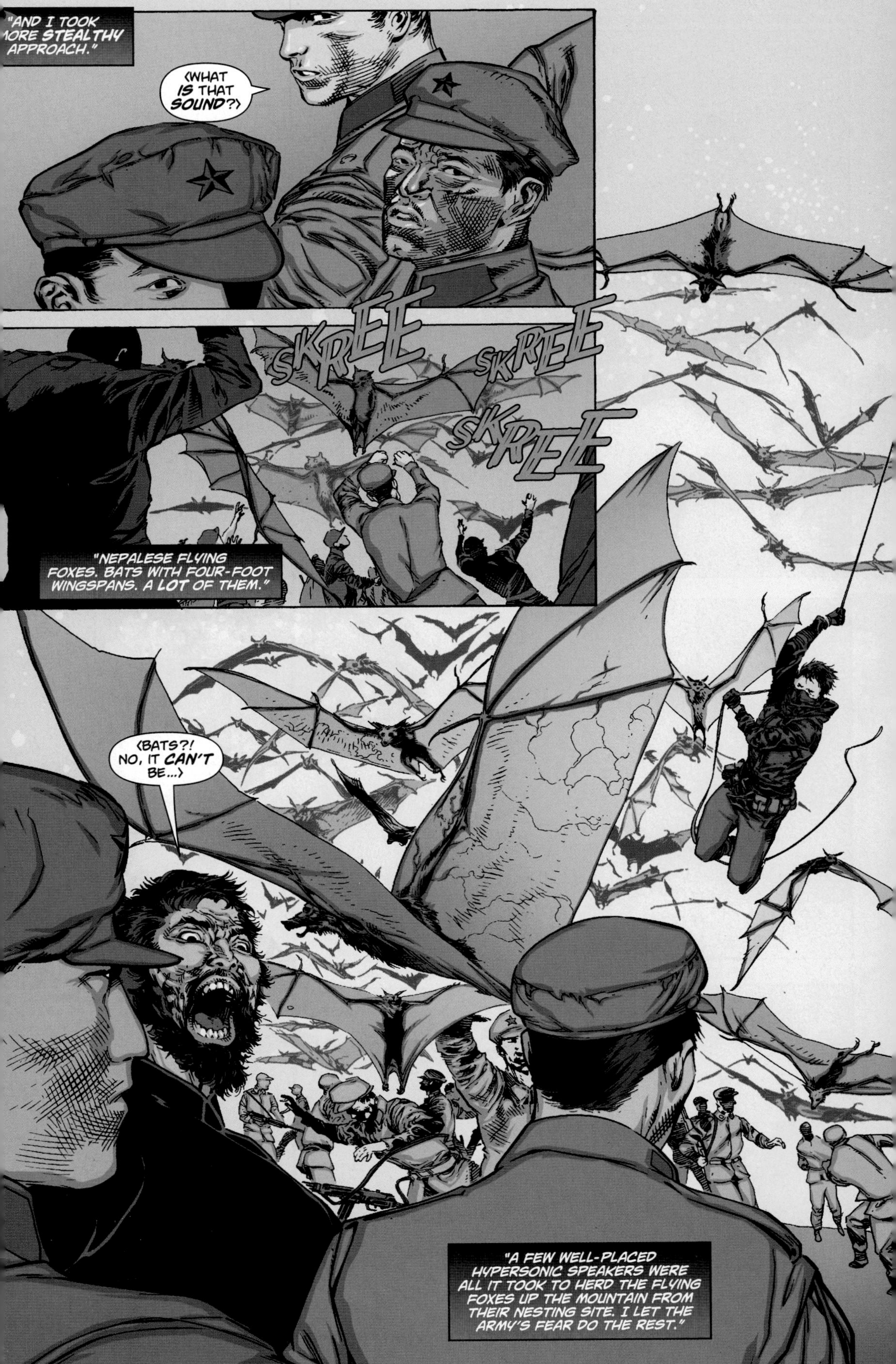
"AND I TOOK
MORE STEALTHY
APPROACH."
‹WHAT IS THAT SOUND?›
SKREE SKREE SKREE
"NEPALESE FLYING FOXES. BATS WITH FOUR-FOOT WINGSPANS. A LOT OF THEM."
‹BATS?! NO, IT CAN'T BE...›
"A FEW WELL-PLACED HYPERSONIC SPEAKERS WERE ALL IT TOOK TO HERD THE FLYING FOXES UP THE MOUNTAIN FROM THEIR NESTING SITE. I LET THE ARMY'S FEAR DO THE REST."

"I HAD BEEN HELPING PEOPLE ALOT OVER THE YEARS, BUT ALWAYS IN SECRET, AT SUPER-SPEED, WITHOUT ANYONE NOTICING."

"I'D FOUGHT CRIMINALS COUNTLESS TIMES IN MY TRAVELS AROUND THE WORLD, BUT NEVER SUCH A LARGE AND ORGANIZED FORCE."

"OPERATING OUT IN THE OPEN LIKE THAT, NOT HIDING WHO AND WHAT I WAS, IT FELT...IT FELT RIGHT."

"BEFORE THAT DAY, I'[D] ALWAYS CONSIDERED CRI[ME-] FIGHTING A ONE-MA[N] OPERATION. BUT SUDDEN[LY I] COULD SEE THE ADVANTA[GE] WORKING WITH A PARTN[ER.]"

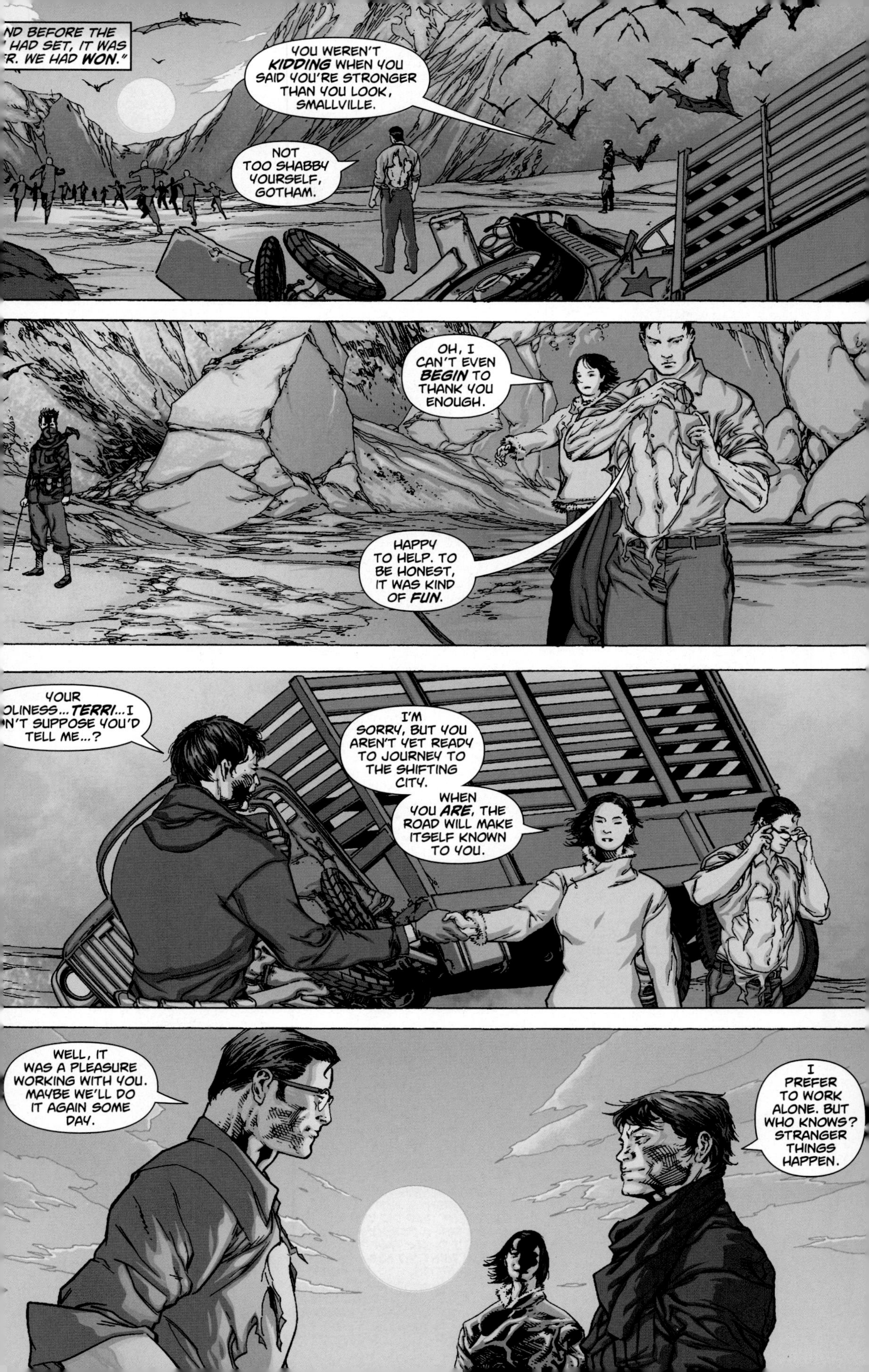
ND BEFORE THE
HAD SET, IT WAS
R. WE HAD WON."
YOU WEREN'T KIDDING WHEN YOU SAID YOU'RE STRONGER THAN YOU LOOK, SMALLVILLE.
NOT TOO SHABBY YOURSELF, GOTHAM.
OH, I CAN'T EVEN BEGIN TO THANK YOU ENOUGH.
HAPPY TO HELP. TO BE HONEST, IT WAS KIND OF FUN.
YOUR
OLINESS... TERRI... I
N'T SUPPOSE YOU'D
TELL ME...?
I'M SORRY, BUT YOU AREN'T YET READY TO JOURNEY TO THE SHIFTING CITY.
WHEN YOU ARE, THE ROAD WILL MAKE ITSELF KNOWN TO YOU.
WELL, IT WAS A PLEASURE WORKING WITH YOU. MAYBE WE'LL DO IT AGAIN SOME DAY.
I PREFER TO WORK ALONE. BUT WHO KNOWS? STRANGER THINGS HAPPEN.

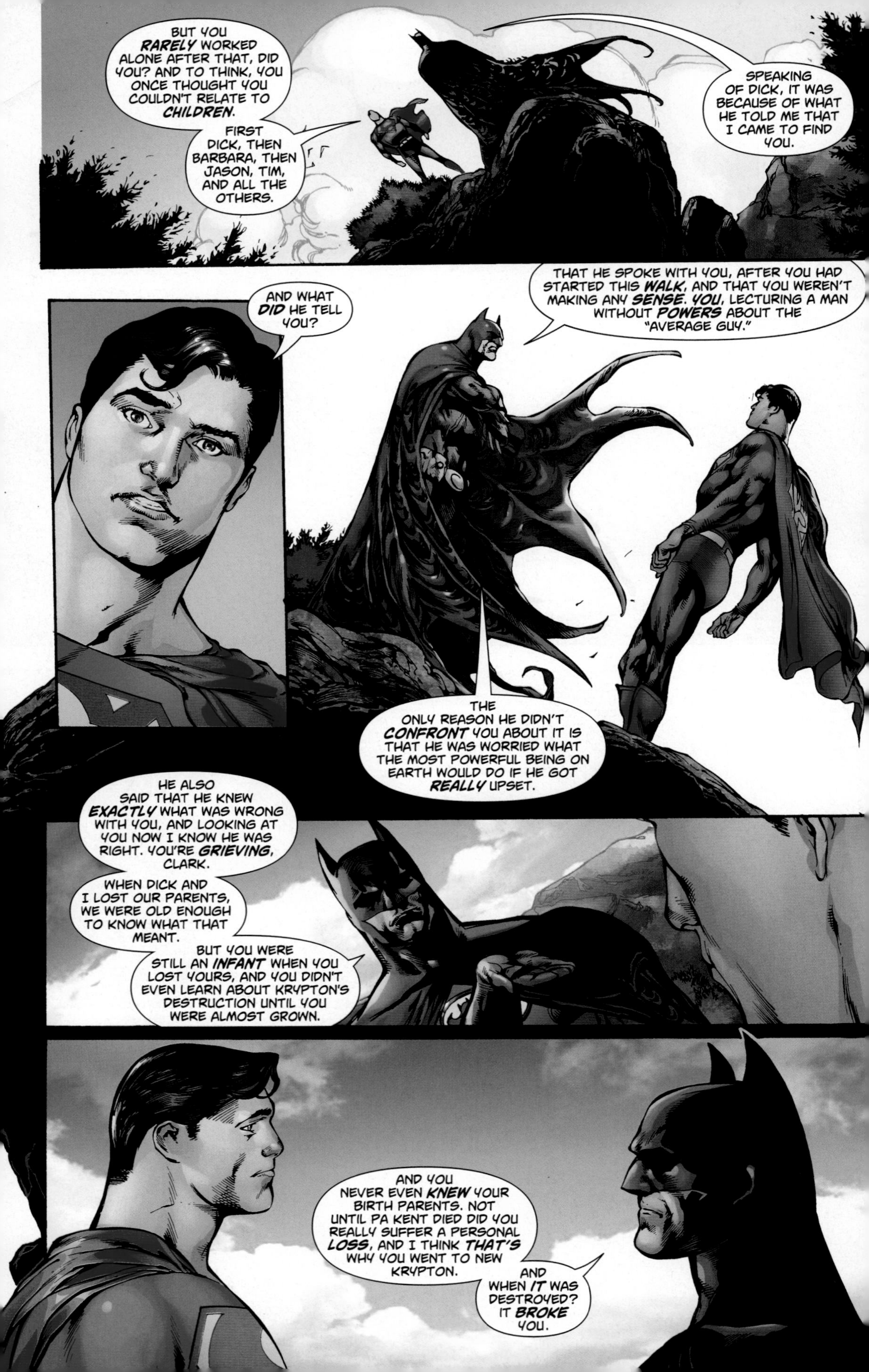
BUT YOU RARELY WORKED ALONE AFTER THAT, DID YOU? AND TO THINK, YOU ONCE THOUGHT YOU COULDN'T RELATE TO CHILDREN.
FIRST DICK, THEN BARBARA, THEN JASON, TIM, AND ALL THE OTHERS.
SPEAKING OF DICK, IT WAS BECAUSE OF WHAT HE TOLD ME THAT I CAME TO FIND YOU.
AND WHAT DID HE TELL YOU?
THAT HE SPOKE WITH YOU, AFTER YOU HAD STARTED THIS WALK, AND THAT YOU WEREN'T MAKING ANY SENSE. YOU, LECTURING A MAN WITHOUT POWERS ABOUT THE "AVERAGE GUY."
THE ONLY REASON HE DIDN'T CONFRONT YOU ABOUT IT IS THAT HE WAS WORRIED WHAT THE MOST POWERFUL BEING ON EARTH WOULD DO IF HE GOT REALLY UPSET.
HE ALSO SAID THAT HE KNEW EXACTLY WHAT WAS WRONG WITH YOU, AND LOOKING AT YOU NOW I KNOW HE WAS RIGHT. YOU'RE GRIEVING, CLARK.
WHEN DICK AND I LOST OUR PARENTS, WE WERE OLD ENOUGH TO KNOW WHAT THAT MEANT.
BUT YOU WERE STILL AN INFANT WHEN YOU LOST YOURS, AND YOU DIDN'T EVEN LEARN ABOUT KRYPTON'S DESTRUCTION UNTIL YOU WERE ALMOST GROWN.
AND YOU NEVER EVEN KNEW YOUR BIRTH PARENTS. NOT UNTIL PA KENT DIED DID YOU REALLY SUFFER A PERSONAL LOSS, AND I THINK THAT'S WHY YOU WENT TO NEW KRYPTON.
AND WHEN IT WAS DESTROYED? IT BROKE YOU.

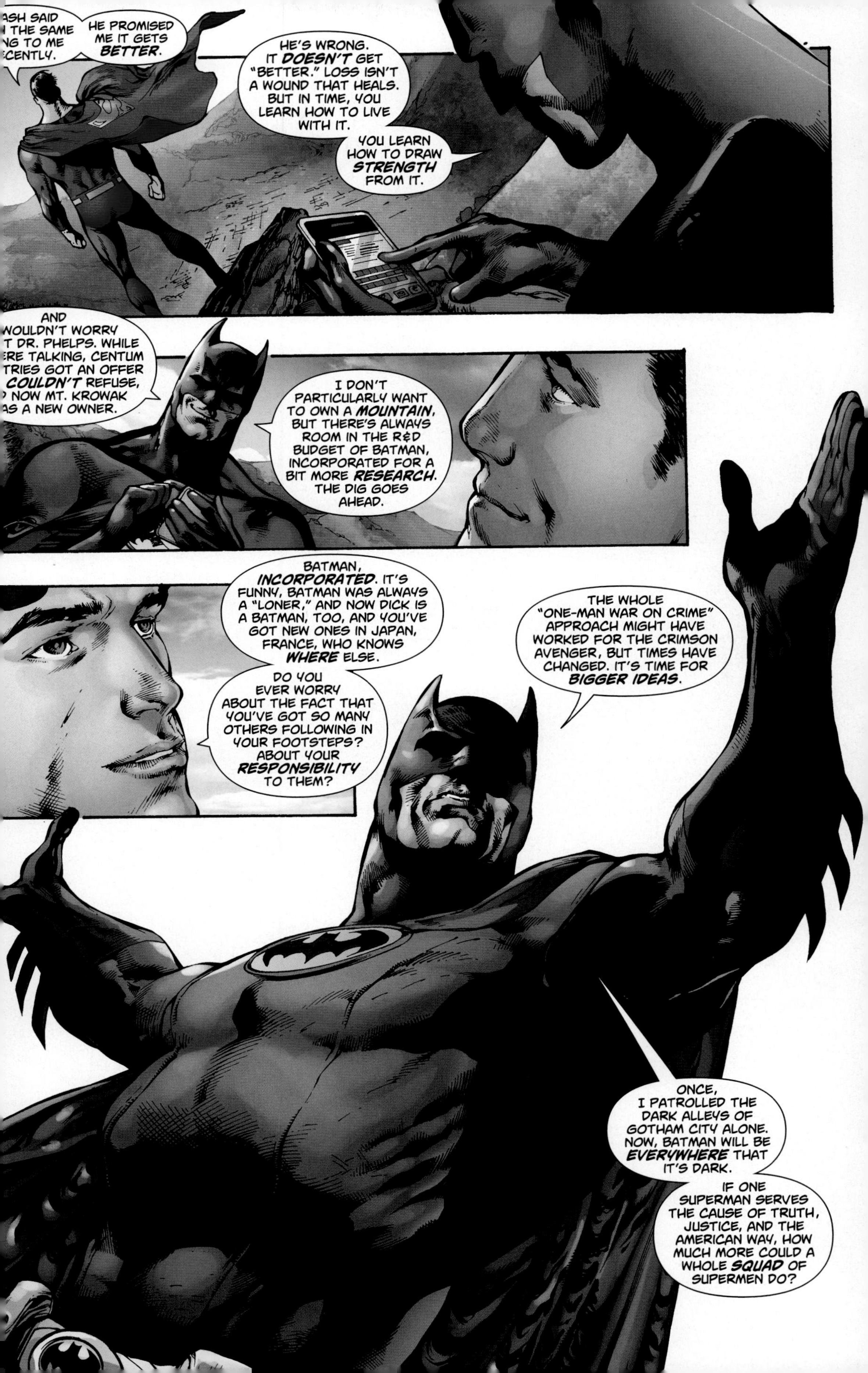

ASH SAID
N THE SAME
NG TO ME
ECENTLY.
HE PROMISED ME IT GETS BETTER.
HE'S WRONG. IT DOESN'T GET "BETTER." LOSS ISN'T A WOUND THAT HEALS. BUT IN TIME, YOU LEARN HOW TO LIVE WITH IT.
YOU LEARN HOW TO DRAW STRENGTH FROM IT.
AND
WOULDN'T WORRY
T DR. PHELPS. WHILE
ERE TALKING, CENTUM
TRIES GOT AN OFFER
COULDN'T REFUSE,
D NOW MT. KROWAK
AS A NEW OWNER.
I DON'T PARTICULARLY WANT TO OWN A MOUNTAIN, BUT THERE'S ALWAYS ROOM IN THE R&D BUDGET OF BATMAN, INCORPORATED FOR A BIT MORE RESEARCH. THE DIG GOES AHEAD.
BATMAN, INCORPORATED. IT'S FUNNY, BATMAN WAS ALWAYS A "LONER," AND NOW DICK IS A BATMAN, TOO, AND YOU'VE GOT NEW ONES IN JAPAN, FRANCE, WHO KNOWS WHERE ELSE.
DO YOU EVER WORRY ABOUT THE FACT THAT YOU'VE GOT SO MANY OTHERS FOLLOWING IN YOUR FOOTSTEPS? ABOUT YOUR RESPONSIBILITY TO THEM?
THE WHOLE "ONE-MAN WAR ON CRIME" APPROACH MIGHT HAVE WORKED FOR THE CRIMSON AVENGER, BUT TIMES HAVE CHANGED. IT'S TIME FOR BIGGER IDEAS.
ONCE, I PATROLLED THE DARK ALLEYS OF GOTHAM CITY ALONE. NOW, BATMAN WILL BE EVERYWHERE THAT IT'S DARK.
IF ONE SUPERMAN SERVES THE CAUSE OF TRUTH, JUSTICE, AND THE AMERICAN WAY, HOW MUCH MORE COULD A WHOLE SQUAD OF SUPERMEN DO?

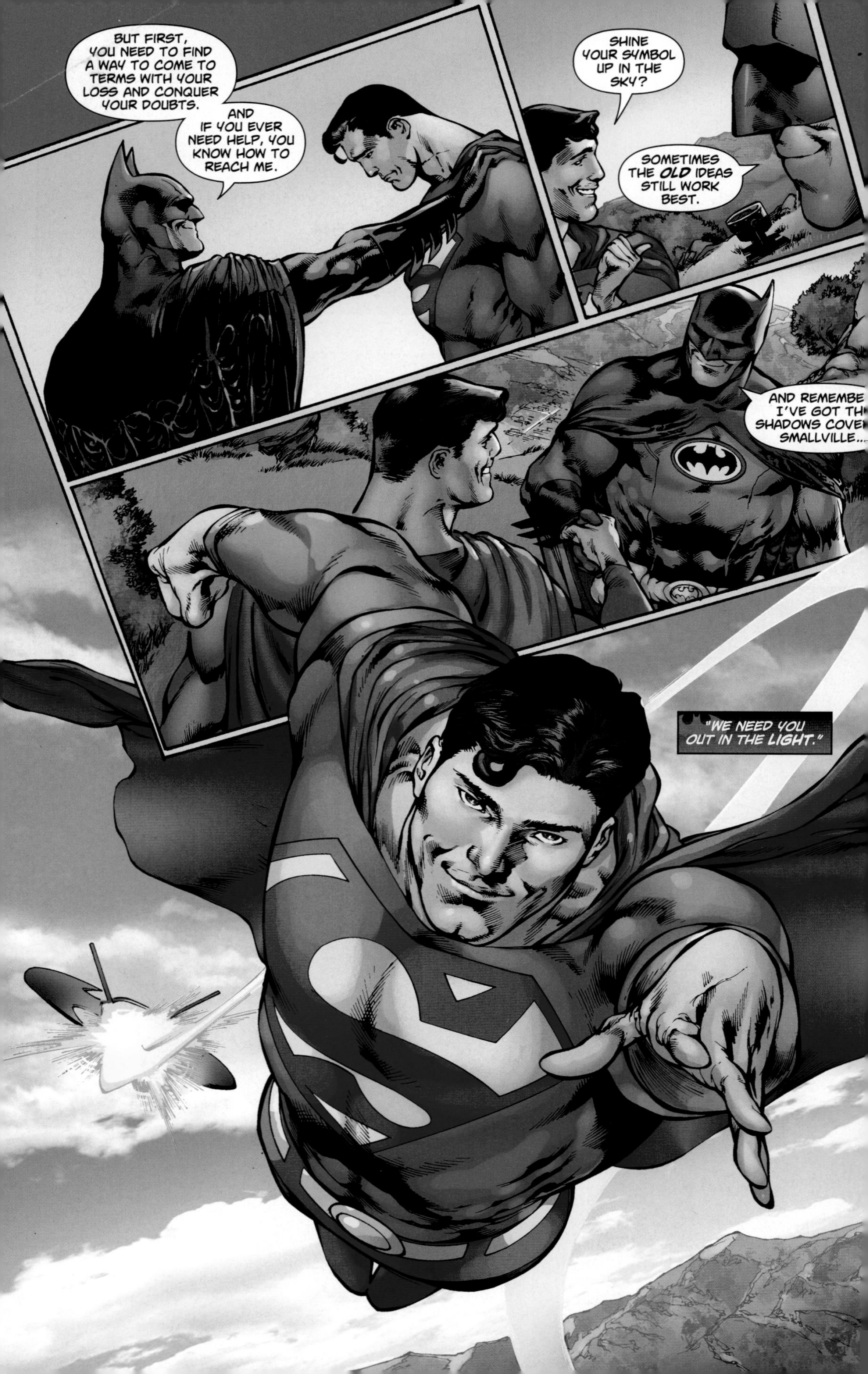
BUT FIRST, YOU NEED TO FIND A WAY TO COME TO TERMS WITH YOUR LOSS AND CONQUER YOUR DOUBTS.
AND IF YOU EVER NEED HELP, YOU KNOW HOW TO REACH ME.
SHINE YOUR SYMBOL UP IN THE SKY?
SOMETIMES THE OLD IDEAS STILL WORK BEST.
AND REMEMBE I'VE GOT TH SHADOWS COVE SMALLVILLE...
"WE NEED YOU OUT IN THE LIGHT."

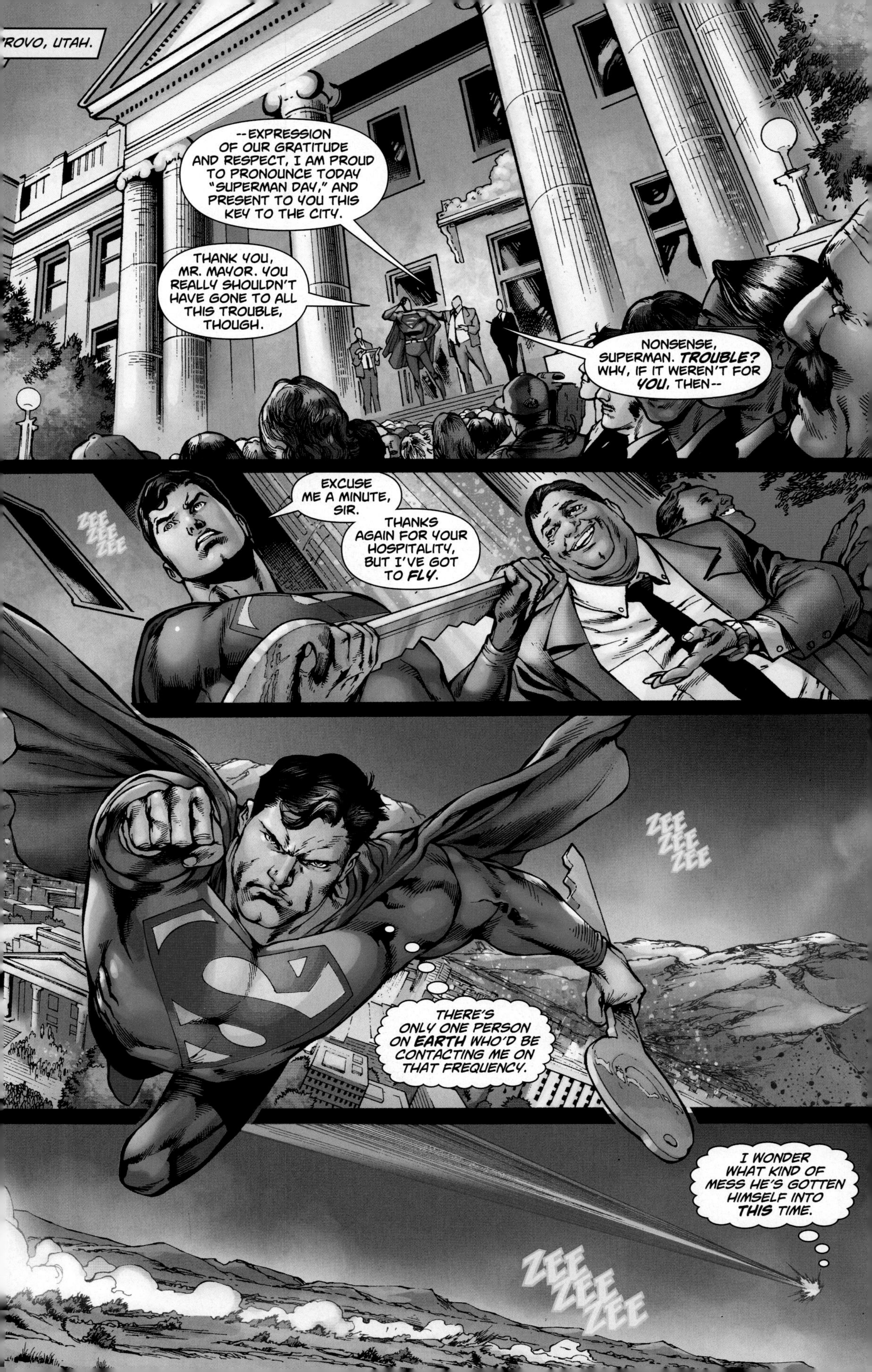

ROVO, UTAH.
--EXPRESSION OF OUR GRATITUDE AND RESPECT, I AM PROUD TO PRONOUNCE TODAY "SUPERMAN DAY," AND PRESENT TO YOU THIS KEY TO THE CITY.
THANK YOU, MR. MAYOR. YOU REALLY SHOULDN'T HAVE GONE TO ALL THIS TROUBLE, THOUGH.
NONSENSE, SUPERMAN. TROUBLE? WHY, IF IT WEREN'T FOR YOU, THEN--
ZEE ZEE ZEE
EXCUSE ME A MINUTE, SIR.
THANKS AGAIN FOR YOUR HOSPITALITY, BUT I'VE GOT TO FLY.
ZEE ZEE ZEE
THERE'S ONLY ONE PERSON ON EARTH WHO'D BE CONTACTING ME ON THAT FREQUENCY.
I WONDER WHAT KIND OF MESS HE'S GOTTEN HIMSELF INTO THIS TIME.
ZEE ZEE ZEE

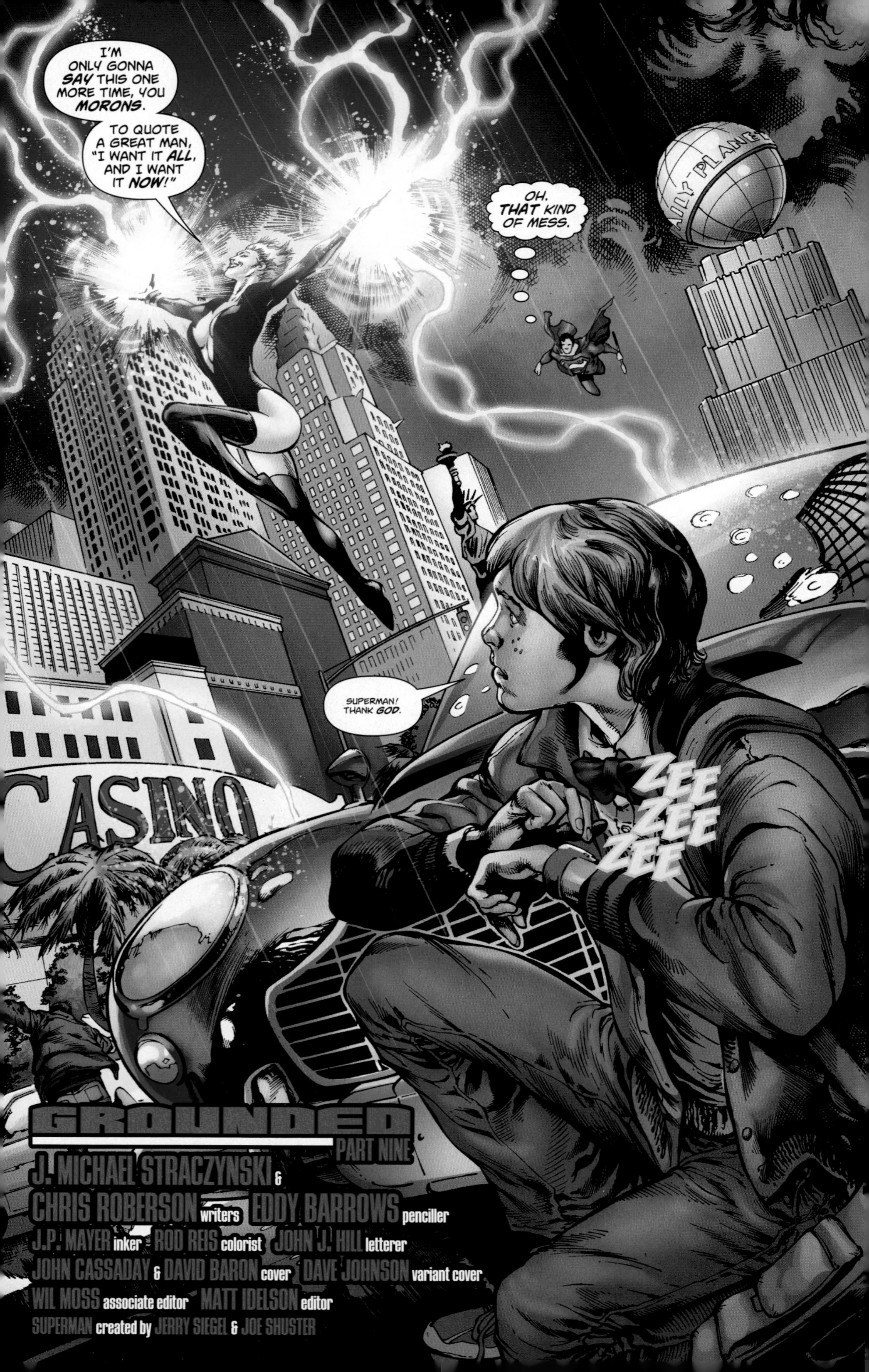
I'M ONLY GONNA SAY THIS ONE MORE TIME, YOU MORONS.
TO QUOTE A GREAT MAN, "I WANT IT ALL, AND I WANT IT NOW!"
OH. THAT KIND OF MESS.
SUPERMAN! THANK GOD.
CASINO
ZEE ZEE ZEE
GROUNDED PART NINE
J. MICHAEL STRACZYNSKI & CHRIS ROBERSON writers EDDY BARROWS penciller
J.P. MAYER inker ROD REIS colorist JOHN J. HILL letterer
JOHN CASSADAY & DAVID BARON cover DAVE JOHNSON variant cover
WIL MOSS associate editor MATT IDELSON editor
SUPERMAN created by JERRY SIEGEL & JOE SHUSTER

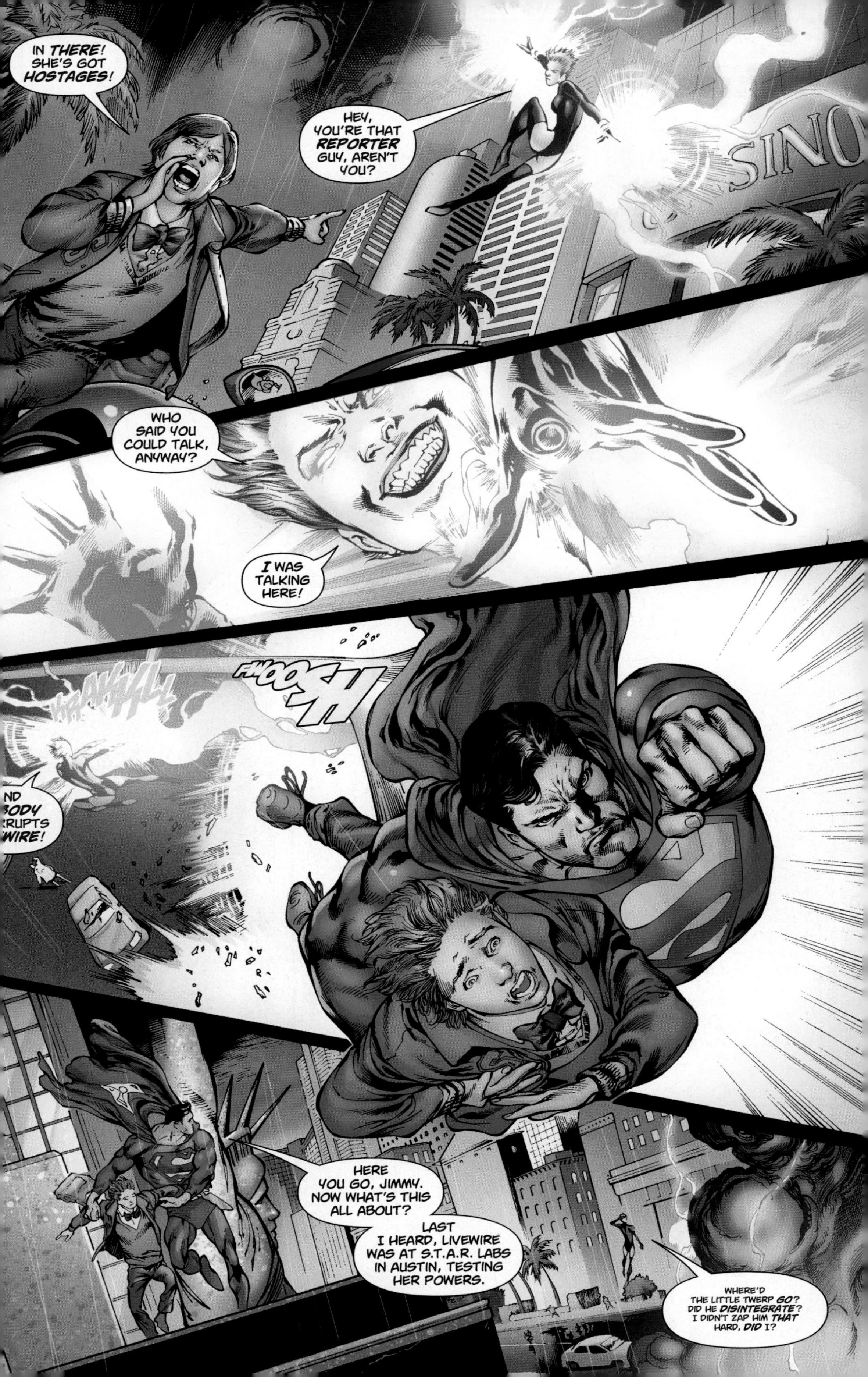
IN THERE! SHE'S GOT HOSTAGES!
HEY, YOU'RE THAT REPORTER GUY, AREN'T YOU?
WHO SAID YOU COULD TALK, ANYWAY?
I WAS TALKING HERE!
KRAKKLL
FWOOOSH
HERE YOU GO, JIMMY. NOW WHAT'S THIS ALL ABOUT?
LAST I HEARD, LIVEWIRE WAS AT S.T.A.R. LABS IN AUSTIN, TESTING HER POWERS.
WHERE'D THE LITTLE TWERP GO? DID HE DISINTEGRATE? I DIDN'T ZAP HIM THAT HARD, DID I?

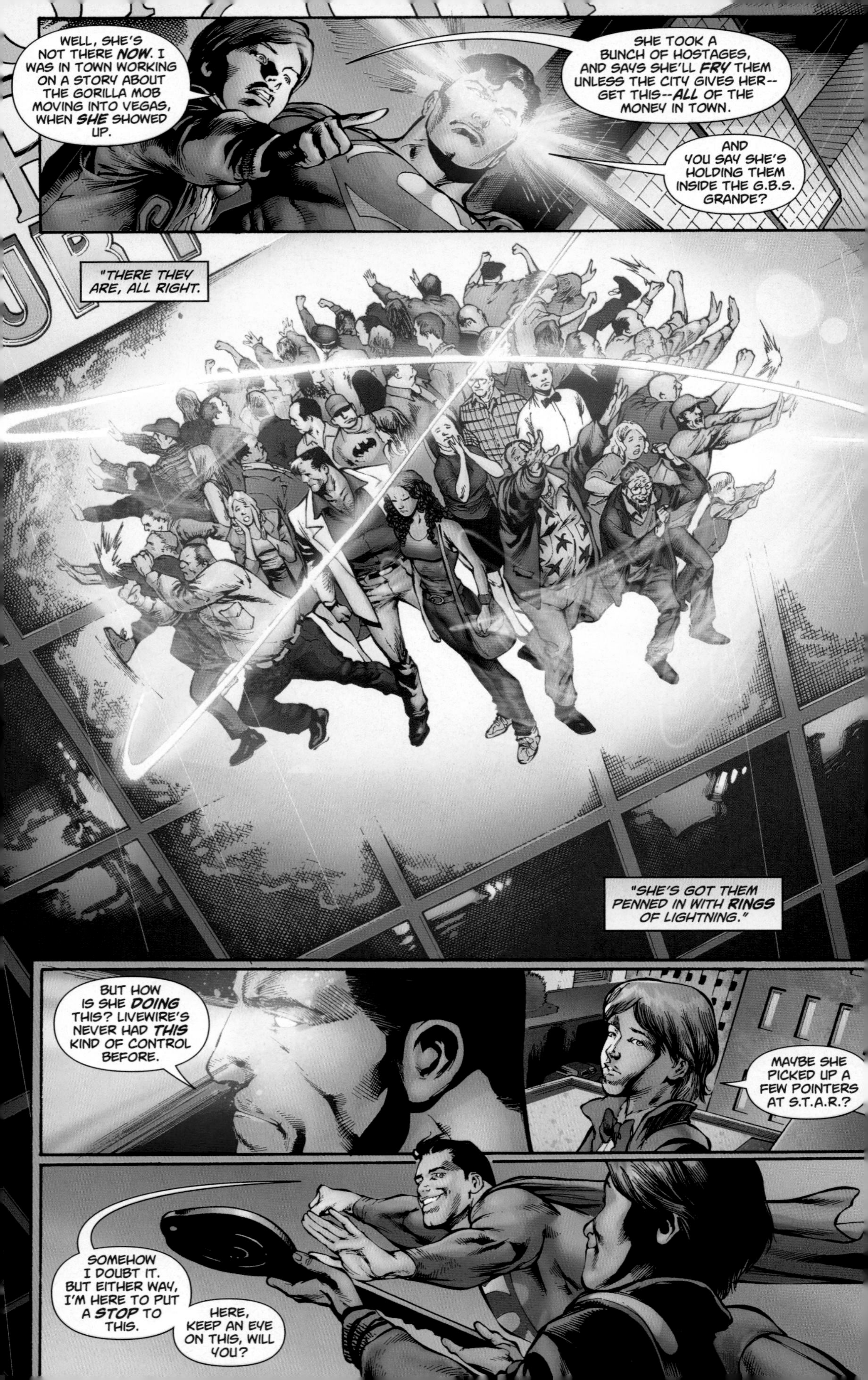
WELL, SHE'S NOT THERE NOW. I WAS IN TOWN WORKING ON A STORY ABOUT THE GORILLA MOB MOVING INTO VEGAS, WHEN SHE SHOWED UP.
SHE TOOK A BUNCH OF HOSTAGES, AND SAYS SHE'LL FRY THEM UNLESS THE CITY GIVES HER-- GET THIS--ALL OF THE MONEY IN TOWN.
AND YOU SAY SHE'S HOLDING THEM INSIDE THE G.B.S. GRANDE?
"THERE THEY ARE, ALL RIGHT.
"SHE'S GOT THEM PENNED IN WITH RINGS OF LIGHTNING."
BUT HOW IS SHE DOING THIS? LIVEWIRE'S NEVER HAD THIS KIND OF CONTROL BEFORE.
MAYBE SHE PICKED UP A FEW POINTERS AT S.T.A.R.?
SOMEHOW I DOUBT IT. BUT EITHER WAY, I'M HERE TO PUT A STOP TO THIS.
HERE, KEEP AN EYE ON THIS, WILL YOU?

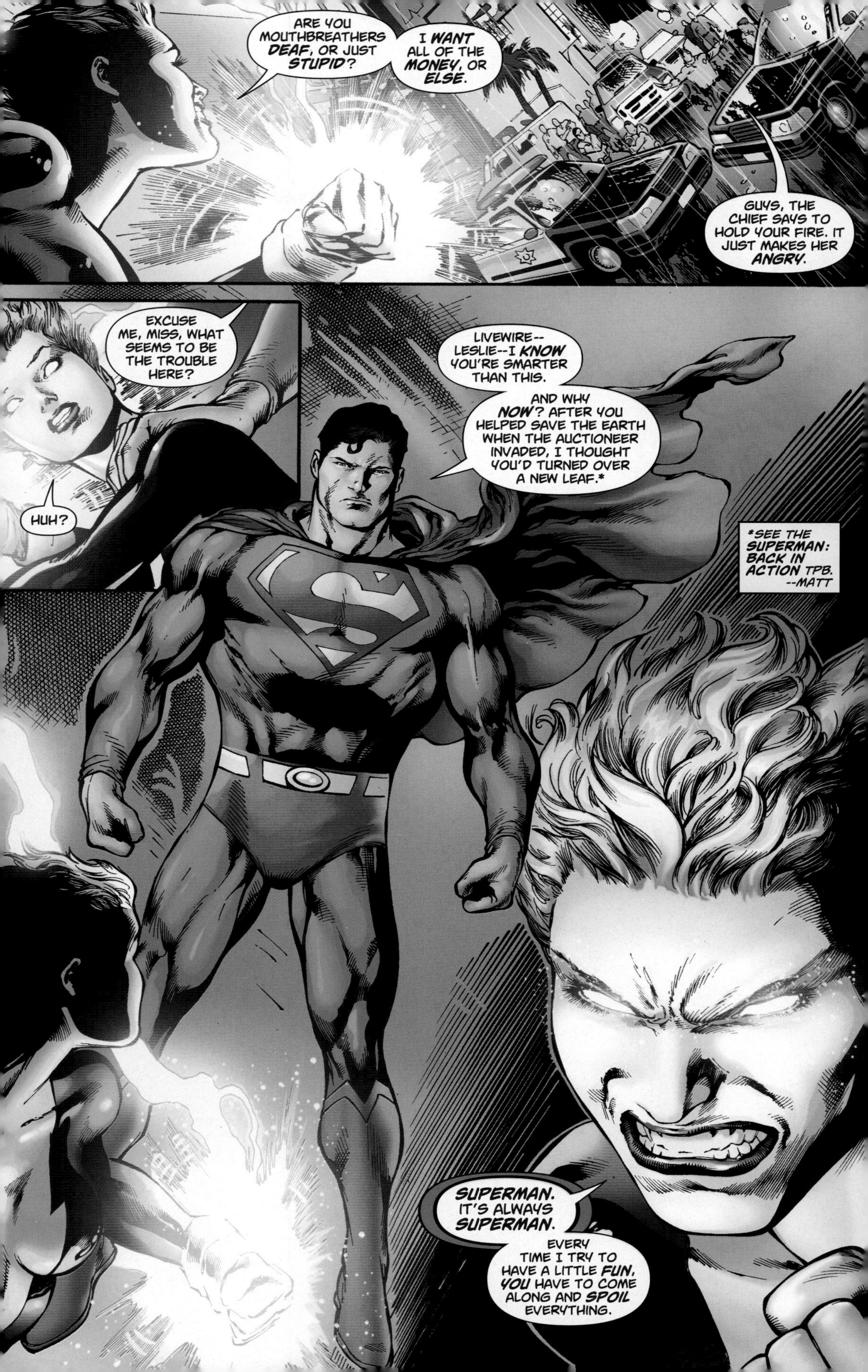

ARE YOU MOUTHBREATHERS DEAF, OR JUST STUPID?
I WANT ALL OF THE MONEY, OR ELSE.
GUYS, THE CHIEF SAYS TO HOLD YOUR FIRE. IT JUST MAKES HER ANGRY.
EXCUSE ME, MISS, WHAT SEEMS TO BE THE TROUBLE HERE?
HUH?
LIVEWIRE--LESLIE--I KNOW YOU'RE SMARTER THAN THIS.
AND WHY NOW? AFTER YOU HELPED SAVE THE EARTH WHEN THE AUCTIONEER INVADED, I THOUGHT YOU'D TURNED OVER A NEW LEAF.*
*SEE THE SUPERMAN: BACK IN ACTION TPB. --MATT
SUPERMAN. IT'S ALWAYS SUPERMAN.
EVERY TIME I TRY TO HAVE A LITTLE FUN, YOU HAVE TO COME ALONG AND SPOIL EVERYTHING.

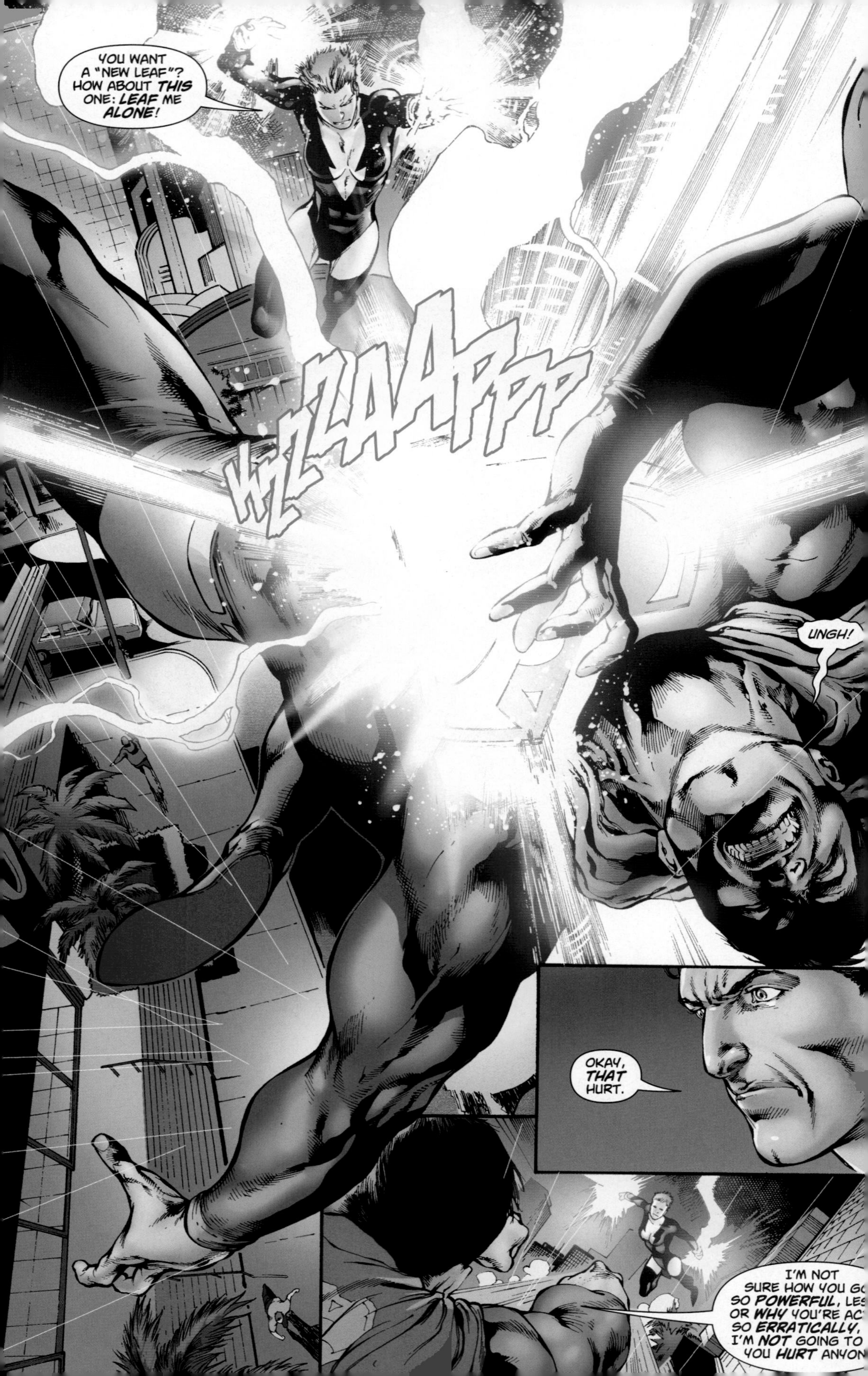
YOU WANT A "NEW LEAF"? HOW ABOUT THIS ONE: LEAF ME ALONE!
WHZZAAPPP
UNGH!
OKAY, THAT HURT.
I'M NOT SURE HOW YOU GO SO POWERFUL, LES OR WHY YOU'RE AC SO ERRATICALLY, I'M NOT GOING TO YOU HURT ANYON

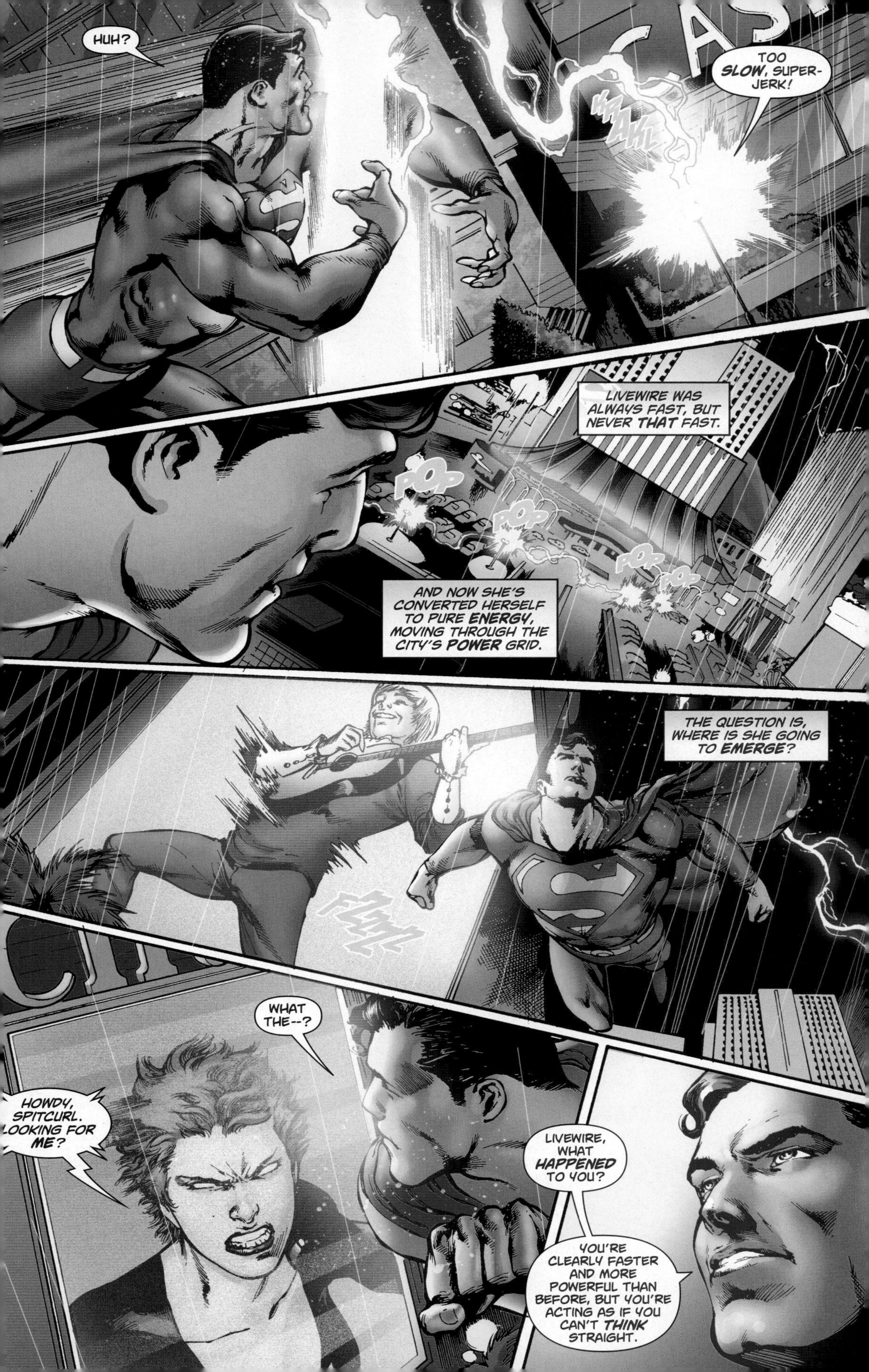
HUH?
KRAKL
TOO SLOW, SUPER-JERK!
LIVEWIRE WAS ALWAYS FAST, BUT NEVER THAT FAST.
POP
POP
POP
POP
AND NOW SHE'S CONVERTED HERSELF TO PURE ENERGY, MOVING THROUGH THE CITY'S POWER GRID.
THE QUESTION IS, WHERE IS SHE GOING TO EMERGE?
FZZZ
WHAT THE--?
HOWDY, SPITCURL. LOOKING FOR ME?
LIVEWIRE, WHAT HAPPENED TO YOU?
YOU'RE CLEARLY FASTER AND MORE POWERFUL THAN BEFORE, BUT YOU'RE ACTING AS IF YOU CAN'T THINK STRAIGHT.

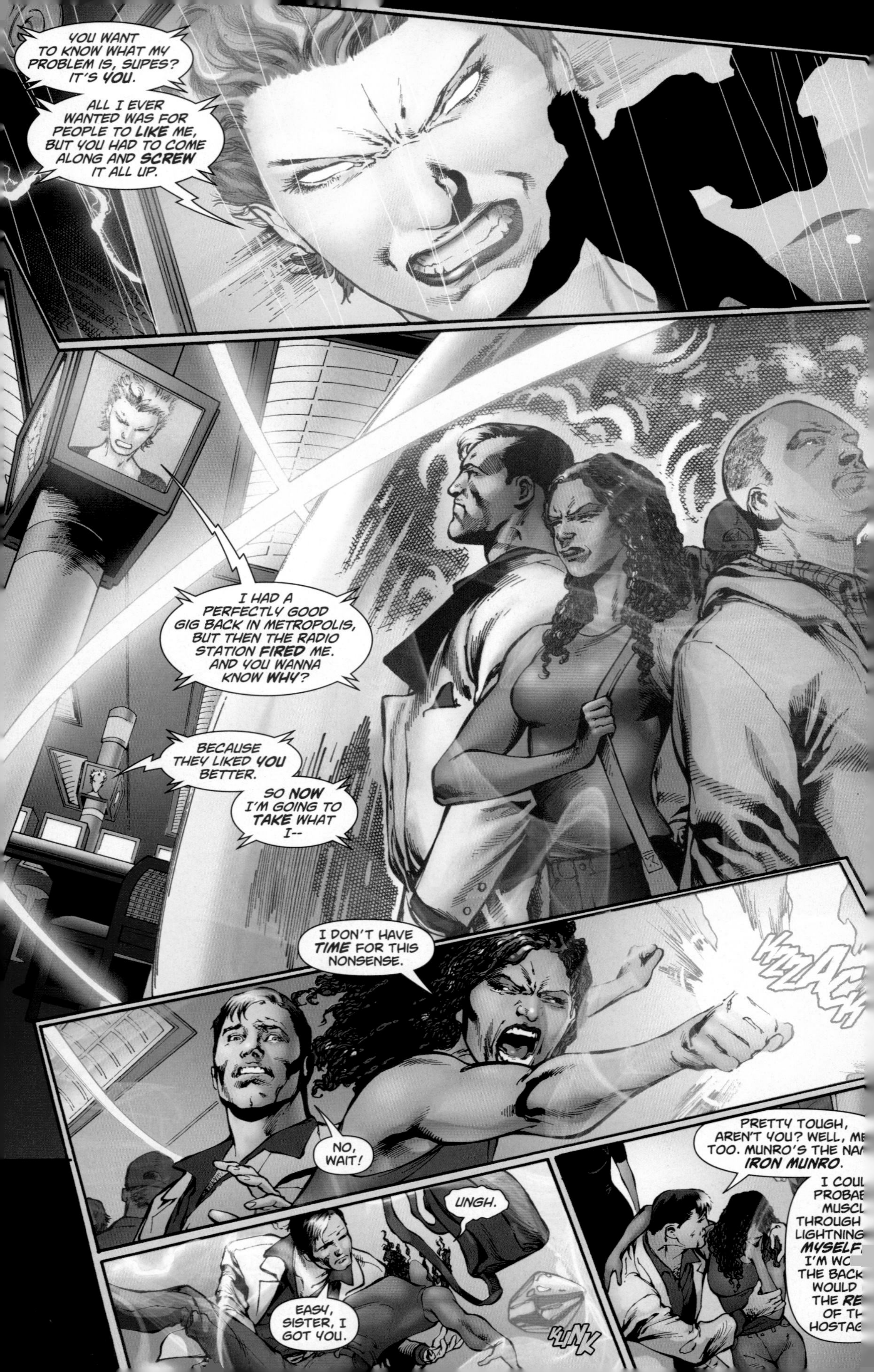
YOU WANT TO KNOW WHAT MY PROBLEM IS, SUPES? IT'S YOU.
ALL I EVER WANTED WAS FOR PEOPLE TO LIKE ME, BUT YOU HAD TO COME ALONG AND SCREW IT ALL UP.
I HAD A PERFECTLY GOOD GIG BACK IN METROPOLIS, BUT THEN THE RADIO STATION FIRED ME. AND YOU WANNA KNOW WHY?
BECAUSE THEY LIKED YOU BETTER.
SO NOW I'M GOING TO TAKE WHAT I--
I DON'T HAVE TIME FOR THIS NONSENSE.
KRZZLACK
NO, WAIT!
UNGH.
EASY, SISTER, I GOT YOU.
KLUNK
PRETTY TOUGH, AREN'T YOU? WELL, ME TOO. MUNRO'S THE NAM IRON MUNRO.
I COUL PROBAB MUSCL THROUGH LIGHTNING MYSELF. I'M WO THE BACK WOULD THE RE OF TH HOSTAG

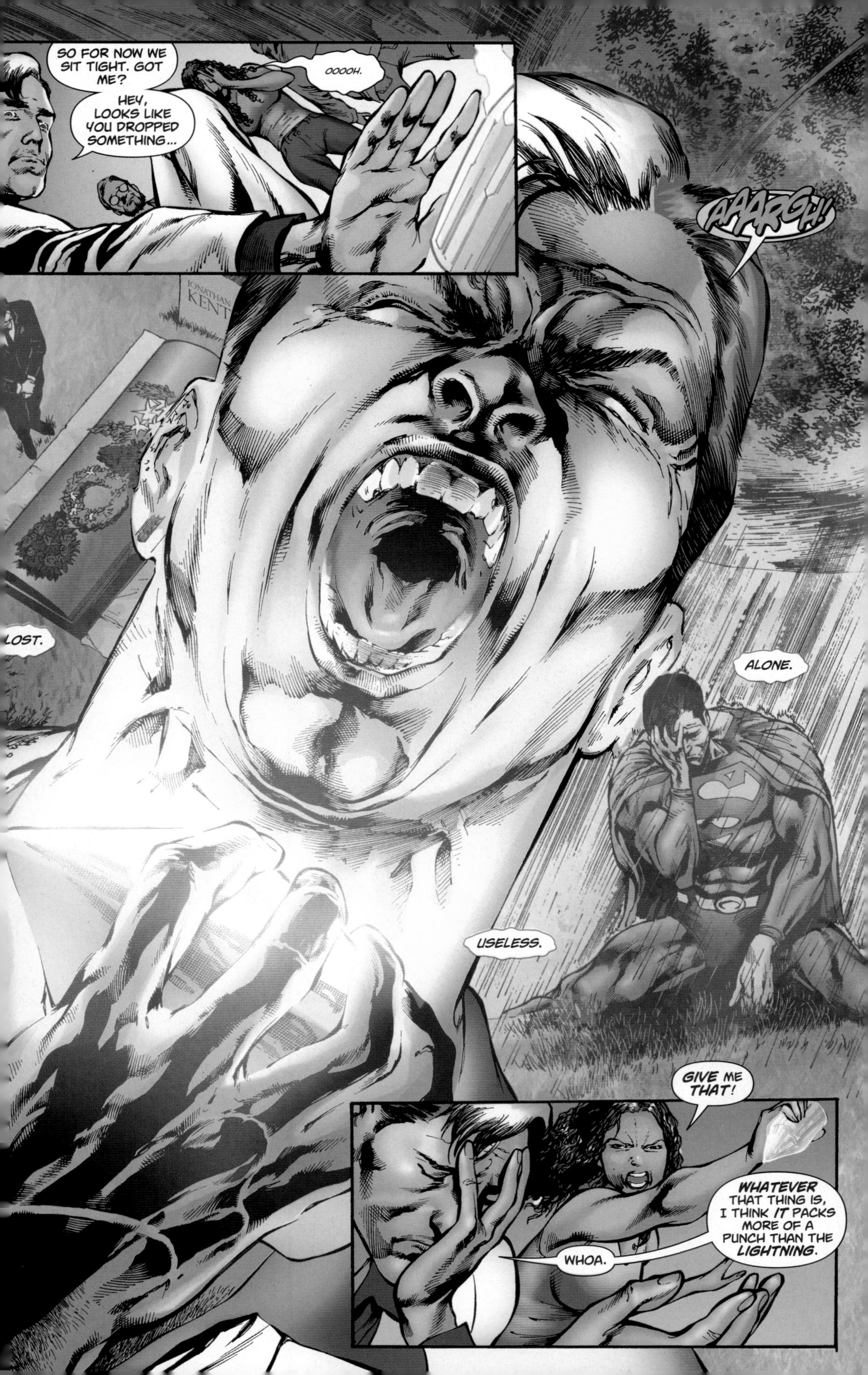

SO FOR NOW WE SIT TIGHT. GOT ME?
HEY, LOOKS LIKE YOU DROPPED SOMETHING...
OOOOH.
AAARGH!
JONATHAN KENT
LOST.
ALONE.
USELESS.
GIVE ME THAT!
WHATEVER THAT THING IS, I THINK IT PACKS MORE OF A PUNCH THAN THE LIGHTNING.
WHOA.

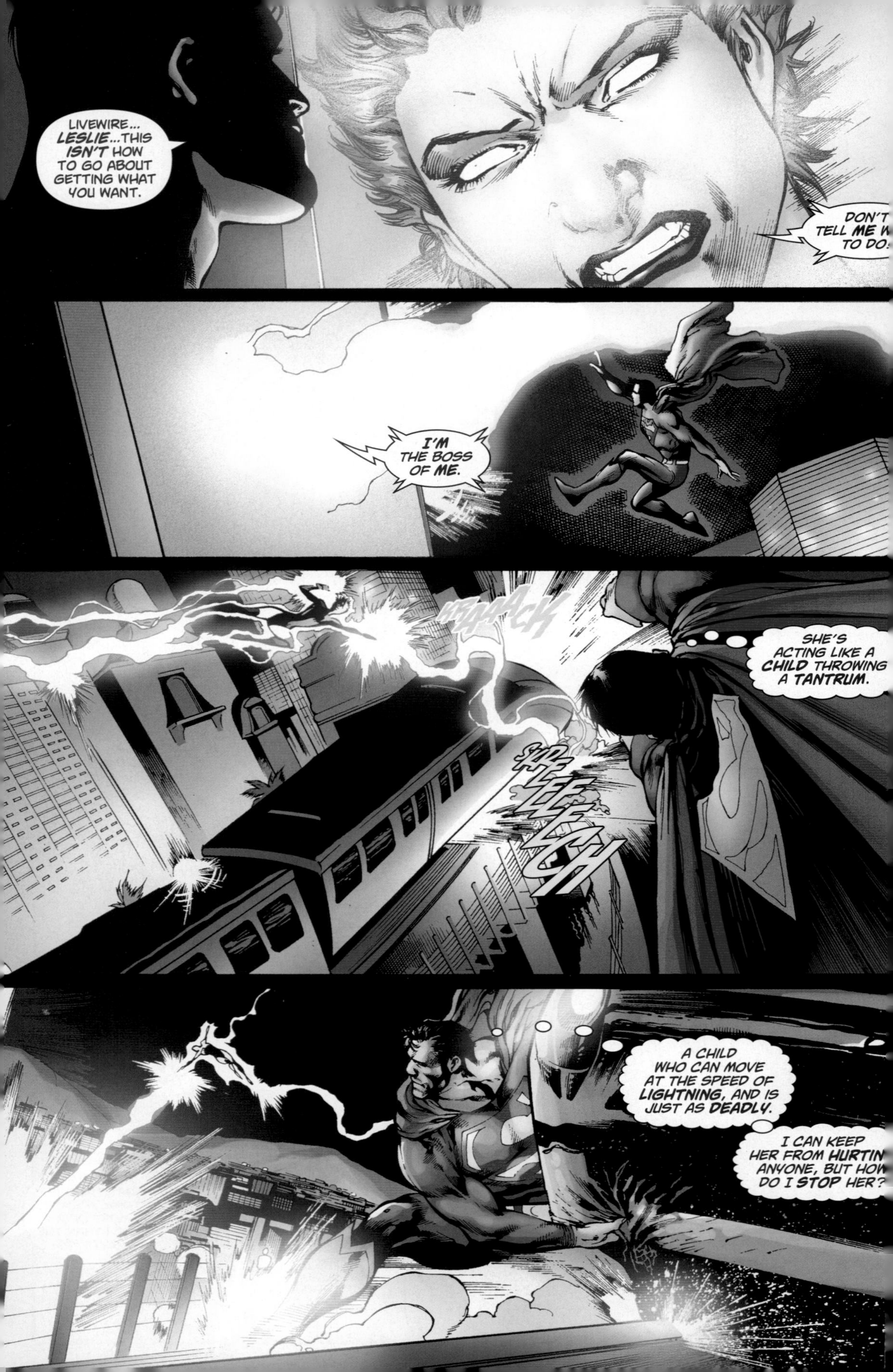
LIVEWIRE... LESLIE...THIS ISN'T HOW TO GO ABOUT GETTING WHAT YOU WANT.
DON'T TELL ME W TO DO
I'M THE BOSS OF ME.
KRAAACK
SHE'S ACTING LIKE A CHILD THROWING A TANTRUM.
SKREEEECH
A CHILD WHO CAN MOVE AT THE SPEED OF LIGHTNING, AND IS JUST AS DEADLY.
I CAN KEEP HER FROM HURTIN ANYONE, BUT HOW DO I STOP HER?

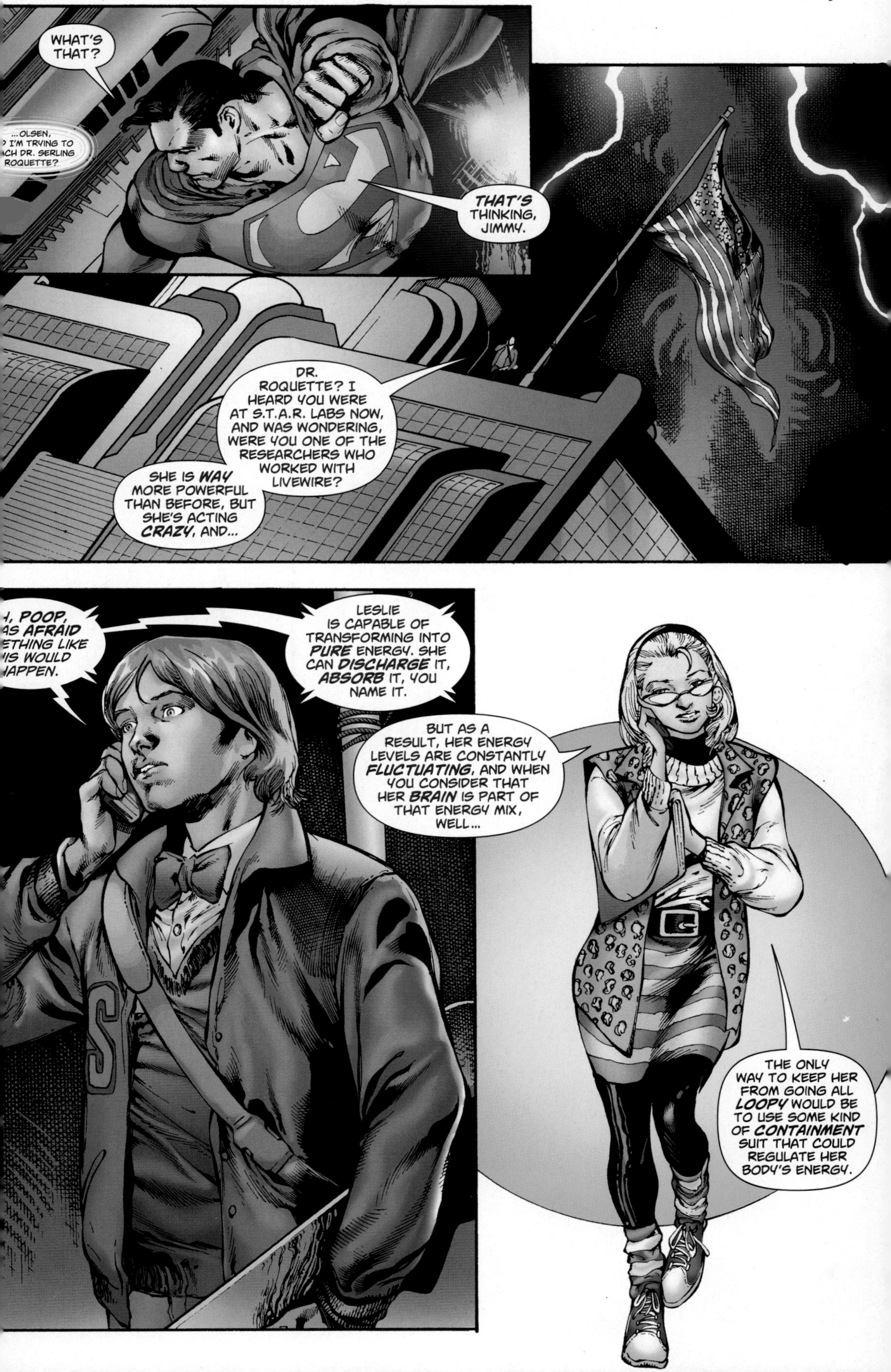
WHAT'S THAT?
...OLSEN, D I'M TRYING TO ACH DR. SERLING ROQUETTE?
THAT'S THINKING, JIMMY.
DR. ROQUETTE? I HEARD YOU WERE AT S.T.A.R. LABS NOW, AND WAS WONDERING, WERE YOU ONE OF THE RESEARCHERS WHO WORKED WITH LIVEWIRE?
SHE IS WAY MORE POWERFUL THAN BEFORE, BUT SHE'S ACTING CRAZY, AND...
H, POOP, AS AFRAID ETHING LIKE IS WOULD HAPPEN.
LESLIE IS CAPABLE OF TRANSFORMING INTO PURE ENERGY. SHE CAN DISCHARGE IT, ABSORB IT, YOU NAME IT.
BUT AS A RESULT, HER ENERGY LEVELS ARE CONSTANTLY FLUCTUATING, AND WHEN YOU CONSIDER THAT HER BRAIN IS PART OF THAT ENERGY MIX, WELL...
THE ONLY WAY TO KEEP HER FROM GOING ALL LOOPY WOULD BE TO USE SOME KIND OF CONTAINMENT SUIT THAT COULD REGULATE HER BODY'S ENERGY.

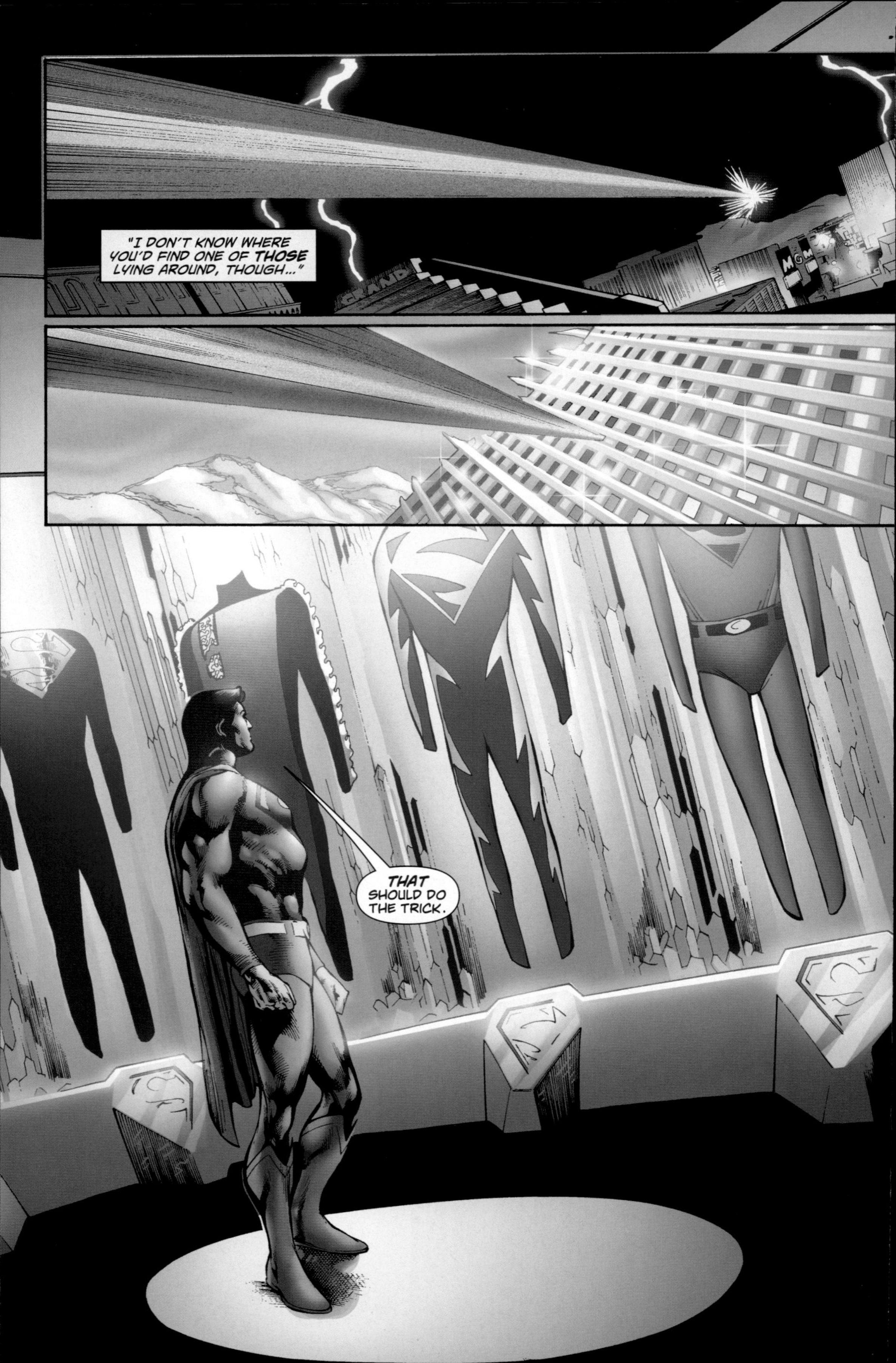
"I DON'T KNOW WHERE YOU'D FIND ONE OF THOSE LYING AROUND, THOUGH..."
GRAND
MGM
THAT SHOULD DO THE TRICK.

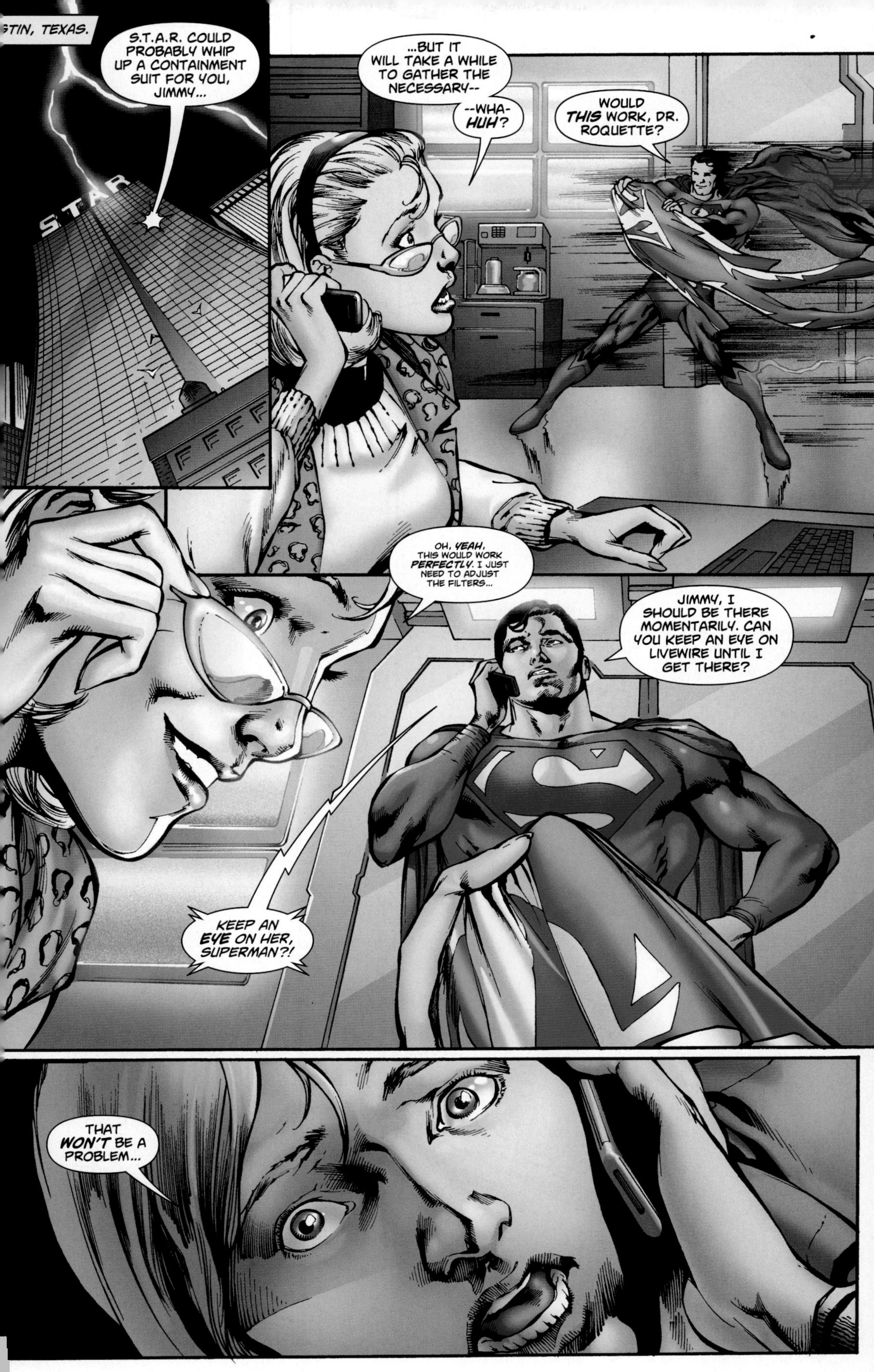

STIN, TEXAS.
S.T.A.R. COULD PROBABLY WHIP UP A CONTAINMENT SUIT FOR YOU, JIMMY...
...BUT IT WILL TAKE A WHILE TO GATHER THE NECESSARY--
--WHA-HUH?
WOULD THIS WORK, DR. ROQUETTE?
OH, YEAH, THIS WOULD WORK PERFECTLY. I JUST NEED TO ADJUST THE FILTERS...
JIMMY, I SHOULD BE THERE MOMENTARILY. CAN YOU KEEP AN EYE ON LIVEWIRE UNTIL I GET THERE?
KEEP AN EYE ON HER, SUPERMAN?!
THAT WON'T BE A PROBLEM...

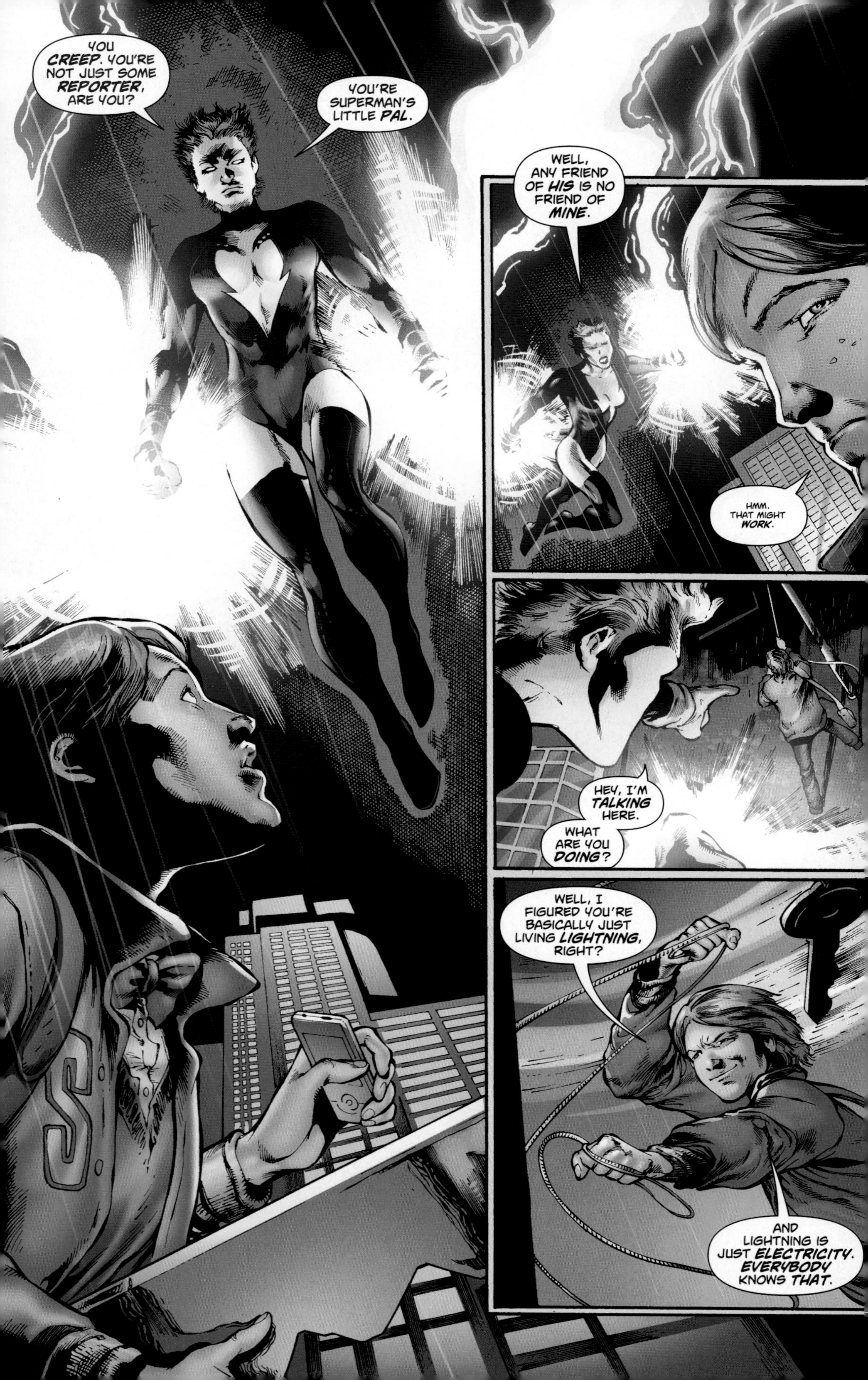

YOU CREEP. YOU'RE NOT JUST SOME REPORTER, ARE YOU?
YOU'RE SUPERMAN'S LITTLE PAL.
WELL, ANY FRIEND OF HIS IS NO FRIEND OF MINE.
HMM. THAT MIGHT WORK.
HEY, I'M TALKING HERE.
WHAT ARE YOU DOING?
WELL, I FIGURED YOU'RE BASICALLY JUST LIVING LIGHTNING, RIGHT?
AND LIGHTNING IS JUST ELECTRICITY. EVERYBODY KNOWS THAT.

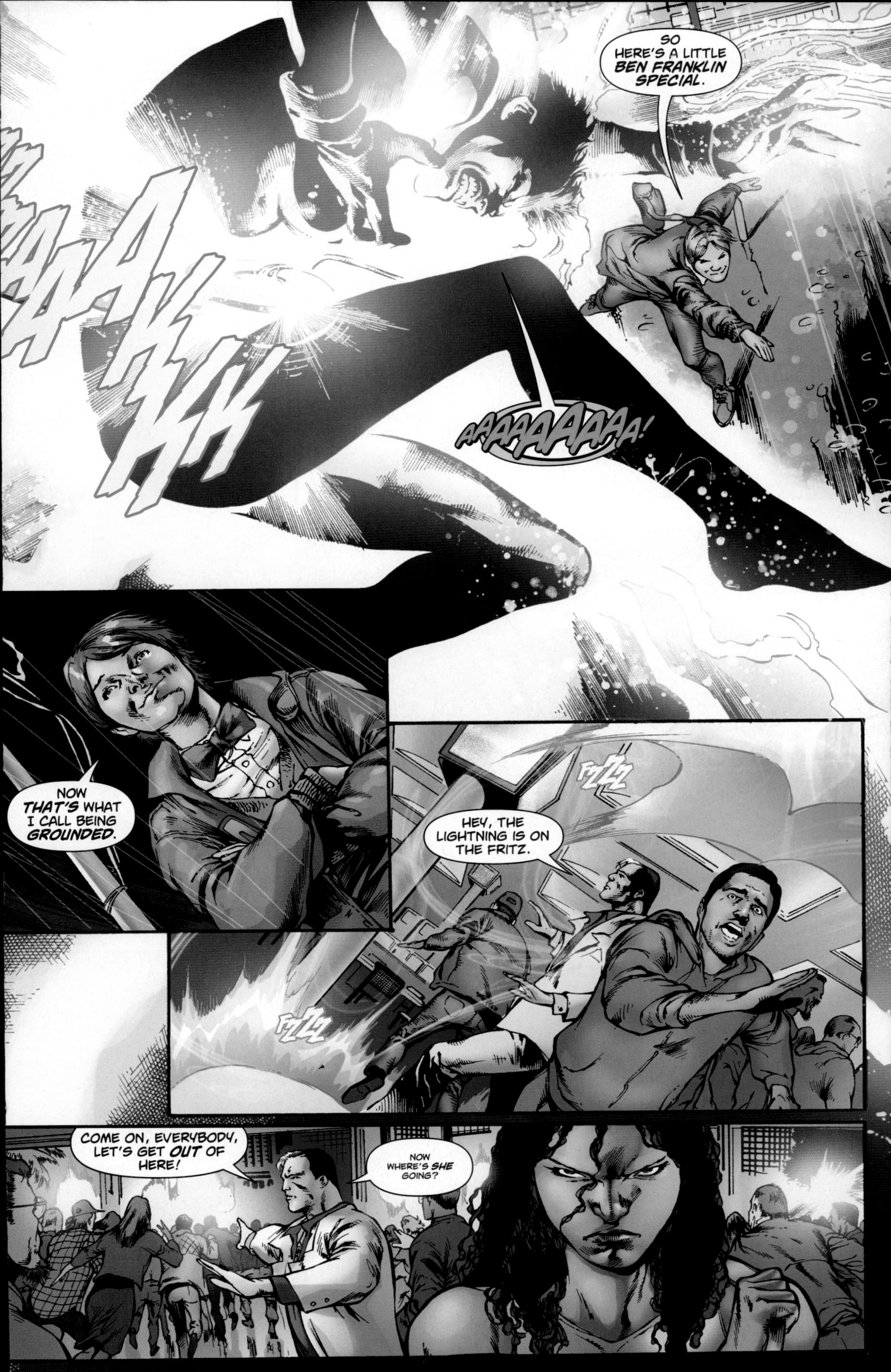
SO HERE'S A LITTLE BEN FRANKLIN SPECIAL.
ZZAAAKKK
AAAAAAAAA!
NOW THAT'S WHAT I CALL BEING GROUNDED.
FZZZ
HEY, THE LIGHTNING IS ON THE FRITZ.
FZZZ
COME ON, EVERYBODY, LET'S GET OUT OF HERE!
NOW WHERE'S SHE GOING?

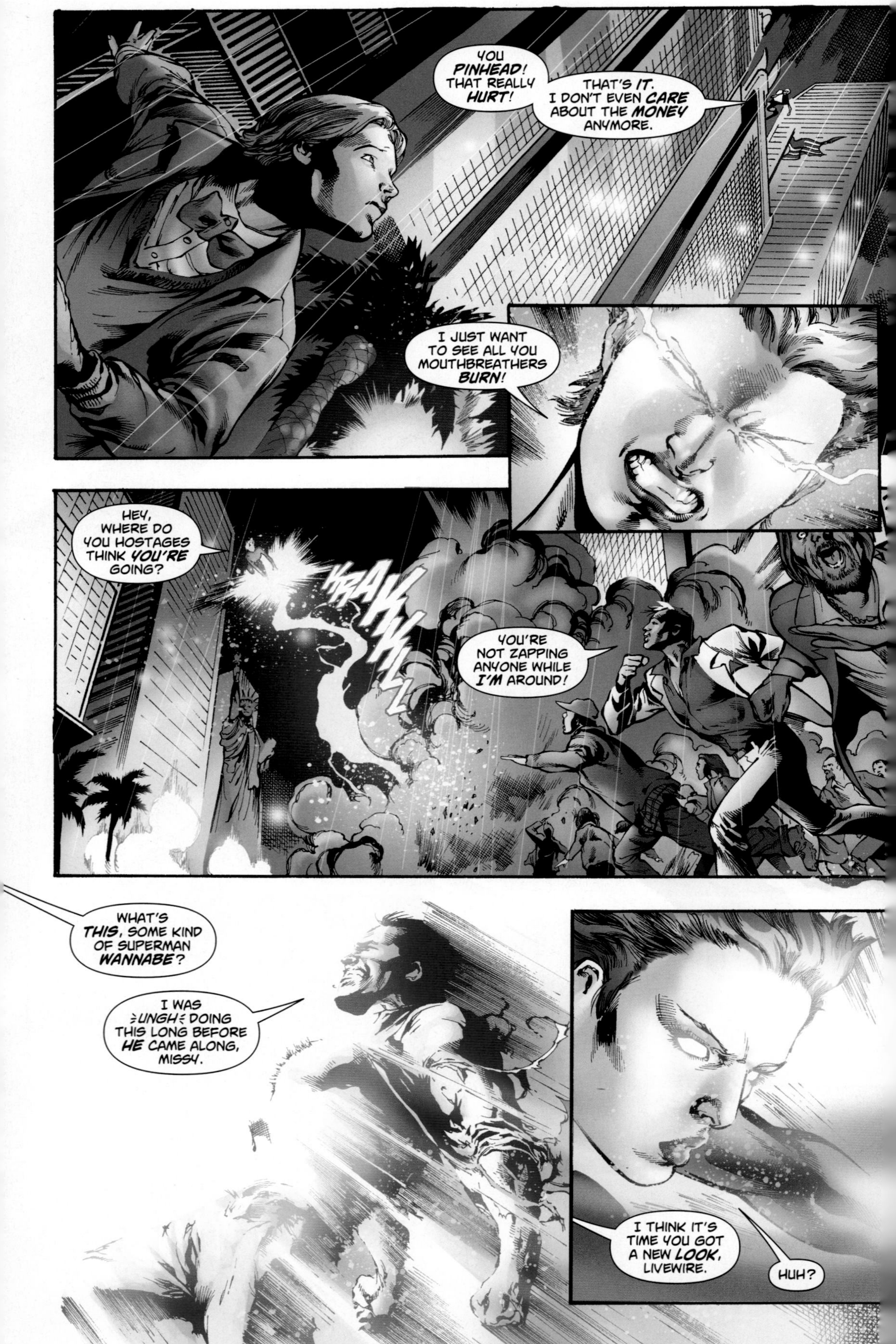
YOU PINHEAD! THAT REALLY HURT!
THAT'S IT. I DON'T EVEN CARE ABOUT THE MONEY ANYMORE.
I JUST WANT TO SEE ALL YOU MOUTHBREATHERS BURN!
HEY, WHERE DO YOU HOSTAGES THINK YOU'RE GOING?
KRAKKKKL
YOU'RE NOT ZAPPING ANYONE WHILE I'M AROUND!
WHAT'S THIS, SOME KIND OF SUPERMAN WANNABE?
I WAS ≷UNGH≶ DOING THIS LONG BEFORE HE CAME ALONG, MISSY.
I THINK IT'S TIME YOU GOT A NEW LOOK, LIVEWIRE.
HUH?

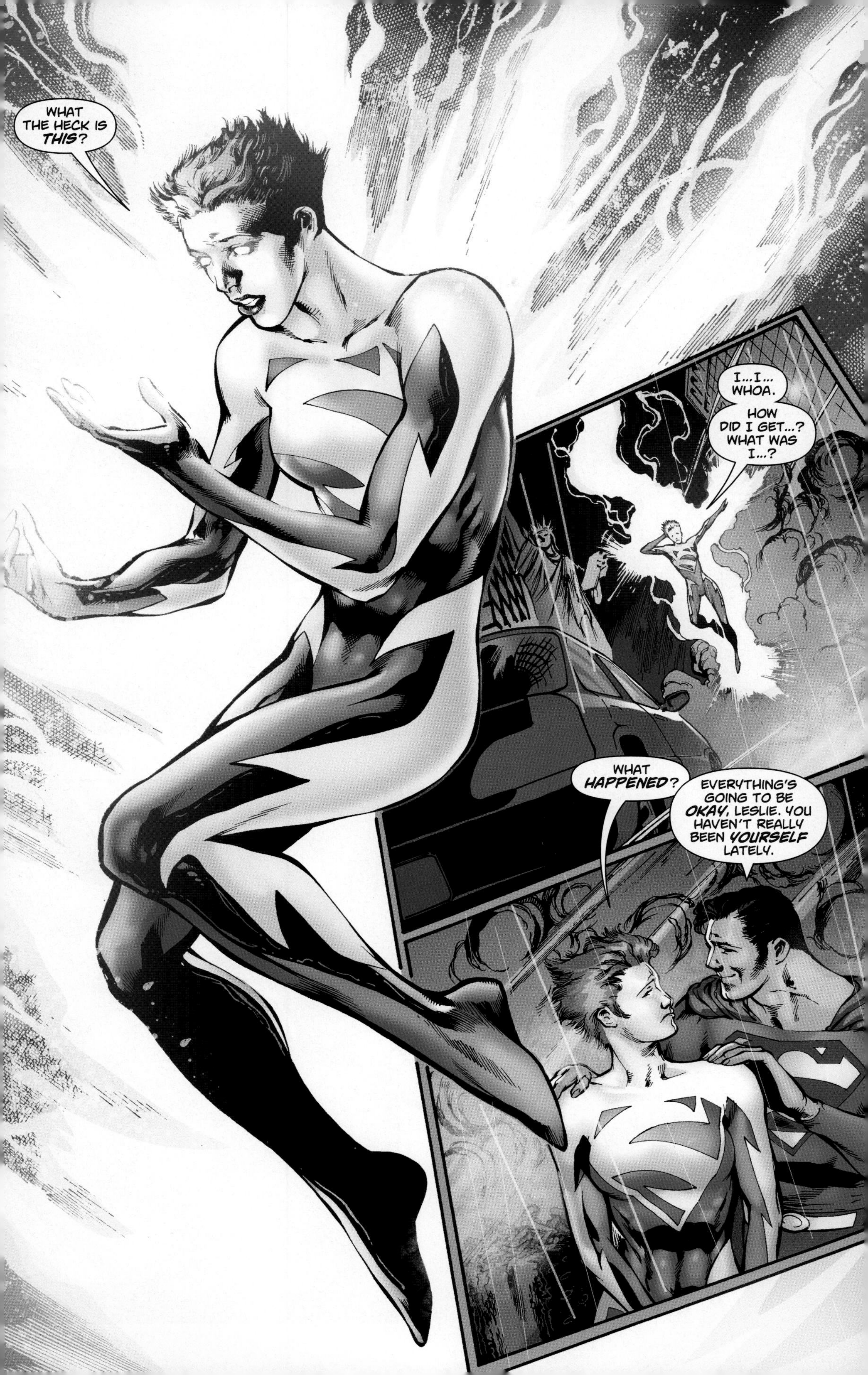

WHAT THE HECK IS *THIS*?
I... I... WHOA.
HOW DID I GET...? WHAT WAS I...?
WHAT *HAPPENED*?
EVERYTHING'S GOING TO BE *OKAY*, LESLIE. YOU HAVEN'T REALLY BEEN *YOURSELF* LATELY.

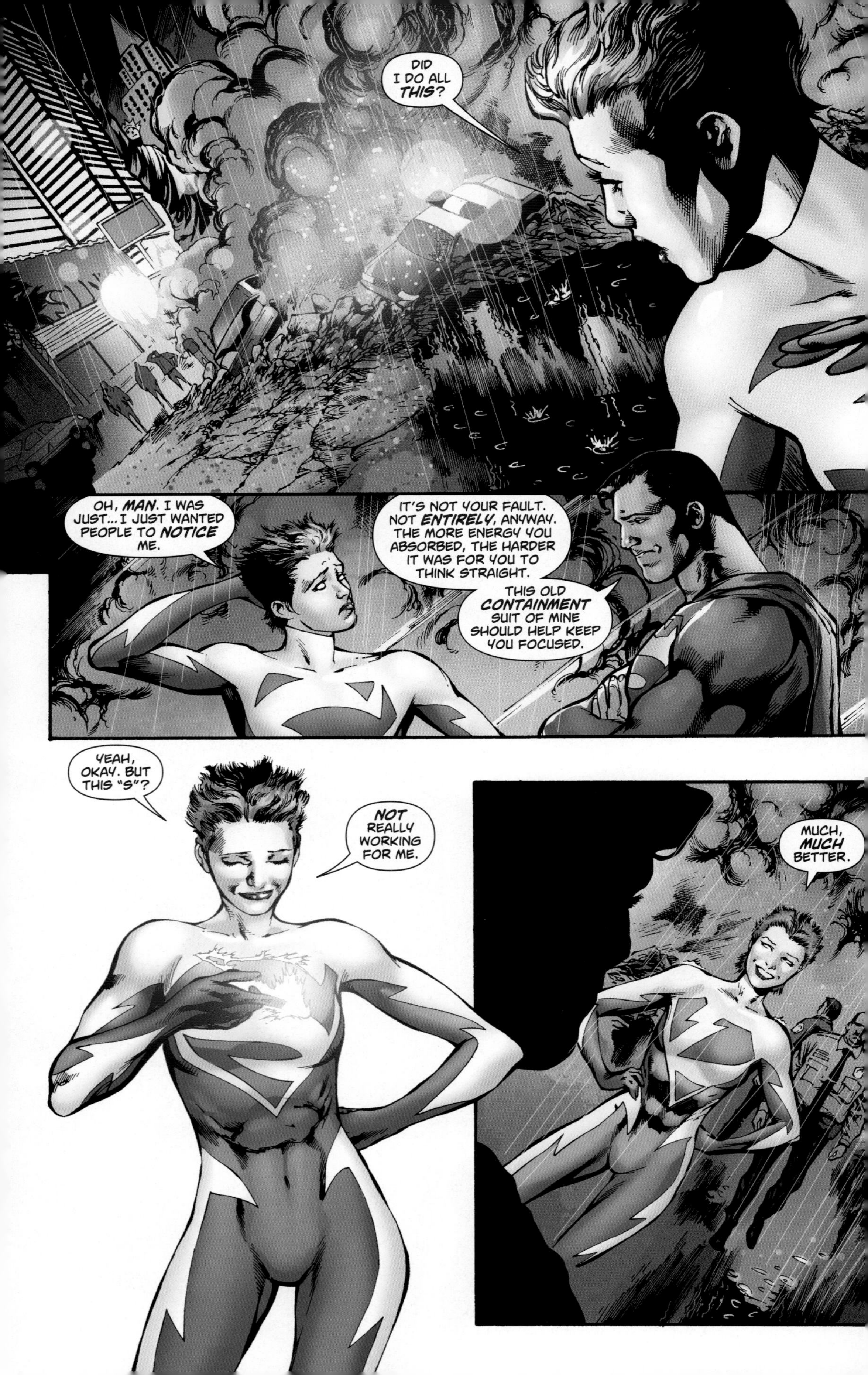

DID I DO ALL THIS?
OH, MAN. I WAS JUST... I JUST WANTED PEOPLE TO NOTICE ME.
IT'S NOT YOUR FAULT. NOT ENTIRELY, ANYWAY. THE MORE ENERGY YOU ABSORBED, THE HARDER IT WAS FOR YOU TO THINK STRAIGHT.
THIS OLD CONTAINMENT SUIT OF MINE SHOULD HELP KEEP YOU FOCUSED.
YEAH, OKAY. BUT THIS "S"?
NOT REALLY WORKING FOR ME.
MUCH, MUCH BETTER.

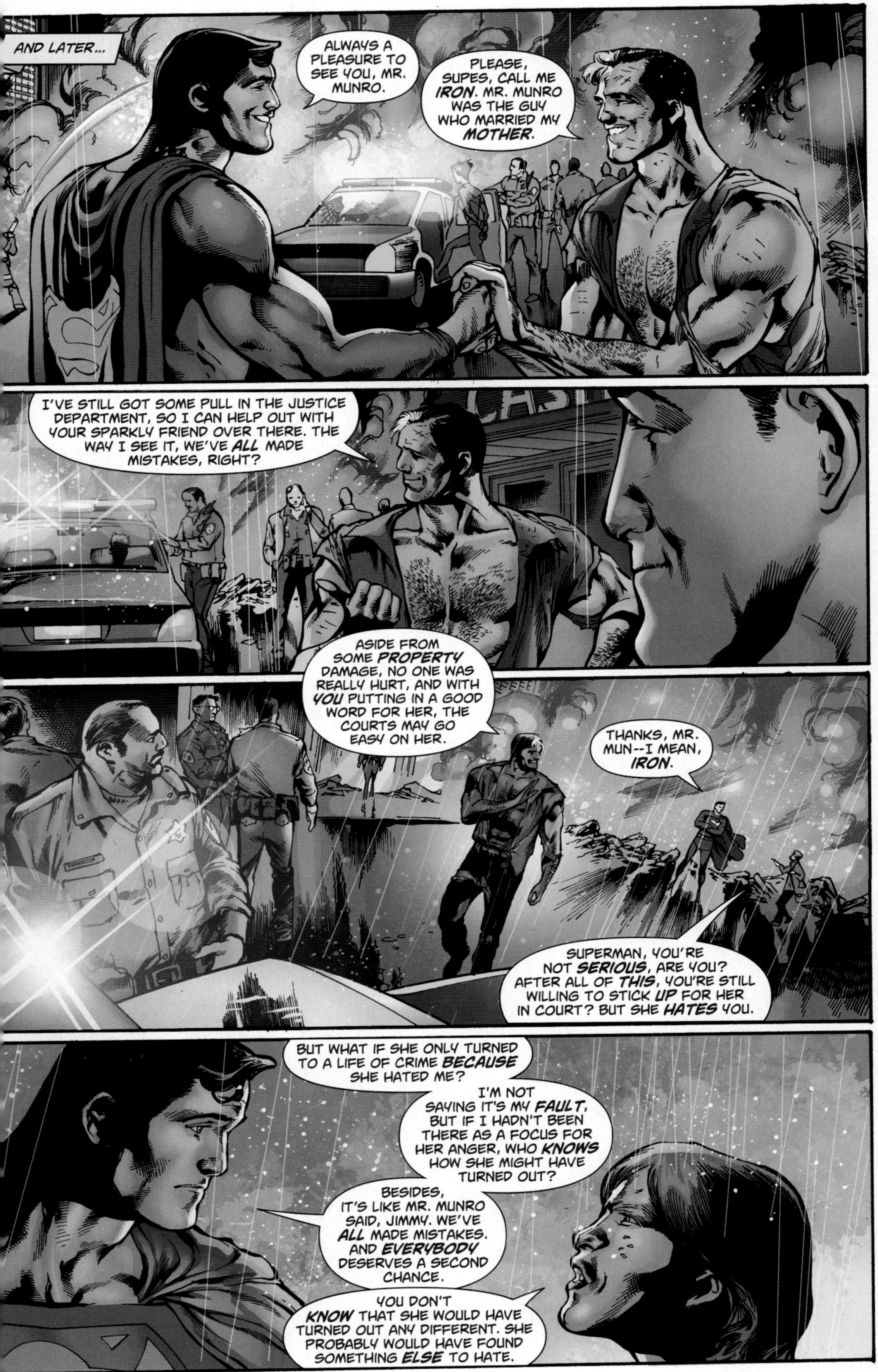
AND LATER...
ALWAYS A PLEASURE TO SEE YOU, MR. MUNRO.
PLEASE, SUPES, CALL ME IRON. MR. MUNRO WAS THE GUY WHO MARRIED MY MOTHER.
I'VE STILL GOT SOME PULL IN THE JUSTICE DEPARTMENT, SO I CAN HELP OUT WITH YOUR SPARKLY FRIEND OVER THERE. THE WAY I SEE IT, WE'VE ALL MADE MISTAKES, RIGHT?
ASIDE FROM SOME PROPERTY DAMAGE, NO ONE WAS REALLY HURT, AND WITH YOU PUTTING IN A GOOD WORD FOR HER, THE COURTS MAY GO EASY ON HER.
THANKS, MR. MUN--I MEAN, IRON.
SUPERMAN, YOU'RE NOT SERIOUS, ARE YOU? AFTER ALL OF THIS, YOU'RE STILL WILLING TO STICK UP FOR HER IN COURT? BUT SHE HATES YOU.
BUT WHAT IF SHE ONLY TURNED TO A LIFE OF CRIME BECAUSE SHE HATED ME?
I'M NOT SAYING IT'S MY FAULT, BUT IF I HADN'T BEEN THERE AS A FOCUS FOR HER ANGER, WHO KNOWS HOW SHE MIGHT HAVE TURNED OUT?
BESIDES, IT'S LIKE MR. MUNRO SAID, JIMMY. WE'VE ALL MADE MISTAKES. AND EVERYBODY DESERVES A SECOND CHANCE.
YOU DON'T KNOW THAT SHE WOULD HAVE TURNED OUT ANY DIFFERENT. SHE PROBABLY WOULD HAVE FOUND SOMETHING ELSE TO HATE.

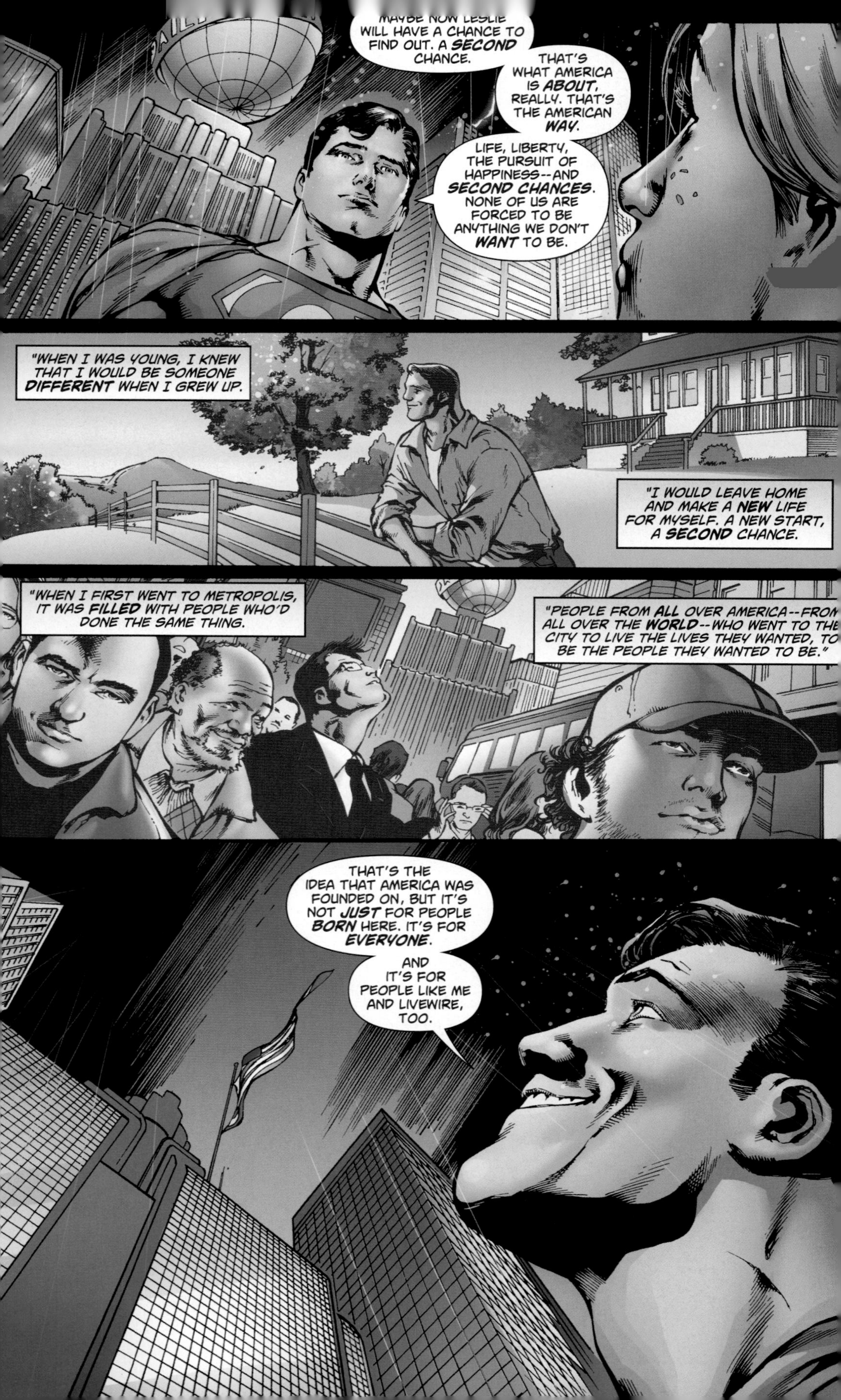
MAYBE NOW LESLIE WILL HAVE A CHANCE TO FIND OUT. A SECOND CHANCE.
THAT'S WHAT AMERICA IS ABOUT, REALLY. THAT'S THE AMERICAN WAY.
LIFE, LIBERTY, THE PURSUIT OF HAPPINESS--AND SECOND CHANCES. NONE OF US ARE FORCED TO BE ANYTHING WE DON'T WANT TO BE.
"WHEN I WAS YOUNG, I KNEW THAT I WOULD BE SOMEONE DIFFERENT WHEN I GREW UP.
"I WOULD LEAVE HOME AND MAKE A NEW LIFE FOR MYSELF. A NEW START, A SECOND CHANCE.
"WHEN I FIRST WENT TO METROPOLIS, IT WAS FILLED WITH PEOPLE WHO'D DONE THE SAME THING.
"PEOPLE FROM ALL OVER AMERICA--FROM ALL OVER THE WORLD--WHO WENT TO THE CITY TO LIVE THE LIVES THEY WANTED, TO BE THE PEOPLE THEY WANTED TO BE."
THAT'S THE IDEA THAT AMERICA WAS FOUNDED ON, BUT IT'S NOT JUST FOR PEOPLE BORN HERE. IT'S FOR EVERYONE.
AND IT'S FOR PEOPLE LIKE ME AND LIVEWIRE, TOO.

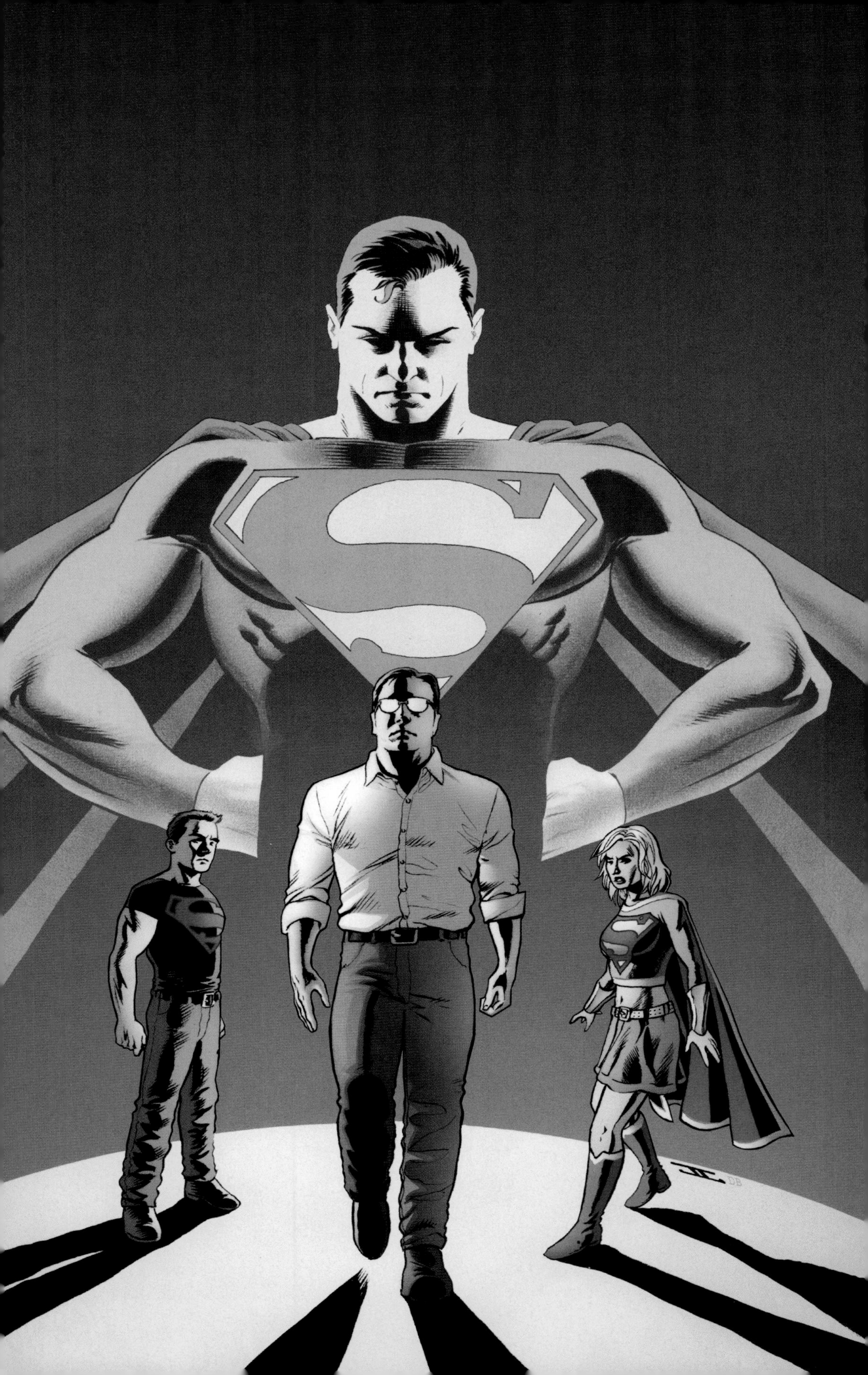

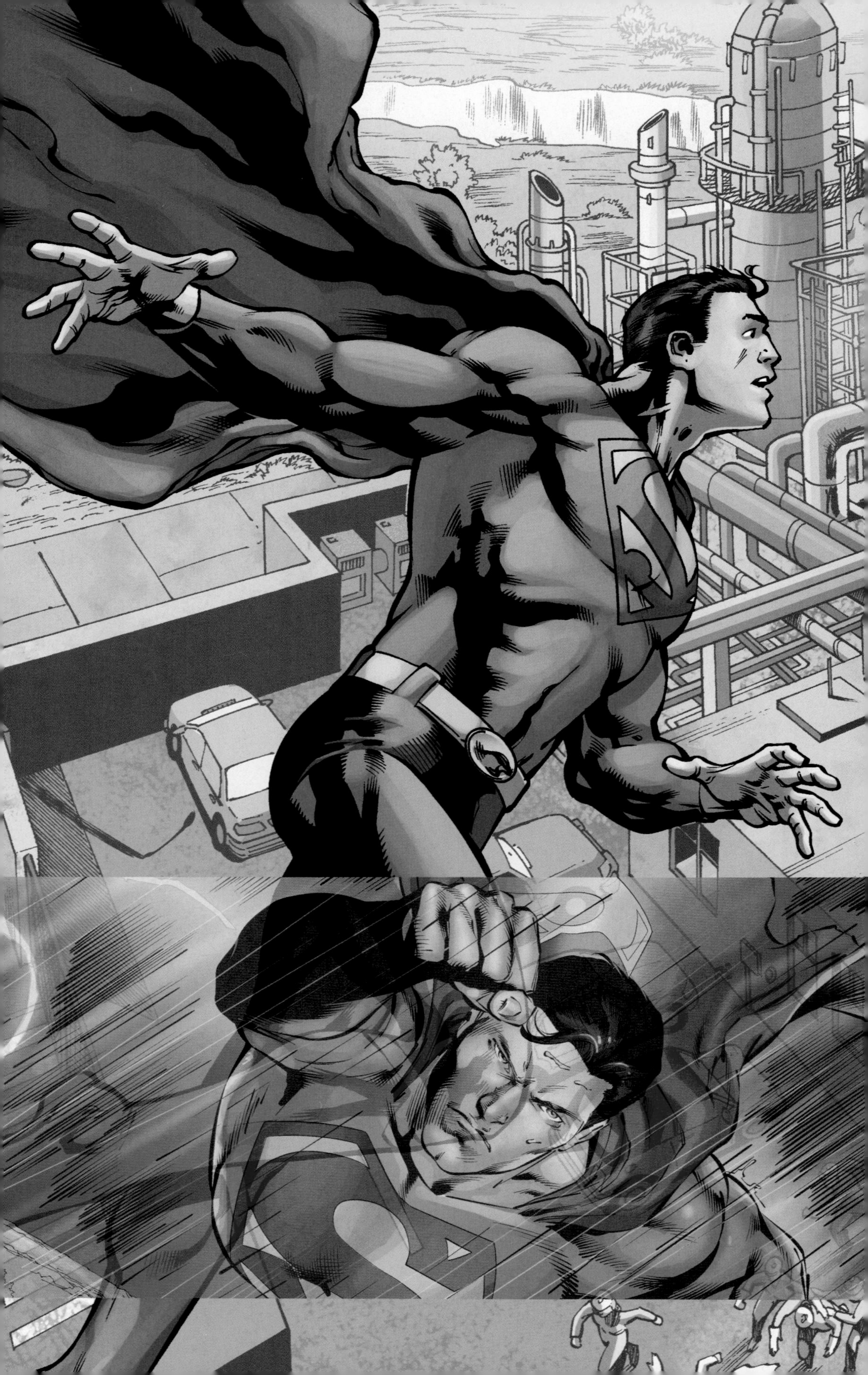

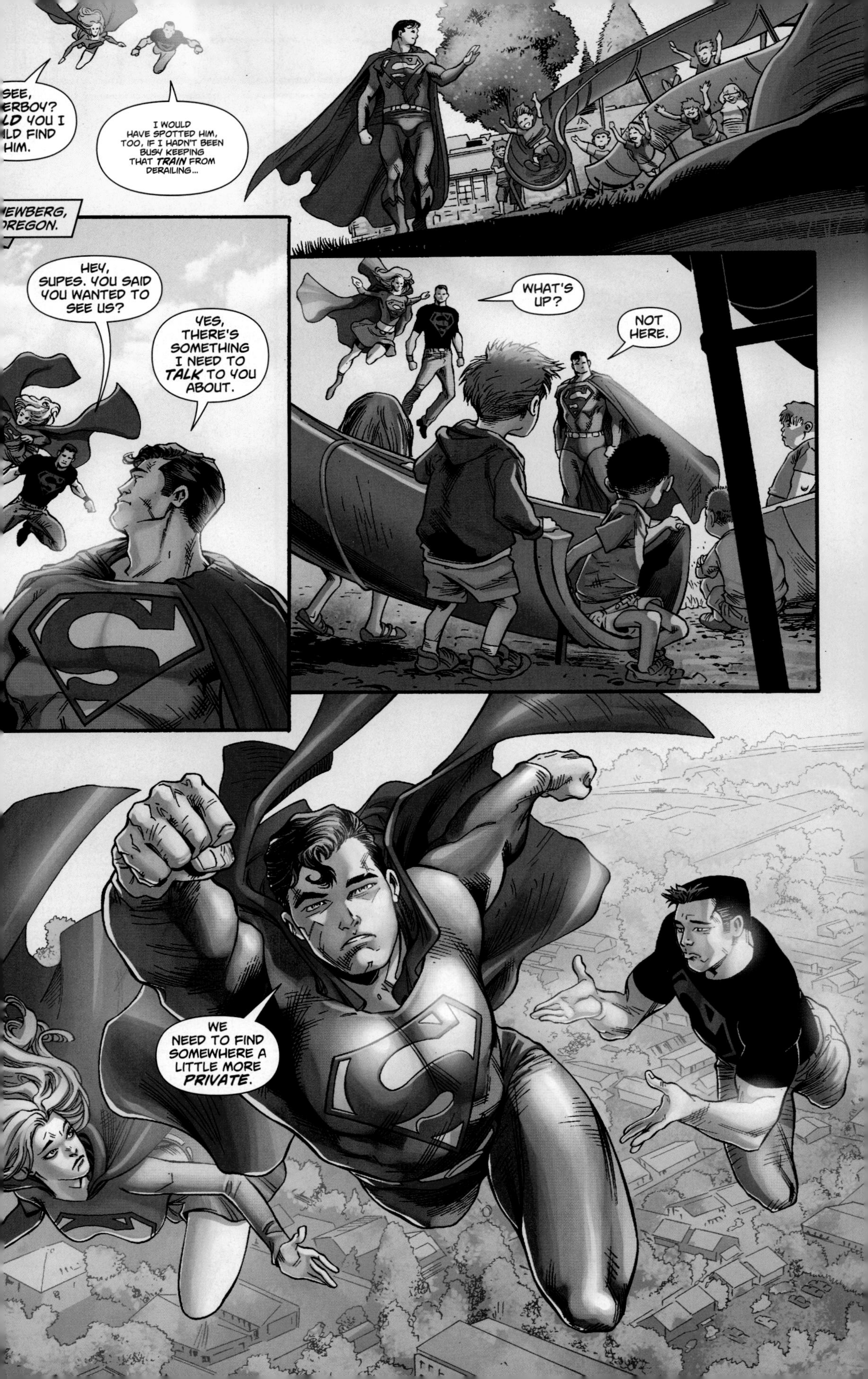
SEE, ERBOY? LD YOU I ILD FIND HIM.
I WOULD HAVE SPOTTED HIM, TOO, IF I HADN'T BEEN BUSY KEEPING THAT TRAIN FROM DERAILING...
EWBERG, OREGON.
HEY, SUPES. YOU SAID YOU WANTED TO SEE US?
YES, THERE'S SOMETHING I NEED TO TALK TO YOU ABOUT.
WHAT'S UP?
NOT HERE.
WE NEED TO FIND SOMEWHERE A LITTLE MORE PRIVATE.

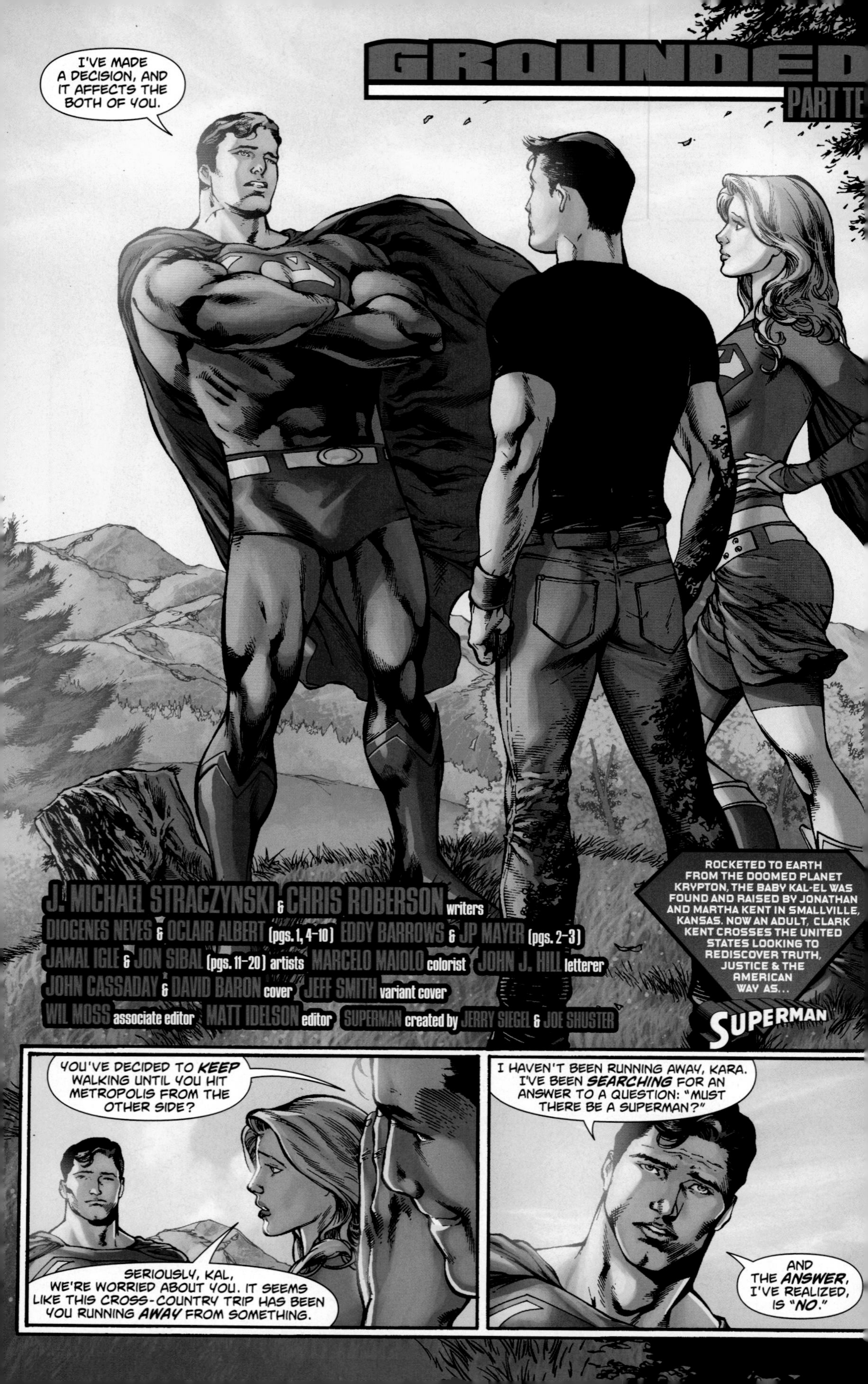

I'VE MADE A DECISION, AND IT AFFECTS THE BOTH OF YOU.
GROUNDED
PART TE
J. MICHAEL STRACZYNSKI & CHRIS ROBERSON writers
DIOGENES NEVES & OCLAIR ALBERT (pgs. 1, 4–10) EDDY BARROWS & JP MAYER (pgs. 2–3)
JAMAL IGLE & JON SIBAL (pgs. 11–20) artists MARCELO MAIOLO colorist JOHN J. HILL letterer
JOHN CASSADAY & DAVID BARON cover JEFF SMITH variant cover
WIL MOSS associate editor MATT IDELSON editor SUPERMAN created by JERRY SIEGEL & JOE SHUSTER
ROCKETED TO EARTH FROM THE DOOMED PLANET KRYPTON, THE BABY KAL-EL WAS FOUND AND RAISED BY JONATHAN AND MARTHA KENT IN SMALLVILLE, KANSAS. NOW AN ADULT, CLARK KENT CROSSES THE UNITED STATES LOOKING TO REDISCOVER TRUTH, JUSTICE & THE AMERICAN WAY AS...
SUPERMAN
YOU'VE DECIDED TO KEEP WALKING UNTIL YOU HIT METROPOLIS FROM THE OTHER SIDE?
SERIOUSLY, KAL, WE'RE WORRIED ABOUT YOU. IT SEEMS LIKE THIS CROSS-COUNTRY TRIP HAS BEEN YOU RUNNING AWAY FROM SOMETHING.
I HAVEN'T BEEN RUNNING AWAY, KARA. I'VE BEEN SEARCHING FOR AN ANSWER TO A QUESTION: "MUST THERE BE A SUPERMAN?"
AND THE ANSWER, I'VE REALIZED, IS "NO."

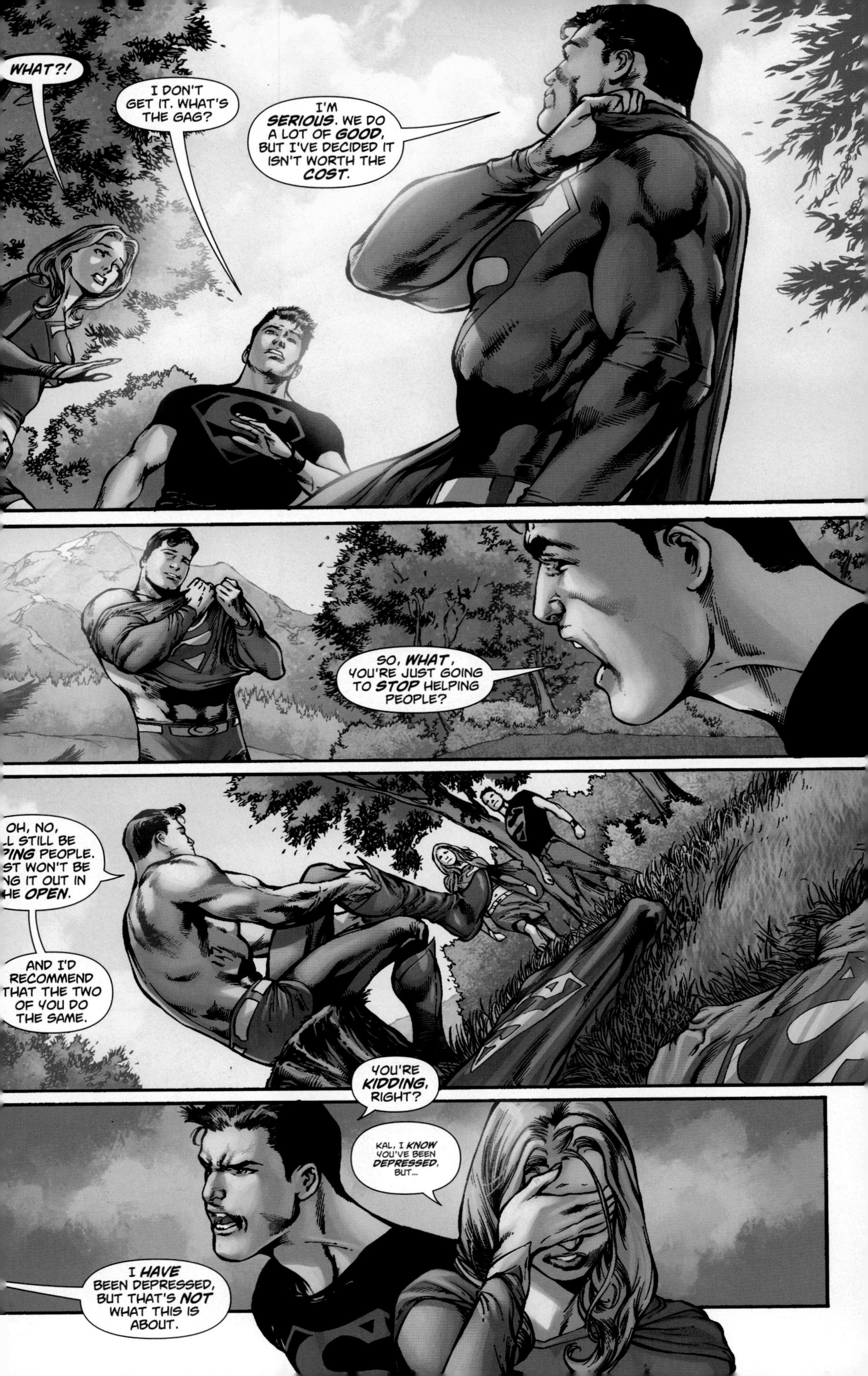
WHAT?!
I DON'T GET IT. WHAT'S THE GAG?
I'M SERIOUS. WE DO A LOT OF GOOD, BUT I'VE DECIDED IT ISN'T WORTH THE COST.
SO, WHAT, YOU'RE JUST GOING TO STOP HELPING PEOPLE?
OH, NO, L STILL BE PING PEOPLE. ST WON'T BE NG IT OUT IN HE OPEN.
AND I'D RECOMMEND THAT THE TWO OF YOU DO THE SAME.
YOU'RE KIDDING, RIGHT?
KAL, I KNOW YOU'VE BEEN DEPRESSED, BUT...
I HAVE BEEN DEPRESSED, BUT THAT'S NOT WHAT THIS IS ABOUT.

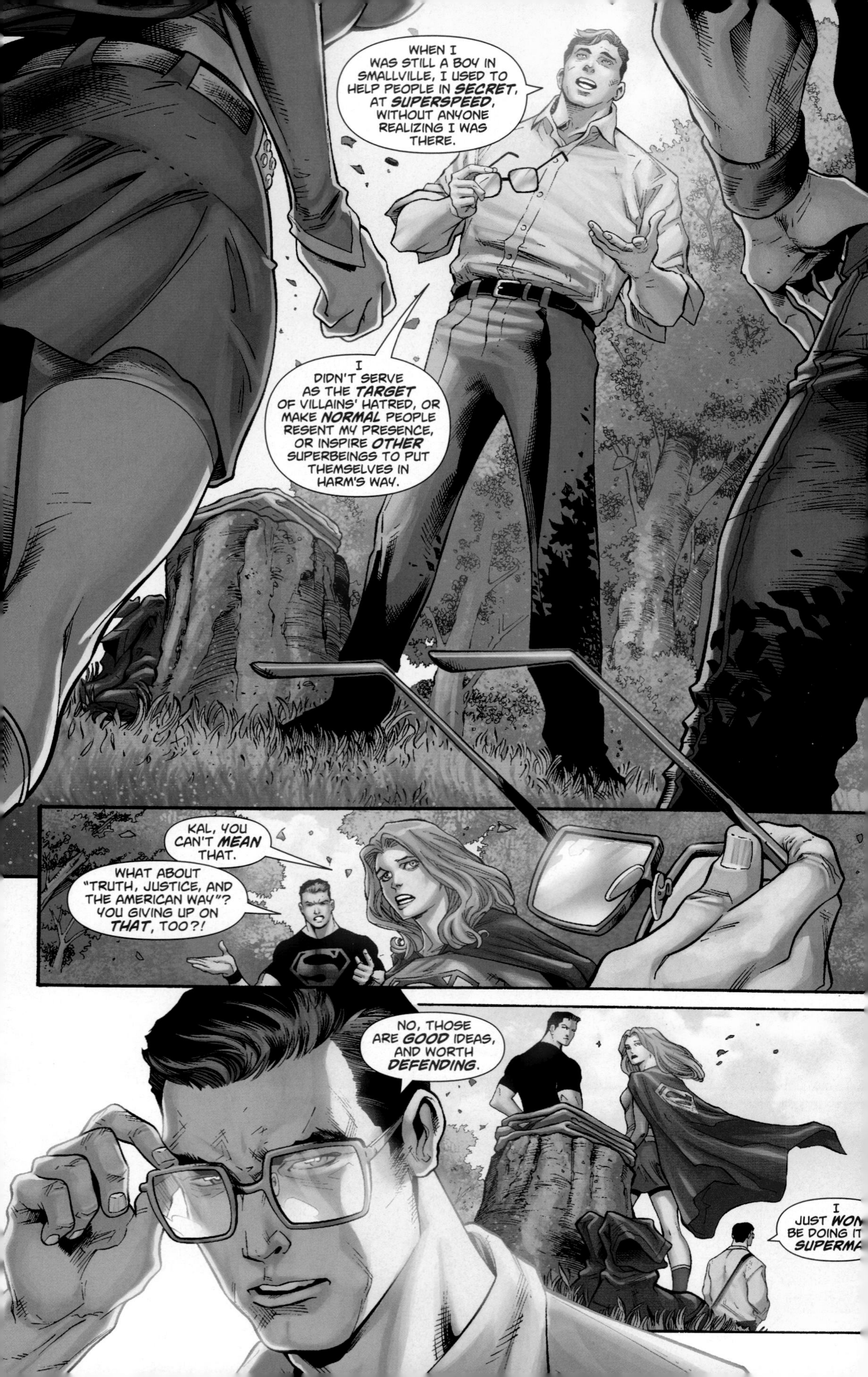
WHEN I WAS STILL A BOY IN SMALLVILLE, I USED TO HELP PEOPLE IN SECRET, AT SUPERSPEED, WITHOUT ANYONE REALIZING I WAS THERE.
I DIDN'T SERVE AS THE TARGET OF VILLAINS' HATRED, OR MAKE NORMAL PEOPLE RESENT MY PRESENCE, OR INSPIRE OTHER SUPERBEINGS TO PUT THEMSELVES IN HARM'S WAY.
KAL, YOU CAN'T MEAN THAT.
WHAT ABOUT "TRUTH, JUSTICE, AND THE AMERICAN WAY"? YOU GIVING UP ON THAT, TOO?!
NO, THOSE ARE GOOD IDEAS, AND WORTH DEFENDING.
I JUST

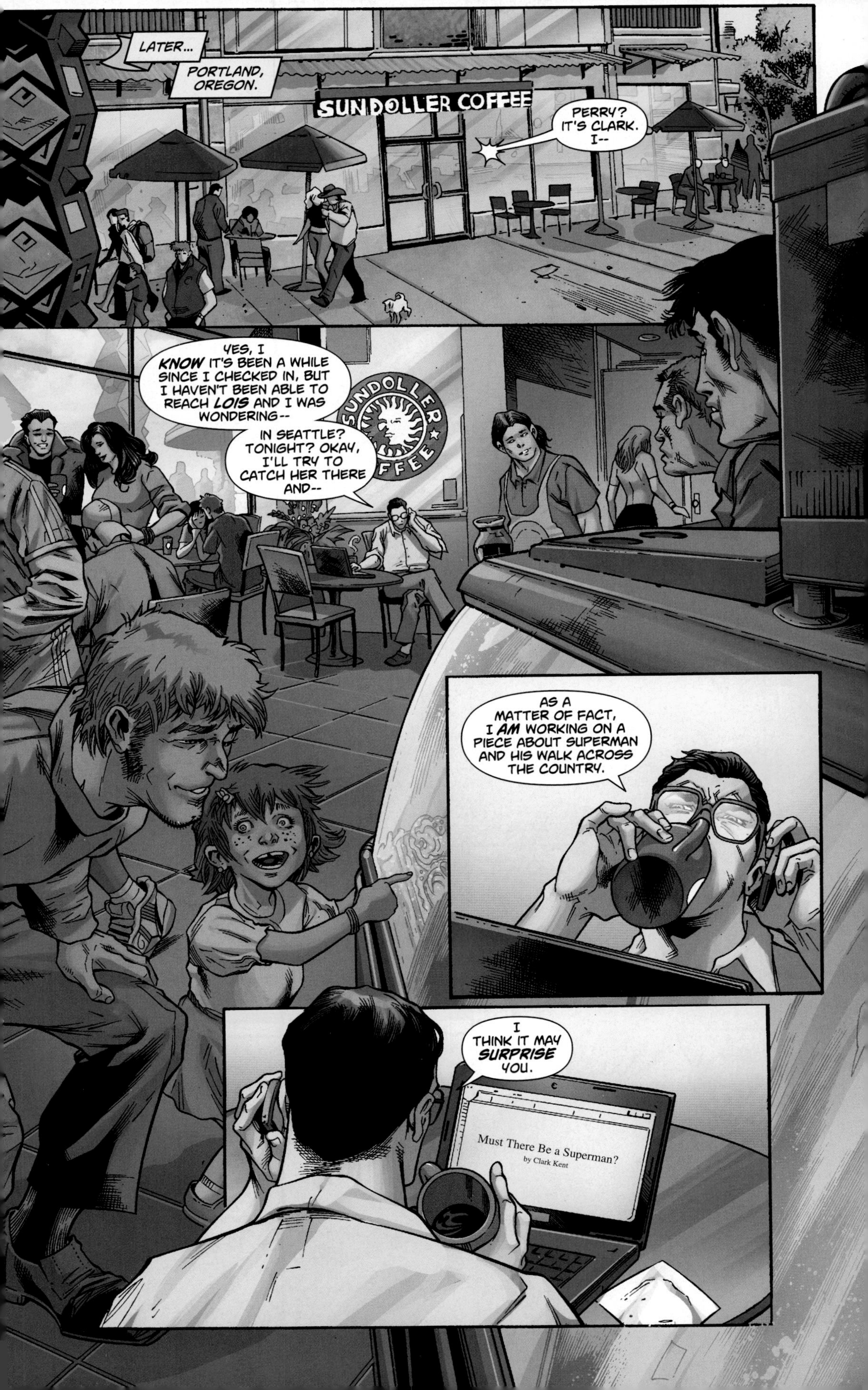
LATER...
PORTLAND, OREGON.
SUNDOLLER COFFEE
PERRY? IT'S CLARK. I--
YES, I KNOW IT'S BEEN A WHILE SINCE I CHECKED IN, BUT I HAVEN'T BEEN ABLE TO REACH LOIS AND I WAS WONDERING--
IN SEATTLE? TONIGHT? OKAY, I'LL TRY TO CATCH HER THERE AND--
AS A MATTER OF FACT, I AM WORKING ON A PIECE ABOUT SUPERMAN AND HIS WALK ACROSS THE COUNTRY.
I THINK IT MAY SURPRISE YOU.
Must There Be a Superman?
by Clark Kent

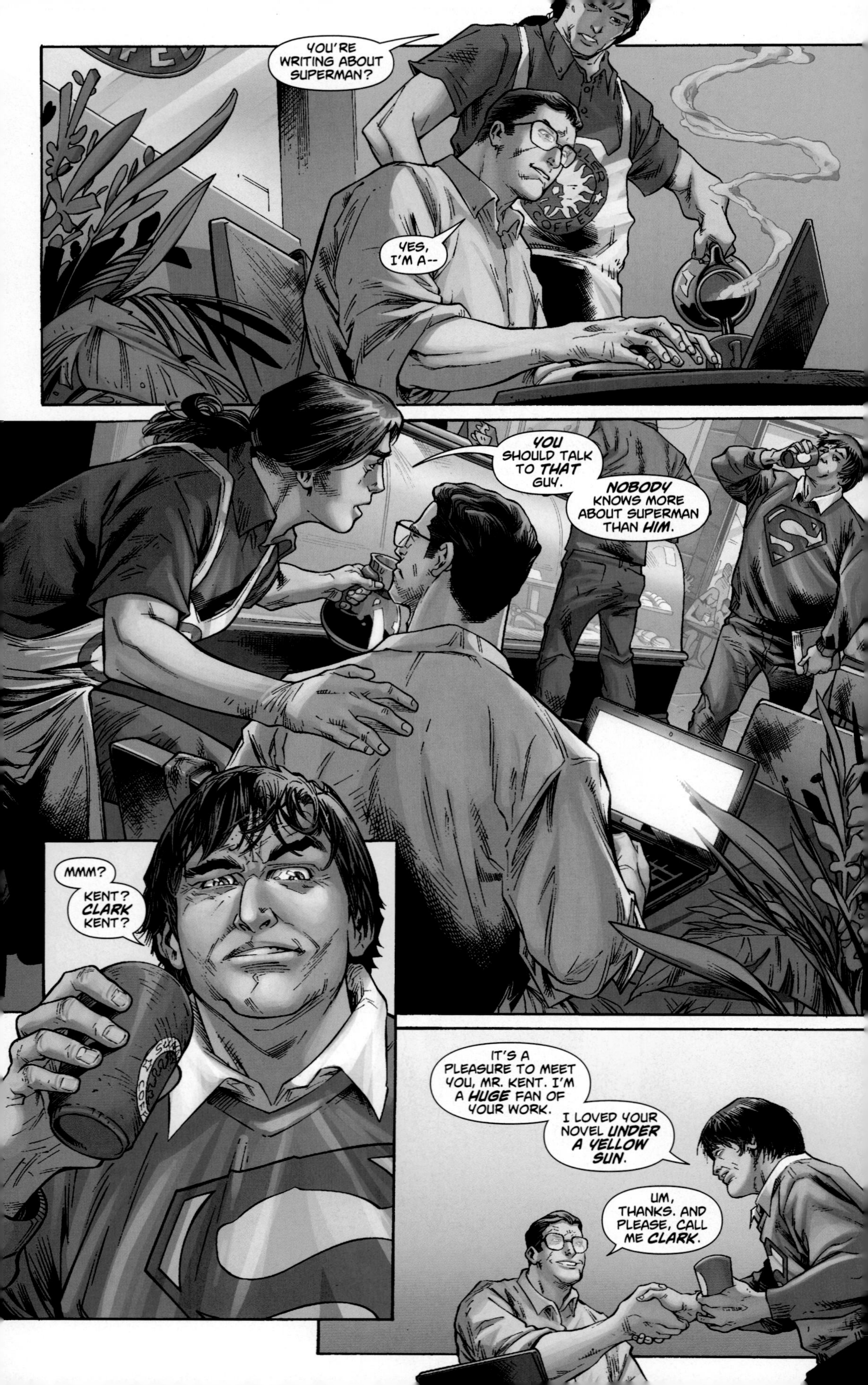
YOU'RE WRITING ABOUT SUPERMAN?
YES, I'M A--
YOU SHOULD TALK TO THAT GUY.
NOBODY KNOWS MORE ABOUT SUPERMAN THAN HIM.
MMM?
KENT? CLARK KENT?
IT'S A PLEASURE TO MEET YOU, MR. KENT. I'M A HUGE FAN OF YOUR WORK.
I LOVED YOUR NOVEL UNDER A YELLOW SUN.
UM, THANKS. AND PLEASE, CALL ME CLARK.

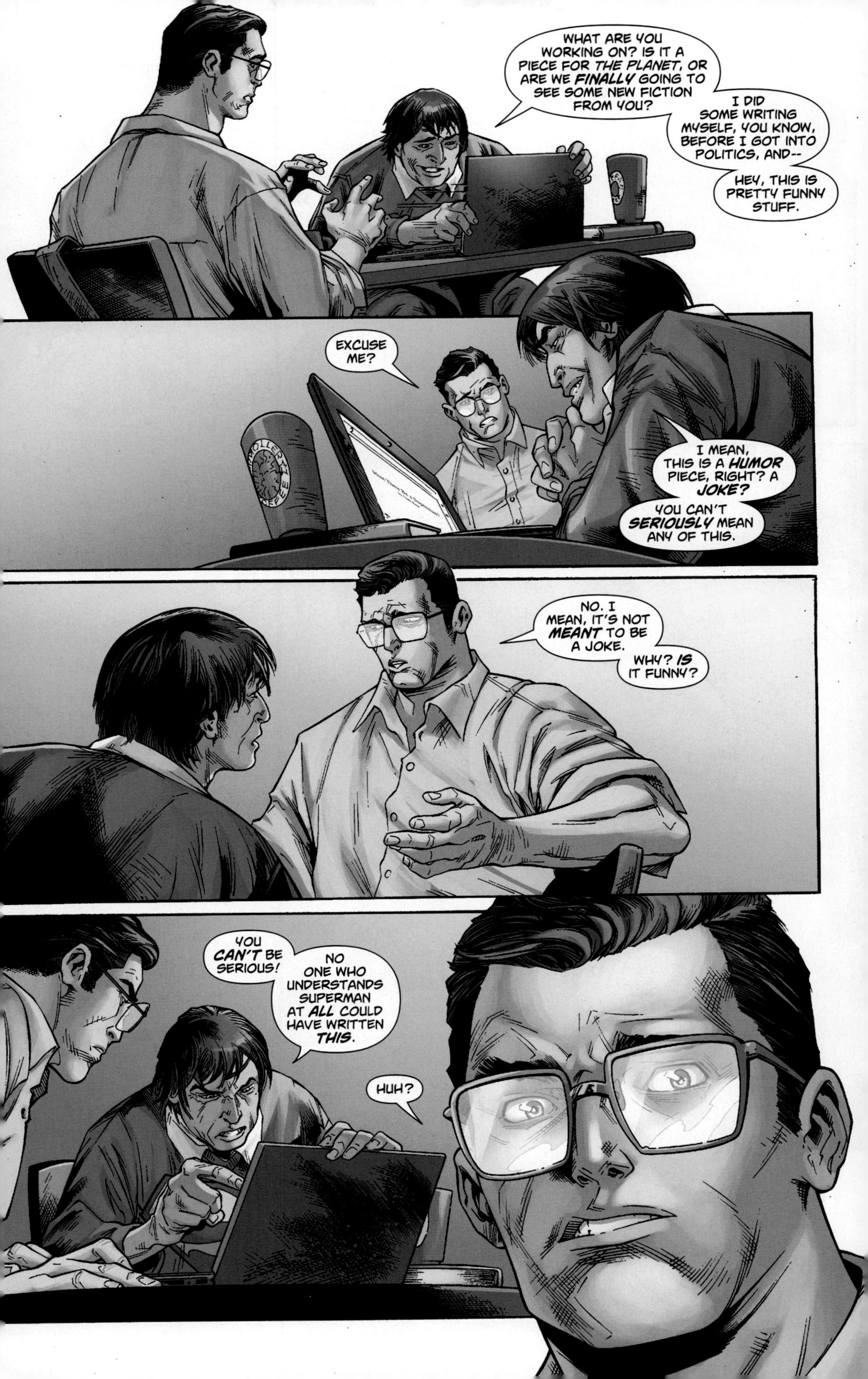
WHAT ARE YOU WORKING ON? IS IT A PIECE FOR THE PLANET, OR ARE WE FINALLY GOING TO SEE SOME NEW FICTION FROM YOU?
I DID SOME WRITING MYSELF, YOU KNOW, BEFORE I GOT INTO POLITICS, AND--
HEY, THIS IS PRETTY FUNNY STUFF.
EXCUSE ME?
I MEAN, THIS IS A HUMOR PIECE, RIGHT? A JOKE?
YOU CAN'T SERIOUSLY MEAN ANY OF THIS.
NO. I MEAN, IT'S NOT MEANT TO BE A JOKE.
WHY? IS IT FUNNY?
YOU CAN'T BE SERIOUS!
NO ONE WHO UNDERSTANDS SUPERMAN AT ALL COULD HAVE WRITTEN THIS.
HUH?

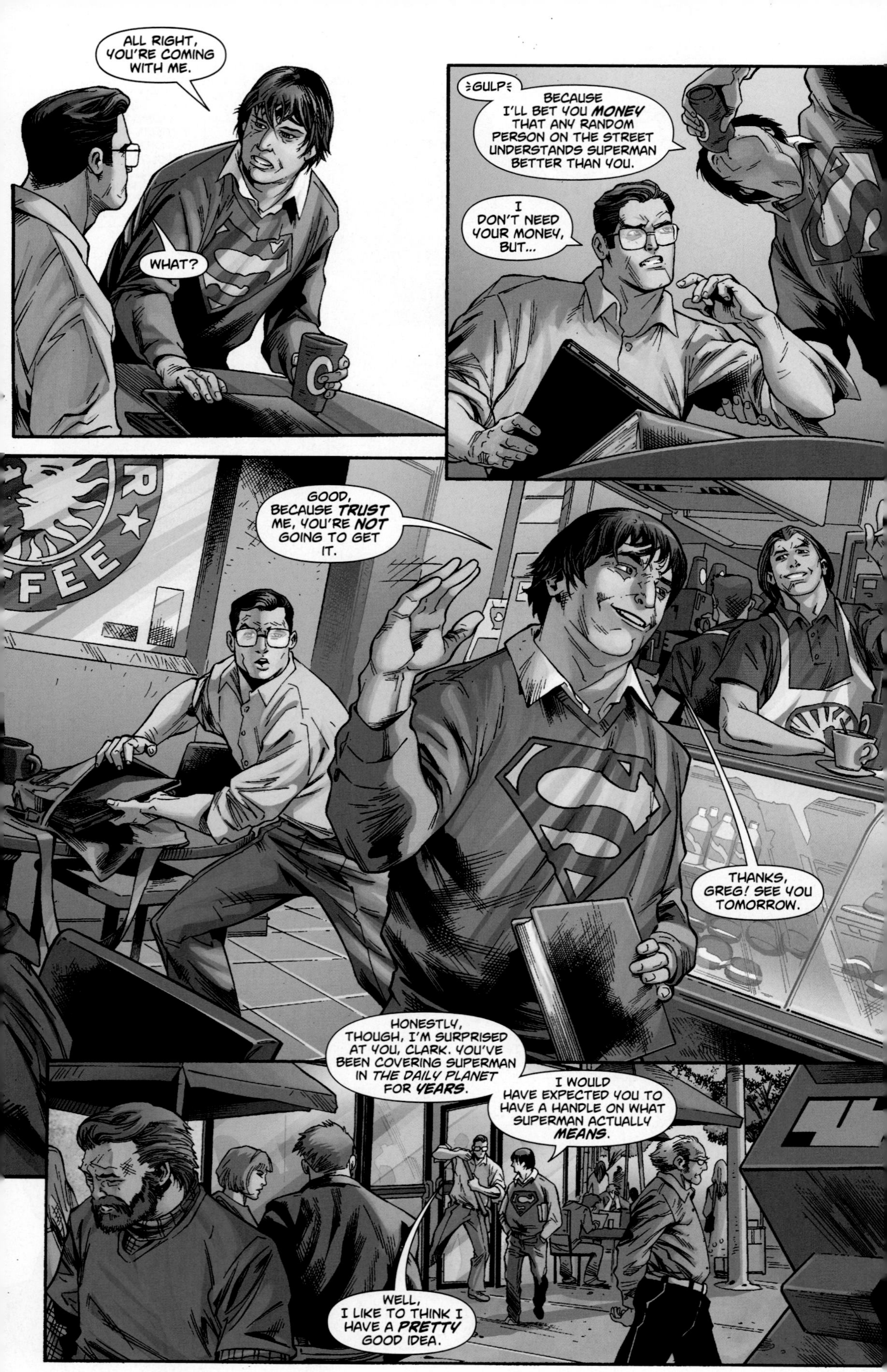
ALL RIGHT, YOU'RE COMING WITH ME.
WHAT?
GULP
BECAUSE I'LL BET YOU MONEY THAT ANY RANDOM PERSON ON THE STREET UNDERSTANDS SUPERMAN BETTER THAN YOU.
I DON'T NEED YOUR MONEY, BUT...
GOOD, BECAUSE TRUST ME, YOU'RE NOT GOING TO GET IT.
FEE
THANKS, GREG! SEE YOU TOMORROW.
HONESTLY, THOUGH, I'M SURPRISED AT YOU, CLARK. YOU'VE BEEN COVERING SUPERMAN IN THE DAILY PLANET FOR YEARS.
I WOULD HAVE EXPECTED YOU TO HAVE A HANDLE ON WHAT SUPERMAN ACTUALLY MEANS.
WELL, I LIKE TO THINK I HAVE A PRETTY GOOD IDEA.

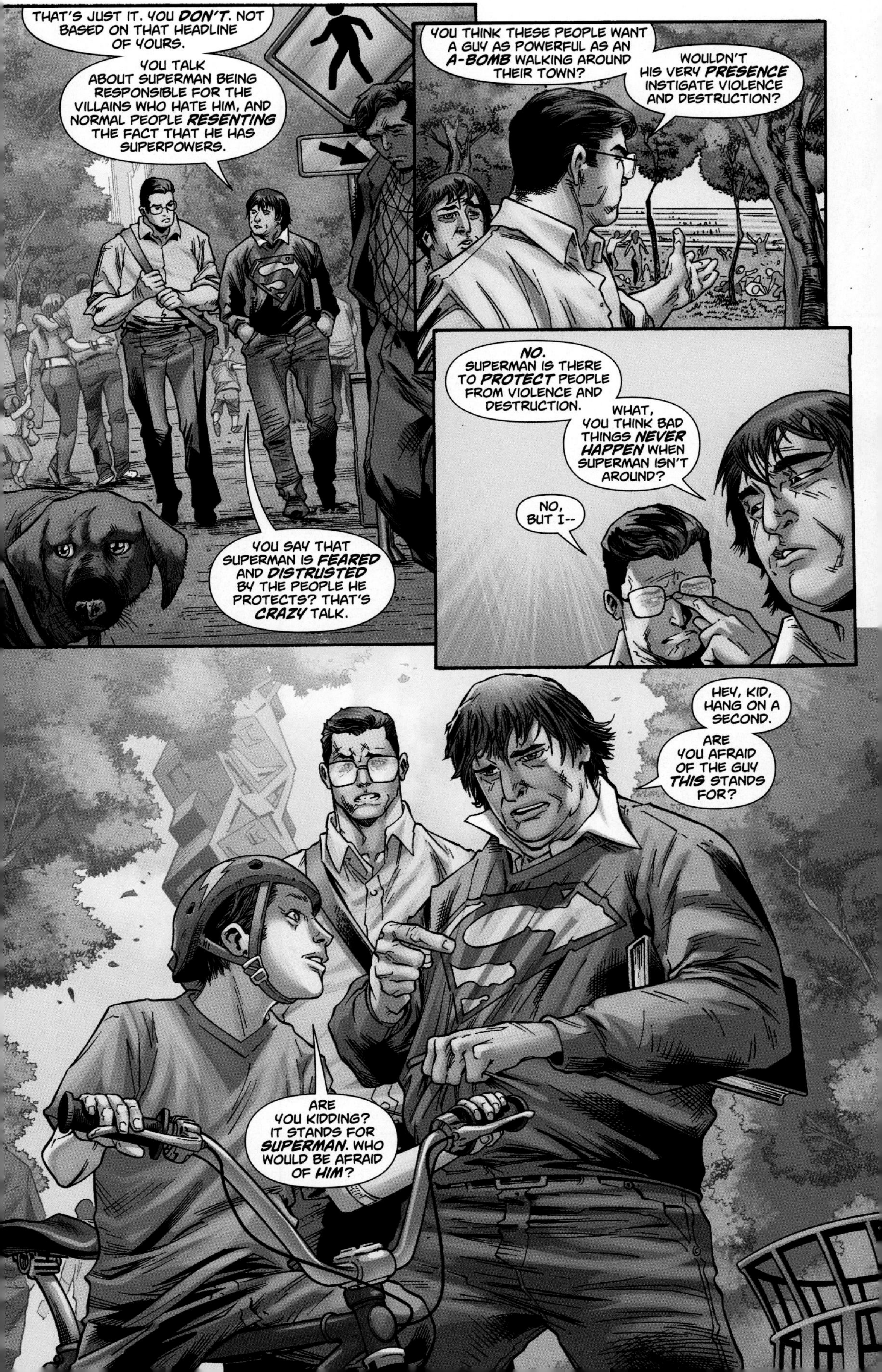
THAT'S JUST IT. YOU DON'T. NOT BASED ON THAT HEADLINE OF YOURS.
YOU TALK ABOUT SUPERMAN BEING RESPONSIBLE FOR THE VILLAINS WHO HATE HIM, AND NORMAL PEOPLE RESENTING THE FACT THAT HE HAS SUPERPOWERS.
YOU SAY THAT SUPERMAN IS FEARED AND DISTRUSTED BY THE PEOPLE HE PROTECTS? THAT'S CRAZY TALK.
YOU THINK THESE PEOPLE WANT A GUY AS POWERFUL AS AN A-BOMB WALKING AROUND THEIR TOWN?
WOULDN'T HIS VERY PRESENCE INSTIGATE VIOLENCE AND DESTRUCTION?
NO. SUPERMAN IS THERE TO PROTECT PEOPLE FROM VIOLENCE AND DESTRUCTION.
WHAT, YOU THINK BAD THINGS NEVER HAPPEN WHEN SUPERMAN ISN'T AROUND?
NO, BUT I--
HEY, KID, HANG ON A SECOND.
ARE YOU AFRAID OF THE GUY THIS STANDS FOR?
ARE YOU KIDDING? IT STANDS FOR SUPERMAN. WHO WOULD BE AFRAID OF HIM?

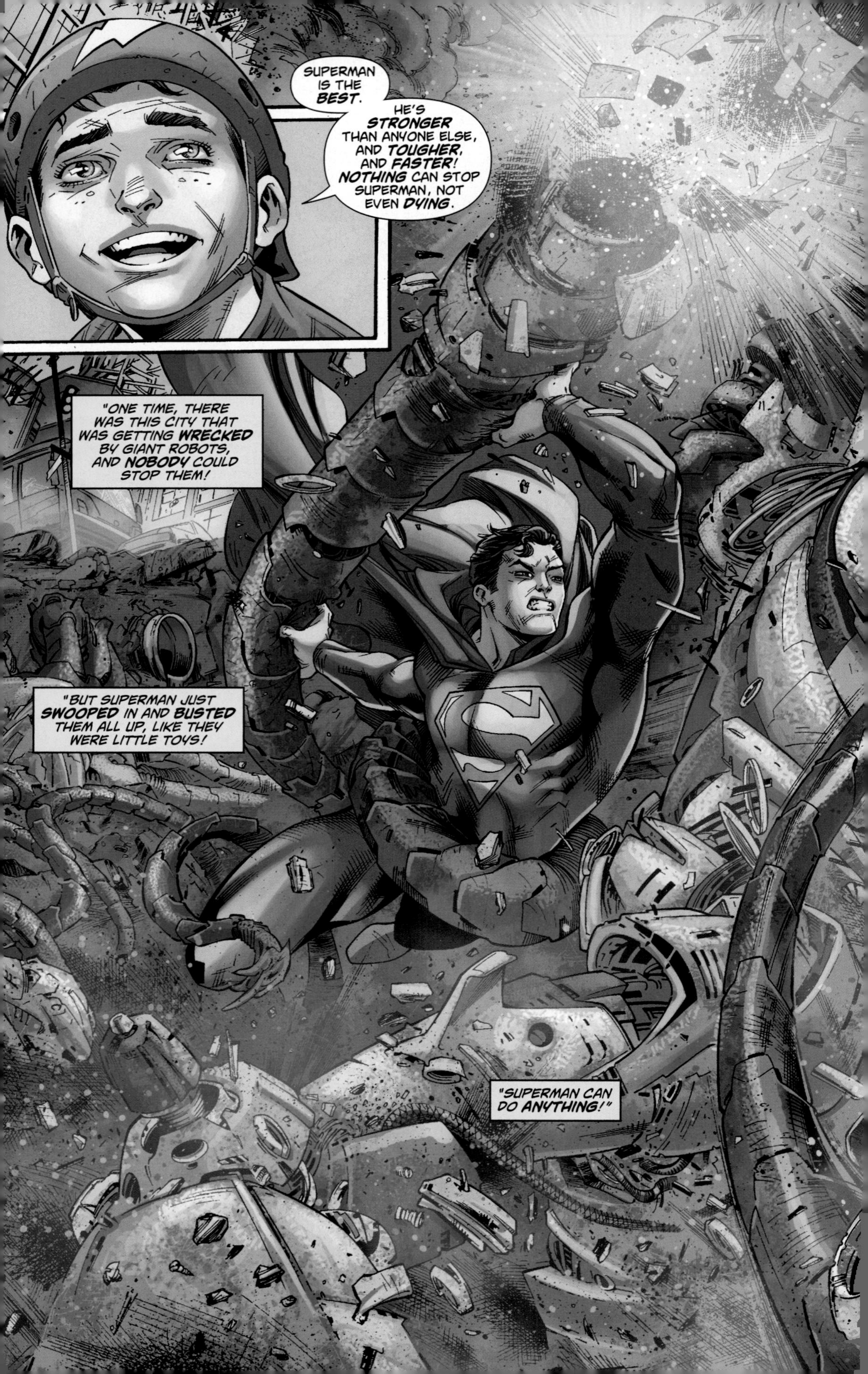
SUPERMAN IS THE BEST.
HE'S STRONGER THAN ANYONE ELSE, AND TOUGHER, AND FASTER! NOTHING CAN STOP SUPERMAN, NOT EVEN DYING.
"ONE TIME, THERE WAS THIS CITY THAT WAS GETTING WRECKED BY GIANT ROBOTS, AND NOBODY COULD STOP THEM!
"BUT SUPERMAN JUST SWOOPED IN AND BUSTED THEM ALL UP, LIKE THEY WERE LITTLE TOYS!
"SUPERMAN CAN DO ANYTHING!"

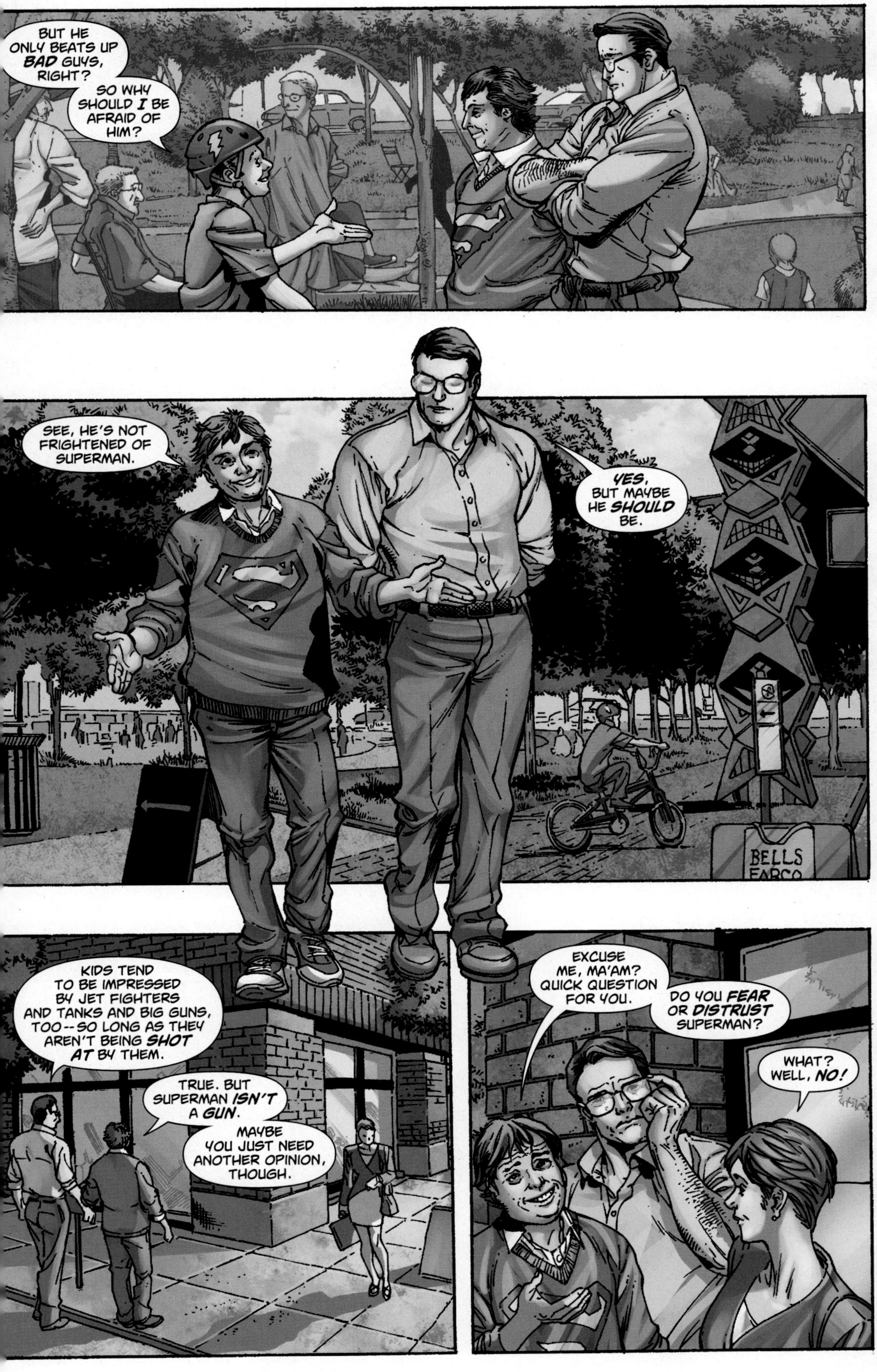
BUT HE ONLY BEATS UP BAD GUYS, RIGHT?
SO WHY SHOULD I BE AFRAID OF HIM?
SEE, HE'S NOT FRIGHTENED OF SUPERMAN.
YES, BUT MAYBE HE SHOULD BE.
BELLS FARGO
KIDS TEND TO BE IMPRESSED BY JET FIGHTERS AND TANKS AND BIG GUNS, TOO--SO LONG AS THEY AREN'T BEING SHOT AT BY THEM.
TRUE. BUT SUPERMAN ISN'T A GUN.
MAYBE YOU JUST NEED ANOTHER OPINION, THOUGH.
EXCUSE ME, MA'AM? QUICK QUESTION FOR YOU.
DO YOU FEAR OR DISTRUST SUPERMAN?
WHAT? WELL, NO!

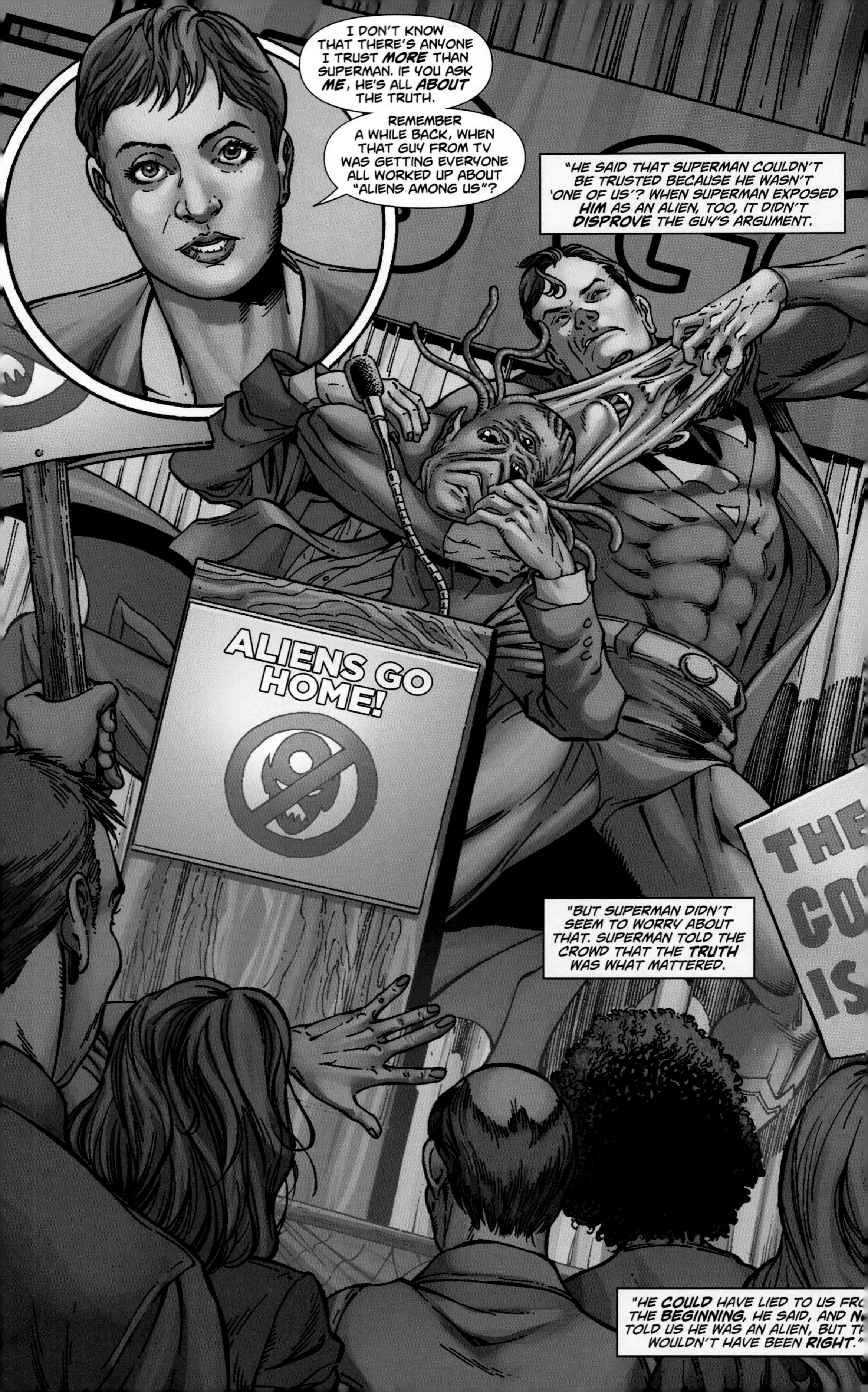
I DON'T KNOW THAT THERE'S ANYONE I TRUST MORE THAN SUPERMAN. IF YOU ASK ME, HE'S ALL ABOUT THE TRUTH.
REMEMBER A WHILE BACK, WHEN THAT GUY FROM TV WAS GETTING EVERYONE ALL WORKED UP ABOUT "ALIENS AMONG US"?
"HE SAID THAT SUPERMAN COULDN'T BE TRUSTED BECAUSE HE WASN'T 'ONE OF US'? WHEN SUPERMAN EXPOSED HIM AS AN ALIEN, TOO, IT DIDN'T DISPROVE THE GUY'S ARGUMENT.
ALIENS GO HOME!
"BUT SUPERMAN DIDN'T SEEM TO WORRY ABOUT THAT. SUPERMAN TOLD THE CROWD THAT THE TRUTH WAS WHAT MATTERED.
"HE COULD HAVE LIED TO US FRO THE BEGINNING, HE SAID, AND N TOLD US HE WAS AN ALIEN, BUT T WOULDN'T HAVE BEEN RIGHT."

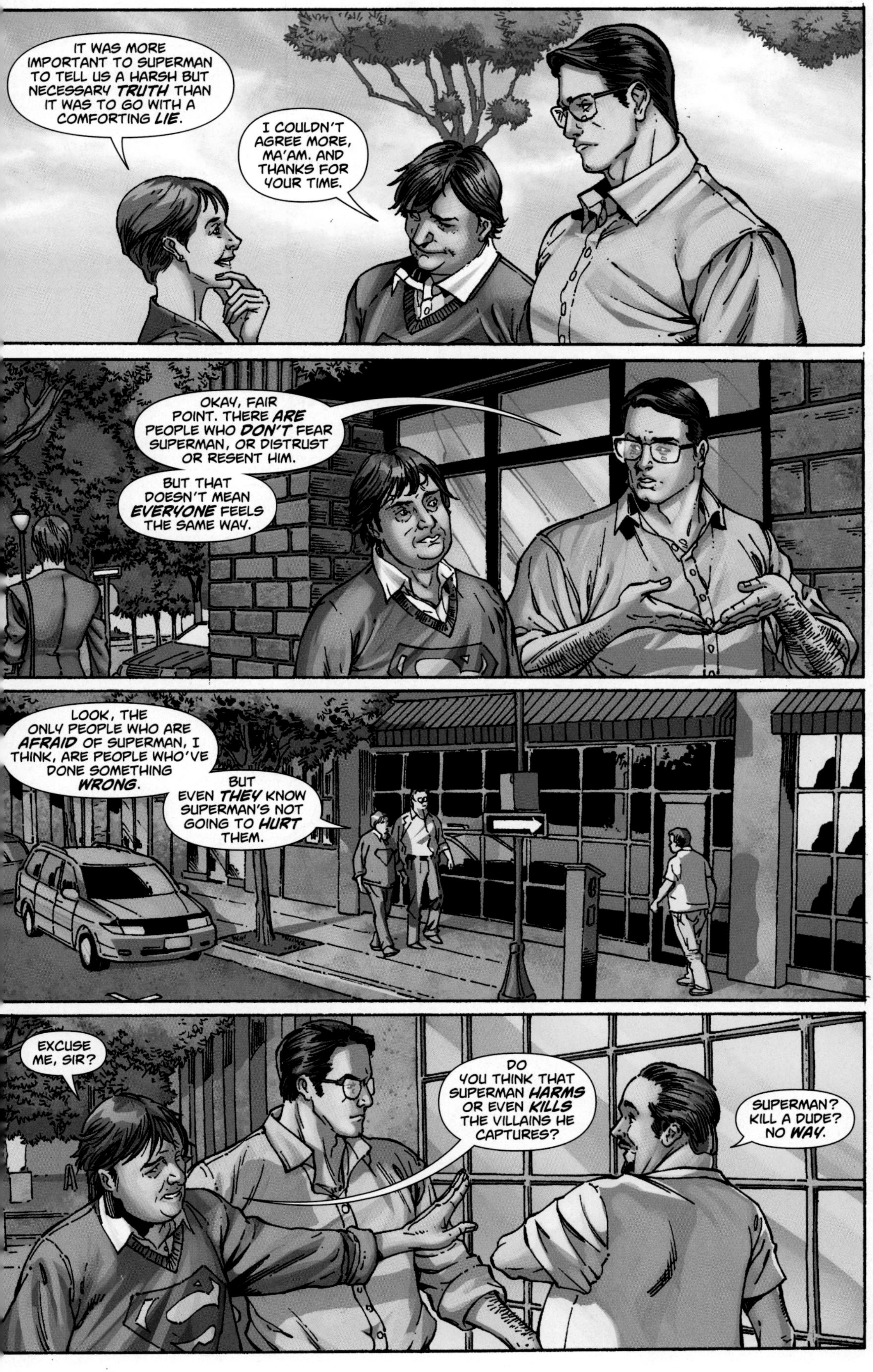
IT WAS MORE IMPORTANT TO SUPERMAN TO TELL US A HARSH BUT NECESSARY TRUTH THAN IT WAS TO GO WITH A COMFORTING LIE.
I COULDN'T AGREE MORE, MA'AM. AND THANKS FOR YOUR TIME.
OKAY, FAIR POINT. THERE ARE PEOPLE WHO DON'T FEAR SUPERMAN, OR DISTRUST OR RESENT HIM.
BUT THAT DOESN'T MEAN EVERYONE FEELS THE SAME WAY.
LOOK, THE ONLY PEOPLE WHO ARE AFRAID OF SUPERMAN, I THINK, ARE PEOPLE WHO'VE DONE SOMETHING WRONG.
BUT EVEN THEY KNOW SUPERMAN'S NOT GOING TO HURT THEM.
EXCUSE ME, SIR?
DO YOU THINK THAT SUPERMAN HARMS OR EVEN KILLS THE VILLAINS HE CAPTURES?
SUPERMAN? KILL A DUDE? NO WAY.

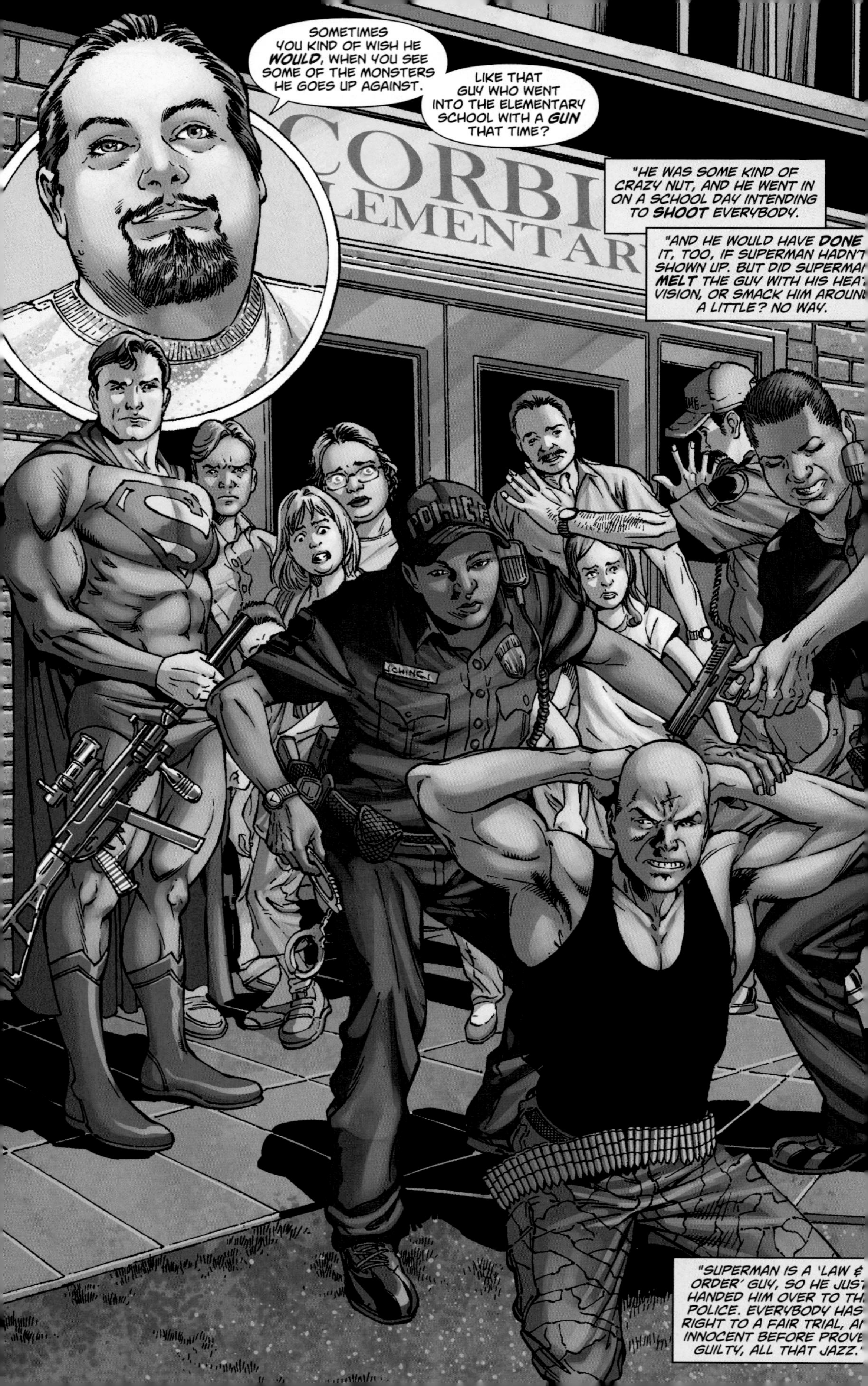
SOMETIMES YOU KIND OF WISH HE WOULD, WHEN YOU SEE SOME OF THE MONSTERS HE GOES UP AGAINST.
LIKE THAT GUY WHO WENT INTO THE ELEMENTARY SCHOOL WITH A GUN THAT TIME?
CORBI
LEMENTAR
"HE WAS SOME KIND OF CRAZY NUT, AND HE WENT IN ON A SCHOOL DAY INTENDING TO SHOOT EVERYBODY.
"AND HE WOULD HAVE DONE IT, TOO, IF SUPERMAN HADN'T SHOWN UP. BUT DID SUPERMAN MELT THE GUY WITH HIS HEAT VISION, OR SMACK HIM AROUND A LITTLE? NO WAY.
POLICE
"SUPERMAN IS A 'LAW & ORDER' GUY, SO HE JUST HANDED HIM OVER TO THE POLICE. EVERYBODY HAS A RIGHT TO A FAIR TRIAL, AND INNOCENT BEFORE PROVEN GUILTY, ALL THAT JAZZ."

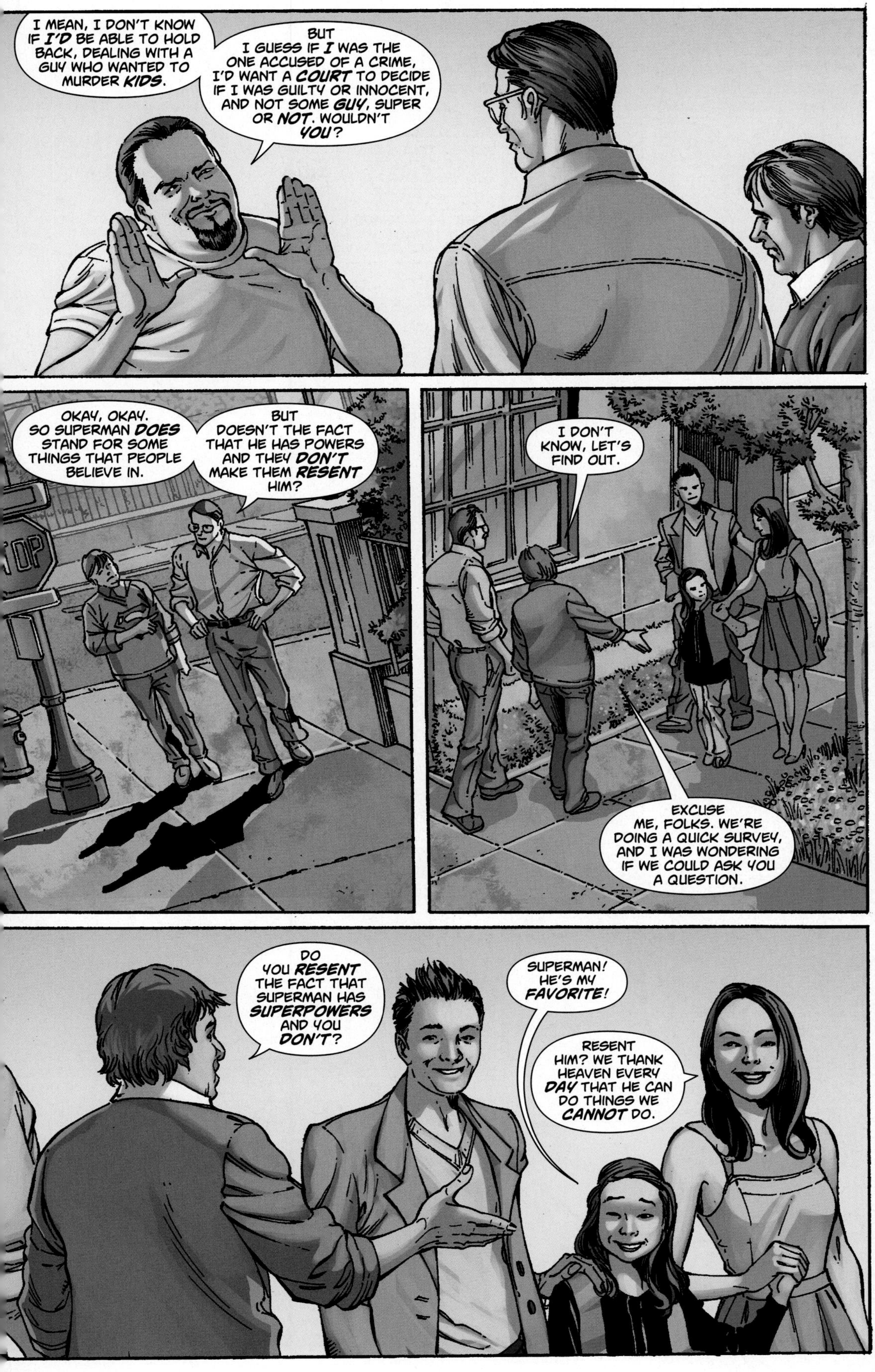
I MEAN, I DON'T KNOW IF I'D BE ABLE TO HOLD BACK, DEALING WITH A GUY WHO WANTED TO MURDER KIDS.
BUT I GUESS IF I WAS THE ONE ACCUSED OF A CRIME, I'D WANT A COURT TO DECIDE IF I WAS GUILTY OR INNOCENT, AND NOT SOME GUY, SUPER OR NOT. WOULDN'T YOU?
OKAY, OKAY. SO SUPERMAN DOES STAND FOR SOME THINGS THAT PEOPLE BELIEVE IN.
BUT DOESN'T THE FACT THAT HE HAS POWERS AND THEY DON'T MAKE THEM RESENT HIM?
I DON'T KNOW, LET'S FIND OUT.
EXCUSE ME, FOLKS. WE'RE DOING A QUICK SURVEY, AND I WAS WONDERING IF WE COULD ASK YOU A QUESTION.
DO YOU RESENT THE FACT THAT SUPERMAN HAS SUPERPOWERS AND YOU DON'T?
SUPERMAN! HE'S MY FAVORITE!
RESENT HIM? WE THANK HEAVEN EVERY DAY THAT HE CAN DO THINGS WE CANNOT DO.

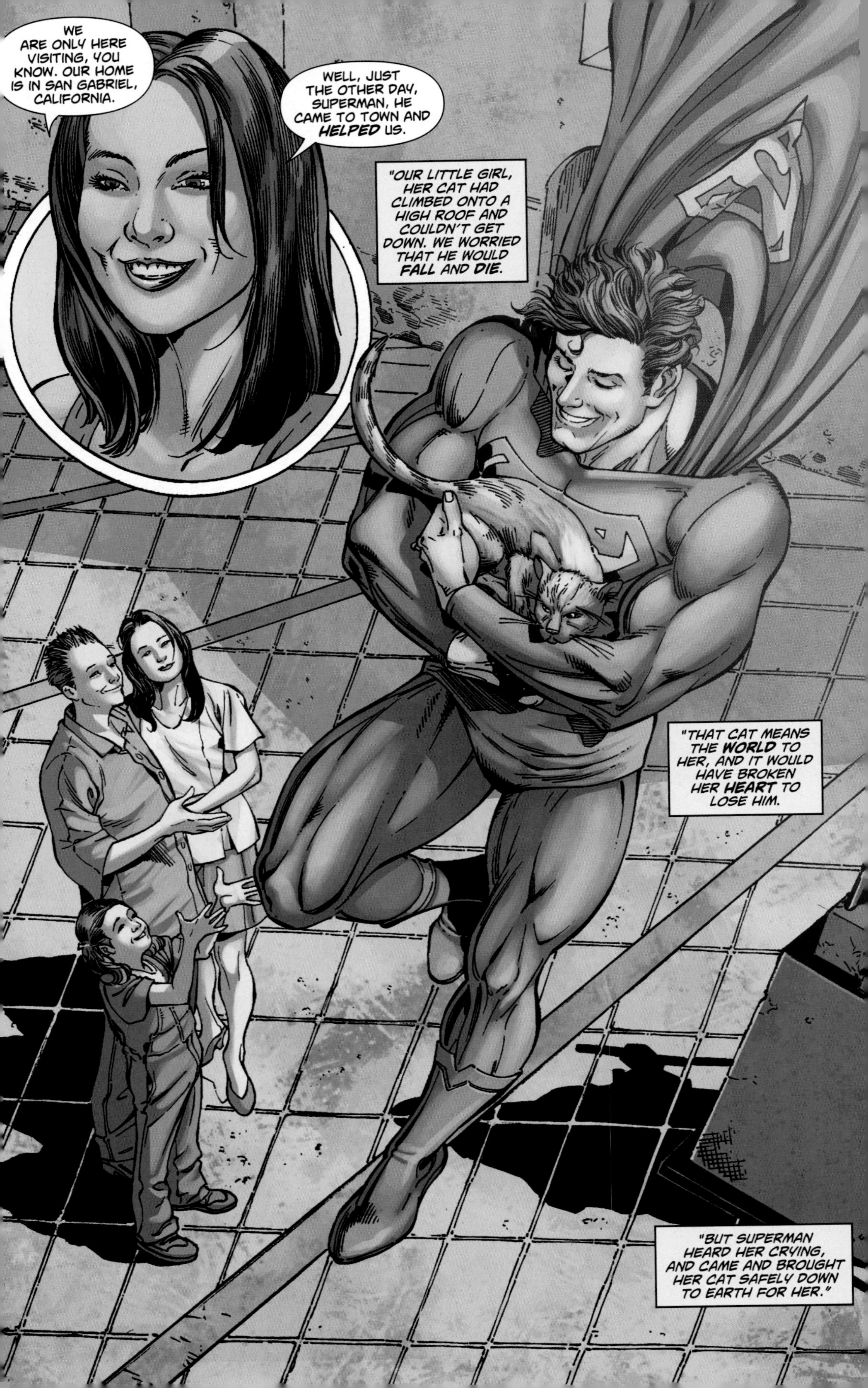
WE ARE ONLY HERE VISITING, YOU KNOW. OUR HOME IS IN SAN GABRIEL, CALIFORNIA.
WELL, JUST THE OTHER DAY, SUPERMAN, HE CAME TO TOWN AND HELPED US.
"OUR LITTLE GIRL, HER CAT HAD CLIMBED ONTO A HIGH ROOF AND COULDN'T GET DOWN. WE WORRIED THAT HE WOULD FALL AND DIE.
"THAT CAT MEANS THE WORLD TO HER, AND IT WOULD HAVE BROKEN HER HEART TO LOSE HIM.
"BUT SUPERMAN HEARD HER CRYING, AND CAME AND BROUGHT HER CAT SAFELY DOWN TO EARTH FOR HER."

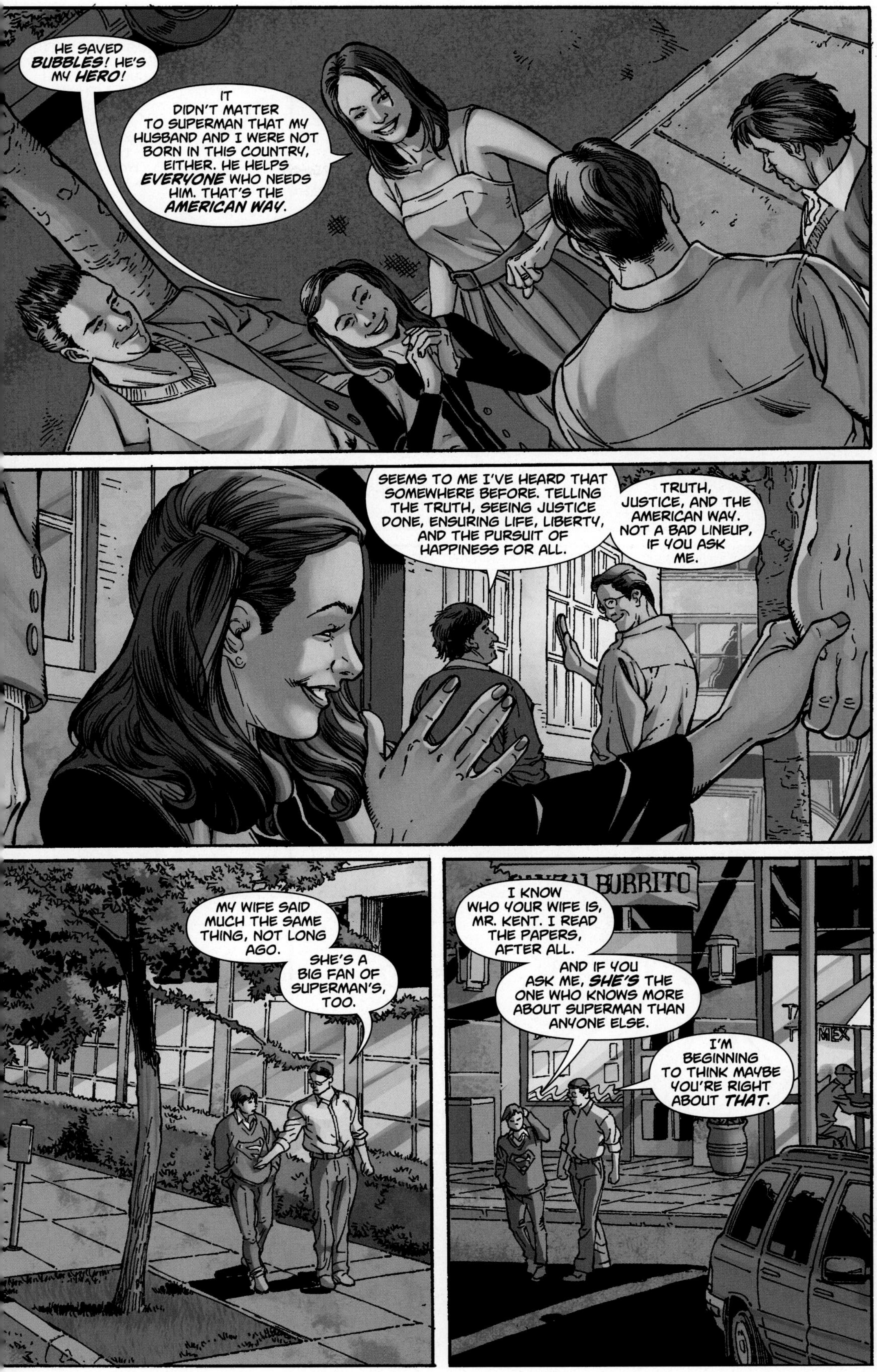
HE SAVED BUBBLES! HE'S MY HERO!
IT DIDN'T MATTER TO SUPERMAN THAT MY HUSBAND AND I WERE NOT BORN IN THIS COUNTRY, EITHER. HE HELPS EVERYONE WHO NEEDS HIM. THAT'S THE AMERICAN WAY.
SEEMS TO ME I'VE HEARD THAT SOMEWHERE BEFORE. TELLING THE TRUTH, SEEING JUSTICE DONE, ENSURING LIFE, LIBERTY, AND THE PURSUIT OF HAPPINESS FOR ALL.
TRUTH, JUSTICE, AND THE AMERICAN WAY. NOT A BAD LINEUP, IF YOU ASK ME.
MY WIFE SAID MUCH THE SAME THING, NOT LONG AGO.
SHE'S A BIG FAN OF SUPERMAN'S, TOO.
BURRITO
I KNOW WHO YOUR WIFE IS, MR. KENT. I READ THE PAPERS, AFTER ALL.
AND IF YOU ASK ME, SHE'S THE ONE WHO KNOWS MORE ABOUT SUPERMAN THAN ANYONE ELSE.
I'M BEGINNING TO THINK MAYBE YOU'RE RIGHT ABOUT THAT.

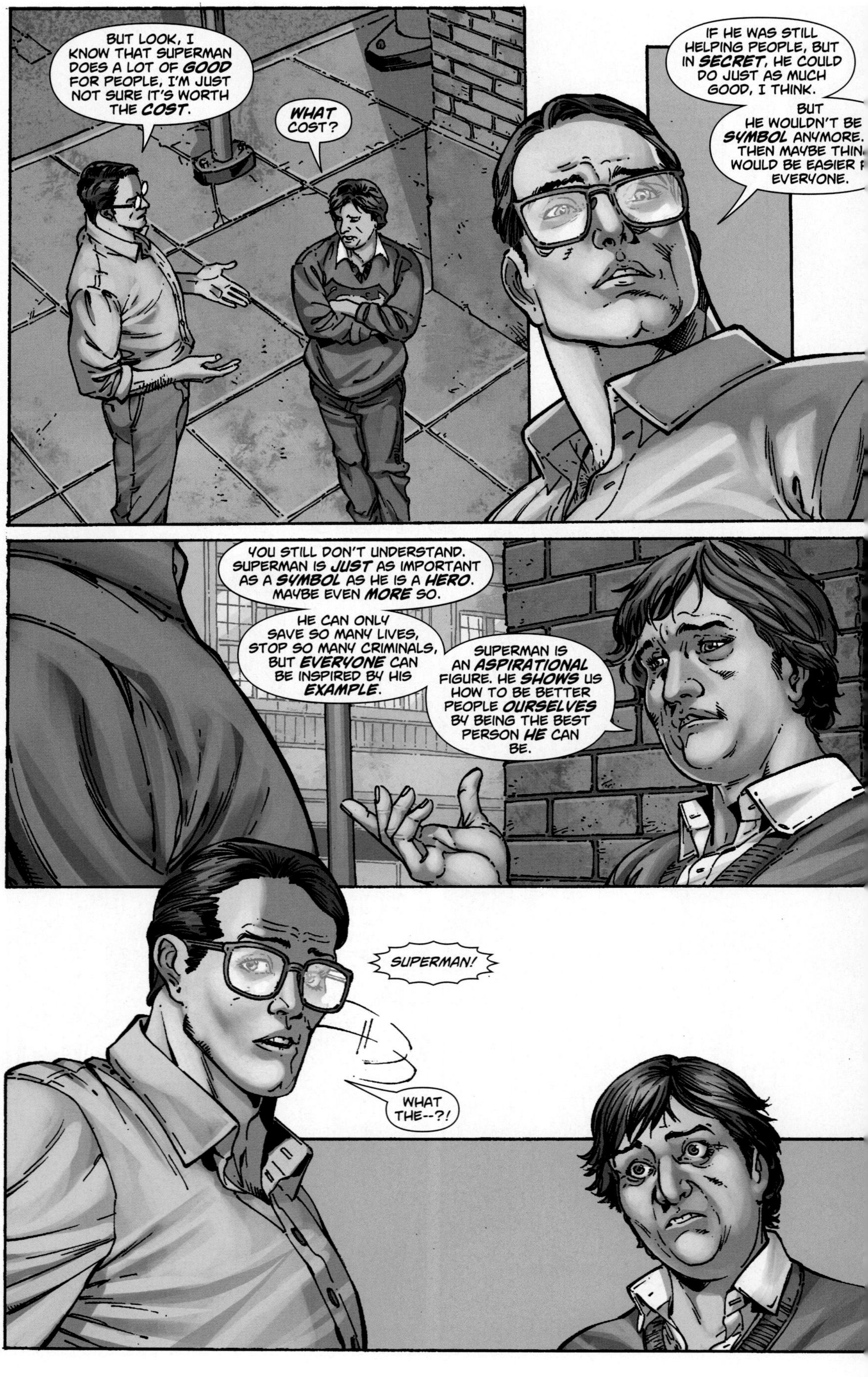
BUT LOOK, I KNOW THAT SUPERMAN DOES A LOT OF GOOD FOR PEOPLE, I'M JUST NOT SURE IT'S WORTH THE COST.
WHAT COST?
IF HE WAS STILL HELPING PEOPLE, BUT IN SECRET, HE COULD DO JUST AS MUCH GOOD, I THINK.
BUT HE WOULDN'T BE
SYMBOL ANYMORE. THEN MAYBE THIN
WOULD BE EASIER
EVERYONE.
YOU STILL DON'T UNDERSTAND. SUPERMAN IS JUST AS IMPORTANT AS A SYMBOL AS HE IS A HERO. MAYBE EVEN MORE SO.
HE CAN ONLY SAVE SO MANY LIVES, STOP SO MANY CRIMINALS, BUT EVERYONE CAN BE INSPIRED BY HIS EXAMPLE.
SUPERMAN IS AN ASPIRATIONAL FIGURE. HE SHOWS US HOW TO BE BETTER PEOPLE OURSELVES BY BEING THE BEST PERSON HE CAN BE.
SUPERMAN!
WHAT THE--?!

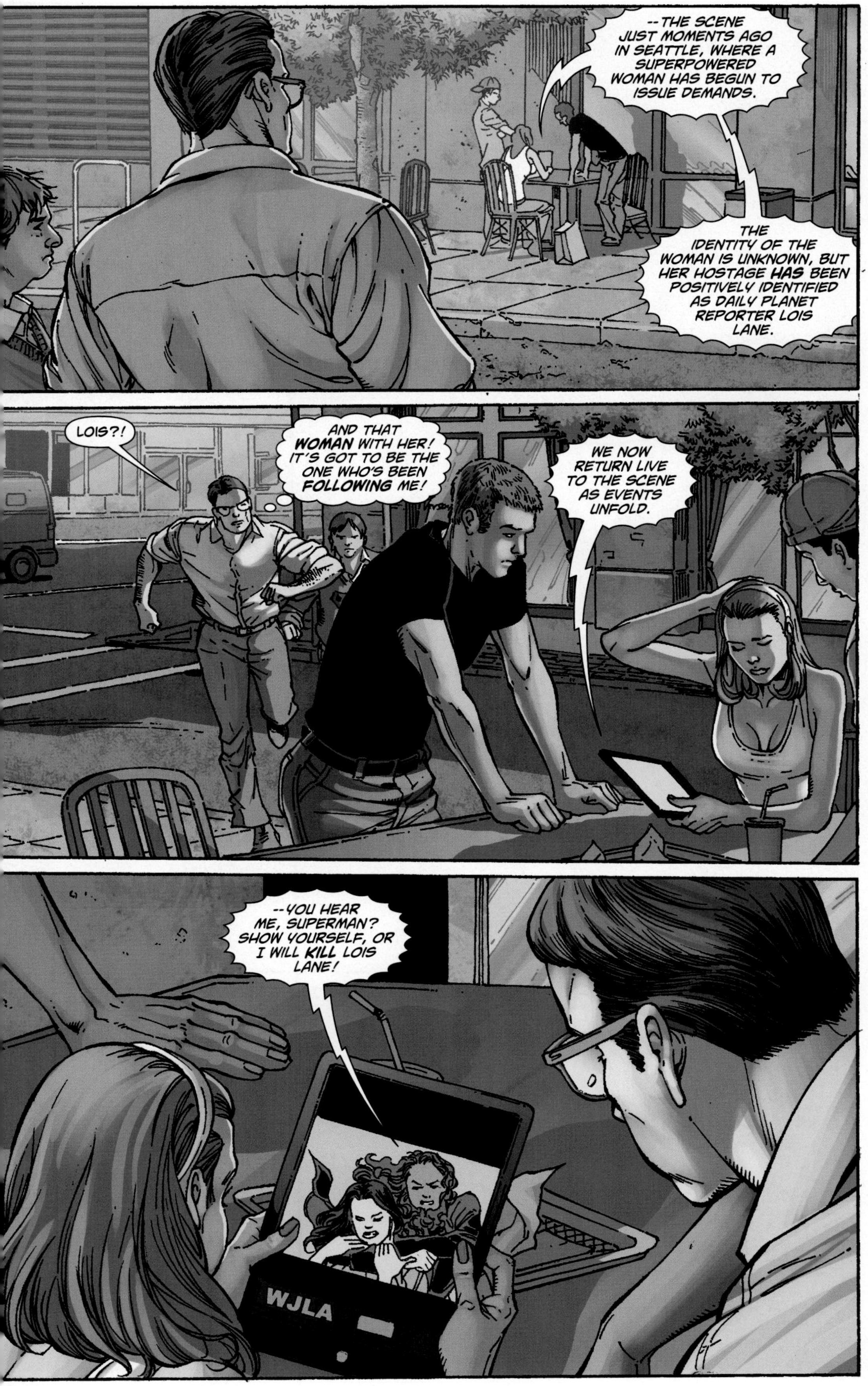
--THE SCENE JUST MOMENTS AGO IN SEATTLE, WHERE A SUPERPOWERED WOMAN HAS BEGUN TO ISSUE DEMANDS.
THE IDENTITY OF THE WOMAN IS UNKNOWN, BUT HER HOSTAGE HAS BEEN POSITIVELY IDENTIFIED AS DAILY PLANET REPORTER LOIS LANE.
LOIS?!
AND THAT WOMAN WITH HER! IT'S GOT TO BE THE ONE WHO'S BEEN FOLLOWING ME!
WE NOW RETURN LIVE TO THE SCENE AS EVENTS UNFOLD.
--YOU HEAR ME, SUPERMAN? SHOW YOURSELF, OR I WILL KILL LOIS LANE!
WJLA

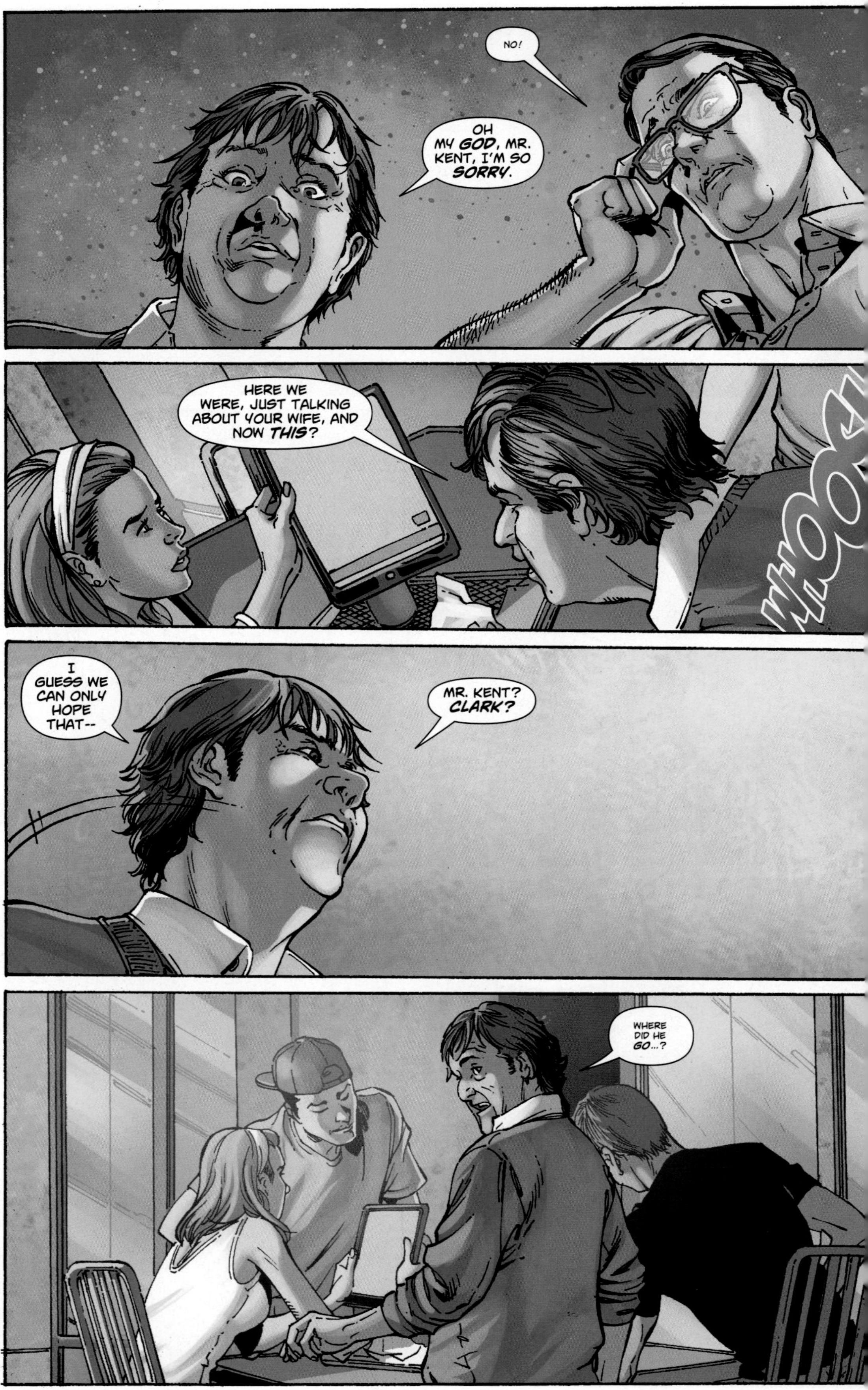
OH MY GOD, MR. KENT, I'M SO SORRY.
NO!
HERE WE WERE, JUST TALKING ABOUT YOUR WIFE, AND NOW THIS?
WHOOSH
I GUESS WE CAN ONLY HOPE THAT--
MR. KENT? CLARK?
WHERE DID HE GO...?

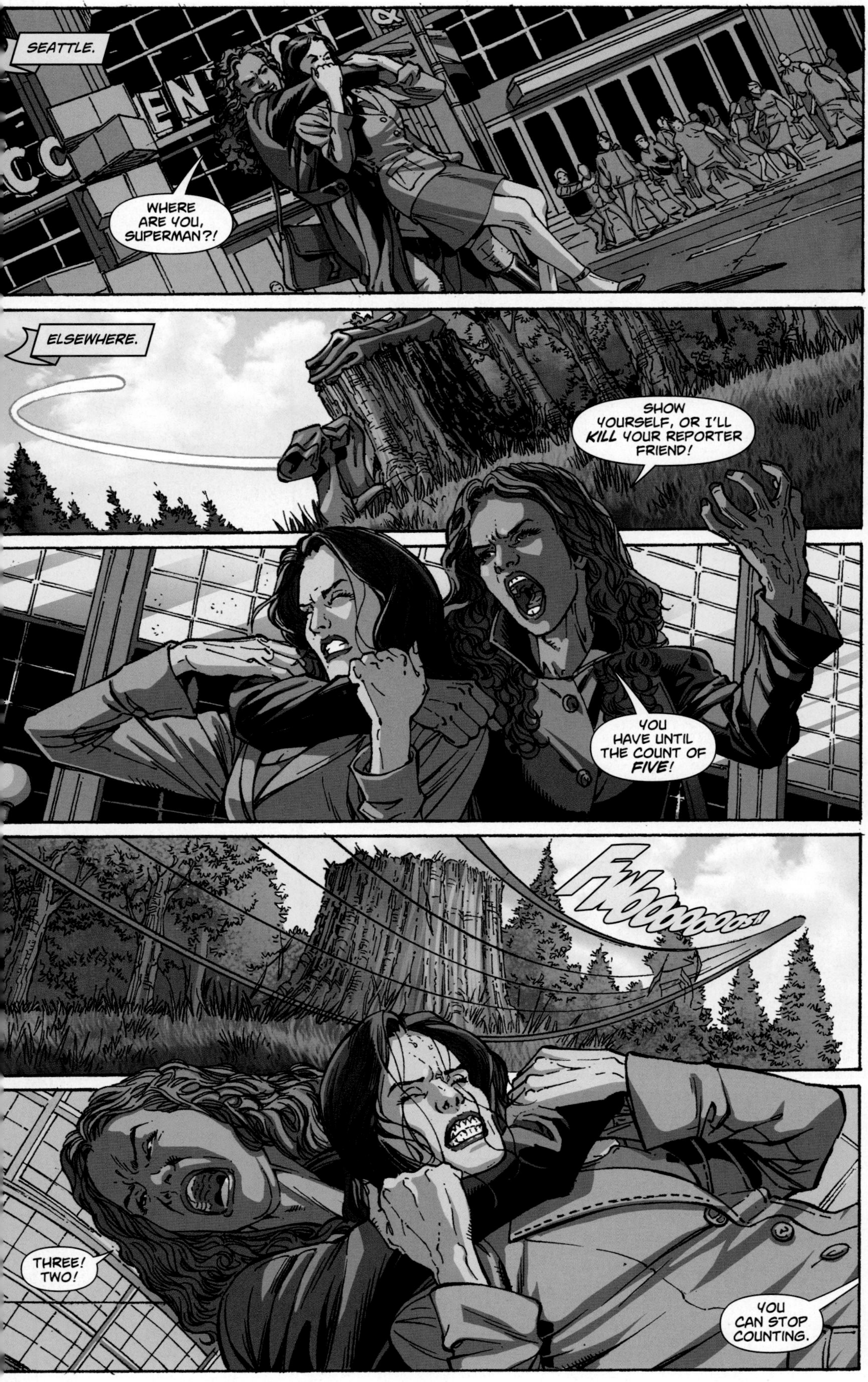
SEATTLE.
WHERE ARE YOU, SUPERMAN?!
ELSEWHERE.
SHOW YOURSELF, OR I'LL KILL YOUR REPORTER FRIEND!
YOU HAVE UNTIL THE COUNT OF FIVE!
FWOOOOOOSH
THREE! TWO!
YOU CAN STOP COUNTING.

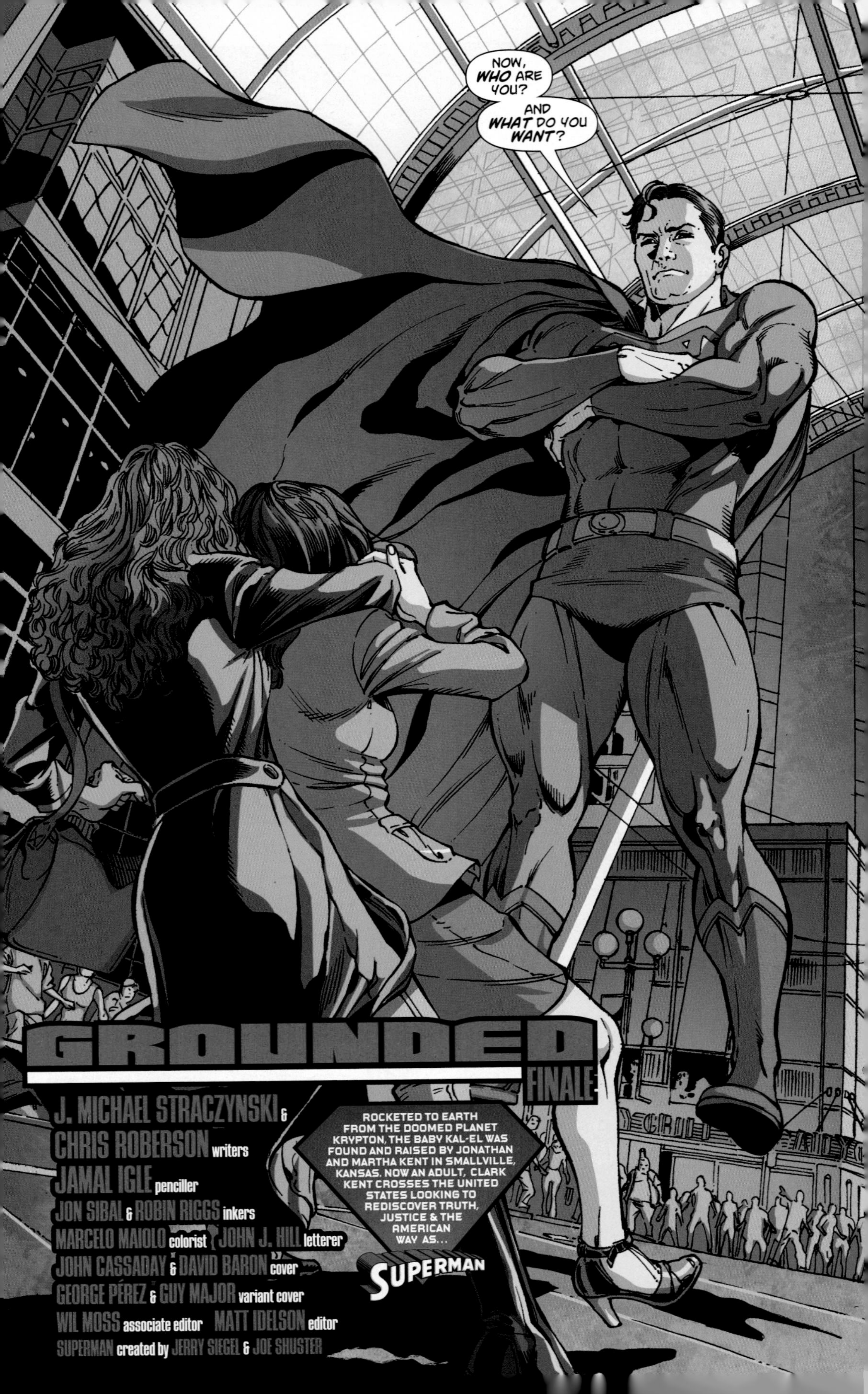
NOW, WHO ARE YOU?
AND WHAT DO YOU WANT?
GROUNDED FINALE
J. MICHAEL STRACZYNSKI & CHRIS ROBERSON writers
JAMAL IGLE penciller
JON SIBAL & ROBIN RIGGS inkers
MARCELO MAIOLO colorist JOHN J. HILL letterer
JOHN CASSADAY & DAVID BARON cover
GEORGE PÉREZ & GUY MAJOR variant cover
WIL MOSS associate editor MATT IDELSON editor
SUPERMAN created by JERRY SIEGEL & JOE SHUSTER
ROCKETED TO EARTH FROM THE DOOMED PLANET KRYPTON, THE BABY KAL-EL WAS FOUND AND RAISED BY JONATHAN AND MARTHA KENT IN SMALLVILLE, KANSAS. NOW AN ADULT, CLARK KENT CROSSES THE UNITED STATES LOOKING TO REDISCOVER TRUTH, JUSTICE & THE AMERICAN WAY AS...
SUPERMAN

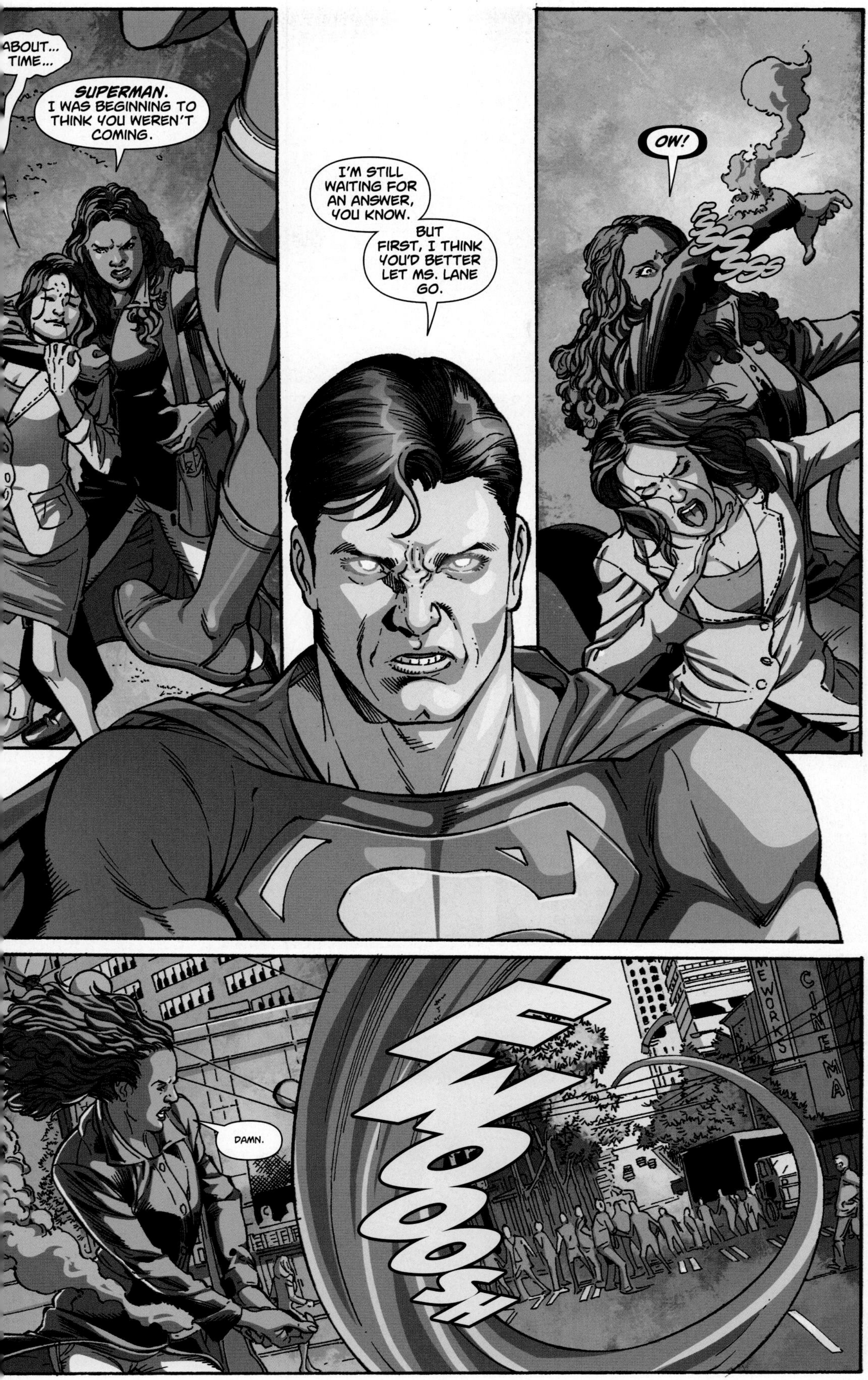
ABOUT... TIME...
SUPERMAN. I WAS BEGINNING TO THINK YOU WEREN'T COMING.
I'M STILL WAITING FOR AN ANSWER, YOU KNOW.
BUT FIRST, I THINK YOU'D BETTER LET MS. LANE GO.
OW!
FSSSSS
DAMN.
FWOOOSH
CINEMA

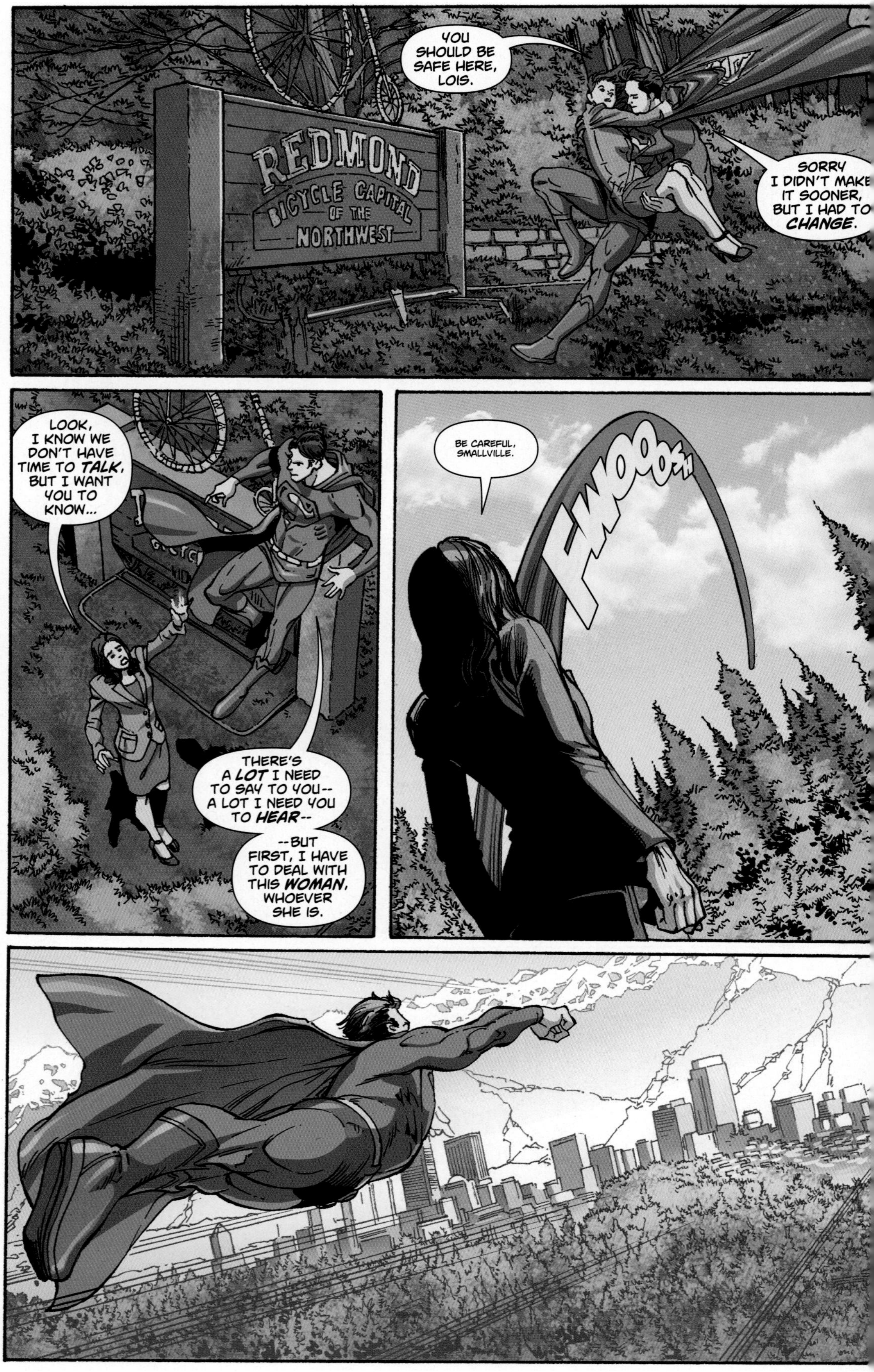
REDMOND
BICYCLE CAPITAL OF THE NORTHWEST
YOU SHOULD BE SAFE HERE, LOIS.
SORRY I DIDN'T MAKE IT SOONER, BUT I HAD TO *CHANGE*.
LOOK, I KNOW WE DON'T HAVE TIME TO *TALK*, BUT I WANT YOU TO KNOW...
THERE'S A *LOT* I NEED TO SAY TO YOU-- A LOT I NEED YOU TO *HEAR*--
--BUT FIRST, I HAVE TO DEAL WITH THIS *WOMAN*, WHOEVER SHE IS.
BE CAREFUL, SMALLVILLE.
FWOOOSH

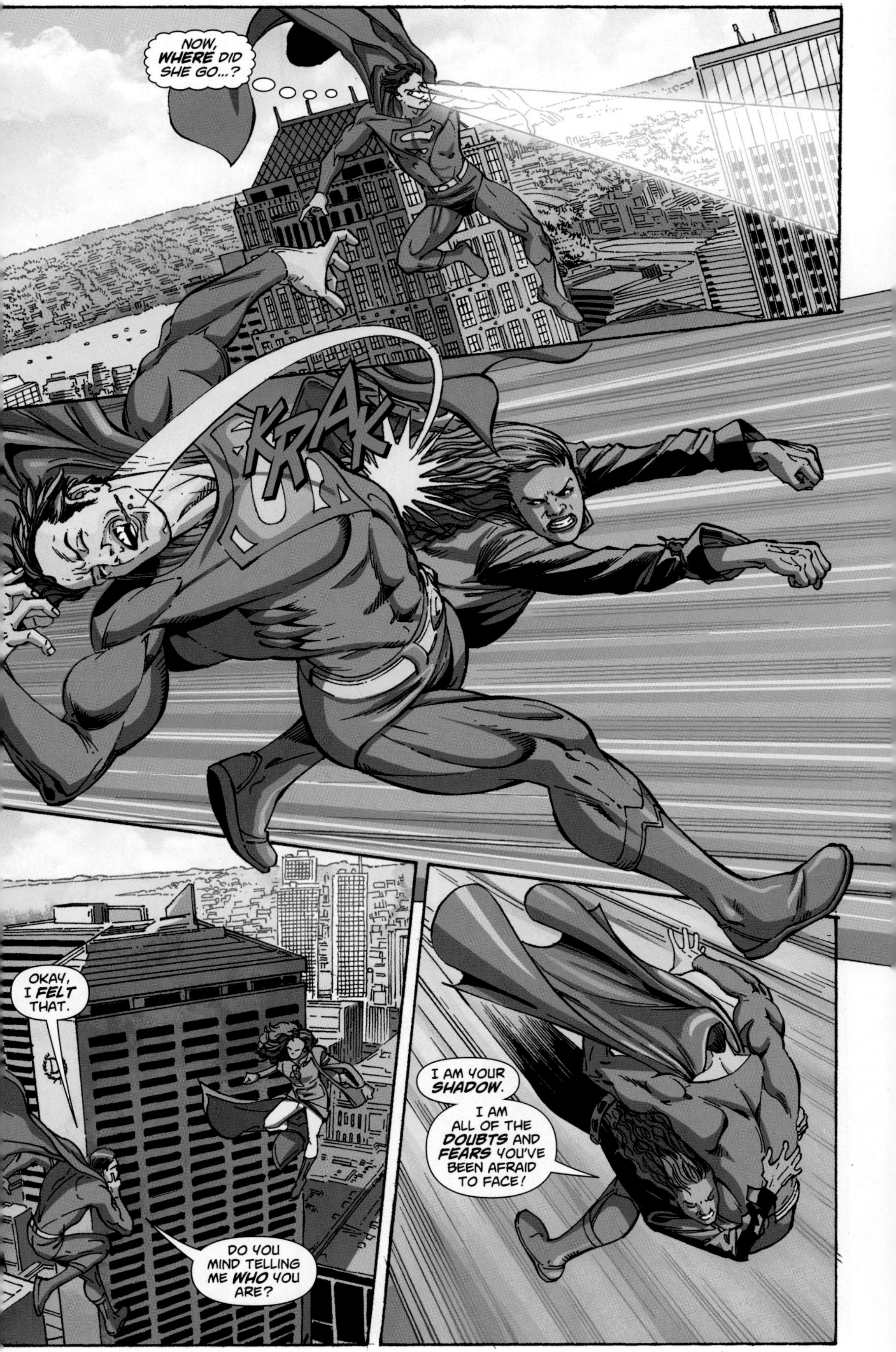
NOW, WHERE DID SHE GO...?
KRAK!
OKAY, I FELT THAT.
DO YOU MIND TELLING ME WHO YOU ARE?
I AM YOUR SHADOW.
I AM ALL OF THE DOUBTS AND FEARS YOU'VE BEEN AFRAID TO FACE!

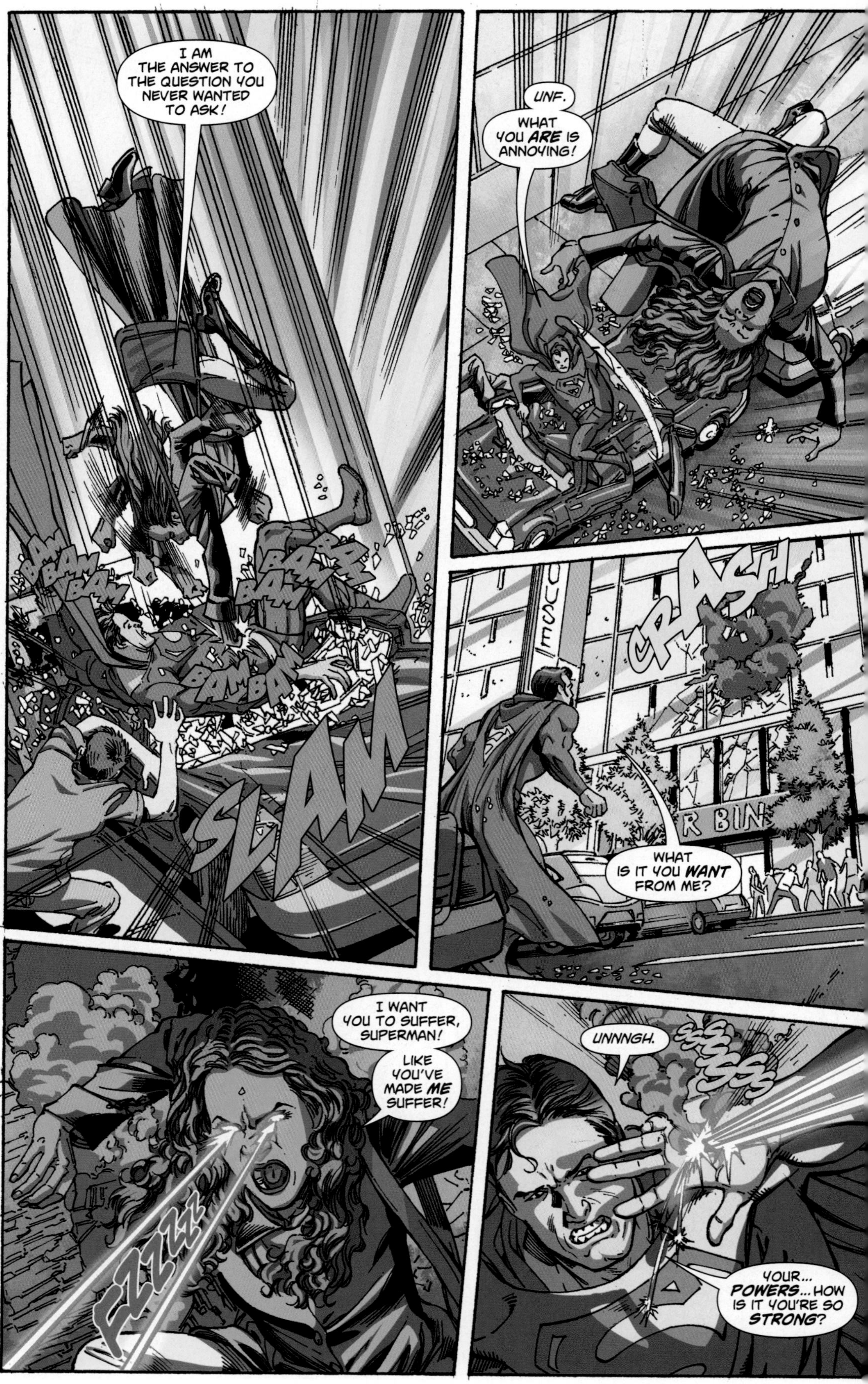
I AM THE ANSWER TO THE QUESTION YOU NEVER WANTED TO ASK!
BAM BAM BAM
BAM BAM BAM
BAM BAM
SLAM
UNF.
WHAT YOU ARE IS ANNOYING!
CRASH
R BIN
WHAT IS IT YOU WANT FROM ME?
I WANT YOU TO SUFFER, SUPERMAN!
LIKE YOU'VE MADE ME SUFFER!
FZZZZZ
UNNNGH.
SSSSSS
YOUR... POWERS... HOW IS IT YOU'RE SO STRONG?

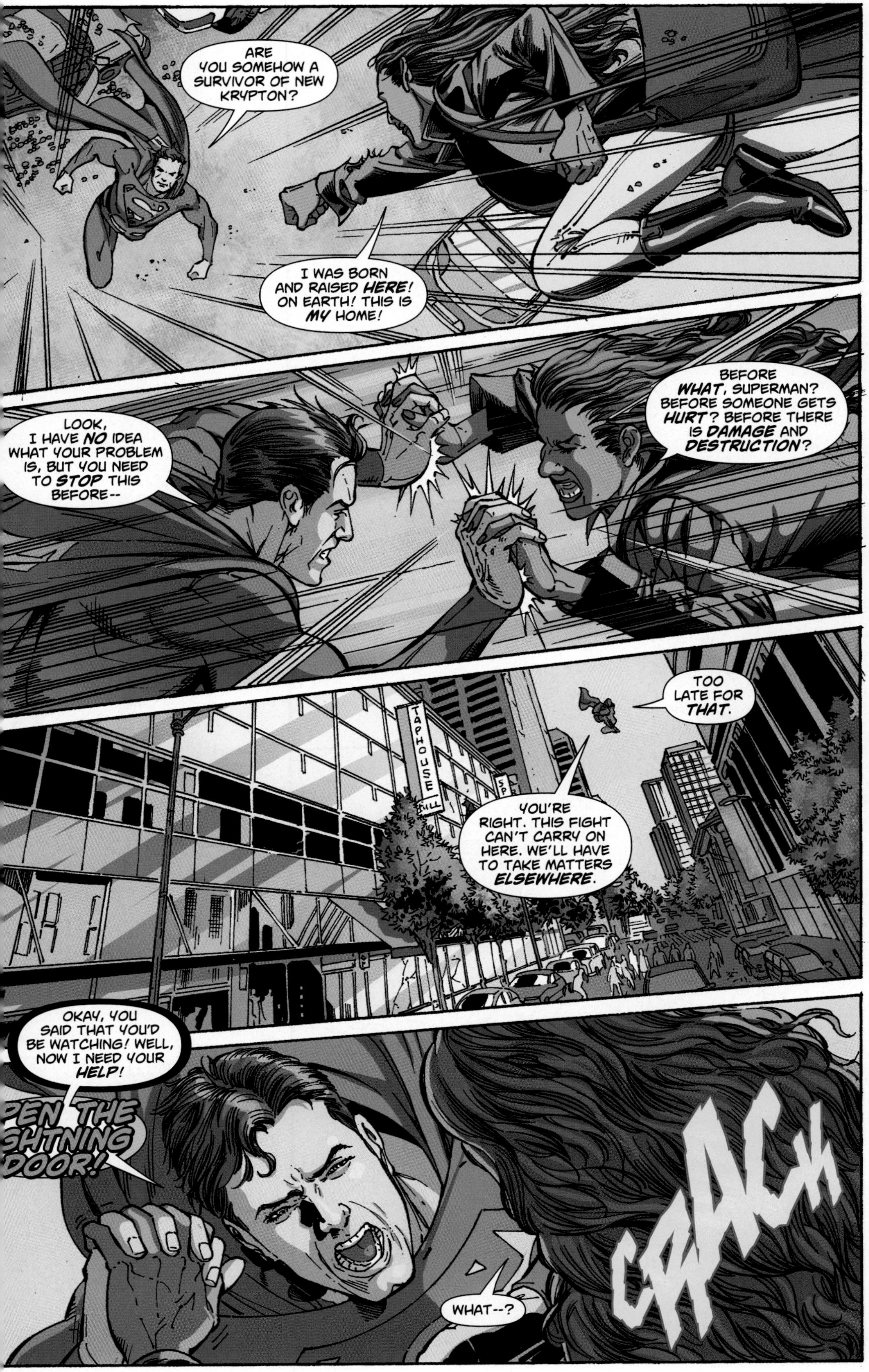
ARE YOU SOMEHOW A SURVIVOR OF NEW KRYPTON?
I WAS BORN AND RAISED HERE! ON EARTH! THIS IS MY HOME!
LOOK, I HAVE NO IDEA WHAT YOUR PROBLEM IS, BUT YOU NEED TO STOP THIS BEFORE--
BEFORE WHAT, SUPERMAN? BEFORE SOMEONE GETS HURT? BEFORE THERE IS DAMAGE AND DESTRUCTION?
TOO LATE FOR THAT.
TAPHOUSE
YOU'RE RIGHT. THIS FIGHT CAN'T CARRY ON HERE. WE'LL HAVE TO TAKE MATTERS ELSEWHERE.
OKAY, YOU SAID THAT YOU'D BE WATCHING! WELL, NOW I NEED YOUR HELP!
PEN THE SHTNING DOOR!
WHAT--?
CRACK

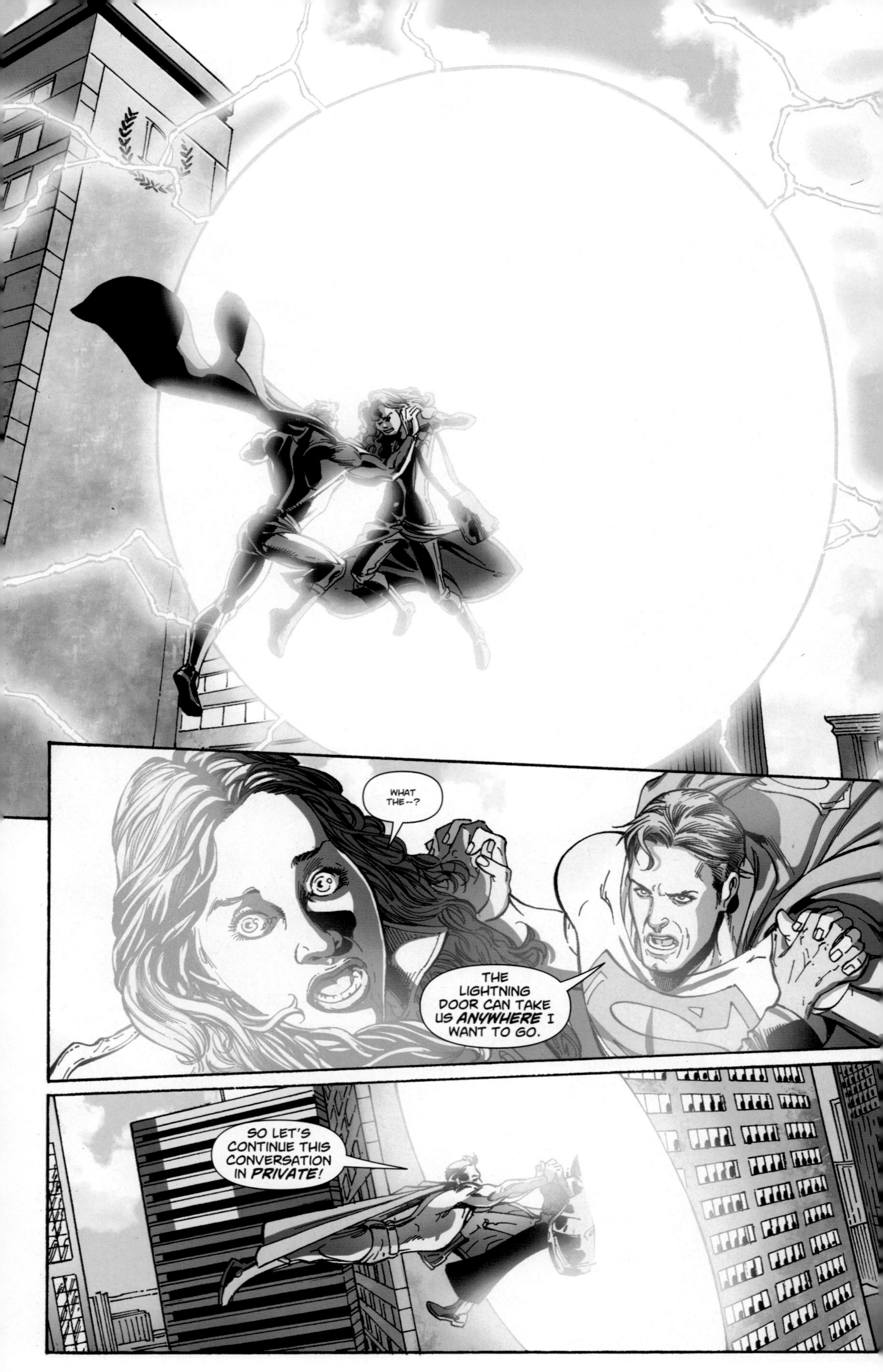
WHAT THE--?
THE LIGHTNING DOOR CAN TAKE US *ANYWHERE* I WANT TO GO.
SO LET'S CONTINUE THIS CONVERSATION IN *PRIVATE*!

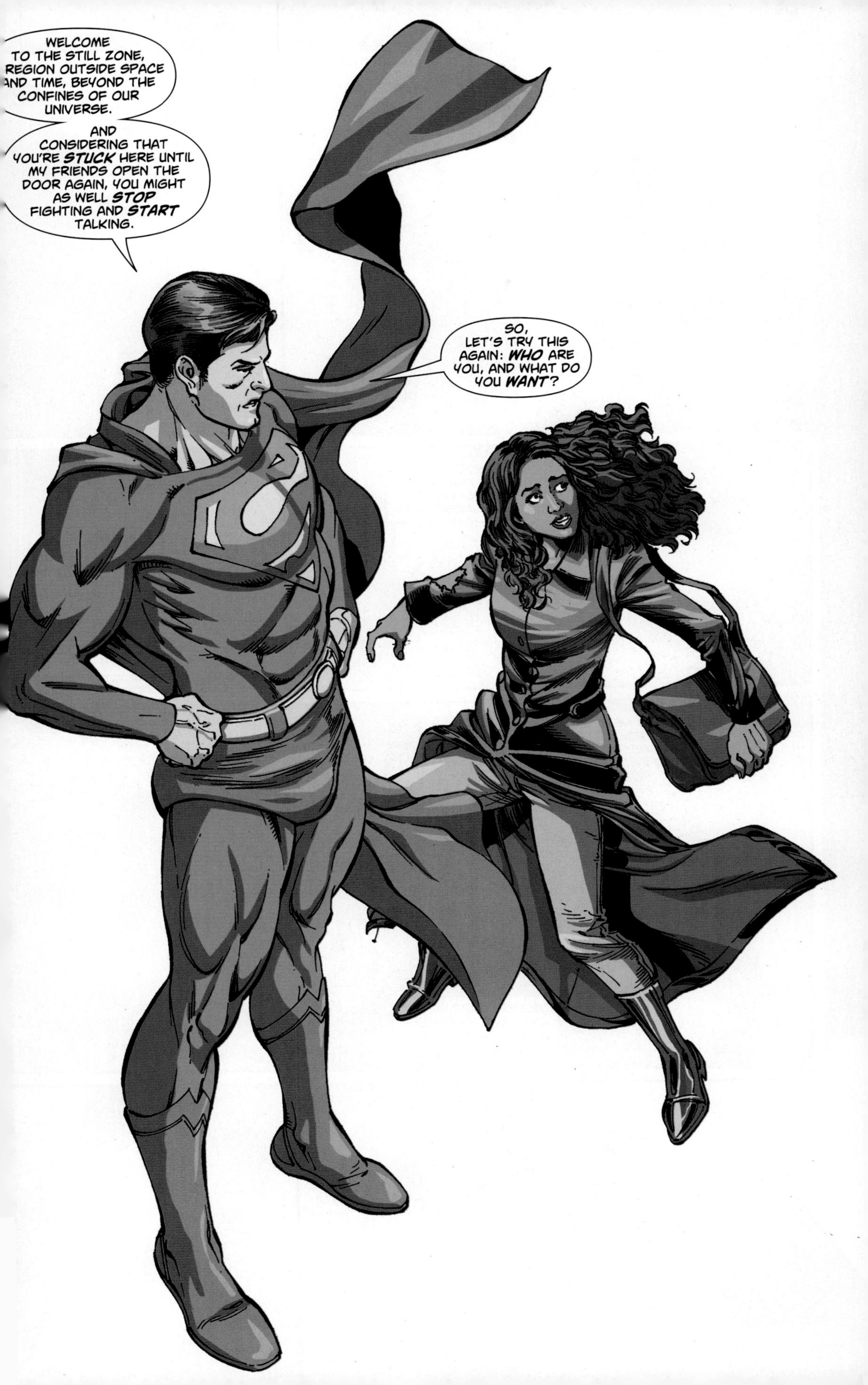

WELCOME TO THE STILL ZONE, REGION OUTSIDE SPACE AND TIME, BEYOND THE CONFINES OF OUR UNIVERSE.
AND CONSIDERING THAT YOU'RE STUCK HERE UNTIL MY FRIENDS OPEN THE DOOR AGAIN, YOU MIGHT AS WELL STOP FIGHTING AND START TALKING.
SO, LET'S TRY THIS AGAIN: WHO ARE YOU, AND WHAT DO YOU WANT?

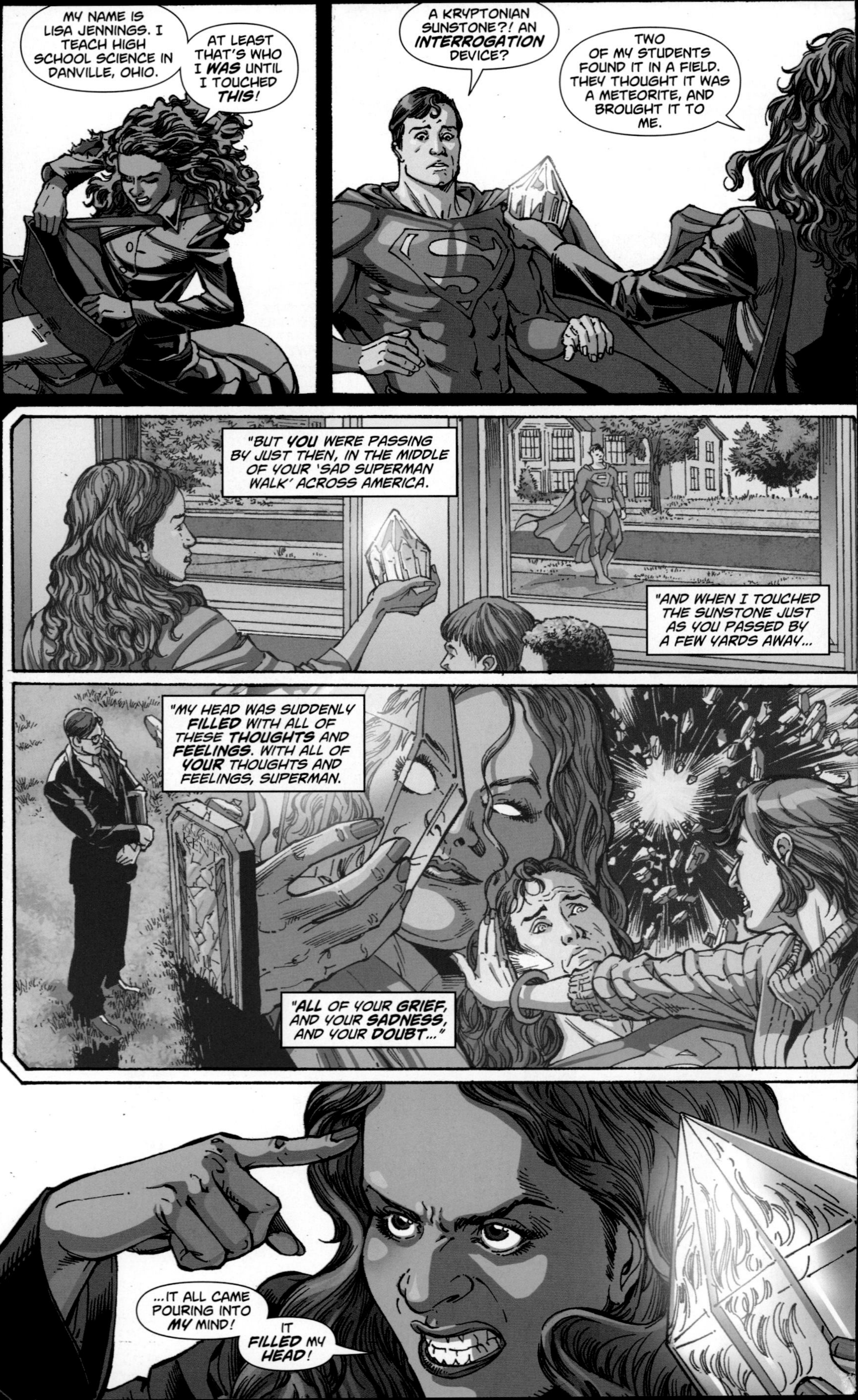
MY NAME IS LISA JENNINGS. I TEACH HIGH SCHOOL SCIENCE IN DANVILLE, OHIO.
AT LEAST THAT'S WHO I WAS UNTIL I TOUCHED THIS!
A KRYPTONIAN SUNSTONE?! AN INTERROGATION DEVICE?
TWO OF MY STUDENTS FOUND IT IN A FIELD. THEY THOUGHT IT WAS A METEORITE, AND BROUGHT IT TO ME.
"BUT YOU WERE PASSING BY JUST THEN, IN THE MIDDLE OF YOUR 'SAD SUPERMAN WALK' ACROSS AMERICA.
"AND WHEN I TOUCHED THE SUNSTONE JUST AS YOU PASSED BY A FEW YARDS AWAY...
"MY HEAD WAS SUDDENLY FILLED WITH ALL OF THESE THOUGHTS AND FEELINGS. WITH ALL OF YOUR THOUGHTS AND FEELINGS, SUPERMAN.
"ALL OF YOUR GRIEF, AND YOUR SADNESS, AND YOUR DOUBT..."
...IT ALL CAME POURING INTO MY MIND!
IT FILLED MY HEAD!

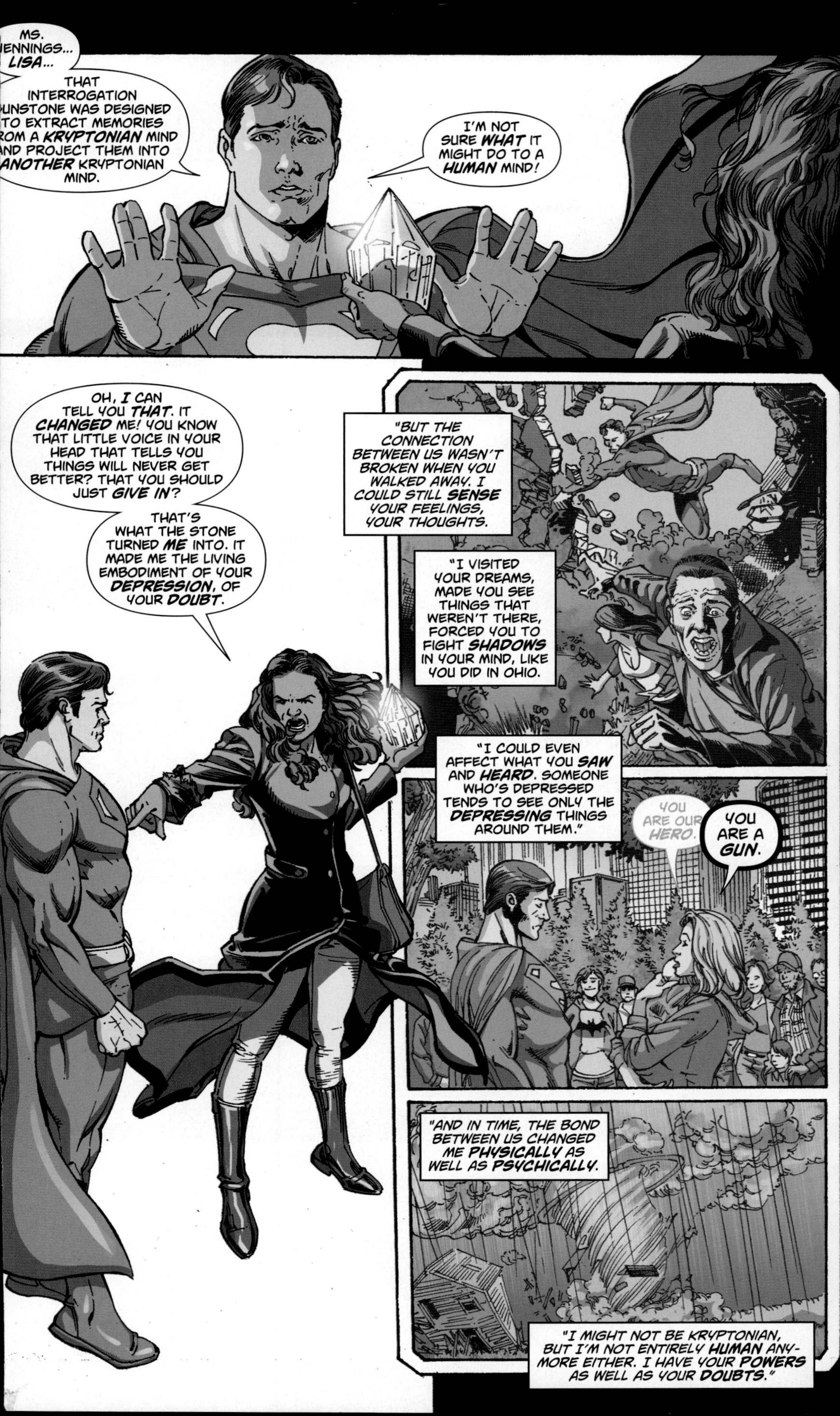

MS. JENNINGS... LISA...
THAT INTERROGATION SUNSTONE WAS DESIGNED TO EXTRACT MEMORIES FROM A KRYPTONIAN MIND AND PROJECT THEM INTO ANOTHER KRYPTONIAN MIND.
I'M NOT SURE WHAT IT MIGHT DO TO A HUMAN MIND!
OH, I CAN TELL YOU THAT. IT CHANGED ME! YOU KNOW THAT LITTLE VOICE IN YOUR HEAD THAT TELLS YOU THINGS WILL NEVER GET BETTER? THAT YOU SHOULD JUST GIVE IN?
THAT'S WHAT THE STONE TURNED ME INTO. IT MADE ME THE LIVING EMBODIMENT OF YOUR DEPRESSION, OF YOUR DOUBT.
"BUT THE CONNECTION BETWEEN US WASN'T BROKEN WHEN YOU WALKED AWAY. I COULD STILL SENSE YOUR FEELINGS, YOUR THOUGHTS.
"I VISITED YOUR DREAMS, MADE YOU SEE THINGS THAT WEREN'T THERE, FORCED YOU TO FIGHT SHADOWS IN YOUR MIND, LIKE YOU DID IN OHIO.
"I COULD EVEN AFFECT WHAT YOU SAW AND HEARD. SOMEONE WHO'S DEPRESSED TENDS TO SEE ONLY THE DEPRESSING THINGS AROUND THEM."
YOU ARE OUR HERO.
YOU ARE A GUN.
"AND IN TIME, THE BOND BETWEEN US CHANGED ME PHYSICALLY AS WELL AS PSYCHICALLY.
"I MIGHT NOT BE KRYPTONIAN, BUT I'M NOT ENTIRELY HUMAN ANY-MORE EITHER. I HAVE YOUR POWERS AS WELL AS YOUR DOUBTS."

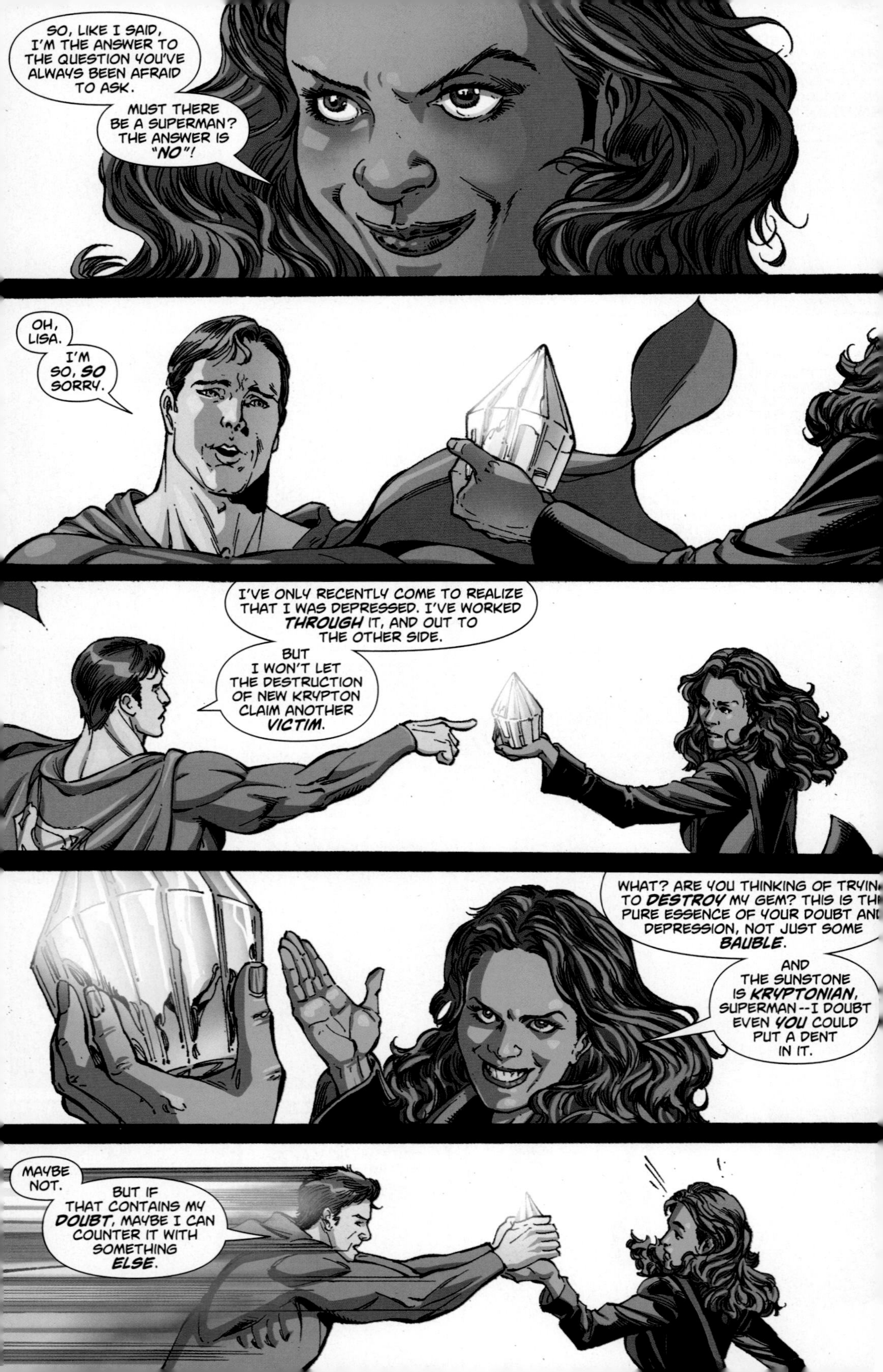
SO, LIKE I SAID, I'M THE ANSWER TO THE QUESTION YOU'VE ALWAYS BEEN AFRAID TO ASK.
MUST THERE BE A SUPERMAN? THE ANSWER IS "NO"!
OH, LISA.
I'M SO, SO SORRY.
I'VE ONLY RECENTLY COME TO REALIZE THAT I WAS DEPRESSED. I'VE WORKED THROUGH IT, AND OUT TO THE OTHER SIDE.
BUT I WON'T LET THE DESTRUCTION OF NEW KRYPTON CLAIM ANOTHER VICTIM.
WHAT? ARE YOU THINKING OF TRYIN TO DESTROY MY GEM? THIS IS TH PURE ESSENCE OF YOUR DOUBT AN DEPRESSION, NOT JUST SOME BAUBLE.
AND THE SUNSTONE IS KRYPTONIAN, SUPERMAN--I DOUBT EVEN YOU COULD PUT A DENT IN IT.
MAYBE NOT.
BUT IF THAT CONTAINS MY DOUBT, MAYBE I CAN COUNTER IT WITH SOMETHING ELSE.
!!
!

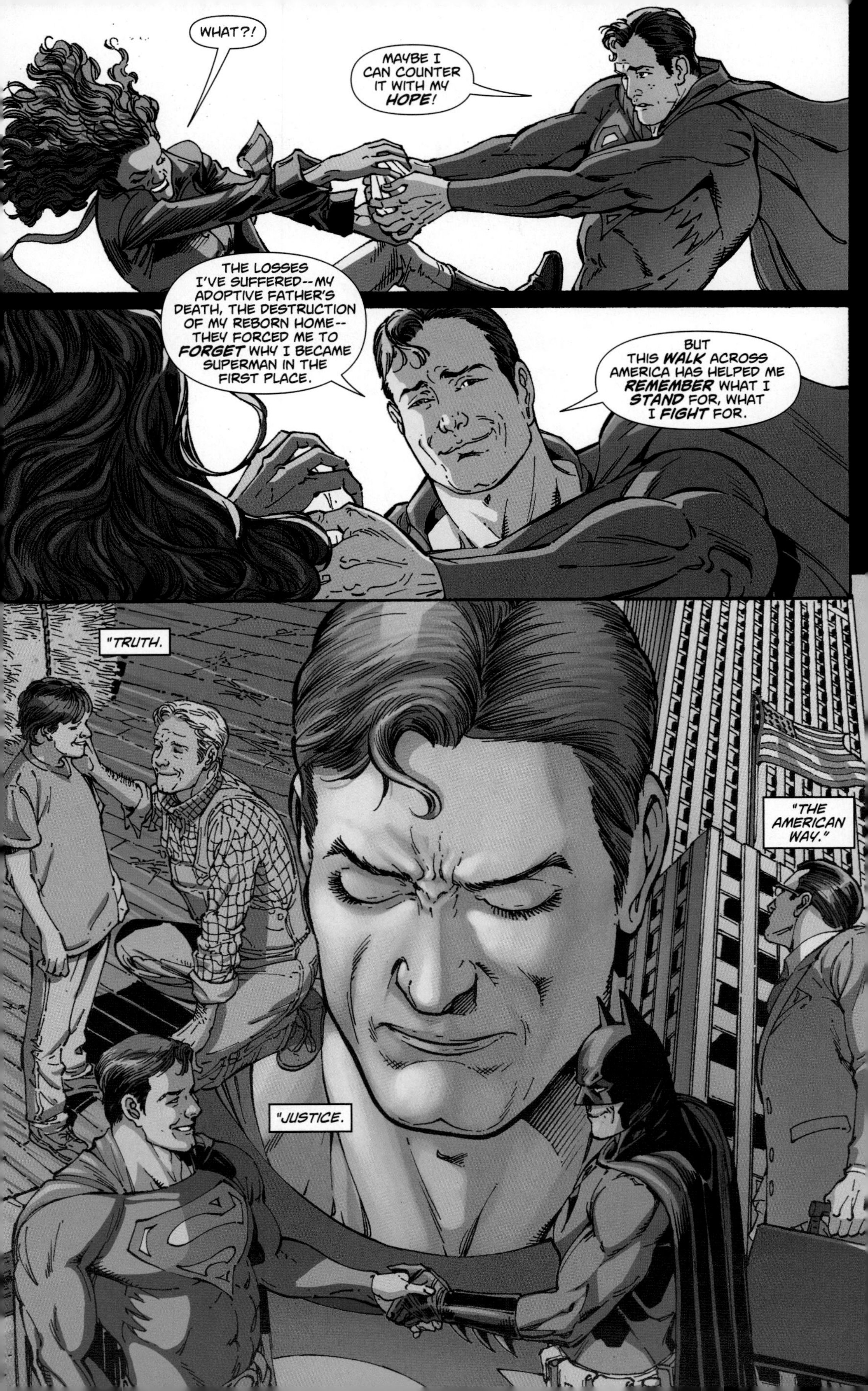
WHAT?!
MAYBE I CAN COUNTER IT WITH MY *HOPE*!
THE LOSSES I'VE SUFFERED--MY ADOPTIVE FATHER'S DEATH, THE DESTRUCTION OF MY REBORN HOME--THEY FORCED ME TO *FORGET* WHY I BECAME SUPERMAN IN THE FIRST PLACE.
BUT THIS *WALK* ACROSS AMERICA HAS HELPED ME *REMEMBER* WHAT I *STAND* FOR, WHAT I *FIGHT* FOR.
"TRUTH.
"JUSTICE.
"THE AMERICAN WAY."

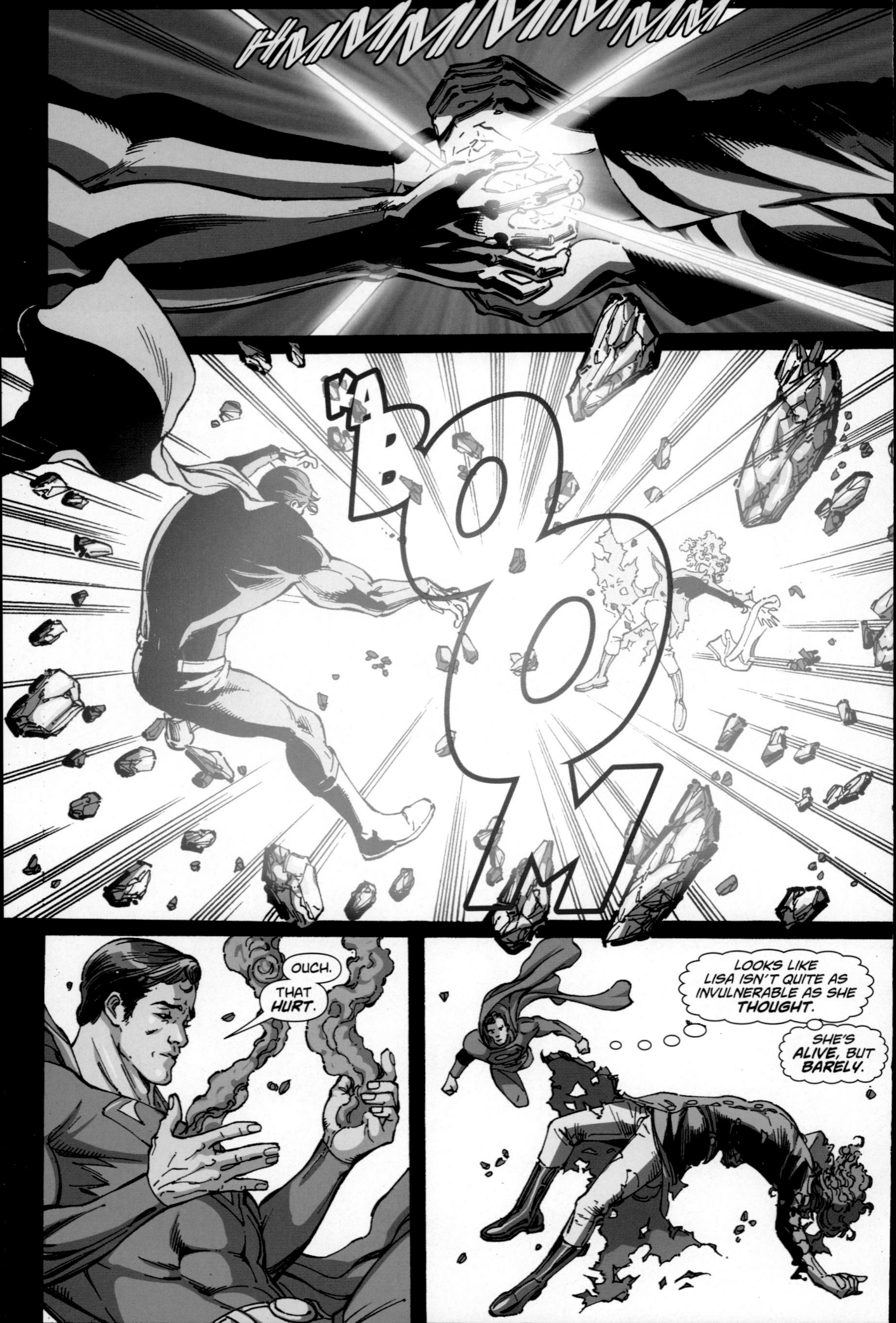
HMMMMMMMMMM
KA-BOOM
OUCH.
THAT HURT.
LOOKS LIKE LISA ISN'T QUITE AS INVULNERABLE AS SHE THOUGHT.
SHE'S ALIVE, BUT BARELY.

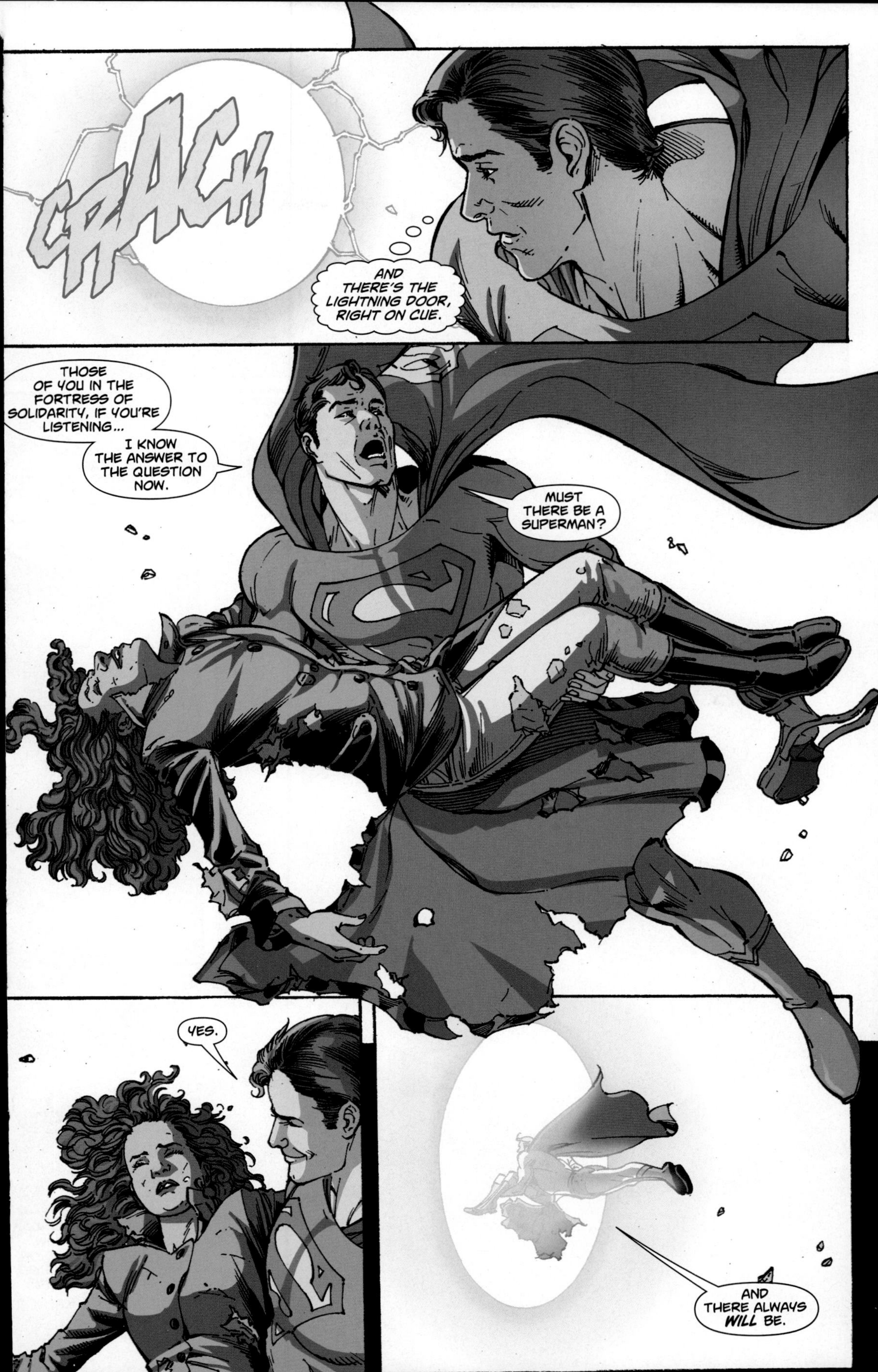
CRACK
AND THERE'S THE LIGHTNING DOOR, RIGHT ON CUE.
THOSE OF YOU IN THE FORTRESS OF SOLIDARITY, IF YOU'RE LISTENING...
I KNOW THE ANSWER TO THE QUESTION NOW.
MUST THERE BE A SUPERMAN?
YES.
AND THERE ALWAYS WILL BE.

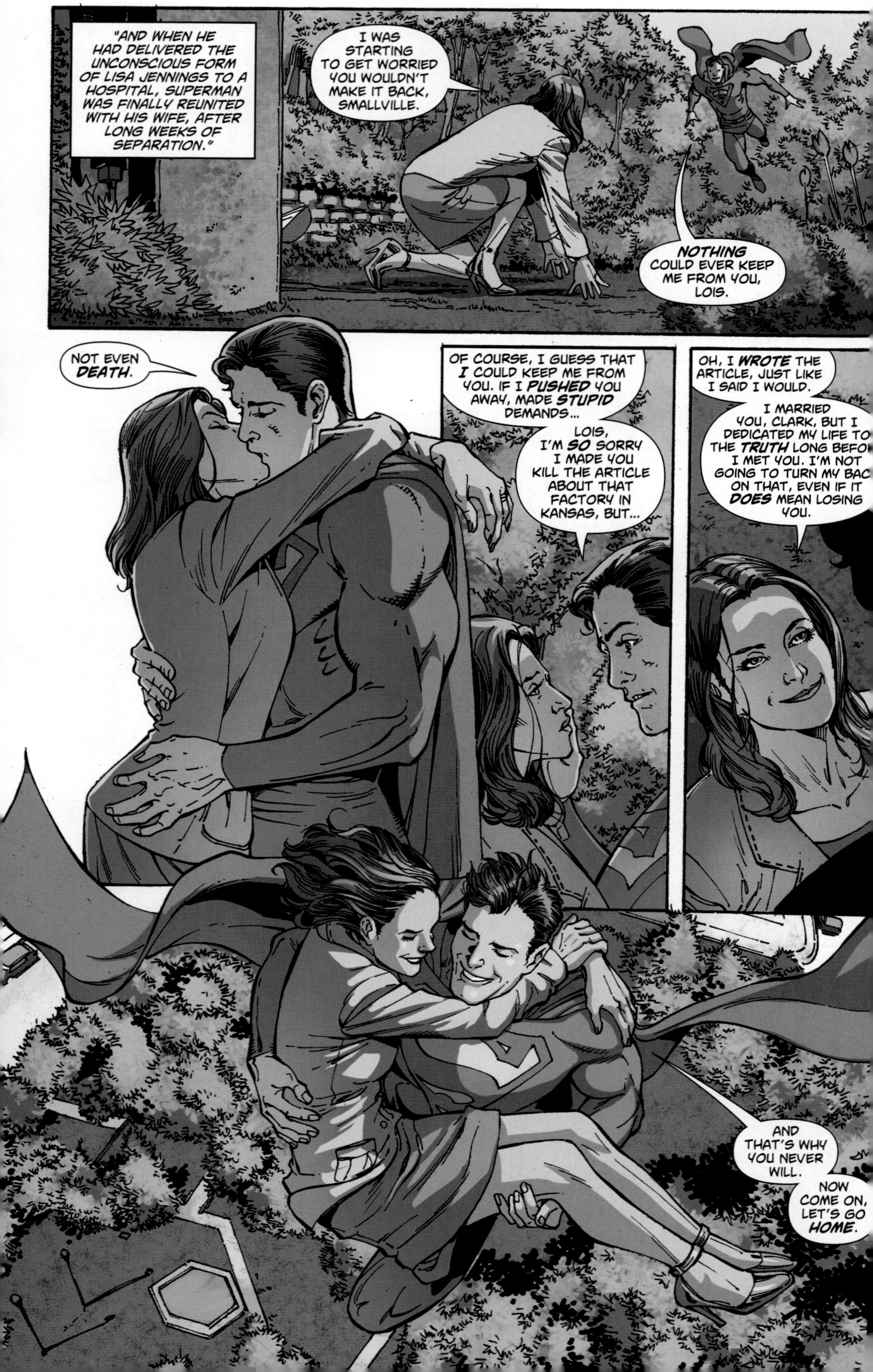
"AND WHEN HE HAD DELIVERED THE UNCONSCIOUS FORM OF LISA JENNINGS TO A HOSPITAL, SUPERMAN WAS FINALLY REUNITED WITH HIS WIFE, AFTER LONG WEEKS OF SEPARATION."
I WAS STARTING TO GET WORRIED YOU WOULDN'T MAKE IT BACK, SMALLVILLE.
NOTHING COULD EVER KEEP ME FROM YOU, LOIS.
NOT EVEN DEATH.
OF COURSE, I GUESS THAT I COULD KEEP ME FROM YOU. IF I PUSHED YOU AWAY, MADE STUPID DEMANDS...
LOIS, I'M SO SORRY I MADE YOU KILL THE ARTICLE ABOUT THAT FACTORY IN KANSAS, BUT...
OH, I WROTE THE ARTICLE, JUST LIKE I SAID I WOULD.
I MARRIED YOU, CLARK, BUT I DEDICATED MY LIFE TO THE TRUTH LONG BEFO I MET YOU. I'M NOT GOING TO TURN MY BAC ON THAT, EVEN IF IT DOES MEAN LOSING YOU.
AND THAT'S WHY YOU NEVER WILL.
NOW COME ON, LET'S GO HOME.

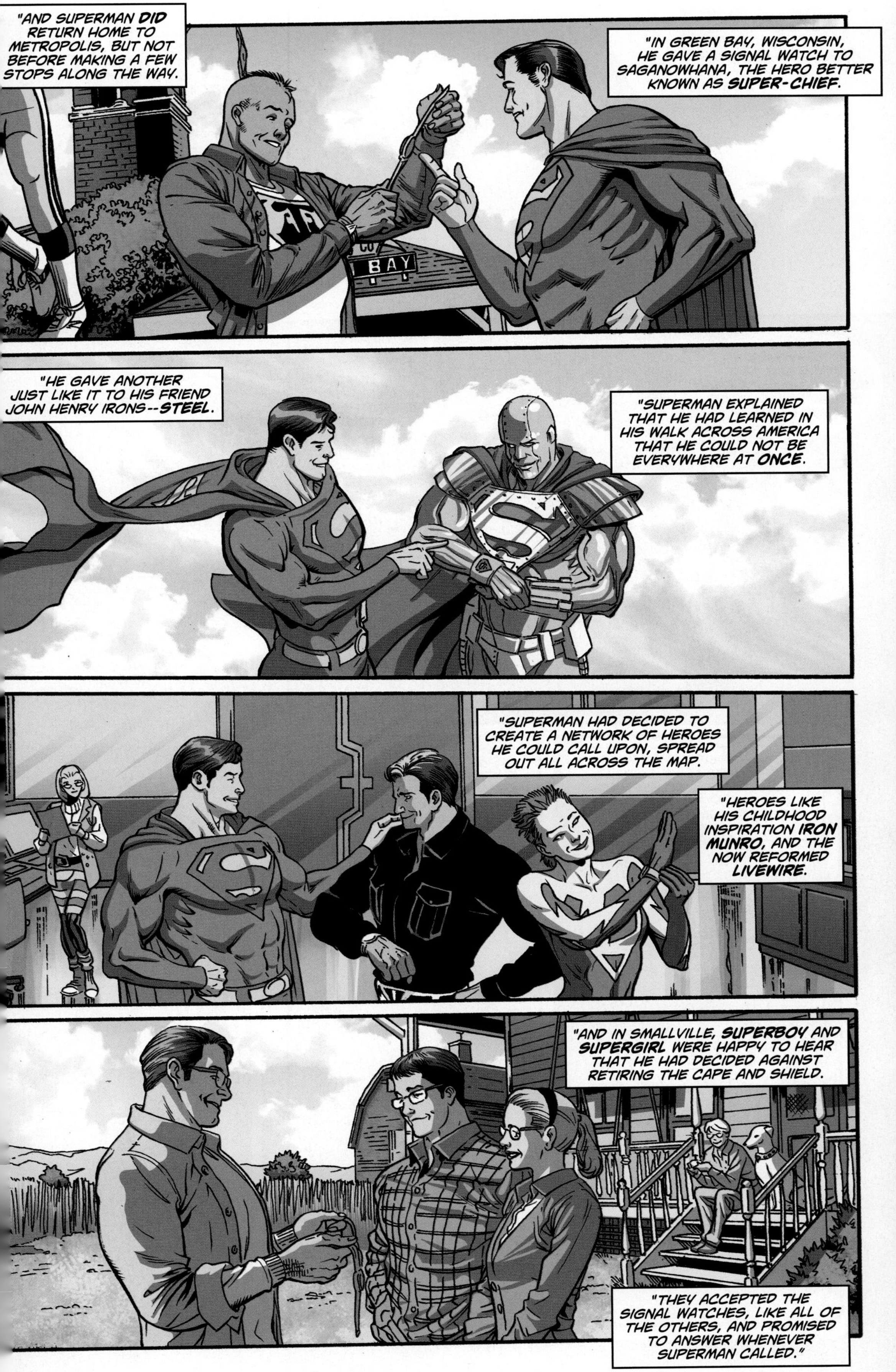
"AND SUPERMAN DID RETURN HOME TO METROPOLIS, BUT NOT BEFORE MAKING A FEW STOPS ALONG THE WAY.
"IN GREEN BAY, WISCONSIN, HE GAVE A SIGNAL WATCH TO SAGANOWHANA, THE HERO BETTER KNOWN AS SUPER-CHIEF.
BAY
"HE GAVE ANOTHER JUST LIKE IT TO HIS FRIEND JOHN HENRY IRONS--STEEL.
"SUPERMAN EXPLAINED THAT HE HAD LEARNED IN HIS WALK ACROSS AMERICA THAT HE COULD NOT BE EVERYWHERE AT ONCE.
"SUPERMAN HAD DECIDED TO CREATE A NETWORK OF HEROES HE COULD CALL UPON, SPREAD OUT ALL ACROSS THE MAP.
"HEROES LIKE HIS CHILDHOOD INSPIRATION IRON MUNRO, AND THE NOW REFORMED LIVEWIRE.
"AND IN SMALLVILLE, SUPERBOY AND SUPERGIRL WERE HAPPY TO HEAR THAT HE HAD DECIDED AGAINST RETIRING THE CAPE AND SHIELD.
"THEY ACCEPTED THE SIGNAL WATCHES, LIKE ALL OF THE OTHERS, AND PROMISED TO ANSWER WHENEVER SUPERMAN CALLED."

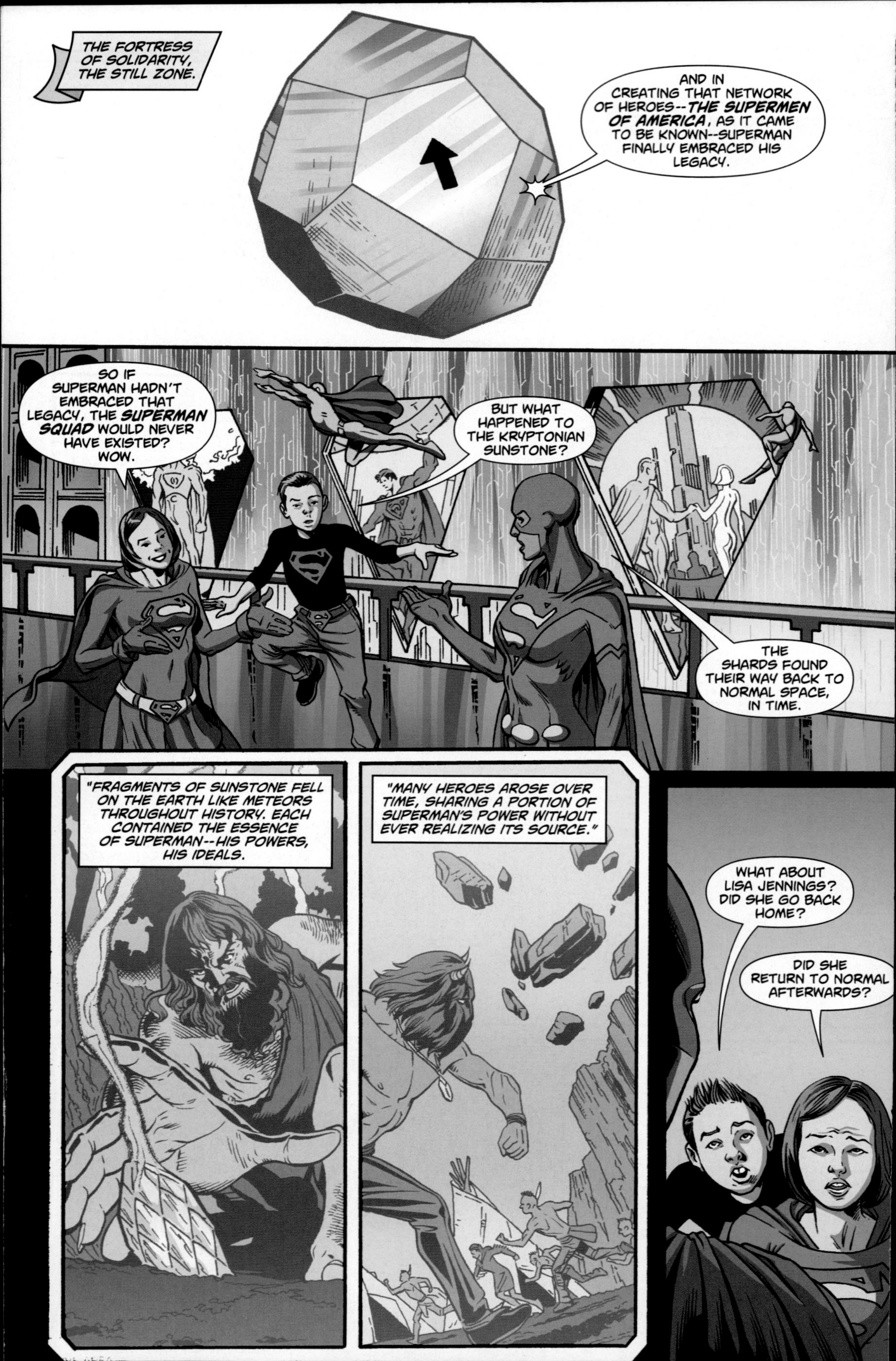
THE FORTRESS OF SOLIDARITY, THE STILL ZONE.
AND IN CREATING THAT NETWORK OF HEROES--THE SUPERMEN OF AMERICA, AS IT CAME TO BE KNOWN--SUPERMAN FINALLY EMBRACED HIS LEGACY.
SO IF SUPERMAN HADN'T EMBRACED THAT LEGACY, THE SUPERMAN SQUAD WOULD NEVER HAVE EXISTED? WOW.
BUT WHAT HAPPENED TO THE KRYPTONIAN SUNSTONE?
THE SHARDS FOUND THEIR WAY BACK TO NORMAL SPACE, IN TIME.
"FRAGMENTS OF SUNSTONE FELL ON THE EARTH LIKE METEORS THROUGHOUT HISTORY. EACH CONTAINED THE ESSENCE OF SUPERMAN--HIS POWERS, HIS IDEALS.
"MANY HEROES AROSE OVER TIME, SHARING A PORTION OF SUPERMAN'S POWER WITHOUT EVER REALIZING ITS SOURCE."
WHAT ABOUT LISA JENNINGS? DID SHE GO BACK HOME?
DID SHE RETURN TO NORMAL AFTERWARDS?

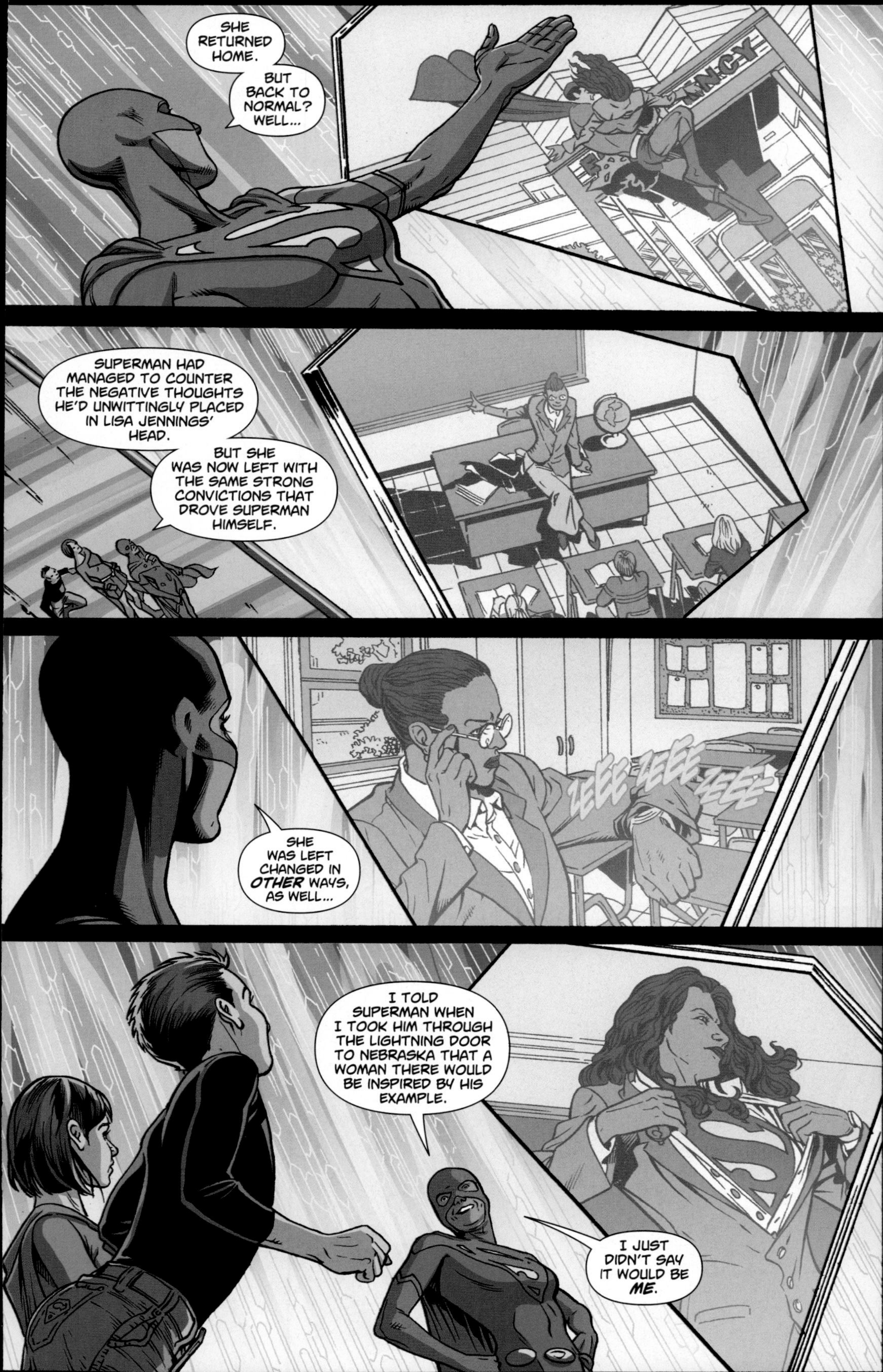
SHE RETURNED HOME.
BUT BACK TO NORMAL? WELL...
SUPERMAN HAD MANAGED TO COUNTER THE NEGATIVE THOUGHTS HE'D UNWITTINGLY PLACED IN LISA JENNINGS' HEAD.
BUT SHE WAS NOW LEFT WITH THE SAME STRONG CONVICTIONS THAT DROVE SUPERMAN HIMSELF.
SHE WAS LEFT CHANGED IN OTHER WAYS, AS WELL...
ZEEE ZEEE ZEEE
I TOLD SUPERMAN WHEN I TOOK HIM THROUGH THE LIGHTNING DOOR TO NEBRASKA THAT A WOMAN THERE WOULD BE INSPIRED BY HIS EXAMPLE.
I JUST DIDN'T SAY IT WOULD BE ME.

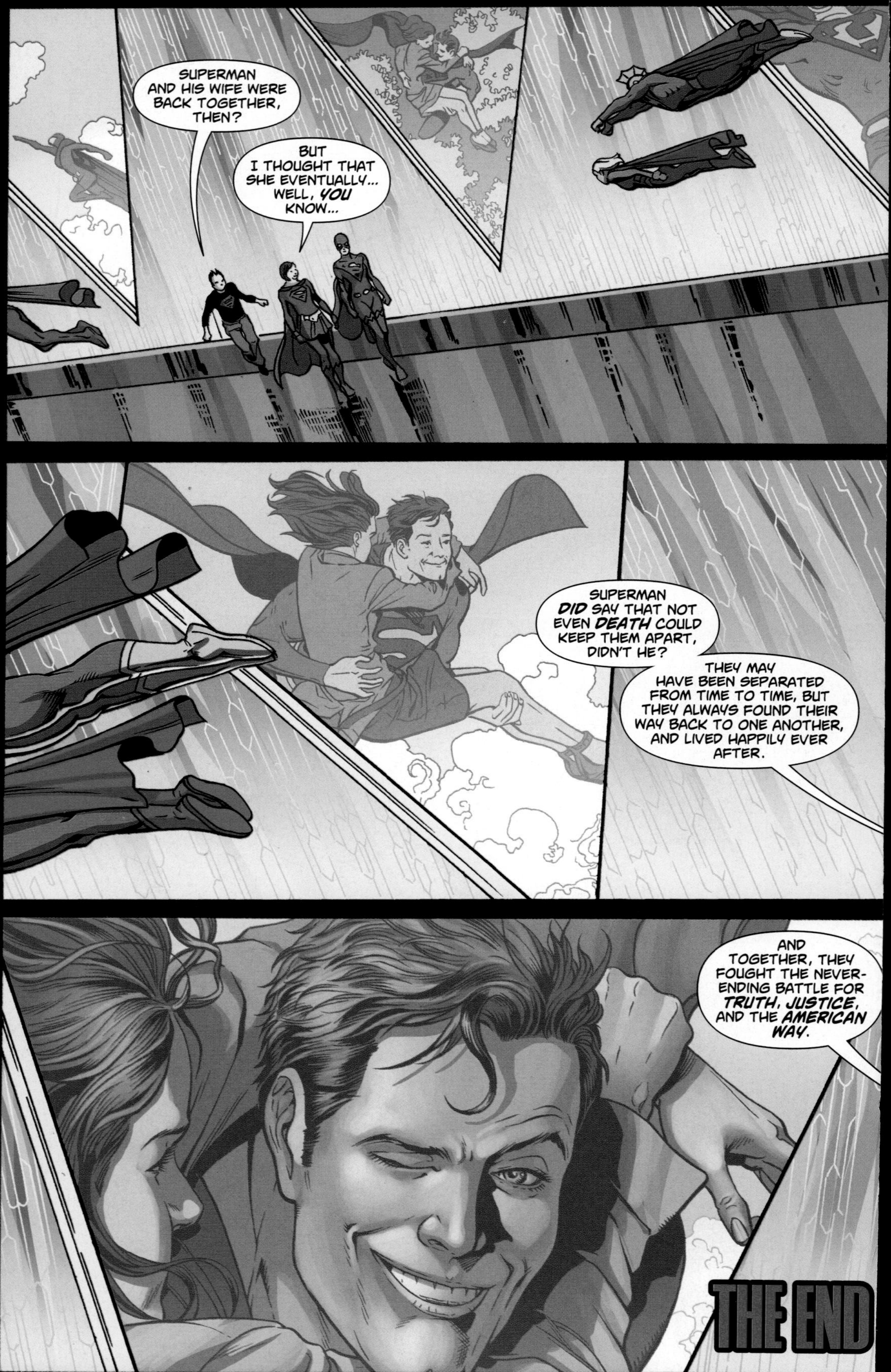
SUPERMAN AND HIS WIFE WERE BACK TOGETHER, THEN?
BUT I THOUGHT THAT SHE EVENTUALLY... WELL, *YOU* KNOW...
SUPERMAN *DID* SAY THAT NOT EVEN *DEATH* COULD KEEP THEM APART, DIDN'T HE?
THEY MAY HAVE BEEN SEPARATED FROM TIME TO TIME, BUT THEY ALWAYS FOUND THEIR WAY BACK TO ONE ANOTHER, AND LIVED HAPPILY EVER AFTER.
AND TOGETHER, THEY FOUGHT THE NEVER-ENDING BATTLE FOR *TRUTH, JUSTICE,* AND THE *AMERICAN WAY.*
THE END

FROM *THE NEW YORK TIMES* #1 BESTSELLING AUTHOR

J. MICHAEL STRACZYNSKI

with SHANE DAVIS

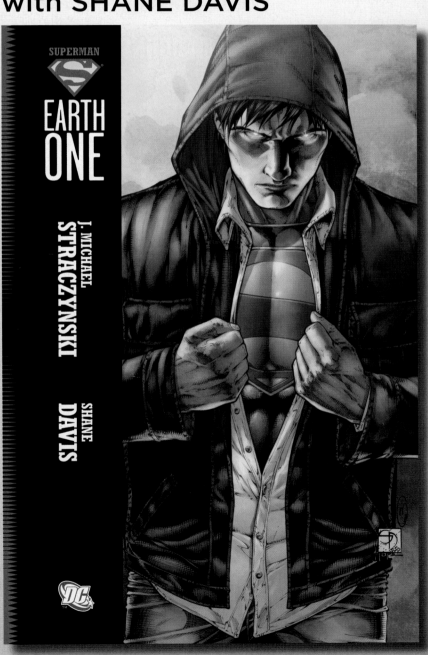

SUPERMAN

EARTH ONE

J. MICHAEL STRACZYNSKI

SHANE DAVIS

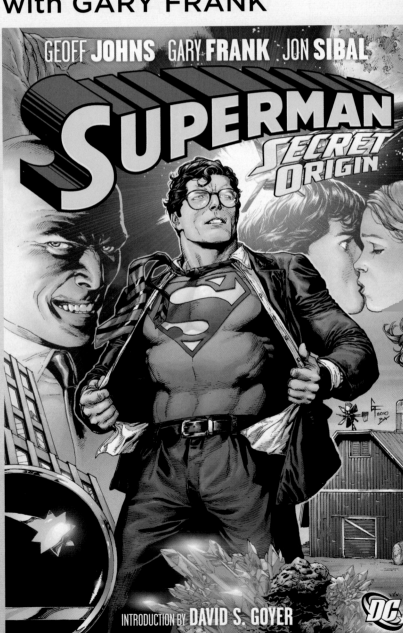